Transatlantic Roots Music

American Made Music Series
Advisory Board

David Evans, General Editor

Barry Jean Ancelet

Edward A. Berlin

Joyce J. Bolden

Rob Bowman

Susan C. Cook

Curtis Ellison

William Ferris

John Edward Hasse

Kip Lornell

Bill Malone

Eddie S. Meadows

Manuel H. Peña

David Sanjek

Wayne D. Shirley

Robert Walser

TRANSATLANTIC ROOTS MUSIC

Folk, Blues, and National Identities

Edited by Jill Terry and Neil A. Wynn

University Press of Mississippi / Jackson

www.upress.state.ms.us

The University Press of Mississippi is a member
of the Association of American University Presses.

Copyright © 2012 by University Press of Mississippi
All rights reserved
Manufactured in the United States of America

First printing 2012

∞

Library of Congress Cataloging-in-Publication Data

Transatlantic roots music : folk, blues, and national identities /
edited by Jill Terry and Neil A. Wynn.
  p. cm. — (American made music series)
Includes bibliographical references and index.
ISBN 978-1-61703-288-2 (cloth : alk. paper) — ISBN 978-1-61703-289-9
(ebook) 1. Folk music—United States—History and criticism. 2. Folk
music—Great Britain—History and criticism. 3. Blues (Music)—History and criticism. 4. Blues (Music)—Great Britain—History and criticism. I. Terry, Jill. II. Wynn, Neil A.
  ML3545.T73 2012
  781.62'13—dc23   2012000869

British Library Cataloging-in-Publication Data available

Contents

vii .... Acknowledgments

ix .... Introduction
          —**Jill Terry and Neil A. Wynn**

3. .... 1. The Historical and Social Background of Transatlantic Roots Music Revivals
          —**Jill Terry and Neil A. Wynn**

20 .... 2. "Early Morning Blues": The Early Years of the Transatlantic Connection
          —**Paul Oliver**

37. .... 3. Dreaming Up the Blues: Transatlantic Blues Scholarship in the 1950s
          —**Christian O'Connell**

57. .... 4. American Balladry and the Anxiety of Ancestry
          —**Erich Nunn**

77. .... 5. Woody Guthrie at the Crossroads
          —**Will Kaufman**

94 .... 6. "It's Not British Music, It's American Music": Bob Dylan and Britain
          —**John Hughes**

119 .... 7. Alan Lomax: An American Ballad Hunter in Great Britain
          —**Ronald D. Cohen**

138 .... 8. Putting the Blues in British Blues Rock
          —**Roberta Freund Schwartz**

153 .... 9. That White Man, Burdon: The Animals, Race, and the American South in the British Blues Boom
   —Brian Ward

179 .... 10. Born in Chicago: The Impact of the Paul Butterfield Blues Band on the British Blues "Network," 1964–1970
   —Andrew Kellett

205 .... 11. "When Somebody Take Your Number and Use It": The 1960s, British Blues, and America's Racial Crossroads
   —Robert H. Cataliotti

227 .... 12. Groove Me: Dancing to the Discs of Northern Soul
   —David Sanjek

246 .... 13. Some Reflections on "Celtic" Music
   —Duck Baker

257 .... Contributors

263 .... Index

Acknowledgments

We would like to thank all our contributors for their work—and their patience. We also appreciate the support and commitment to the project of Craig Gill at the University Press of Mississippi and input of our readers, Professor David Evans and an anonymous reviewer, both of whom offered valuable suggestions and corrections. In some cases the chapter author and we, as editors, took a different line in the interest of academic debate. Thanks are also due to Anne Stascavage and Will Rigby at the press for their outstanding editorial work.

We have both been influenced and encouraged by other people who have played a part in "roots" music. Jill particularly thanks Mitch (Gerald) Mitchell, who for forty years has been an inspiration, friend, guide, singer, dancer, oral historian, and collector of folk, blues, and jazz and who was there, in the London clubs, when the roots scene really blossomed—lucky him! Paul Oliver not only took part in the conference from which these papers sprang, but also offered the chapter included here; his influence can be seen in many of the chapters in the book, but the fact that his work is itself the subject of one speaks volumes for his importance.

—Jill Terry
University of Worcester

—Neil Wynn
University of Gloucestershire

Introduction

—Jill Terry and Neil A. Wynn

This collection of articles originally began as a series of conference papers on the subject of "The Transatlantic Routes of Roots Music" held at the University of Worcester, England, in September 2009. The event brought together prominent authorities on British and American roots music from both sides of the Atlantic, who collectively engaged in discussion of this phenomenon as it appeared in folk and blues music emanating from Europe and the USA. Its aim, and the aim of this volume, was (and is) to consider exchanges and dialogues about folk music, often referred to now in the expanded term as "roots" music—that is, the (originally) unwritten traditional music of ordinary people. As knowledge of the music and culture of the non-English-speaking, nonwhite, non-European, and non-American world grew, folk music broadened into "world" and then "roots" music.[1] Recognizing the plurality of musical strands even within the European/North American world, the collection explores not just the interconnectedness of folk/roots music on either side of the Atlantic, but also issues of discovery, rediscovery, and representation of such musical forms.

While many of the papers focused on African American music, particularly the blues and its influence on white popular transatlantic culture in the 1960s, the conference also included papers on white American and British folk music. One of the aims of the conference was to bring these two aspects of roots music together—as indeed they generally were historically—both in "revivals" and in everyday performance. Many performers, ranging from the Mississippi Sheiks through to Sonny Terry, Leadbelly, Big Bill Broonzy, and Josh White, sang blues *and* folk songs, and played and recorded with people such as Woody Guthrie and Pete Seeger. While our predominant theme is how music crossed from one side of the Atlantic to the other, and with what effect, one of the central concerns that comes out of these discussions is the relationship between different folk music forms or genres and questions of identity: individual, national, regional, racial, and social. What emerges from these questions is thus an examination of the quest for authenticity which has led collectors of folk and blues, as well as those engaged in performance, marketing, and consumption of the music, to assert a claim of pure lineage. The essays collected here demonstrate the vital significance that regional, national, and racial identifications have had in twentieth-century reproductions of roots music and for the performers' and audiences' own authentication of roots.

Not surprisingly, our contributors focus mainly on the postwar years, when first jazz and then folk and blues music gained in popularity on both sides of the Atlantic. This was a period when there was a growing interest in African American culture in Europe, particularly Britain; this interest was then exported back to the USA. However, the volume addresses issues of origin in folk music raised by the first collectors, Child, Sharp, the Lomaxes, and many others, which continued not just about black song, but also about all folk music. How folk music was perceived by those who recorded it for posterity as well as by those who performed it continues to be a matter of interest and debate. Several new publications touch on such matters either directly or indirectly. New or forthcoming biographies of Alan Lomax, Pete Seeger, and Woody Guthrie reveal continuing interest in folk music and the discussion surrounding it.[2] Broader matters are dealt with in many others, such as Ronald Cohen's *Rainbow Quest: The Folk Music Revival & American Society, 1940–1970*; Benjamin Filene's *Romancing the Folk: Public Memory and American Roots Music*; Karl Hagstrom Miller's *Segregating Sound: Inventing Folk and Pop Music in the Age of Jim Crow*; and William Roy's *Red, White and Blues: Social Movements, Folk Music and Race in the United States*.[3] Picking up on the recurring question of identity, Roy talks of folk music in Europe being "associated with nationalist sentiment" while American folk music, according to Alan Lomax ("the most influential definer of what American folk music is"), "'mirrors the unique life of this western continent' and 'a culture of the common man.'" However, as Roy reminds us, the very concept of *folk* music "is socially constructed":[4] who the "folk" were, what they sang, and what it meant was the subject of outside interpreters, the American and British collectors and recorders from Francis James Child and Cecil Sharp through to the Lomaxes, John and Alan, and Paul Oliver, all names that, with others, figure in almost all of the essays included here. The performance of traditional music, the appropriation of form and lyrics, as well as the adoption of "authentic" personas have been critical factors in debates about authenticity that reverberated throughout the folk revivals led by its performers such as Ewan MacColl, Pete Seeger, Martin Carthy, Woody Guthrie, and Bob Dylan, all of whom make frequent appearances throughout this book. The essays in this collection thus allow us to understand the continuing emphasis on authenticity on both sides of the Atlantic.

Child, Sharp, the Lomaxes, and Oliver compiled and collected both blues and folk, sometimes both from a single singer, and the approach to music taken in this volume emphasizes the connection between folk and blues traditions because their genealogies have much in common, as do the debates on authenticity that surround them. The transatlantic connections within and between these British and American roots musics have been intrinsic to their collection, performance, and reception from the earliest recorded oral histories through to circulation and reproduction in folk clubs, on vinyl, in radio broadcasts, and into the digital age. The most recent revival in roots music popularity, showcased in the 2001 PBS documentary *American Roots Music* and the BBC's *Late Junction* series, is also manifested in the enormous expansion of the folk, blues, and world music festival scenes in the twenty-first century, from Britain's Womad to the Chicago Blues Festival. If the first folk revival occurred at the end of the nineteenth and early twentieth centuries (1890s-1920s), the second in mid-twentieth century (1945–1960s), then it could be said that we are in the era of the "Third Revival."[7]

Chapter 1, by Terry and Wynn, offers an overview of some of the major debates and issues about folk/roots music, and its meaning and place as a genre, identified by the collectors and authorities who both preserved the historical musical record and at the same time posed the questions of meaning and authenticity that were to become a major feature of "revivals" of both folk and blues music in later years. That such questions were important can be seen in the disappearance (from academic memory and discourse at least) of African American performers such as Florence Mills who were enormously popular in the 1930s and 1940s and yet did not easily fit the descriptions of blues or jazz performers. The authors also address the causes of folk/blues revivals and attempt to place them historically before returning again to the fundamental question of definition and meaning.

In "Early Morning Blues" a leading world authority, Paul Oliver, provides a broad historical overview of the development and transatlantic movement of African American roots music from minstrelsy through to the blues. Some of those musical forms were evident in the plantation reviews discussed in chapter 1, but others were linked to the growth of jazz and blues, which soon developed a small but devoted following and a growing body of journals and scholarship that provided an intellectual basis for the blues revival of the 1960s in Britain. The impact and meaning of this writing, particularly that of Oliver himself, is explored by Christian O'Connell in his chapter, "Dreaming Up the Blues: Transatlantic Blues Scholarship in the 1950s." For O'Connell and for other writers in Britain and elsewhere, those who write about a musical form often become the arbiters of what is or is not "authentic," perhaps ignoring what is, or is not, "popular." Thus it is the recorder/historian who determines what blues or folk music is rather than the musicians or "folk" themselves.

The musical origins of particular folk songs and the manner of their interpretation by scholars, recorders, and performers is taken further by Erich Nunn in his discussion of the work of one of the most famous authorities on American folk music, black and white, John Lomax, and in the particular case study of Bradley Kincaid's telling and retelling of the acquisition of a "hound dog guitar." Nunn looks at cowboy and mountain songs and their reading by first Lomax and then Kincaid in terms of an "Anglo-Saxon ancestry" that demonstrates the manner in which investments in racial difference structure the way folk music is understood as it is formed and re-formed across the Atlantic at different times.

Will Kaufman's chapter on Woody Guthrie explores the different meanings and interpretations of one of the most influential American folk singers of the 1930s and 1940s. Kaufman implicitly addresses the issue of what "folk" music means and looks particularly at the notion that Guthrie's music was "proletarian," reflecting the views of the Okies, Arkies, and trade unionists, or whether it was shaped instead more by middle-class, urban audiences. This chapter also looks at the issue raised in chapter 1 of the relationship between folk and popular music and the extent to which recorded, as opposed to performed, music also led to different meanings. Addressing the examination of origins and influences, Kaufman sees Guthrie standing at the intersection of many "crossroads" analyzed in this volume.

While in many ways an archetypal American folk musician, Guthrie's song lyrics have provided much of the material that was developed in 1960s revivals that drew on both sides of the Atlantic for inspiration, not least by Bob Dylan. Dylan's songwriting craft is examined in John Hughes's chapter, which traces the complex influence and genealogies of Dylan's compositions throughout the 1960s as he crossed the Atlantic in person. Hughes documents the inspiration of Child Ballads and other British folk song on Dylan's writing and then considers Dylan's eventual return in 1965 to the American tradition, as redrawn by Guthrie, as he adopted an American provenance. At the same time, Hughes locates Dylan in a literary and poetic tradition.

In his chapter on Alan Lomax, Ronald Cohen provides crucial biographical detail of Lomax's time in Great Britain during the 1950s. Substantially sourced from his own research in Lomax's letters, Cohen's examples enable us to appreciate the impact that Lomax had on the circulation of American folk, blues, and jazz through his BBC broadcasts from London. Lomax not only continued the tradition of recording indigenous folk songs of Ireland and Scotland while in Britain but was also instrumental in facilitating the performances of American singers such as Big Bill Broonzy in appearances alongside traditional British singers in both public and radio performances. Cohen documents the significance of these transatlantic music exchanges, including the African American source material that would be so significant to developments in popular music.

This theme is taken up in chapter 8 by Roberta Freund Schwartz, who examines the fusion of blues and rock in the 1960s heyday of what has variously been termed "blues rock," "British blues," or "R&B." Describing the ways in which bands such as the Rolling Stones, the Yardbirds, and the Animals adopted style and lyrics from the recorded music of Chicago blues performances such as Broonzy and others, Schwartz demonstrates the revolutionary impact of the fusions that were the result of the British exposure to American blues.

The specific example of the Animals, examined by Brian Ward in chapter 9, demonstrates the processes at work for one band in the context that Schwartz describes. The Animals rose to fame in the 1960s, and their success, Ward argues, reflected the 1960s enthusiasm for African American–derived sounds. By tracing the provenance of the Animals' rendition of "The House of the Rising Sun" through its complex genealogy, Ward describes the following "fetishization" of blues authenticity. This essay illuminates controversies about white popular musics' appropriation of Civil Rights era radicalism as well as tendencies toward the stereotyping of black Americans that arose in part due to the recording industry's impact on British popular culture.

Andrew Kellett examines the response of the Chicago blues band led by Paul Butterfield to the British blues invasion and their appearance of greater musical authenticity than that of the British "invaders." He argues that in the course of this rivalry British musicians stopped trying so hard to sound American (to say nothing of "black") and that, as a result, blues rock music truly became a transatlantic dialogue. By examining the mutually constitutive relationship between Butterfield's band and the British bluesmen, Kellett addresses core issues such as authenticity, creativity, and identity construction and seeks to explain the roles they played in this extraordinary cultural call-and-response. Similar issues are explored in chapter 11 by Robert Cataliotti's broader discussion of the contribution of British blues to the construction of a racial nexus between black and white Americans during the 1960s. Taking the careers of B.B. King and Eric Clapton as a starting point, he looks at the impact of the music produced by such British artists as Clapton, the Rolling Stones, John Mayall, Fleetwood Mac, and Van Morrison, along with the research of scholars like Paul Oliver, on the consciousness of American artists and audiences.

While Ward, Kellett, and Cataliotti all describe mainstream developments of black musical influence, a different version of African American music's impact on British culture comes from David Sanjek's examination of Northern Soul in chapter 12. Focusing on a specific geographic region, and a particular moment in time, the 1970s, Sanjek examines the ways in which the actual audience gathered around identification with U.S. soul music, and asks why this music became the focus of this particular "imagined community."

All of the above essays deal with the collection, reproduction, performance, and reception of transatlantic roots music. For the final word we invited a musician to give his own take on an aspect of the transatlantic. Duck Baker, an American living in Britain who plays both U.S. and British roots music and fusions of the two, adds his reflections on Celtic music and, in so doing, joins our other writers in debating the central issue of authenticity. Baker's piece is a salutary reminder that this issue is bound up with an honest desire on the part of roots musicians to value and nurture tradition from whenever and wherever that tradition comes. That is, after all, how and why the music survives.

Notes

1. Thus American roots music includes traditional white folk music, African American blues, and the music of Native Americans, Mexican Americans, Cajuns, and others. See "American Roots Music" at www.pbs.org./americanrootsmusci/pbs_arm_itc_historical_background.html (accessed 15/07/2011). More broadly the term "roots music" as commonly used, incorporates all of folk music, as well as its popularized

forms (e.g., commercial blues) and popular forms that draw on folk and "world" music (e.g., rockabilly, reggae).

2. See for example Ron Cohen's edited collection, *Alan Lomax, Assistant in Charge: The Library of Congress Letters, 1935–1945* (Jackson: University Press of Mississippi, 2011); John Szwed, *Alan Lomax: The Man Who Recorded the World* (New York: Viking, 2010) [in the UK as *The Man Who Recorded the World: A Biography of Alan Lomax* (London: William Heinemann, 2010)]; Alan Winkler, *"To Everything There is a Season": Pete Seeger and the Power of Song* (New York: Oxford University Press, 1999); Alec Wilkinson, *The Protest Singer: An Intimate Portrait of Pete Seeger* (New York: Vintage, 2010); and Will Kaufman, *Woody Guthrie American Radical* (Chicago: University of Illinois Press, 2011). Bob Riesman's *I Feel Good: The Life and Times of Big Bill Broonzy* (Chicago and London: University of Chicago Press, 2011) provides a perfect example of a singer who blurred the distinctions between blues and folk. On the British side, *Electric Eden: Unearthing Britain's Visionary Music by Rob Young* (London: Faber & Faber, 2010) is the most related recent work.

3. Ronald Cohen, *Rainbow Quest: The Folk Music Revival and American Society, 1940–1970* (Amherst and Boston: University of Massachusetts Press, 2002); Benjamin Filene, *Romancing the Folk: Public Memory and American Roots Music* (Chapel Hill and London: University of North Carolina Press, 2010); Karl Hagstrom Miller, *Segregating Sound: Inventing Folk and Pop Music in the Age of Jim Crow* (Durham and London: Duke University Press, 2010), William G. Roy, *Red, White and Blues: Social Movements, Folk Music and Race in the United States*, (Princeton and Oxford: Princeton University Press, 2010).

4. Roy, *Red, White and Blues*, 2–3.

Transatlantic Roots Music

1

The Historical and Social Background of Transatlantic Roots Music Revivals

—Jill Terry and Neil A. Wynn

> I guess all songs is folk songs. I never heard no horse sing 'em.
> —Big Bill Broonzy, "Folk singing," *Time*, 23 November 1962.[1]

The distinction between folk music and popular music is often blurred. Indeed, from the 1940s on folk songs often made the charts and could therefore be classed as popular; and as the broadcasting and recording industries grew, this became ever more the case. However, "roots" music (sometimes also "world" music to include non–English language music), is the focus of this volume, which demonstrates the growing appreciation of a "transatlantic world" and the interconnectedness of folk forms that resulted from the cultural transfer between Europe, Africa, and the Americas. The flow of people from Britain, Ireland, Europe, Mexico, and Africa into the United States of America helped shape American folk music, that is, the music performed (at least originally) by ordinary people (rather than professional musicians) reflecting upon their everyday life and work as well as their hopes, traditional tales, and romances. Often based on songs and melodies from the Old World, their original authors mostly unknown, this new music emerged among the rural workers, farmers, and miners of the East Coast and Appalachia, the plantations (and prisons) of the South, black urban communities, the cowboys and ranchers of the plains, lumberjacks in the far West and Northeast, itinerant workers and hoboes, and industrial laborers of northern cities in the nineteenth and twentieth centuries. As Marty Stuart remarks in the PBS television series *American Roots Music*, the diversity of roots music—including as it does everything from Scottish, Irish, and English ballads, to fiddle music, sea shanties and songs, hillbilly and cowboy songs, country and western, and blues—represents more of a root system than a unified whole. Not all of this system can be represented in this book. By way of introduction here, we want to present some of the key debates about roots/folk music, provide an overall chronology of the development of folk music on both sides of the Atlantic, and offer a case study of some individuals who were not always recognized as folk singers and indeed have often been lost to history despite their popularity in both the United States and Britain, and whose repertoire often fell between "folk" and "popular."

Frequently associated with a "lost" pre-industrial world and known variously as folk, country, cowboy, labor, or blues, American folk music was subsequently "discovered" and "rediscovered" on both sides of the Atlantic in successive folk revivals through the twentieth century. However, the revivals often prompted discussion and debate about the origins and authenticity of the songs and their connection with similar musical forms in the Old World, and the interest in folk music became a transatlantic phenomenon as scholars and musicians investigated and adopted not just their own traditional music, but also that of their distant relatives across the ocean.

The commercialization of the music industry and incorporation of folk music into broader pop music led to the spread of folk beyond its original geographical confines, increasingly blurring national and regional distinctions; and as music crossed back and forth across the Atlantic, the questions of "authenticity," origin, and "authorship" became ever more complex. As Benjamin Filene points out, "the notion held by early folklorists . . . of an unselfconscious, unmediated, and wholly un-commercial mode of music expression strikes me as fundamentally flawed: almost all musicians, after all, are influenced by others and make use of their talent in social settings. Given the explosion of mass media, rigid definitions of folk music become especially illusory when applied to the twentieth century."[2] Contemporary critics such as Elijah Wald and Karl Hagstrom Miller (echoing earlier scholars such as Alan Lomax, D. K. Wilgus, and Archie Green) have pointed out that distinctions between folk and popular music are often artificial, imposed by intellectuals rather than the people who perform the music. Miller quotes Johnny Shines, a friend of the famous bluesman Robert Johnson who, Shines insisted, would play "ANYTHING that he heard . . . popular songs, ballads, blues, anything."[3] Wald points out further that Johnson's fame is based more on the work of later white writers and performers than the response of audiences at the time who were limited in number precisely because Johnson made so few records and never had a big hit.[4] However, as Filene argues, the harder it is to locate and define cultures, the more value is placed on musical "authenticity" to create an idea of roots.[5]

On both sides of the Atlantic one vital element in the routes that this music has taken is race. While color has been harnessed as the authenticating factor in the performance and marketing of folk and blues, we are also reminded of the role of music in race relations, especially in the South, as well as the influence that black performers have had on white musical styles in both folk and popular music whether in the United States or Europe. In examining the transatlantic routes of American roots music, we therefore are confronted by the importance of race in musical cultures and in claims for authenticity. A contentious example is that of Leadbelly, who was presented by John Lomax as the epitome of the primitive Negro—while Lomax himself, in his autobiography *Adventures of a Ballad Hunter*, described himself as belonging to a family of "po' white trash." Neither characterization was accurate. But in his aim to find unsullied, "authentic" black music Lomax visited most of the Southern penitentiaries in the 1930s to "feel carried across to Africa . . . as if I were listening to the tom-toms of savage blacks" in his quest for the "idiom of the Negro common people."[6]

Early Folk Revival Collectors

The practice of compiling, collecting and recording traditional vernacular songs was a transatlantic affair. Although it began in Britain early in the eighteenth century and continued through into the nineteenth with Walter Scott's collection, *Minstrelsy of the Scottish Border* (1802–3), it was an American, Francis James Child, professor of medieval studies and English literature at Harvard College, who published the first major compilation of British folk song: *The English and Scottish Popular Ballads* (1882–98), originally in ten (later five) volumes of ballad lyrics that were believed to predate the printing press or existed outside of the printed medium. His work often formed a point of reference of British songs for later collectors seeking the origins of folk music in the United States. With another Harvard professor, William Wells Newell, Child also helped to establish the American Folklore Society in 1888. Ironically, while this American popularized British folksong, it was an English folklorist, Cecil Sharp (1859–1924), founder of the English Folk Dance Society—forerunner of the English Folk Dance and Song Society (EFDSS)—who, influenced by the work already undertaken by Olive Dame Campbell of North Carolina, became the equivalent of Child in the USA. In 1916, assisted by Maud Karpeles, Sharp "discovered" British folk music in the Appalachians. The result was the publication of *English Folk Songs of the Southern Appalachians* in 1917, a work that includes forty Child ballads.[7] Cecil Sharp was purely interested in collecting song and dance in England and in the southern United States from the "source"; he advocated folksongs as "racial products" and took the view that "the only musical source of cultural improvement was pure folksong."[8] Sharp's expedition in 1916 to the Appalachian Mountains supported his thesis that Appalachian musical culture clearly demonstrated its antecedents in English, Irish, and Scottish folksong.

While Sharp and others were searching for surviving British ballads in the South, John Lomax, a Texan, collected black and white material, cowboy (including black and Mexican cowboys), blues, Cajun, Mexican American, hillbilly, and prison songs, as well as spirituals. He published *Cowboy Songs and Other Frontier Ballads* in 1910. The continued growth in interest in American folk music after World War I was reflected in a growing number of folk festivals in the 1920s and the creation of the Library of Congress Archive of American Folk Song in 1928. In 1933 Lomax became the curator of the Library of Congress collection; that same year he and his son Alan Lomax began the first of several field trips to the southern states collecting material that appeared as *American Ballads and Folk Songs* in 1934. Alan Lomax was to become exceptionally prolific in published and recorded output of his collections of roots music throughout the United States, Europe, and beyond, and was a major influence in reviving interest in folk music on both sides of the Atlantic.

Cecil Sharp and John Lomax's searches for authentic folk music in the Appalachians were governed by their own specific prescriptions to seek out examples of "pure" Scottish and English folk ballads, in the process masking the fact that the intermixing of national and racial traditions had been continuous. Their "folk" music needed to be uninfluenced by the commercial mass media. To this end, John Lomax deliberately sought out the most isolated black men he could find in the penitentiaries in the South, while Sharp located the most isolated white singers in the Appalachians. The segregation of roots music into black or white, blues or folk was recognized by collectors, although some, such as the writer Carl Sandburg, were vaguer as to origins. While his *American Songbag* (1927) was clearly intended as a celebration of Americana, Sandburg confessed that the origins of songs could be complex: the very first in his collection, "He's

Gone Away," was, he wrote "of British origin marked with mountaineers and southern negro [sic] influences."[9]

Second Generation Folk Revival Musicians

Like Cecil Sharp, Alan Lomax also made frequent Atlantic crossings. He had an idea of folk music that it need not be specific to a group but could be shared by a nation. As Benjamin Filene has argued in *Romancing the Folk*, "most Americans would have been surprised to hear that America *had* any folk music.... Rural musicians had had no reason yet to think of themselves as 'the folk' or of their music as 'folk' music."[10] Lomax's work resulted in the first great published collections of American folksong and made it clear that the repertoire of songs and dance tunes from Britain to be found on both sides of the Atlantic was prolific, diverse, and very rich. The young Pete Seeger was his assistant in compiling a *Checklist of Recorded Songs in the English Language in the Archive of American Folk Song to July, 1940* and Seeger also compiled *American Folk Song and Folklore: A Regional Bibliography*.[11] Alan Lomax's work as folk collector/ethnographer offers an important window on transatlantic folk exchanges. One significant example was his 1959 trip to the Deep South accompanied by English folk singer Shirley Collins. He sought out singers and musicians from both sides of the color line, recording everything from black chain gangs to white shape-note singers, and this previously unrecorded music is meticulously preserved and available among the vast collections in the Library of Congress Lomax Archives.[12] While Cecil Sharp thought of folk music in terms of its survival from the past and recorded it by transcribing it in written form, Lomax made audio recordings and was interested in the music as a living force. Both these methods continued to some extent later in the twentieth century in the work of people like Paul Oliver and Samuel Charters who transcribed songs from recordings.

The transatlantic crossings of these and earlier collectors were continued through radio broadcasters such as Alistair Cooke, who immigrated to the United States in the 1930s and produced a series of radio programs for the BBC. For *I Hear America Singing* (1938) Cooke used field recordings from the Lomax collection. Lomax meanwhile traveled to London in the 1950s to escape the repressive climate of Cold War America and achieved extensive exposure for both American and British folk and blues recordings in several series of BBC radio and TV programs, creating the first television series in the UK, *Song Hunter*, in which source singers and traditional folk songs had significant exposure. In an obituary following Alan Lomax's death in 2002, David Gregory writes that Lomax's production of *Negro Sinful Songs performed by Leadbelly* was the first commercial album of African American folk songs and was followed by release of *The Midnight Special: Songs of Texas Prisons* and Woody Guthrie's *Dustbowl Ballads*.[13]

Karl Hagstrom Miller argues that folklorists "helped to naturalize segregation by insisting that important aspects of African American or white folk culture were those that showed no sign of cultural miscegenation," thus "forming the basis of the musical color line." The recording industry's desire to produce "race" and "hillbilly" records reinforced this segregation through their selection of performers and songs. Indeed, to meet Ralph Peer's requirements performers "employed racialized sounds," deliberately affecting the popular black blues sound or the white hillbilly sound regardless of their own race.[14] Talented "hillbilly" mountaineers have capitalized on this since the 1920s recordings by Ralph Peer that eventually led to an explosion of performers heading to Nashville, the celebrated home of white country music; once identified as the true white roots of America, this music did not return to or acknowledge its British or its black roots.

The availability of source material in print and on record facilitated the folk revivals on both sides of the Atlantic, motivated by what Robert Cantwell describes as a nostalgic "generational longing" for a sense of connection with an enduring past and a rooted sense of belonging in an imagined community.[15] The revivals established strict criteria to facilitate a project that can be seen to be a response to a need for the reproduction of "Englishness" in England in the post–World War II era, and to establish a version of "Americanness" in the Cold War climate in the United States. While the political climate in the States saw Alan Lomax seeking refuge in England, it also contributed to a deep fracture in the British folk revival scene then being led by folk singer Ewan MacColl: "We were intent on proving that we had an indigenous folk-music that was as muscular, as varied and as beautiful as any music anywhere in the world. We felt it was necessary to explore our own music first, to distance ourselves from skiffle with its legion of quasi-Americans."[16]

MacColl's stance is reinforced by his claim that the "main objective" of his hugely successful radio series, *Ballads and Blues*, was "to demonstrate that Britain possessed a body of songs that were just as vigorous, as tough and as down-to-earth as anything that could be found in the United

States."[17] MacColl's wife, the American folk singer Peggy Seeger (half sister of Pete), criticized British singers of American folk songs: "[But] when I hear a British person singing a folk song from America I feel that there's an anachronism, a spiritual anachronism, if you want to put it that way, there's something which is not quite right."[18] As Ben Harker writes,

> MacColl's policy was "purposefully provocative and inevitably divisive. The paradox behind the British folk revival's attitude to American culture was widely recognised. Certain types of American music—particularly the work of Woody Guthrie, Leadbelly, Big Bill Broonzy—had in the second half of the 1950s kick-started a movement that often defined itself in opposition to 'commercialism,' and particularly the American and Americanised manifestations of commercialism that dominated the pop charts at the time . . . the policy was, for MacColl, a way of declaring that phase over."[19]

In the United States, Pete Seeger begged his audiences to listen to traditional musicians and recommended, as Dick Weissman notes, "Always mentioning the original sources of the songs that you performed; not using 'modern' chords, but rather sticking to the sort of chord progressions that traditional blues or country musicians played, and a certain non dramatic dryness of performance styles."[20]

Roots revival musicians thus sought to deny the transatlantic roots and routes of their repertoires as they strove to establish the authenticity of traditions and to resist the processes of musical migrations as well as racial crossovers that comprise the histories of U.S. roots music, whether performed in America or in Britain and Europe. As David Whisnant documents in *All That Is Native and Fine*, the American festivals of the 1930s, such as the White Top Festival in Virginia, "brought performers out of their isolated surroundings. . . . Confronted by the beauty and authenticity of the 'real thing,' the audience would be moved to forsake vulgar commercial imitations." The Festival promoted purely white national culture based on Anglo-Saxon folk music.[21]

Folk clubs and festivals proliferated throughout the sixties and seventies and blossomed further in the festival scene in the 1980s; but in the words of Michael Brocken, "the [British] folk club coterie of the 1970s transformed the folk revival by acting out a fantasy of authenticity that their own time denied them."[22] In both Britain and the United States the revivalists saw themselves as renewing connections with a strain of democratic experience that modern life was threatening to destroy. "As communists we have a special interest in the folk revival," wrote A. L. Lloyd in 1962, "seeing it as a valuable popular weapon with which to combat the brain-softening commercial culture that the masters think fit for the masses."[23]

African American Music Revivals

One significant element of the Lomaxes' work was the inclusion of African American songs, and in 1936 they published *Negro Folk Songs as Sung by Leadbelly*, a collection of songs performed by Huddie Ledbetter aka Leadbelly. The Lomaxes were not the first to compile and publish songs from the black community: John Wesley Work Jr., professor at Fisk University, collected slave songs and produced *The Folk Song of the American Negro* in 1907. Scholarly interest was also evident through the 1920s in the work of people like Howard Odum, professor of sociology at the University of North Carolina; Newman White, professor of English at Duke University; the writer/professor Dorothy Scarborough; and in the publication of W. C. Handy's *Blues: An Anthology* (1926), perhaps the first collection to describe and analyze blues.[24]

One of the issues surrounding African American music was its definition. It is clear that black and white musicians borrowed from one another. Just as blues songs often included elements of popular music, many African American performers had a wide repertoire including folk ballads and other popular songs as well as blues; others were identified simply as "blues singers." As African Americans moved northward out of the South from World War I on, blues and jazz spread into the major industrial centers of the North, where they took on forms classified as rhythm and blues, which in turn became a shaping force in the emergence of rock 'n' roll, blurring even further questions of definition. At the same time the folk revivals in both the USA and UK during the 1950s led to a rediscovery of "authentic" classic or rural blues, that is, the blues of the period prior to World War II.

The blues revival of the 1950s and early 1960s went alongside the folk revival—performed in the same venues and attracting the same audiences, but escalated by the appearances in England and Europe of black blues artists such as Big Bill Broonzy, Brownie McGhee, Sonny Terry, and Muddy Waters. The American Folk Blues Festival toured Europe and England from 1962 through 1972, and after a gap, began again in the 1980s.[25]

A foremost early British venue for blues was the Ballads and Blues Club in London, later to be called the Singers' Club, run by Ewan MacColl and A. L. Lloyd. The folk revival in the United States was at its height in the early 1960s and became closely associated with the civil rights movement, especially through the involvement of Pete Seeger and Joan Baez. The second folk music revival mingled great new songs of the civil rights and antiwar movements with old ones, as African American spirituals were re-created on the front line of protests.[26] Pete's younger half brother Mike Seeger was an important figure in the following generation in the United States as he tried to re-create the style of folk music performance from half a century earlier. He was one of several folklorists making trips to the South to search out white performers who had recorded in the 1920s and 1930s, while other folklorists and performers were focusing their attention on the music of black blues guitarists.

It is due to these American musicians and others, as well as the later success of rhythm and blues, that British audiences and musicians encountered African American music. From the Beatles to the Rolling Stones to the Animals, many British bands turned to black music for inspiration and "authenticity." The history of this development has been outlined by a number of authors, including another contributor to this volume, Roberta Freund Schwartz, author of *How Britain Got the Blues: The Transmission and Reception of American Blues Style in the United Kingdom*. Several of the chapters here deal with aspects of the transatlantic flow that turned music originating in the American South into an international form. However, African American music already had a significant presence in Britain, and many of the writers dealing with the growing influence of African American music in Britain have outlined a narrative that seems to separate different forms of black performance into distinct categories. Thus while it is recognized that different forms of black music came to Britain and the rest of Europe with performers such as blackface minstrel troupe the Ethiopian Serenaders in the 1840s, and religious music with the Fisk Jubilee Singers beginning in the 1870s, it was jazz that developed as a major influence from the end of World War I on. Beginning with the Original Dixieland Jazz Band in 1919, visiting American jazz bands and touring groups appeared through the interwar years, culminating in the appearances of Louis Armstrong and Duke Ellington in the early 1930s.

A growing number of British jazz bands played versions of American jazz/swing. Some of these, already adopting the mantle of "traditionalists" or "purists," were leading a revival of New Orleans or Dixieland jazz.

Even this early, debates about authenticity in black music were emerging in the columns of the British music press. A lengthy article in the leading music weekly, *Melody Maker* on February 27, 1943, discussed whether Bessie Smith sang jazz or blues, while a piece the previous week by the leading music writer Edgar Jackson pondered "Is Basie Jazz or Swing?" In the March 20, 1943, issue Bill Elliott and Jeff Aldan noted that there had been "so very few examples of genuine blues singing" issued in Britain, but pointed to the popularity of Bessie Smith, Rosetta Howard, Trixie Smith, and Ida Cox as well as Pete Johnson and Joe Turner in readers' surveys. "Blues and boogie woogie," they remarked, "were on the up-grade in the affections of this country's jazz lovers." However, the arguments about what was and was not jazz or blues continued—interestingly with a discussion in January 1947 of Josh White's rendition of "House of the Risin' Sun," which, according to the reviewer, was "not quite blues" but still an "almost perfect record," if not quite as powerful as the version White had performed on the BBC "a while back." The review also noted that Alan Lomax had said that until White's performance, "We have heard it sung only by southern whites." This signaled much of the discussion about White that was to persist in later years, as well as raising some of the issues about the origins of "House of the Risin' Sun" discussed in this collection by Brian Ward.

The debates about what was "real" jazz or what constituted blues indicate the rather simplistic categorization of musical forms that led some African American musical influences to altogether disappear from the sight of experts and later "evangelists." So much has this been the case that Brian Ward asks, "Why Does Nobody Remember the Most Popular African American Entertainer of the Interwar Years?"[27] As Paul Oliver indicates in his chapter, many black American performers visited Britain and Europe in the inter-war period, but the entertainer Ward is discussing was Florence Mills, a star of the "plantation revues" such as *Dover Street to Dixie* and *Blackbirds of 1926*. Mills scored great success in the latter when it came to Ostend, Paris, and London; the Prince of Wales apparently saw the show twelve times. She achieved even greater acclaim in *Blackbirds of 1927* in London, and for a while "Mills mania" led to the production of Mills dolls and stockings in the Florence Mills shade. The song most associated with Mills was "I'm a Little Blackbird Looking for a Bluebird," interpreted by some people as a thinly veiled call for equality. The song became a jazz standard when recorded by Eva Taylor, herself a well-known jazz-blues singer, accompanied by a band including Sidney Bechet and Louis Armstrong in 1924.[28]

Tragically, Mills died at the height of her success in 1927, possibly from exhaustion. Although her performances might be dismissed as reflecting the stereotyped expectations of white audiences, her funeral was nonetheless the largest ever in Harlem until then. She was succeeded by Adelaide Hall, a Brooklyn-born singer who first performed professionally in the all-black Broadway musical *Shuffle Along* in 1921. Like Mills and others of her contemporaries, Hall does not fall neatly into any simple categorization of musical performer: her hit song from *Blackbirds* was "I Can't Give You Anything but Love," and her repertoire ranged from "I Got Rhythm" and "I'm in the Mood for Love" through to "Lover Man" and "Minnie the Moocher." She performed with the likes of Josephine Baker, Lena Horne, and Ethel Waters, and recorded with, among others, Louis Armstrong, Cab Calloway, Duke Ellington (most famously scat singing on "Creole Love Call," a song judged scandalous in its day and of which writer Edmund Wilson is said to have exclaimed on hearing it, "I'll never believe in God again, I'll never believe in anything again"[29]), Fats Waller, and Art Tatum, and yet was equally happy in the musical and vaudeville tradition, and with popular song generally. A two-year world tour beginning in 1931 made Hall one of the United States' wealthiest black women. With her husband, Bert Hicks, a British West Indian, Hall opened a nightclub in Paris in the thirties before moving to Britain in 1938 where they established the Florida club in Mayfair. As well as roles in West End musicals, in 1940 Hall made a cameo appearance in Alexander Korda's Oscar-winning film, *The Thief of Bagdad*. She was so successful in Britain that she remained in London until her death in 1993. She became the first black star to have a long-term contract with the BBC and in 1941 was reported to be the highest-paid entertainer in the country. Through her radio shows, records, and many public performances—including entertaining the troops as a member of ENSA (Entertainers' National Service Association), she was said to be second only to Vera Lynn in popularity. Hall continued to perform on both sides of the Atlantic through the 1950s, and although her career went into decline after the emergence of rock 'n' roll, she was still active into the 1990s. In 1980 Hall was among those who took part in the Newport Jazz Festival's celebration "Blues is a Woman," and she was recognized personally in 1991 by the Guinness Book of Records as the most durable recording artist, having performed over eight consecutive decades.

Almost as successful as Hall was Elisabeth Margaret Welch, another New York–born singer who performed in Eubie Blake's *The Chocolate Dandies* with Josephine Baker in 1924 but who really emerged in

Blackbirds in 1928 with Hall and Bill "Bojangles" Robinson. Welch came to Paris with *Blackbirds* in 1929 and returned as a cabaret performer in 1930. In 1933 she moved to London and made a name singing "Stormy Weather" in the revue *Dark Doings*, and scored another hit singing "Solomon" in Cole Porter's *Nymph Errant*. Having appeared at the London Palladium with Cab Calloway in 1934, Welch was a regular performer on BBC radio. In 1935 she had further success in *Glamorous Night* singing Ivor Novello's "blues melody," "Far Away in Shanty Town." She also co-starred with Paul Robeson in the movies *Song of Freedom* in 1936 and *Big Fella* in 1937. Like Hall, Welch remained in Britain during the war and entertained the public and service personnel as well as making a number of stage appearances as an actor. After the war she appeared in a number of successful revues, continued to sing and act in radio broadcasts, and emerged as a television actor in plays and musicals right through to the 1970s. Her last professional appearance was in September 1996 in a British Channel 4 television documentary entitled *Black Divas* singing "Stormy Weather." She died in 2003.

The fact that performers like Mills, Hall, and Welch are often now forgotten is undoubtedly in part because they became popular, mainstream performers and did not remain simply blues or jazz singers. Nonetheless, they did help introduce non-American audiences to African American music. Perhaps more surprising is the fact that the war years themselves are left out of discussion of transatlantic cultural transfers. Not only did the war encourage an interest in "peoples' music," it also brought a flood of American music across the Atlantic as American and African American service personnel came first to Britain and then to Europe, bringing not just their records and V-discs, but also their bands. At its height the American invasion of Britain numbered about two million, approximately 130,000 of them African Americans. For many Britons this brought firsthand encounters with African Americans and their culture. Paul Oliver has recalled the seminal moment when he overheard black GIs singing in Suffolk in 1942: "It was the strangest, most compelling singing I'd ever heard," and it began his lifelong interest in black music.[30]

Sociological, Ideological, and Political Motivations for Roots Music Revivals

What caused these revivals? Georgina Boyes suggests that revivals function as an antidote to industrial capitalism, war, and modernity, and that the English revival was presented as "a direct and urgent response to a cultural crisis," namely the passing of oral and other folk traditions with the growth of urban and industrial society.[31] Such concerns were evident earlier in the Romantic movements at the end of the eighteenth century; they too were associated with the quest to form national identity both in Britain and in continental Europe in the nineteenth and twentieth centuries. Ironically, folk music could also point to diversity and be associated with forms of dissident national identity: Scottish, Irish, Welsh, in Britain; Breton or Corsican in France; Basque or Catalan in Spain; Sicilian and Sardinian in Italy; and so on.

In the twentieth century the rise of new technologies such as records, radio, and later television all helped spread and encourage interest in different, sometimes forgotten types of music. While many of those interested in folk tradition were students of language and literature, the rise of the social sciences, particularly sociology and anthropology, in the late nineteenth century gave new impetus for the study of tradition and supposedly pre-industrial societies. These intellectual trends continued, reinforced by the rise of working-class organizations, which produced yet more music of "the people" in the form of labor songs, but also by the rise of left-wing political organizations that identified with "the people" and their culture. This identification increased during the Depression years, as economic collapse saw a shift in politics toward the ordinary people, in Franklin Roosevelt's words, "the forgotten man." In Nazi Germany the identification of workers, *volk*, and nation took on an overtly racist aspect. While working people were often celebrated in the painting and murals of artists employed by the New Deal's Works Progress Administration (WPA), their songs and oral histories were also collected by the same organization.

The Depression also spawned new or revived folk music in the labor conflicts associated with the rise of industrial unions spearheaded by the Congress of Industrial Organizations (CIO) and in response to the economic collapse of farming and the environmental disaster of the Dust Bowl. In his songs Woody Guthrie explicitly addressed many of the issues relating to folk music, its origins, and significance, but above all located it with the ordinary working person. World War II only spurred on the "age of the common man" as fighting for a common cause brought a great democratic spirit—in theory, at least. As the Allied powers banded together to defeat Hitler's Germany, they celebrated one another's folk cultures—thus the BBC during World War II was to broadcast not only American folk music, but also that of the Soviet Union. The African American singer Paul Robeson, who supported left-wing causes in many ways, personified the trends of the 1930s and 1940s, becoming an international star whose repertoire included spirituals, African American and international folk songs, as well as concert music. Equally representative was the creation in London of the International Folk Music Council 1947 (now the International Council for Traditional Music) as an affiliated organization of UNESCO with Ralph Vaughan Williams as its president until 1958, when he was succeeded by Maud Karpeles.

The Cold War in the USA witnessed a tide of anti-unionism and discouraged overt sympathy with working people as "left-wing"—Pete Seeger famously was hauled before the House Un-American Affairs Committee in 1955, as was Paul Robeson in 1956. Nonetheless, folk music continued to be popular, reaching wider audiences with the Weavers' recording of Leadbelly's "Goodnight Irene" in 1950 (also recorded by, among many others, Frank Sinatra) and in 1958 with the Kingston Trio's hit "Tom Dooley." The continued appeal of folk music was due to a considerable extent, as Ron Cohen has pointed out, to the evangelical work of people like Pete Seeger who, having worked on Armed Forces Radio Service during the war to "advance the cause of freedom," returned home determined to continue the campaign in support of labor causes and the maintenance of a reform agenda. At the same time, Alan Lomax was promoting international roots music through publications and recordings. A new record company, Disc Records, was succeeded by Folkways in 1949 and large recording companies like RCA Victor also produced some folk releases.

Although developments in postwar folk music are often seen as separate from the rock 'n' roll craze that began in the mid-fifties, young people often identified with the songs because they were anti-establishment and hinted of a grittier world that existed before the rise of suburbia and the affluent society. But the simplicity of folk music also had an impact: many budding young musicians of the emerging postwar teenage generation learned their first guitar chords picking "On Top of Old Smokey" or "Goodnight Irene." In Britain the link was more direct as the success of people like Lonnie Donegan—a banjo player with Chris Barber's jazz band who sang in the intermissions and had an enormous hit with "Rock Island Line"—led to the skiffle boom that presaged the British rock 'n' roll explosion.

The war years, then, accelerated the loosening of traditional cultural barriers and introduced a wider British (and European) audience to American and African American musical forms. It is not surprising that in the postwar years, first jazz and then folk and blues music gained in popularity on both sides of the Atlantic. What is interesting is the growing interest in African American culture in Europe, particularly Britain, and the way in which that was exported back to the USA. This flow of musical influence has occasioned much debate. At the same time, issues about folk music raised by the first collectors, Child, Sharp, the Lomaxes, and many others continued, not just about black song but also about all folk music.

The most recent, or third, revival of what we now describe as roots music celebrates both the global and the local and ranges across the entire spectrum of ethnicities, whether defined as world music or specifically American, which now includes Celtic, klezmer, southern, Cajun, zydeco, Tex-Mex, and Native American, to name a few. This revival also is profoundly affected by the scope of technological availability. Recorded catalogues of traditional music are digitally available, for example through the Smithsonian Global Sound Collection. Musicians now independently record and distribute via YouTube. In 2007 critic Thomas Gruning reflected: "Folk is no longer a type of music. Rather, it is symptomatic of a dynamic confluence of ideas, ideals, and ideologies within which . . . tradition, lived experience, community, economy, tourism (both literally and figuratively), and technology intertwine in a convoluted web of significance."[32] One important home of what could be called the third revival wave is also the festival scene.

The essays in this volume do not necessarily offer final answers, but they point to the variety of questions that the transatlantic roots and routes of "roots" music pose. In the end the discussions may be simply academic and all music, as Bill Broonzy suggested, should be judged as folk. But "folk" music as such has often seemed likely to disappear, swallowed up into the wider commercial world of popular music. As an important part of our heritage, its meaning, impact, and interconnectedness need to be kept alive and explored; the various revivals should be seen and understood at least in that context, and as a reviewer of a recent study of English folk music notes, "Folk, be it traditional, mystical, mythical, radical or experimental, is a living breathing form. . . . It is everywhere, in all the music we hear, in every song we sing."[33]

Notes

1. Quoted in Karl Hagstrom Miller, *Segregating Sound: Inventing Folk and Pop Music in the Age of Jim Crow* (Durham and London: Duke University Press, 2010), 275.

A. L. Lloyd also attributes what he calls the "dreary axiom" to Louis Armstrong in *Folk Song in England* (London: Lawrence & Wishart, 1968), 12.

2. Benjamin Filene, *Romancing the Folk: Public Memory and American Roots Music* (Chapel Hill and London: University of North Carolina Press, 2010), 3.

3. Miller, *Segregating Sound*, 1.

4. Wald, *Escaping the Delta: Robert Johnson and the Invention of the Blues* (New York: Amistad, 2004), xv.

5. Filene, *Romancing the Folk*, 55.

6. John A. Lomax, *Adventures of a Ballad Hunter* (New York: Macmillan, 1947).

7. See Ronald D. Cohen, *Folk Music: The Basics* (New York: Routledge, 2006), 19–26, for a fuller account of Cecil Sharp.

8. Georgina Boyes, *The Imagined Village: Culture, Ideology and the English Folk Revival* (Manchester: Manchester University Press, 1993), 66.

9. Carl Sandburg, *The American Songbag* (New York: Harcourt, Brace, 1927), 29.

10. Filene, *Romancing the Folk*, 9.

11. In his introduction to the Southern Folk Heritage Series (Atlantic Records), Alan Lomax notes: "Some of the songs date back to European and African origins. Others were created in the pioneer period. Still others were born yesterday. The whole collection is a testament to the folk tradition of the Southern states where the country folk—Negro and white—continue to sing the deep songs of our country."

12. The Lomax family collection is in the Center for American History at the University of Texas, and the collections of the Archive of Folk Culture, American Folklife Centre of the Library of Congress.

13. David E. Gregory, *Folk Music Journal* 8, no. 4 (2003): 548–64, 549.

14. Miller, *Segregating Sound*, 4, 81, 119.

15. Robert Cantwell, *When We Were Good: The Folk Revival* (Cambridge: Harvard University Press, 1966), 36.

16. Ewan MacColl, *Journeyman* (London: Sidgwick & Jackson, 1990), 272.

17. MacColl, *Journeyman*, 299.

18. Cited in Michael Brocken, *The British Folk Revival: 1944–2002* (Aldershot, UK: Ashgate, 2003), 79.

19. Ben Harker, *Fakesong: The Manufacture of British 'Folksong' 1700 to the Present Day* (Oxford: Oxford University Press, 1985), 160.

20. Dick Weissman, *Which Side Are You On?: An Inside History of the Folk Music Revival in America* (New York: Continuum, 2005), 79.

21. David Whisnant, *All That is Native and Fine: The Politics of Culture in an American Region* (Chapel Hill: University of North Carolina Press, 1983), 191–93.

22. Brocken, *The British Folk Revival*, 116.

23. Ben Harker, *Class Act: The Cultural and Political Life of Ewan MacColl* (London: Pluto Press, 2007), 166. Although not discussed here, A. L. Lloyd, and especially his book *The Singing Englishman* (London: Workers' Music Association,

1944), championed the democratizing of "folk" to include music emanating from the industrial north of England.

24. Howard W. Odum (1884–1954), *The Negro and His Songs* (Chapel Hill: University of North Carolina Press, 1925) and *Negro Workaday Songs* (Chapel Hill: University of North Carolina Press, 1926); Newman I. White (1892–1948), *American Negro Folk Songs* (Cambridge: Harvard University Press, 1928); Dorothy Scarborough (1878–1935), *On the Trail of Negro Folk Songs* (Cambridge: Harvard University Press, 1925) and *Song Catcher in Southern Mountains: American Folk Songs of British Ancestry* (New York: Columbia University Press, 1937).

25. Details of the American Blues Festivals can be found on the several compilation albums and the itineraries of the tours are listed at www.wirz.de/music/afbffrm.htm.

26. See David King Dunaway and Molly Beer, *Singing Out: An Oral History of America's Folk Music Revivals* (Oxford: Oxford University Press, 2010), chapter 7.

27. Paper given to the Historians of Twentieth Century USA (HOTCUS) Music and Popular Culture Symposium, University of Reading, 4 March 2010.

28. The details of Florence Mills's career can be found in Bill Egan, *Florence Mills: Harlem Jazz Queen* (Lanham, MD: Scarecrow Press, 2004).

29. Wilson is quoted in the only biography of Hall: Iain Cameron Williams's *Underneath a Harlem Moon: The Harlem to Paris Years of Adelaide Hall* (London and New York: Continuum, 2002), 115. Further information on Hall in Britain can be found in Stephen Bourne, *Sophisticated Lady: A Celebration of Adelaide Hall* (London: Hammersmith & Fulham Ethnic Communities Oral History, 2001).

30. Paul Oliver, *Blues Off the Record* (Tunbridge Wells: Baton Press, 1984), 3.

31. Boyes, *The Imagined Village*, 1.

32. Dunaway and Beer, *Singing Out*, 186.

33. Dan Cairns, "Tripping through the music of time," reviewing Rob Young's *Electric Eden: Unearthing Britain's Visionary Music* (London: Faber, 2010), in (London) *Sunday Times*, Culture section, 8 August 2020, 35.

2

"Early Morning Blues"

The Early Years of the Transatlantic Connection

—**Paul Oliver**

For the purposes of this chapter, the term *roots music* relates essentially to folk traditions of African American song and music in their many forms. These include the religious idioms, notably the spirituals, that were widely acknowledged from the mid-nineteenth century, and the later gospel songs, which were influenced by secular music idioms. Of these, ragtime was important, being initially based on banjo playing of the earlier minstrelsy, and subsequently on the syncopated piano music, which was so termed. Considered in the roots music context, ragtime and its "Stride" derivative referred to the compositions and playing of such pianists as Scott Joplin and Thomas "Fats" Waller (who played stride piano, a later form of ragtime), who were African American. A number of compositions were by white musicians, but they each had their own distinctive musical characteristics, frequently recognized by Europeans who were inspired by them. The questions arise as to how the latter became aware of these types of African American music, and how these crossed the Atlantic as formulated musical genres.

Implicit in the music of North America is the assumption that the musical forms were essentially adopted by the English-speaking peoples, but the evidence of contemporary writing and recording indicates that these idioms were widely performed in Germany, the Low Countries, France, Scandinavia and, to some extent, in Italy, Spain, and Russia. However, it must be recognized that the question of musical roots also applied in the opposite direction—for example, in the adoption of the ballad tradition that Irish immigrants brought to North America, and the influence on spirituals and gospel music of the hymns and sacred songs composed by British churchmen who migrated west.

To a considerable extent the questions, which are promoted by the transmission of these forms of aesthetic expression and the skills in their presentation from America to Europe, remain unresolved. The present discussion is concerned with African American roots music, especially blues, and how the idioms were conveyed, received, and adopted in Europe. To be assimilated, a musical idiom with such a specialized origin had to be both recognized and welcomed. Consequently, how the ground was prepared and African American creativity and expression were recognized and appreciated, as the anticipated new forms were being created, also needs consideration.

Complex though the phenomena may be, the music and related aspects of performances by African American artists, on stage or in clubs, have a history of promotion and appreciation in Europe that grew for a century from the early 1870s. Audiences of that period had witnessed the transition from the emergence of minstrelsy, with its white exponents, to the development of theatrical entertainment by way of groups and troupes, and eventually, to duets and soloists that gave prominence to blues artists. Prior to this there had been many minstrel companies that had followed the tradition established by Dan Emmett and his fellow entertainers early in the nineteenth century. A feature of the minstrel company was that its performers were customarily white, but were masked in "blackface," usually by applying burnt cork. Eventually, African American minstrels became numerous, many of them also using blackface, with exaggerated red lips. Such companies sang, danced, and exchanged witticisms with a central figure, "the interlocutor." Performing in line, they included several banjo players, together with "endmen" of the line who played tambourine and rattled "bones."

Several black American minstrel troupes performed in Britain. An early black minstrel was Master Juba (William Henry Lane), who was famed as a reel-and-jig dancer and was heard in 1842 by Charles Dickens in the Five Points District of New York. Also accomplished as a banjo and tambourine player, Master Juba worked in minstrel shows, joining Richard Eli's company, the Ethiopian Serenaders, and traveling to England with them in 1846. They were suspected by some listeners as being white entertainers "blacked up," authentic black minstrels still being rare, although their numbers were increasing. Minstrel show entertainments often illustrated life on the plantations but during the post–Civil War years some depicted military units, as did Callender's Minstrels with their burlesque Georgia Brigadeers, renamed the Ginger Blues in 1877.

A contemporary show, the Haverly Colored Minstrels, had a very successful tour in England in 1880–81. Included was the black composer James Bland who had worked with the highly regarded minstrels Sam Lucas and Billy Kersands, joining them in Sprague's Georgia Minstrels. Bland wrote several hundred songs, including many that became major hits, such as "Dem Golden Slippers" and "Carry Me Back to Old Virginny." Managing his own black minstrel companies, which were very well received in Germany as well as in Britain, James Bland remained for a decade in Europe. Returning to the United States in 1890 he was far less popular, and died a pauper in Philadelphia.

European responses to the African American music forms that entertainers and instrumentalists brought with them from the United States were generally appreciative. Although details of the musical transmission may be lengthy and dependent on the identification of the American singers and musicians who visited Europe, the diversity of artists and the numbers of players of specific instruments, and the countries, cities, concert halls, and other locations where they performed over the years, are substantial evidence of the extent of the positive and informed reception of their music in several countries. Europeans were attracted by the expressive music and vocals that they heard, commenting upon the rhythms, instrumental qualities and entertainment value of the musicians and singers who performed as well as on the lively group and solo dancing in which many also engaged.

Generally, however, blues was not acknowledged as a significant new form of musical expression associated with black Americans until the end of the first decade of the twentieth century, with the publication of the compositions of W. C. Handy, Chris Smith, and others. Identification of specific blues singers in the United States came even later, with just a few recordings of female singers such as Rosa Henderson, Lizzie Miles, and Sara Martin, some under pseudonyms, being issued in Britain during the 1920s. None of those mentioned performed in Europe at the time, but the quality of African American music was already widely recognized, following the visits of exponents of black sacred music. Of these, the Fisk Jubilee Singers were among the earliest. The Fisk Singers constituted a company of mature students of the Fisk University of Nashville, Tennessee, which was dedicated to the advanced education of black Americans. The university was facing financial problems, and the students who formed the group of Jubilee Singers made a successful tour in the eastern and northern United States in order to raise money for the university project. More money still was raised when, under direction, they toured Europe during 1895–96. A singular event that drew wide recognition on both continents was their singing in a Royal Command Performance before Queen Victoria of England.

There was more than one troupe of the Fisk Singers, and soon there were other companies visiting Europe, including the Norfolk (Virginia) Jubilee Company. The term *jubilee* reflected the days of celebration of Emancipation that followed the Civil War. These troupes were of different sizes and had varied repertoires. From one body of Jubilee Singers emerged the American Troubadours, a secular group of singers that established themselves independently when their Jubilee Company performed in Germany in 1898. Minstrelsy continued well into the late twentieth century—for example, in the British television and music hall *Black and White Minstrels Show*, which ran from 1958 until 1978—and is considered by some historians of the subject to have been the longest-lasting form of popular music, terminated only because it was increasingly perceived as racist. Nevertheless, some black minstrel troupes were impressive, like the Bohee Brothers' Colored Minstrel Company (including a few white players among its thirty artists), which was reported to have played to enthusiastic audiences in 1889 at the International Hall, Piccadilly Circus. Numerous black minstrels, such as the previously mentioned Billy Kersands and Sam Lucas, were much sought after and featured in diverse shows. By the late 1890s a new trend was marked with the writing and production of a musical show that owed little to minstrelsy, namely Bob Cole and J. R. Johnson's *A Trip to Coontown*, in which Sam Lucas was featured.

From the larger minstrel companies and jubilee singers, the emphasis moved to smaller groups and quartets. Subsequently, as a result of working more closely together, these were largely replaced by duets and single, star performers. Some had already made their mark, as was the case with Edgar Jones, a solo entertainer who played fruit bottle (jug) and other homemade instruments, whose show ran for six months in London and in the provinces for several years. During much of the same period others performed in Sweden, Germany, Denmark, and eventually in most countries in Europe. At the turn of the century the New Orleans–born instrumentalist, Seth Weeks, who played banjo, mandolin, and guitar, was performing in France while a black company, the Louisiana Troupers, was playing to audiences in Vienna, Austria. A popular entertainer in 1902 was dancer and singer Belle Davis, known as the "Greatest Coon Cantrice," who was accompanied by four children who were able dancers and entertainers, often termed her "PickChicks," a term derived from pickaninny. They performed in London and in many other British cities, as well as in European countries, including Belgium, Germany, and Bohemia. By this time the term *coon* (derived from raccoon) was often applied to black entertainers.

In February 1903 the celebrated team of Bert Williams and George Walker produced the musical *In Dahomey* with music by Will Marion Cook as well as some by Williams. Later that year Cook took the show to London, where it played at the Shaftesbury Theatre, featuring the comedian, harmonica player, and dancer Pete Bowman. After a period back in the States he returned to London where he made a large number of recordings for Odeon and Edison Bell. Some years later, he toured extensively throughout Europe and beyond, even playing in Russia, India, and North Africa. Meanwhile, Cook brought Ernest Hogan's Tennessee Students to London to play at the Palace Theatre, and on to Paris and Berlin. Cook's use of folk instruments and folk music made Britain and Europe even more aware of the creativity of black musicians and the qualities of their performances. At the end of the decade, Cook took his New York Syncopated Orchestra, with fifty artists, including the brilliant young clarinetist Sidney Bechet, to the Albert Hall, London. While in England they played for the royal family before the company toured throughout Europe.

In contrast to the large companies that Will Marion Cook favored, an increasing number of small groups were featured in the States, and soon worked in Britain. In 1912, for instance, the African American group the Five Musical Spillers arrived in Liverpool, where they played at the Alhambra Theatre before entertaining the following year at the London Hippodrome. During the second decade several groups followed them, most notably the Southern Syncopated Orchestra, which played in London from 1919, almost immediately after the "Great War" (later termed World War I).

Although direct links with blues and jazz were limited, the presence of black musicians and singers in popular music prepared the way for performers of the new idioms. Visits by early blues artists were not numerous, but a few may have come in another capacity, as did the pianist Jimmy Yancey, who originally came to Europe as a tap dancer. He claimed to have been engaged in a royal performance, as indeed were several other black artists in the following decades.

A number of female singers and entertainers, in whose repertoires blues played a part, did come to Europe. Prominent among them were the singers Alberta Hunter and Ethel Waters. The former had worked in vaudeville and cabaret for some years before. Hunter had composed blues and recorded them in the United States and this may have helped her obtain engagements in London, Monte Carlo, and Nice in the late 1920s. After a short period in Drury Lane, she returned to Paris to perform at the Grande Carte and the Chez Florence Jones Cabaret. Back in the United States for a while, she worked in Chicago and Harlem, but Europe still appealed to her and she revisited London and Paris before singing in clubs in Amsterdam, Copenhagen, and (during the mid-1930s) Russia and Egypt. Ethel Waters's overseas visits were less extensive but, after appearing in numerous revues in New York, Philadelphia, and Chicago, she too was to perform in London and, in 1929, for several months at the Cafe de Paris.

Among the American visitors in the mid-1920s and early 1930s, dance orchestras were prominent. Noble Sissle's Colored Entertainers, which played the Plaza in London in 1926, were very popular, and Sissle's reconstituted orchestra played dates in Austria, Germany, and other European venues. Sissle also worked with pianist Eubie Blake, composing a number of songs together and being successful with their celebrated *Shuffle Along* show of 1921. Also featuring Paul Robeson and Josephine Baker in minor roles, it was the first major black musical show to play on Broadway. Sissle and Blake also wrote songs for *The Chocolate Dandies* a year later. Referred to as "The American Ambassadors of Syncopation," Sissle and Blake were engaged by Charles B. Cochran to write songs for his show, *Still Dancing*, in 1925–26.

While in London, Eubie Blake played at the celebrated Kit Kat Club, where the current Prince of Wales (later King Edward VIII) came and played drums. Blake joined Andy Razaf in writing the score for *Blackbirds of 1930*. He kept on writing, playing ragtime piano, and recording until his death in 1983, at the age of 100. In his life and his work he spanned the era of the "roots" and made highly effective use of all the "routes" by which African American music could be enjoyed between continents.

The issue arises as to what enabled Europeans to develop their values and knowledge of the music, facilitating their recognition and appreciation of black blues singers. Undoubtedly, sheet music played an important part, especially in early years, as it had with minstrelsy. The initial publication of W. C. Handy's *Saint Louis Blues* and its many successors played a significant role, but the music as written seldom conveyed the qualities of sound and expression to be heard in live performances. Undoubtedly a large number of black entertainers worked in England with several remaining to tour further in Europe.

Recognition of the sounds of the blues and the development of the idiom might not have persisted had it not been for the availability of the phonograph. Many records were made as wax cylinders in the late nineteenth century, eventually to be replaced by 78 rpm (revolutions per minute) flat discs. In the early 1920s these were limited, but the major record companies rapidly expanded in both the United States and in Britain, such as the American Victor, which was linked with the British HMV (His Master's Voice) and American Columbia, associated with Parlophone. Sometimes these companies released blues and jazz issues in Britain. Among them in the 1920s, were items by Bessie Smith, Lizzie Miles, the Dixieland Jug Blowers and many more, some being released in the segregated "race" catalogues. Such record issues were few in number but became much sought after, following the visits of American musicians and singers and greater awareness of records. This was soon widely accepted, even King George V himself having a large collection of Duke Ellington records. Sales of Bessie Smith issues in Britain were in sufficient numbers for Parlophone to pay for what was to become, in 1933, her last recording session. The resultant records were issued in Britain as a memorial album following her death in an automobile accident.

During the late 1930s, the popularity of boogie-woogie, the eight (beats)-to-the-bar piano idiom enhanced by evident passages of improvisation, grew among jazz enthusiasts. This inspired the release in Britain of titles by the pianists Pete Johnson, Albert Ammons, and Meade Lux Lewis, some featuring the powerful blues singer Joe Turner. The growing enthusiasm for blues based on the twelve-bar structure led to the release of titles by "Pinetop" Smith and Jesse James, among others, on Brunswick and Vocalion. The names of the performers and the titles of some of their "numbers," in addition to the distinctive features of their instrumental techniques, vocal qualities, and the content of their verses, stimulated the curiosity and pleasure of a great many European record collectors.

The availability of records was greatly limited by World War II; the materials employed in 78 rpm discs were needed for military manufacturing. After the end of the war and a few years of recovery, a number of enthusiasts began to produce records themselves, "dubbed" (copied) from items in personal collections. Issues on Tempo, Jazz Collector, and Esquire, among other "labels" as the new record companies were termed, enabled aspiring collectors to obtain previously rare blues items. These were reviewed and discussed in jazz magazines, notably *Jazz Journal*, edited by Sinclair Traill and with regular blues columns and articles by Derrick Stewart-Baxter, and *Jazz Monthly*, edited by Albert McCarthy, who commissioned blues reviews and articles by myself, and subsequently, by Tony Russell. Specialist magazines such as *Jazz News* included significant and groundbreaking articles by Max Jones, Ernest Borneman, and others, and the increasing readership was an incentive for the record companies to issue yet more blues. I was urged by Charles Chilton, the editor of *Music Mirror*, to write a series of articles based on my blues collection and those of friends and fellow enthusiasts. The series, *Sources of Afro-American Music*, appeared monthly in the mid-1950s, the research involved eventually taking book form.

In 1963 the first magazine dedicated to blues appeared, namely *Blues Unlimited*, issued monthly in Britain by Simon A. Napier, who was the principal editor, which he shared with Mike Leadbitter. Well in advance of the American publication *Living Blues*, it produced 150 issues, with a rich variety of articles, interviews, and reviews, a model that has been followed by numerous blues publications. Concluding eventually, it was succeeded by *R & B Monthly*, then edited by Mick Vernon, to which Mike Leadbitter, John Broven, Neil Slaven, and others, including myself, contributed. Interviews and narratives by visiting blues singers, including Otis Spann, Curtis Jones, and Aleck Miller, known as Sonny Boy Williamson No. 2, were published in it. In 1965 British collector Bob Groom initiated yet another magazine, *Blues World*, and in those pre-Web days readership was substantial enough for all to flourish. Each would supplement articles on blues with discographies, extensive coverage of book and record reviews, and amendments to information when necessary.

Although blues was essentially a vocal form sung in English, many of the collectors and writers on the subject were based in other European countries. Jacques Demetre wrote blues columns for the Paris-based journal *Jazz Hot*. In France there was a measure of rivalry between the followers of Charles Delauney and those of Hughes Panassie, but both were important in promoting interest in the music, and valuable in the thorough nature of their research. Record collections were not exclusively based on European releases; many were augmented by discs owned by overseas American servicemen who sold their American records when they were to return to the States. Many continued to trade fragile 78 rpm records by airmail, often exchanging them for issues featuring European dance bands. Meanwhile, in France, Charles Delauney was building another collection:

that of the information borne on the record labels of the blues and jazz discs, including the names of the artist and the song titles—to which he sometimes added the names of the composers. Of great importance was the issue number and, in particular, the less evident matrix number of each recorded item. Noted in company files, matrix numbers often indicated the dates, location, participants, and session sequence position of each title. Seeking the file information where possible, with painstaking research on recording dates, locations, and personnel, Delauney eventually published in 1941 what he termed the *Hot Discography*. It had omissions, of course, but it stimulated other research that slowly supplied the missing data by way of specialist magazines, including *Discophile* and *Matrix*, published in Britain.

Further discographies of individual performers, specific record company issues, and other classifications were produced in Britain and in several other European countries. Of significance were the jazz and dance band discographies prepared by Brian Rust, formerly of the BBC, notably his two-thousand-page *Jazz Records 1897–1942*. Most important in the present context is the *Blues and Gospel Records* discography, compiled by R. M. W. Dixon and the late John Godrich, later augmented by Howard Rye. Other discographies were compiled of post–World War II blues issues—including *Blues Records 1943 to 1970*, initially edited by Mike Leadbitter and Neil Slaven—and of gospel music; this extensive European documentation made a major contribution to the international comprehension of recorded jazz, blues, gospel, and related music. But, while all this was valued, the lack of any live performances by blues singers was disappointing. For a decade or two of recovery after the end of the war there was relatively little change in this situation. The possibility of any blues singers coming to Europe seemed minimal, even though many enthusiasts hoped that it could happen. The French writer Hughes Panassie sought to solve the problem by visiting the United States with the booking of jazz performers particularly in mind, but also of blues singers. In fact, it was Panassie who encouraged Leadbelly to come and perform in France. But, owing to bad health, he was obliged to return to the United States, where he died a few months later. Soon after, Panassie arranged for the blues singer Big Bill Broonzy to come to France, where he toured from Paris to Calais.

In Britain other promoters, most notably Howard Davison, also had the booking of blues singers in mind. Eventually Josh White, the singer from the Carolinas who had a unique style of both singing and playing, was engaged. Some of the items he chose to perform were disappointing for many British listeners, being sung at the time with little "blues feeling." It was the expressive form and content of the blues with its repeated first line of each verse, and their personalized content, together with distinct vocal qualities, and partly improvised instrumental accompaniment, often by the singer himself, that had so much appeal for European enthusiasts. In the early 1950s the celebrated guitarist Lonnie Johnson was booked to perform in England, but his selection of "I Left My Heart in San Francisco," among other non-blues titles, suggested that the briefing of both these singers had not been appropriate, their chosen themes having been among those that they played in New York "folk" clubs. Fortunately, this was not the case with Big Bill Broonzy when he was booked to perform in Kingsway Hall, London, in September 1951, promoted by the London Jazz Club.

Big Bill was brought to the Hall by Max Jones and was introduced by Alan Lomax, who had been living in England and broadcasting for the BBC. The choice may have seemed appropriate but, to the disappointment of many in the audience, Lomax monopolized much of the time of the event before he introduced the blues singer. Nevertheless, when Big Bill performed, the experience of hearing him was unforgettable. His vocal blues were moving in their content and expression, brilliantly supported by the quality and sensitivity of his guitar playing. After a highly successful tour, Broonzy returned to England in 1955–56 with the publication of his autobiography. Sadly, he died in 1958, a victim of throat cancer. It seemed as if there could be no replacement for Big Bill.

A dispute between the American Federation of Musicians and the Musicians Union in Britain forbade the booking of groups and bands from the "other" country. Intermission artists and variety entertainers were permitted however, and the inspiration of the leader of the most popular British jazz band, Chris Barber, ensured that listening to live, authentic blues could continue. In place of Big Bill he booked Carolina blues guitarist Brownie McGhee and the incomparable blind harmonica player Sonny Terry. Their interplay of strings and mouth harp was variously in accord and in contrast, making their appearances stimulating, whether in concerts or in clubs. Terry and McGhee returned on several occasions, but Chris Barber had other blues artists in mind. Among them were the veteran pianists Roosevelt Sykes and Eurreal "Little Brother" Montgomery and, eventually, one of the most celebrated of blues singers in the United States at the time: McKinley Morganfield, known as Muddy Waters. His electric guitar playing did not appeal to those who favored the traditional acoustic instrument, but it exhilarated many others with its intimations of the contemporary music of the Chicago blues clubs. Muddy was supported by his modest but skilled pianist, Otis Spann, and later by the electric harmonica-player, "Little Walter" Jacobs. By now, visits of blues singers were being anticipated by large numbers of enthusiasts; many toured Britain, France, Germany, Scandinavia, and even in Russia.

Inevitably, there were European enthusiasts who sought to sing or play blues themselves. They included the French jazz guitarist Django Reinhardt, whose crippled fingers imparted a unique sound to his playing, and the capable violinist Stephane Grappelli. As might be expected, the blues vocalists were principally British. They included George Melly, a strong singer with an art background, and the female "classic blues" singer Beryl Bryden, who sometimes worked together in a vaudeville-style duet. More folk blues–directed was the playing and singing of guitarist Alexis Korner, some of whose supporting instrumentalists eventually became significant in the rock music trend. Also "down home" was Cyril Davies, who played twelve-string guitar in the manner of the now legendary Leadbelly. Vocalist "Long John" Baldry was one of the several aspiring British blues singers who performed in the Barrelhouse and Blues Club run by Korner and Davies in Piccadilly, Central London. Some of the visiting blues singers were invited to attend the club, although in view of contractual obligations they were not asked to perform. But some volunteered nevertheless, memorably including Muddy Waters.

Profiting from the appreciation of British and Continental enthusiasts for their music, a number of blues singers who visited Europe chose to stay, glad to leave behind the racial discrimination they experienced in the United States. Prominent among them was the ex-boxer "Champion" Jack Dupree. A firm blues and boogie player with a sense of humor, the New Orleans–born pianist lived for a while in different parts of Britain, Scandinavia, and Germany where he died in 1992. With a comparable stay of several years, another blues pianist, Peter Chatman, known as Memphis Slim, resided in a suburb of Paris. Aware of his audience's curiosity, he would replay aspects of the history of blues piano. Peculiar to pianists, European residence was also sought by the Chicagoan Eddie Boyd, who lived in Sweden, and the modest but exploratory piano player Curtis Jones, who moved through several European countries, even spending a while in North Africa.

Toward the end of the 1950s, there seemed little likelihood that any other blues singers would be invited to perform in Europe. Aware that there were many Chicago bluesmen that had not been approached, and conscious that the European contexts were very different from those of urban U.S.A., the French writer Jacques Demetre, with companion discographer Marcel Chauvard, decided to do research in the States in the summer of 1959. They concentrated on Detroit and Chicago, where they documented the clubs on Hastings Street in Detroit and on the South Side of Chicago, among other locations where blues singers were still working. The trip was written up in *Jazz Hot* and published in book form many years later. Their accounts and photographs of singers like Howling Wolf indicated that blues was still active in the northern cities. At much the same time, the Belgian collector Georges Adins also made a research trip, extending this to East St. Louis, where he met Sonny Boy Williamson No. 2 among other singers. It was clear that more had to be done, in particular with finding and interviewing blues singers in the South, which I resolved to do in 1960. Accompanied by my wife, we joined California-based Chris Strachwitz in Memphis, Tennessee, from where we made an extended trip that included Mississippi, Louisiana and Texas. In these states we were able to meet, interview, and record many blues singers in their familiar environments. Chris founded his record company Arhoolie (which means field holler) with the issue of many of these recordings.

On return to Britain I was invited by the American embassy to design a large blues exhibition, which would be shown in 1964. In those days the embassy was accessible and host to a great many arts events. *The Story of the Blues* exhibition was assembled from my collection of photographs, including those taken during the U.S. trip. Mounted on two dozen large panels, the exhibition of over five hundred items covered the ground floor of the new embassy building in Grosvenor Square. It was visited by all members of the Alvin Ailey Dance Company, by black American writers including Langston Hughes, and by a number of blues singers, Lightnin' Hopkins and Little Walter among them. By this time a dramatic change had taken place, and live blues was to be heard in Europe to an unprecedented degree. "Ein Konzert mit den besten Blues-Sängern Amerikas" as the publication *American Folk Blues* declared. The size of a twelve-inch "long-play" record, it was the brochure of a Folk Blues Festival organized by two German promoters, Horst Lippmann and Fritz Rau, of Frankfurt am Main. They were apprehensive of an impending decline in recognition of the blues but also well aware that many blues singers were still alive and active. After a couple of years in which they had minor concerts, learning to manage and to meet the needs of both musicians and audiences, they initiated a series of American Folk Blues Festivals in 1963. Their concerts presented remarkable casts of performers that included the guitarists Lonnie Johnson, Big Joe Williams, Matt Murphy, and Muddy Waters; pianists Memphis Slim and Otis Spann; harmonica player Sonny Boy Williamson No. 2, backed where required by drummer Bill Stepney and string bass player Willie Dixon who also supported the younger of the "classic" blues women singers, Sippie Wallace and Victoria Spivey. The experience of hearing so many major singers and players was beyond belief for many blues enthusiasts.

Willie Dixon was responsible for more than playing bass: he had worked with many singers in Chicago clubs, and was now able to provide the necessary contacts, helping Lippman and Rau in engaging singers for subsequent festivals. The following year, 1964, saw "a Documentation of the Authentic Blues featuring the best blues artists of America." It was not an unjustified claim; the company included the veteran guitarist Sleepy John Estes, and his harmonica accompanist, Hammie Nixon. The little-known guitarist John Henry Barbee found himself in the company of the powerful Chicago club singer Chester Burnett, known as Howlin' Wolf, who played both guitar and harmonica. Unexpected was the inclusion of guitarist Lightnin' Hopkins from Houston, Texas, while piano blues was represented by Albert "Sunnyland Slim" Luandrew. Harmonica player "Sonny Boy Two" (as Williamson was sometimes called) and Willie Dixon had been in the previous festival, but the 1965 concerts included the celebrated John Lee Hooker, veteran Fred McDowell, and the promising Chicagoan Buddy Guy, among many others.

The Folk Blues Festivals attracted capacity crowds to the Royal Albert Hall and other locations in England and Scotland. Cities in Germany, France, Belgium, the Netherlands, Scandinavia, Switzerland, Spain, and elsewhere all featured concerts. The living blues were brought to virtually all parts of Europe, and the tours were disappointing only in the limited representation of female singers, the slim young singer Sugar Pie Desanto being the exception in 1964. The formidably large but kindly Big Mama Thornton performed in the 1965 session, as did the young singer Ko Ko Taylor. The last of the original classic blues singers, Sippie Wallace, appeared in the 1966 festival, but these were the only women to follow Victoria Spivey.

New to the festivals in 1966 were Junior Wells, Otis Rush, Big Joe Turner, Yank Rachell, and pianists Roosevelt Sykes and Eurreal "Little Brother" Montgomery. It seemed as if the series must be coming to a conclusion but, with the exceptional lineup of 1967 the festivals reached a peak. The selection included a few familiar personalities, who had been featured before and who gave a sound base to the festival, such as Brownie McGhee and Sonny Terry. Important participants were the guitarist Hound Dog Taylor and the electric harmonica player Little Walter (Jacobs). But the strongest feature of the 1967 festival was the presence of singers of an earlier generation, who were born in the very first years of the twentieth century and who represented links with the past history of the blues. Significantly, they were from Mississippi, and included Booker T. Washington White, known as Bukka White, who played memorable slide guitar. Also performing was Eddie "Son" House, a guitarist from Clarksdale who had been a close associate of the "father" of Mississippi blues, Charley Patton, and the legendary Nehemiah "Skip" James, with his perfect integration of vocal, guitar, and lyrics. For experienced and musically knowledgeable blues enthusiasts of the time, a better combination of veteran blues singers could hardly be conceived.

In this period rock music was dominant and blues, for many listeners, seemed an indication of music from the past. Nevertheless, the final American Folk Blues Festival, held in 1970, was optimistic, with subtle indications of the borrowings from contemporary blues of the current "rock" players. The team included John Lee Hooker and Big Joe Williams as representatives of the background; Curtis Jones and Walter "Shakey" Horton as the middle generation; and "T-Bone" Walker (even though ten years older and recording earlier than Horton), Jimmy Reed, and the Eddie Taylor Blues Band as the shapers of the new blues.

While 1970 was the final season of the festivals, it was not the last of Lippman and Rau's creations. Back in 1965 they had commenced spiritual and gospel festivals, with Bishop Samuel Kelsey leading the "authentic documentation of Negro church music in concert." The participants that year included the well-known vocal group the Original Five Blind Boys of Mississippi; Inez Andrews and the Andrewettes from Chicago gave due opportunities for female gospel singers, while Sister Lena Philips and Reverend John Little brought some of the congregation of Bishop Kelsey's Temple Church of God in Christ from Washington, D.C., to the event. Other spiritual and gospel festivals followed, that of 1966 including the Gospelaires of Dayton, Ohio; the Dorothy Norwood Singers of Atlanta, Georgia; and the Harmonizing Four of Richmond, Virginia, with Gospel Joe Williams. By this time the Lippmann and Rau Concert Büro of Frankfurt am Main was also organizing the Festival Flamenco Gitano and the Deutsches Jazz Festival. In addition, they were associated with Norman

Granz's multinational tours of the Oscar Peterson Trio, Ella (Fitzgerald) and Oscar (Peterson), the Dave Brubeck Quartet, B.B. King and Orchestra, and other promotions. Concerts were presented in Frankfurt, Strasbourg, Paris, Düsseldorf, Hamburg, Rotterdam, Amsterdam, as well as in London and many other British cities. They even hosted a tour by Duke Ellington and His Orchestra in the mid-sixties. In 1970 they attempted to bring some of these ventures together with The American Folk, Blues and Gospel Festival, which featured Bukka White, Jack Dupree, Brownie McGhee and Sonny Terry, as well as the splendid Sister Rosetta Tharpe with her gospel guitar.

Although the focus of virtually all their enterprises was African American musical forms and their artists, Lippmann and Rau also presented a festival of American Folk and Country Music, which was of white performers, including the New Lost City Ramblers, Roscoe Holcomb, the Clinch Mountain Boys, and Cyp Landreneau's Cajun Band. It was successful, but the performers did not have the exhilaration of the Blues Festivals. Lippmann and Rau were fatigued by their many enterprises and eventually the festivals were withdrawn.

This may seem an unduly detailed account of the Lippmann and Rau concerts, but the singers they engaged and the festivals that they promoted played a large part in the popularization of blues, and to an extent jazz, gospel, and country music as well. For their events to be successful they needed large audiences and press coverage as well as specialized reviews and accounts. The remarkable enterprises of Lippmann and Rau were certainly among the most important in the identification of the "roots" of African American folk music and the "routes" by which they were disseminated in Europe. As a result of their work and that of their predecessors, most enthusiasts in Europe heard more live performances than did their counterparts in the United States.

As for the routes that they took to Europe, these were literally, made by air, and for this they had the support of Air India, which brought many of the musicians over to Europe and back to the States. Their large advertisements declared: "Swingin the Blues to the land of THE BLUES aboard *AIR-INDIA*. Daily Europe USA, of course."

In terms of major expositions of the roots of blues, and the exercise of the various "routes" by which blues singers and their music and song became known and acknowledged, promoters, writers, discographers, and recorders throughout Europe, as well as in Britain, all played an immense part. Visits by blues singers continued; the last of the early Mississippians, nonagenarian "Honey Boy" Edwards, played in Britain in 2010. The founding of the European Blues Association, with headquarters in central Gloucester, offers the current "routes" by which the thorough documentation and presentation of the blues and its related musical forms from its earliest "roots" can be accessed, shared, studied and, thanks to the development and persistence of recording, much of the "early morning blues" can still be heard and enjoyed.

Selective Bibliography and References

Bean, Annemarie, James V. Hatch, and Brooks McNamara, eds., *Inside the Minstrel Mask: Readings in Nineteenth Century Minstrels*. Hanover, NH: Wesleyan University Press, 1996.

Bigsby, C. W. E., ed., *Superculture: American Popular Culture and Europe*. London: Paul Elek, 1995.

Charters, Ann, *Nobody: The Story of Bert Williams*. New York: Da Capo, 1983.

Cockrell, Dale, *Demons of Disorder: Early Blackface Minstrels*. Cambridge: Cambridge University Press, 1997.

Dixon, R. M. W.. John Godrich, and Howard Rye, *Blues and Gospel Records 1890–1943*, 4th ed. Oxford: Clarendon Press, 1997.

Finson, Jon W., *The Voices That Are Gone. Themes in 19th-Century American Popular Song*. New York: Oxford University Press, 1994.

Fletcher, Tom, *100 Years of the Negro in Show Business*. New York: Burdge, 1954.

Hamm, Charles, *Yesterdays. Popular Song in America*. New York: W. W. Norton, 1979.

Jasen, David A., and Gene Jones, *Spreadin' Rhythm Around. Black Popular Songwriters, 1880–1930*. New York: Schirmer, 1998.

Lotz, Rainer, *Black People. Entertainers of African Descent in Europe and Germany*. Bonn, Germany: Birgit Lotz Verlag, 1997

Marsh, J. B. I., ed., *The Story of the Fisk Jubilee Singers—With Their Songs*. London: Hodder and Stoughton, 1877.

Mellers, Wilfred, *A Darker Shade of Pale. A Backdrop to Bob Dylan*. London: Faber & Faber, 1984.

Nathan, Hans, *Dan Emmett and the Rise of Early Negro Minstrelsy*. Norman: University of Oklahoma Press, 1962.

Oliver, Paul, "Blue-Eyed Blues: The Impact of Blues on European Popular Culture." In Bigsby, *Superculture*, 227–40.

Oliver, Paul, "Overseas Blues: Europeans and the Blues." In Daniel W. Patterson, ed., *Sounds of the South*. Chapel Hill: University of North Carolina Press, 1991. 57–72.

Oliver, Paul, "Taking the Measure of the Blues." In Neil A. Wynn, ed., *Cross the Water Blues. African American Music in Europe*. Jackson: University Press of Mississippi, 2007. 23–38.

Sampson, Henry T., *Blacks in Blackface. A Sourcebook on Early Black Musical Shows*. Metuchen, NJ: Scarecrow Press, 1980.

Southern, Eileen, *The Music of Black Americans. A History*. New York: W. W. Norton, 1971.

Southern, Eileen, "The Georgia Minstrels: The Early Years." In Bean et al., *Inside the Minstrel Mask*. 163–75.

Toll, Robert C., *Blacking Up. The Minstrel Show in Nineteenth-Century America*. London: Oxford University Press, 1974.

Walser, Robert. ed., *Keeping in Time. Readings in Jazz History*. Oxford: Oxford University Press, 1999.

Woll, Allen, *Black Musical Theatre. From Coontown to Dreamgirls*. Baton Rouge: Louisiana State University Press, 1989.

Wynn, Neil A., ed., *Cross the Water Blues. African American Music in Europe*. Jackson, University Press of Mississippi, 2007.

3

Dreaming Up the Blues

Transatlantic Blues Scholarship in the 1950s

—Christian O'Connell

For those with a newly discovered ear for the blues and a desire to know more about the music, a library search will quickly lead to the work of Paul Oliver. For more than half a century he has published books about the music, written articles in the music press and journals, written record sleeve notes, broadcast on radio, and even designed record covers for blues records. He is regarded as one of the leading blues scholars, and for many the publication of *Blues Fell This Morning: The Meaning of the Blues* (1960) marked the beginning of "serious scholarship on the genre."[1] Oliver has published some of the best-known work, such *Conversation with the Blues* (1965), *The Story of the Blues* (1969), and *Savannah Syncopators* (1970). It is no surprise that for the ethnomusicologist David Evans, "it would hardly be an exaggeration to state that most of our present understanding of the blues is based on the work of Paul Oliver."[2] Oliver's interest in African American music was sparked by an encounter with American GIs who were singing while working in Suffolk in the summer of 1942.[3] Writing about this encounter years later, he recalled that ". . . the air seemed split by the most eerie sounds . . . and the back of my neck tingled."[4] However much this recollection has been touched by the hand of nostalgia, it captures the impact of the music on Oliver as a teenager, and possibly mirrors the first experience most aficionados had with the music. Oliver's first experience is particularly significant given that it occurred during World War II, as it provides an example of the influence of African American troops in the diffusion of African American music during the war period.

What may surprise new blues enthusiasts is that Oliver is British and that he is a professor of architecture, meaning he began writing about the blues as an enthusiast rather than an expert. Following his first experience Oliver began collecting all the records of African American music he could find in British junk shops and record stores, particularly blues. In the immediate postwar period, those who shared his enthusiasm were very few, and the majority of British writing on African American music focused on jazz, with blues mentioned in occasional chapters primarily as a branch of jazz.[5] Only Derek Stewart-Baxter's regular column "Preaching the Blues" in *Jazz Journal* dealt with blues on a regular basis, and seemed to provide Oliver with inspiration to deepen his knowledge of the music.[6] The lack of any widespread interest in blues after World War II is probably one of the main reasons for the relative ease with which he began publishing articles during this decade, although it does signify a growth in appreciation of the music in Britain.[7] Another reason is probably that the period was characterized by a resurgent interest in folk music and tradition in Britain, what Georgina Boyes terms the "second folk revival."[8] Oliver's subject matter presented a different type of folk music from that characterizing the British revival, but it nonetheless stemmed from a distinct rural folk heritage, something Oliver was often keen to emphasize. The relative obscurity of blues, coupled with the increasing interest in folk music, gave Oliver a certain amount of freedom with which to approach his work. It obviously proved popular: his articles became regular features in *Music Mirror*, *Jazz Journal*, and *Jazz Monthly*, and the decade also saw the publication of two books by Oliver, the biography *Bessie Smith* (1959) and his classic study of the genre, *Blues Fell This Morning* (1960).

The beginning of Oliver's writing on blues in the early 1950s demonstrates that the music was being studied from across the Atlantic as early as the immediate postwar period, and that an audience for blues existed in Britain prior to the highly publicized 1960s blues revival (the period of the British blues boom and the so-called British invasion bands).[9] The revival has come under severe scrutiny in recent studies which take a deconstructive approach to blues scholarship and reveal the romanticism that has characterized interpretations of the blues in the postwar era. Elijah Wald and Marybeth Hamilton, for instance, argue that the work of white researchers during the 1960s often took on "the hues of romance" due to their reverence for the music, thus ignoring important historical evidence such as record sales.[10] Consequently, the lack of "methodological rigour" of amateur scholars resulted in much of blues history, particularly Delta blues, being invented as much as it was discovered.[11] However, by placing emphasis on the scholarship of the blues revival, Wald and Hamilton's work omit some major elements worthy of investigation for understanding the construction of ideas about the music in the 1950s and 1960s: the contribution of the most prolific and probably the most influential writer on the subject, the European contribution to blues scholarship that represents the transatlantic diffusion of the music, and writing published on blues prior to the revival.

The latter point is of particular significance, as the nature of blues writing in the period preceding the 1960s can help clarify some of the revivalist approaches to blues scholarship that followed. This article will consider Oliver's writing in Britain during the 1950s for magazines such as *Music Mirror* and *Jazz Monthly*, in order to understand the nature of the engagement between scholar and music during the early period of transatlantic interest in blues. Rather than rejecting romanticism as an obstacle to historical truths or as an element that invalidates the research of the blues revival, this article will demonstrate that Oliver's interpretations in the fifties indicate a great deal about the transatlantic reception of the blues in the postwar era. Looking back on his own work and that of fellow blues scholars during the revival, Jeff Todd Titon stated: "by our interpretive acts, we constructed the very thing we thought we had found."[12] By focusing on what Titon refers to as "interpretive acts" and Oliver's engagement with the music, this article aims to demonstrate the ways in which transatlantic visions of the blues emerged in the 1950s. Moreover, it will argue that romanticism was part of the process of analyzing and understanding the music and, importantly, not limited to white American revivalists but to some extent predated by the leading British blues scholar.

Transatlantic Blues: Can White People Understand the Blues?

For some blues scholars, not being African American and not coming from the same social, cultural, and historical context of the blues was a barrier to a true understanding of the music, putting white blues enthusiasts at a huge disadvantage.[13] For Jon Michael Spencer it was simply that whites had never experienced the brutality of racism, and therefore could never appreciate the real significance of a black music such as the blues.[14] This perspective is understandable given the harsh realities of African American life within which the blues emerged. However, what is more important is that regardless of the validity of the white research into black life, white scholars have written about the music and their work has informed much of what Evans called "our present understanding." The music has been able to communicate to those outside the physical and cultural borders of the USA, and some of these people became leading figures in blues scholarship. Indeed, for African American author Richard Wright there were "certain psychological advantages in an outsider examining [the blues]," and the physical and cultural distance separating Oliver from the milieu of the blues was seen as an advantage.[15] For Wright, this distance allowed Oliver the freedom to work without the pressures of the American social and physical climate, allowing a more objective and unbiased analysis.[16]

The distance between Oliver and the land where the blues began was thus regarded as "empty" in the sense that it was devoid of American sociocultural influences that may have clouded his objectivity. This would seem to complement Oliver's own approach to his writing: "I tend to keep myself out of the text, so that there's a focus on the subject of blues or blues singers, without any intrusion."[17] However, one of the characteristics of Oliver's writing for magazines in the 1950s is that this distance was filled by an array of influences derived from the writer's engagement with the music through the primary process of listening and the secondary analysis of texts related to the music and African American culture. If, as Hamilton states, "every landscape is a work of the mind,"[18] then Oliver made contact with the blues by imagining that landscape. An important factor in this process is the role of listening, which ironically is overlooked in many studies of music. Characterized by certain imaginative qualities and the role of the listener's imagination in the interpretation of the music, the significance of listening should not be underestimated. Despite seeing numerous live performances by visiting blues singers in the 1950s, Oliver's experience of blues in this period was highly dependent on the collection and transcription of records as well as interviews with some of the performers he saw. As Titon argues, the "fascination with the recorded artifact produced a distancing that the 'real thing' (hearing the music live) couldn't quite dislodge."[19] His reliance on records was due to the fact that Oliver was not able to visit the land of the blues until 1960, when he would eventually meet and interview a large number of singers in what was deemed their natural environment.[20] The consequence of the physical, historical, and cultural distance separating Oliver from the music was that a large part of the experience was left to the imagination, and by imagining the blues there was also the possibility for exaggeration, marginalization, and to a large extent, invention.

Invention and Imagination

Invention in blues scholarship, as argued by Wald and Hamilton, occurs mainly as a consequence of the combination of two factors: the failure to consider important empirical evidence, and the influence of romanticism, which "obscures as much as it illuminates."[21] This represents a variation from the invention, as argued by the historian Eric Hobsbawm, based on a larger social scale: "The invention of tradition" is a conscious process which, in seeking to establish continuities with "a suitable historic past," is representative of the desired ends of certain ideologies.[22] In music studies, this form of invention is clearly demonstrated by Boyes in her analysis of the British folk revival. Here, invention is an attempt on behalf of collectors and cognoscenti of the folk tradition, such as the British folk song collector Cecil Sharp, to forge a national identity by instituting links with an idealized and imagined past at a time when that very identity was under threat.[23] In another study of the postwar folk revival, Mitchell demonstrates how invention plays an important role in nation building, more significantly in the "idea" of a nation.[24] In terms of folk music then, invention is inherently intertwined with politics.

Invention, as it appears in Oliver's writing and in a large proportion of blues scholarship, differs from the examples mentioned above. Oliver has often been praised for relying on "facts and evidence" and for his research being "carefully documented."[25] There is no direct intention to embellish or romanticize the music as, for instance, in the blues writing of Samuel Charters.[26] Rather than being the reflection of certain political or ideological notions of a national identity, the way the blues is imagined in Oliver's writing of the 1950s is derived from the scholar's involvement with his subject as both an enthusiast and author. If the scholar's work becomes the subject of analysis as part of the deconstruction of blues scholarship, it is therefore necessary to approach Oliver's writing as a body of literature where the lines between fact and fiction are sometimes blurred. It is then possible to appreciate the "literary imagination" of the writer, which creates "fictive elements" in his narrative.[27] This is not to say that Oliver's writing on blues is fictional, because this is far from the case; it is based on a detailed knowledge of African American society, history, and culture. However, the point of the present article is to demonstrate the possibility of an alternative reading of his work in which the various unknown elements of blues scholarship combined with the interpretive processes of listening and research helped construct transatlantic ideas about the blues in the 1950s.

Oliver in the 1950s

In his very first article in 1952, dealing with the topic of religious music in African American churches, Oliver began to depict what he would often refer to as the "Negro world."[28] For Oliver, the further removed the African American was from the influences of the white world, where the places were of a "darker hue," the more it was possible for him to be "unashamedly himself."[29] The distance between black and white, and the separation of the races were fundamental to an understanding of African American music. Ironically, the distance separating the races in the United States was mirrored by the distance separating Oliver from his subject matter. He argued that the cultural and historical distance of the Negro world from the surrounding world was difficult to cross for the "outsider." An example is given in an article on Blind Lemon Jefferson, where there is a specific reference to the singer's anonymity in white America. This was in contrast to the "Negro world" where "the blues singer was valued and loved, for [Blind Lemon Jefferson] spoke to them who were members of his race."[30] (It is ironic to think that Blind Lemon may well have been less anonymous in the United Kingdom than in white America at this point). Similarly, when discussing the significance of Peetie Wheatstraw's blues, it was clear to Oliver that the music spoke strictly through racial lines: "Peetie's blues appealed to his coloured audience because they made no compromise. He sang in their language, he sang of his life which was their lives."[31] The question that arises here is how the writer could draw such conclusions about music in the "Negro world." For Oliver, although accessing this world was difficult, it was not impossible: "there are, of course, exceptions as "[Wheatstraw's] work tends to appeal only to the 'hardened' collector who has allowed himself to be absorbed by the idiom."[32] There is no doubting that Oliver was completely "drenched in his subject."[33] This can be corroborated by the evidence from his personal notebooks from this era which reveal hours upon hours of laborious transcription from records, and the endless listing and referencing of record serial numbers.[34] However, closer examination of his writing exposes the means by which Oliver became absorbed into the "Negro world" by the blues.

By analyzing blues lyrics, talking to visiting musicians such as Big Bill Broonzy and Brother John Sellers, and reading enormous amounts on all aspects of African American life and culture, Oliver gained insights into the world from which the blues emerged. However, one of the most striking seems to have been his use of African American literature, particularly that of Richard Wright, Claude McKay, and Ralph Ellison, which he believed could allow the blues collector "a clearer insight into the environment that produced [the blues singer's] music than he can find in any descriptive work of non-fiction."[35] Although the realism and immediacy that characterize the writing of these authors make this claim more than plausible, it is by no means unproblematic. For instance, despite the naturalist shades of Wright's autobiography *Black Boy*, the narrative "is so consciously shaped and framed, editing out many aspects of Wright's actual life, and reshaping others, that it needs to be considered a fiction, despite the fact that most of the major incidents actually occurred."[36] Wright's autobiography was a literary work molded by the hands of memory and the creative imagination of the author, where the boundaries between fact and fiction were often blurred. By making use of the realism in African American literature, the empty space provided by Oliver's distance from the milieu of the blues was filled by the subjective interpretation of the "Negro world" as these African American writers saw it—meaning objectivity, in Oliver's case, was no longer possible.

Ellison's *Invisible Man* in particular seems to have exerted a certain amount of influence on Oliver. Apart from direct references to the novel in his two articles on Peetie Wheatstraw, there are other, more indirect but nonetheless significant references. For instance, in the novel the invisible man encounters a man on the streets of New York who later turns out to be Wheatstraw:

> Close to the kerb ahead I saw a man pushing a cart piled high with rolls of blue paper and heard him singing in a clear ringing voice. It was a blues, and I walked behind him remembering the times I had heard such a singing at home. It seemed that there are memories slipped around my life at the campus and went far back to things I had long ago shut out of my mind. There was no escaping such reminders.[37]

The song evokes memories of the past, of home, and "far back" in the protagonist. The blues plays the role of guiding the invisible man toward self-realization, one point among many in the novel in which he is in "movement toward identity."[38] The music touches an innate, natural, but hidden part of his identity. This sense of African American atavism seems to be of fundamental importance in Oliver's depiction of music in African American life. For example, in his first article he mentions that music "is so essentially a part of the coloured man's nature";[39] dancing was described as a "natural form of expression."[40] In talking about the Delta singer Muddy Waters, he argues that "it was as natural to him as the desire to eat . . . [to] want to learn to play and sing the blues."[41]

Oliver portrayed the music as being both the symbol and practice of a folk heritage that went deep into the heart of the African American experience, depicting blues and music as being as natural as breathing for African Americans. The examples demonstrate the manner in which Oliver's own imagination as a writer merged with the literary memory of the African American author in a layering process. The "Negro world" is therefore imagined—as it can only be, considering the physical distance separating Oliver from the African American South. This is not to say it is inaccurate, as it is also based on nonfictional material, but that it exists in an imagined, and to a large extent exaggerated, form in the mind of the writer.

One of the major consequences of imagining this world is that it can also be idealized, and in Oliver's writing the evidence of this can be seen in his depiction of the "Negro folk." He often made reference to the blues as "the common folk song of the African American Negro,"[42] and those who sang "the music of their people" were most often regarded as being more authentic and worthy of attention.[43] The explanation for this reasoning lies in the fact that, for Oliver, the blues was inextricably linked to the African American's racial strife: "The Negro knows the blues. He can talk with the blues, walk with the blues. And for the coloured man confounded by his environment, puzzled and disappointed, the blues is not just an unwelcome associate: the blues give him consolation, enough to continue the fight."[44]

Blues enabled a "liberating catharsis" that helped both singer and audience deal with the pressures of African American life.[45] However, rather than forming a way of fighting back against racial discrimination or defying Jim Crow laws as in Robin Kelley's "theatres of resistance,"[46] music in Oliver's Negro world was a coping strategy, a "safety-valve" for the release of tension and hardship.[47] When Blind Lemon Jefferson sang about the problems of "his people," he was a "true folk artist" displaying the folk heritage of African Americans.[48]

It is never completely clear what Oliver means by the Negro folk, and it has often been a criticism of those studying folklore that ambiguity in defining the term can result in *folk* meaning whatever the researcher says it means.[49] What is clearer, however, is that in Oliver's depiction of the Negro world, true Negro folk music was in its purest form where white influence was lowest, but paradoxically was dependent upon the racial oppression of the white world. This depiction becomes clearer in Oliver's consideration of what blues was *not*.

Later in the decade, at the time of the skiffle craze in Britain, Oliver aimed various criticisms at British musicians attempting versions of African American songs. British musician Ken Colyer was described as "singing without feeling," and Lonnie Donegan's failure to impress was given to the fact he was not "born of a folk heritage."[50] It is evident that Oliver, as well as other "blues evangelists" and proselytizers of this period, had developed a clear notion of "how it was imagined the music of rural African Americans ought to sound," and clearly whites, especially British, were not able to replicate it.[51] It is also clear from this evidence why Oliver would be disappointed by the singers Josh White and Lonnie Johnson, who, on their first visits to Britain in the 1950s, played songs that were seen as pandering to a wider audience at the expense of the blues repertoire of their records.[52] In any case, in a later article Oliver would attribute the interest in Negro folk music to the fact that whites had long since lost their own culture, and thus needed to "borrow" from another.[53] It therefore seems apparent that African American folk culture contained elements Western white culture had lost.

Fascination with African American folk culture characterizes much of Oliver's writing, and seems to mirror the attitudes of African American intellectuals such as W. E. B. Du Bois.[54] Oliver's description of the music's function in the Negro world echoes the sentiments expressed by Du Bois: "the true Negro folk-song still live[d] . . . in the hearts of the Negro."[55] This fascination could suggest that music as a form of meaningful expression had become "unnatural" for the white man, as Negro folk culture in its purest form was considered "unpalatable" for the white Western observer.[56] The blues of Blind Lemon Jefferson, although appearing primitive, crude, and unrefined to the white world, was "starkly dramatic, stripped of all superfluities" and "uncompromising" to the African American.[57] Peetie Wheatstraw "sings for the coloured people with no thought for discographers or a white world."[58] For Oliver, then, the true folk blues singer consciously rejected materialism or even (white values of) commercial success.[59] Oliver's Negro folk culture is defined by its opposition to white culture as Oliver saw it in the 1950s. British musicians like Donegan and Colyer could attempt African American songs, but in his eyes they would never be able to match the real thing, as it was not natural for them; so they had to either learn or rediscover their folk heritage. Overall, Oliver idealizes African American folk music and culture in opposition to the commercialism and artificiality of white culture, which was attempting to replicate and appropriate an authentic culture through imitation by skiffle musicians.

Blues is interpreted as a product and expression of Negro folk culture. This is demonstrated by Oliver's treatment of blues lyrics as the direct expression of the hardships of the African American experience, the primary method adopted in *Blues Fell This Morning* and widely used in subsequent research. He justifies this by stating that "[t]he blues singer is seldom inhibited by any thoughts of the more delicate sensibilities of his listeners and his statements are frank and forthright."[60] Despite coming in for some criticism for the method's reduction of blues to a mere report or description of reality that denies it poetic value,[61] according to Oliver the blues singer's "subjective realism" paints an accurate picture of African American life.[62] This "forthright" realism Oliver imparts to the blues is also represented in many of the illustrations he produced to accompany his articles in the 1950s. Figure 3.1, for instance, is an illustration of two African Americans working on the riverside. Their body language shows dejection, their facial expressions convey fatigue as well as melancholy, and the paddle steamers seem to suggest a bygone era. On the other hand, Figure 3.2, which accompanied an article on the living conditions of African Americans, is a representation of urban family life in a tightly cramped living space. Oliver writes, "'Hot-bed' apartments are rented by three families at once, each using the bed and room for eight hours of the day."[63] In the illustration, a despondent elder member of the family sits on the bed with young children. The clean clothes hanging on the line over the bed seem futile considering the griminess of the walls. The image is reminiscent of a scene in Wright's *Black Boy*:

> Another change took place at home. We needed money badly and Granny and Aunt Addie decided that we could no longer share the entire house, and Uncle Tom and his family were invited to live upstairs at a nominal rental. The dining room and the living room were converted into bedrooms and for the first time we were squeezed for living space. We began to get on each other's nerves . . . Rattling pots and pans in the kitchen would now awaken me in the mornings.[64]

The similarity to Wright's autobiography is coincidental. However, Oliver's illustrations show a distinct resemblance to the social photo-documentary style of Wright's *12 Million Black Voices*.[65] These illustrations,

Figure 3.1. "Sources of Afro-American Folk Song 1—Down the Line," *Music Mirror*, May 1954

Figure 3.2. "Chocolate to the Bone," *Music Mirror*, November 1954

which Oliver drew as a pastime during his early years as a blues writer, are the fruit of his absorption into the Negro world.[66] They are a representation of the subjective realism of blues lyrics, but also point toward Oliver's sociological interpretation of the naturalism in the literature of writers such as Wright and McKay. The illustrations are literary images, works of the imagination that aim to present the reality of African American life, but instead, like much realism in art, are closer to *re*-presentations of that reality.

This portrayal of the realism in blues lyrics and their relevance to African American life seems to be an attempt to validate the music as being worthy of more attention. Indeed, Oliver even bemoaned the way northern African American intellectuals snubbed the music for being "backward," claiming "they have yet to recognize the beauty of their own tradition."[67] It is ironic, given the influence of his literature on Oliver's work, that early in his career even Wright regarded blues as being only a "naïve" and "mundane" form of expression.[68] Nonetheless, Oliver was probably referring to the black northern intellectuals of the Harlem Renaissance who renounced blues and jazz as popular entertainment that did not conform to their standards of high civilized art.[69] A notable example would be Alain Locke's New Negro movement to whom "Afro-American music had always been a source of embarrassment . . . [and their] feelings about urban spirituals—the blues—and about jazz sometimes verged on the unprintable."[70] Oliver's sentiments seem to mirror those of the poet Langston Hughes, who regarded blues and related black music as a rich source of heritage and culture. Hughes was one of the few exceptions, along with Zora Neale Hurston, to the predominant view of the low art credentials of African American music, and "was noted as one of the first poets to celebrate the beauty of the blues as an American art form."[71] It is characteristic of those who study folk cultures to feel the need to rescue that culture from extinction;[72] feeling that the blues were being disregarded and forgotten, Oliver defiantly declared that "it has not gone yet" and "there is still time . . . Blind Willie McTell still walks the streets of Atlanta with his guitar and his tin cup."[73] This was a cry, not only for preservation, but for research that consisted of direct contact with the people involved because at the time it was still "living folk-lore."[74]

Interviews and encounters with blues musicians were to become an important part of Oliver's career as a blues scholar, and in the 1950s he began the process of interviewing visiting blues singers in Britain. Among them were Brother John Sellers, Eddie Boyd, Sonny Terry and Brownie McGhee, Big Bill Broonzy, and Jimmy Rushing. Although recordings formed the basis for most of Oliver's research in this period, he acknowledged at the time that the transcription of records could never fully account for all the subtle qualities the recordings contained.[75] He also often stressed the fact that African American folk music was rooted in the oral tradition of the folk culture, in which improvisation was the "golden rule."[76] Therefore, analysis of records could only do so much, and oral history could have a large part to play, especially considering the idiom was fighting for survival and only a handful of its exponents were still alive. Consequently, the large amount of biographical information in articles that focused on singers, especially those from the more distant past, such as Blind Lemon Jefferson and Ma Rainey, were dependent on the recollections and reconstructions from interviews with other musicians such as Big Bill Broonzy.

Oliver often acknowledges that the interviewees could not always guarantee certainty in their recollections, and were liable to exaggerate or exclude certain facts. These are common consequences of using oral history. In blues scholarship physical evidence is often limited to recordings; available information on singers and their lives is scarce, and therefore Oliver's advocacy for oral history can be appreciated. Interestingly, however, the absence of empirical evidence highlights the immeasurable possibilities presented by the enigmatic lives of singers and by the unknown element in the music's history, "for therein lies much of [the blues'] fascination":[77]

> But as the blues collector stares at the record label or listens whilst the needle summons again three lost minutes of a man's life some thirty years ago, he cannot help but speculate at times on the possible chain of circumstances that finally brought him from the city sidewalk and before the crude recording apparatus. . . . Where did he come from; who were his parents; when did he leave home? One wanders and falters, as the limitations of one's own personal experience make it almost impossible to imagine.[78]

This passage not only provides an example of the stimulus given by the unknown to the blues collector, but also highlights Oliver's acknowledgment of the imaginative qualities of listening as an activity. In a study on the role of radio in African American society, Hangen argues that the role of listening through radio allowed African American listeners to "renegotiate racial boundaries."[79] The reliance of the medium on the individual's imagination allowed entry into a sensory experience that could ignore racial barriers, something not as easily tangible in the reality of the South, for example. It can be argued that listening to records was a similar experience in the sense that it could allow Oliver to transcend the transatlantic gulf separating him from the South. Listening was also a key factor in the recording of oral history. Interviews with singers often led to recollections of obscure singers from a lost era who were never recorded, leading Oliver to dwell on the identity of those on record label discographies labeled "unknown."[80] The lack of physical material to discover the unknown elements may have facilitated and perhaps motivated the quantity of guesswork. However, the fascination of enthusiasts with the more obscure elements of blues history could help to explain the enormous interest in singers such as Robert Johnson during the blues revival. Stories vary dramatically on the singer's life and death, and the paucity of empirical evidence to substantiate these has facilitated the creation of myths and legends.[81]

Blues history, then, is a puzzle in which a large portion of the pieces are missing, which the blues scholar strives to unearth. In other words, there are numerous black holes the writer's imagination cannot help filling, and this has two main forms of expression in Oliver's writing. First, the reliance on oral accounts that come from musicians, as described earlier, allows the entry of memory and all its biases into the writing. Second, in the absence of empirical evidence the writer subconsciously constructs a series of narratives and images gathered from his experience of the music through research, interviewing, and listening. An example can be seen in Oliver's exploration of the theme of departure in blues lyrics.

> Coming home when the sun goes down, hand thrust deep in empty pockets, gunny sacks tied about his feet, he pauses before his clapboard shack. The holes in the walls are patched with packing cases and rats live unmolested beneath the floor boards. His children greet him solemn-eyed. Their bellies are swollen with pellagra. Now busy with the hominy grits in the skillet his woman is waiting for him. Only partially does she appreciate why the pay packet is small and why so much of that is spent in the gin-mill at the back of town.[82]

The characters are literal inventions, as they do not refer to any particular singer. Oliver's writing here is not socio-historical or academic but more akin to a fictional literary style. The subtleties of the man's pause, the children's greeting, and the woman's attitude are imagined and seek to create the situation in which a typical bluesman would feel the need to depart. This example is complemented by two further illustrations that depict a man leaving his family (see Figs. 3.3 and 3.4). It would be difficult to find a more stereotyped image of the wandering bluesman leaving his troubles behind and taking to the road. This style is highly representative of Oliver's articles in the 1950s, and considering the writing is journalistic, the creative literary writing style could be understood as attempts to engage the reader. Nonetheless, they manifest the ways in which the writer himself

Figures 3.3 and 3.4. "Another Man Done Gone," *Music Mirror*, Vol. 1, No. 4 (August 1954)

was engaging with the object of his research and the manner in which the blues was being received and interpreted in the early 1950s.

Oliver's interpretive methods for the analysis of blues—the sociological interpretation of African American literature, the subjective realism of blues lyrics, the use of oral history, the activity of listening—allowed him to transcend the "cultural separation"[83] that separated him from the land of the blues. It was then possible to imagine a "Negro world" very different from his own, a world where the blues functioned to help singers and audiences cope with the strains imposed by the harsh realities of life in the American South. Music functioned as both a practice that allowed the African American to go on, and as a symbol of the undying folk heritage of the African American community, defiant in the face of white capitalist oppression. By contrast, the music was reliant upon the white world pushing the Negro world further into obscurity. Ironically, while the blues existed within a place that seemed dislocated from the modern world, modern methods of record transcription and listening to records allowed Oliver and other enthusiasts to become absorbed by it.

The reader of Oliver's work from the 1950s is presented with images of a world where the boundaries between historical fact and the fictive elements of the writer's imagination are often unclear. This lack of clarity is created by the romanticism for a music beset by the enigmatic lives of singers, combined with a sense of loss of folk heritage in the white world. Importantly, however, the influence of romanticism in Oliver's blues writing is not to be understood as a trait that devalues the worth of his research, but instead should be interpreted as one of the underlying features of the nature of blues scholarship of the period. The level of personal involvement in Oliver's writing in the 1950s reflects the personalized experience of the listening process and demonstrates the difficulty the blues writer faces in disengaging with his tastes. Oliver's early career as a blues writer provides an insight into the transatlantic movements of the blues years before the revival of the 1960s, when the names of Robert Johnson and Charley Patton as beacons of authentic blues would become the norm, and the British invasion bands would begin paying homage to their idolized blues masters. Oliver's scholarship during the 1950s was pivotal to British conceptions of blues in this period, as one of the few (but undoubtedly the largest) sources of information and commentary on the music. His work not only provided a socio-historical context to the music for record collectors, but also went on to influence the following generation of scholars, both American and non-American.[84]

Notes

1. Roberta Freund Schwartz, *How Britain Got the Blues: The Transmission and Reception of American Blues Style in the United Kingdom* (Aldershot, UK: Ashgate,

2007), 114. Oliver's book was not the first on the blues, as American writer Samuel Charters published *The Country Blues* in 1959.

2. Quoted in *The Paul Oliver 70th Birthday Tribute* www.bluesworld.com/pauloliver.html, retrieved 22/08/2009.

3. Paul Oliver, *Blues Off the Record: Thirty Years of Blues Commentary* (Tunbridge Wells: Batton Press, 1984), 2.

4. Oliver (1984), 3.

5. See Max Jones, "On Blues," in Albert J. McCarthy, ed., *The PL Yearbook of Jazz* (London: Nicholson & Watson, 1946); Iain Lang, *Jazz in Perspective: The Background of the Blues* (London: Hutchinson, 1947).

6. Roberta Freund Schwartz, "Preaching the Gospel of the Blues: Blues Evangelists in Britain," in Neil A. Wynn, ed., *Cross the Water Blues: African American Music in Europe* (Jackson: University Press of Mississippi, 2007), 149.

7. Oliver (1984), 4.

8. Georgina Boyes, *The Imagined Village: Culture, Ideology, and the English Folk Revival* (Manchester, UK: Manchester University Press, 1993), 198.

9. Although Schwartz acknowledges the pre-1960 blues interest in Britain, it is not the focus of analysis for the reception or study of blues. More has been written on the popularity of jazz in Britain in the interwar period; see, for example, Catherine Parsonage, *The Evolution of Jazz in Britain 1880–1935* (Aldershot, UK: Ashgate, 2005). However, interest in blues music in Britain before 1960 has received little attention.

10. Elijah Wald, *Escaping the Delta: Robert Johnson and the Invention of the Blues* (New York: Amistad, 2004); Marybeth Hamilton, *In Search of the Blues: Black Voices, White Visions* (London: Jonathan Cape, 2007).

11. Hamilton, 8–9; Wald also points to this trend of ignoring commercial record sales by revivalist writers, with the principal result being the idolization of a singer such as Robert Johnson, who sold relatively little and was largely unknown to African Americans in his own time, at the expense of singers who were more successful commercially, and therefore more significant, such as the earlier Leroy Carr; the term "invented" is adapted from Wald's book title.

12. Jeff Todd Titon, "Reconstructing the Blues: Reflections on the 1960s Blues Revival," in N. V. Rosenberg, ed., *Transforming Tradition: Folk Music Revivals Examined* (Chicago: University of Illinois Press, 1993), 223.

13. James H. Cone, *The Spirituals and the Blues* (New York: Seabury, 1972), 124.

14. Jon Michael Spencer, "Blues and Evil: Theomusicology and Afrocentricity," in Robert Sacré, ed., *Saints and Sinners: Religion, Blues and (D)evil in African American Music and Literature* (Liège, Belgium: University of Liège, 1996), 47.

15. Richard Wright, "Foreword," in Paul Oliver, *The Meaning of the Blues* (New York: Collier, 1959) 11 (originally published as *Blues Fell This Morning: Meaning in the Blues*).

16. Interestingly, objectivity is a characteristic for which Oliver has often been praised (see Evans, *Paul Oliver 70th Birthday Tribute*).

17. Oliver (1984), 2.

18. Hamilton, 3.

19. Titon, 223.

20. This field trip led to the publication of Oliver's *Conversation with the Blues* in 1965; Oliver met and interviewed over seventy singers, including Muddy Waters, J. B. Lenoir, John Lee Hooker, Sunnyland Slim, Roosevelt Sykes, and St. Louis Jimmy.

21. Wald, xxiii; the empirical evidence ignored by blues revivalists, as well as record sales, is the findings of early fieldwork conducted by folklorists such as Howard B. Odum.

22. Eric Hobsbawm, "Introduction: Inventing Traditions," in Eric Hobsbawm and Terence Ranger, eds., *The Invention of Tradition* (Cambridge: Cambridge University Press, 1983), 1.

23. Boyes, 22–24.

24. Gillian Mitchell, *The North American Folk Music Revival: Nation and Identity in the United States and Canada, 1945–1980* (Aldershot, UK: Ashgate, 2007), 6.

25. Evans, *Paul Oliver 70th Birthday Tribute*; Schwartz, *How Britain Got the Blues*, 114;

26. In the introduction to the 1975 edition, Charters openly admits that he sought to enrich and embellish the music and the musicians so that more people would take notice. Samuel B. Charters, *The Country Blues* (1959; rpt. New York: Da Capo, 1975), x.

27. Hayden White, "Historical Text as Literary Artefact," in Hayden White, ed., *The Tropics of Discourse: Essays in Cultural Criticism* (London: Johns Hopkins Press, 1978), 99.

28. Paul Oliver, "Match Box Blues: Blind Lemon Jefferson," *Jazz Review* (July 1959), reprinted in *Blues Off the Record*, 69; the term *Negro* was used at Oliver's time of writing as the term *African American* is used in the present day, and did not carry today's offensive connotations. The use of the term in the present article is only to represent Oliver's work accurately and consistently, and in order to avoid confusion.

29. Paul Oliver, "Give Me That Old Time Religion," *Jazz Journal* (February 1952), reprinted in *Blues Off the Record*, 14–15.

30. Oliver, "Match Box Blues: Blind Lemon Jefferson," 69.

31. Paul Oliver, "Peetie Wheatstraw: Devil's Son-in-Law," *Jazz Monthly* (May 1959), reprinted in *Blues Off the Record*, 193.

32. *Ibid.*

33. Wright, "Foreword" to *The Meaning of the Blues*, 11.

34. The personal notebooks were made available to the author by Paul Oliver.

35. Paul Oliver, "Devil's Son-in-Law," *Music Mirror* vol. 3, no. 2 (March 1956): 8.

36. John Lowe, "Palette of Fire: The Aesthetics of Propaganda in *Black Boy* and *In the Castle of My Skin*," *Mississippi Quarterly* vol. 61, no. 4 (Fall 2008): 565.

37. Ralph Ellison, *Invisible Man* (Harmondsworth, UK: Penguin, 1952), 141.

38. Raymond M. Olderman, "Ralph Ellison's Blues and 'Invisible Man,'" *Wisconsin Studies in Contemporary Literature* vol. 6, no. 2 (Summer 1966): 11.

39. Oliver, "Give Me That Old Time Religion," 15.

40. Paul Oliver, "Strut Yo' Stuff," *Music Mirror* vol. 2, no. 3 (March 1955): 4.

41. Paul Oliver, "Muddy Waters: Hoochie Coochie Man," *Jazz Monthly* (January 1959), reprinted in *Blues Off the Record*, 259.

42. Paul Oliver, "Sources of Afro-American Folk Song 1: Down The Line," *Music Mirror* vol. 1, no. 1 (May 1954): 42.

43. Paul Oliver, "In the Sticks," *Music Mirror* vol. 2, no. 4 (April 1955): 4. The references here are to the female singers such as Ma Rainey who, although more involved with the world of entertainment, are praised by Oliver for retaining the quality of singing the "music of their people."

44. Paul Oliver, "Got the Blues," *Music Mirror* (May 1955), 8.

45. Cone, 125.

46. Robin Kelley, "'We Are Not What We Seem': Rethinking Black Working-class Opposition in the Jim Crow South," in *Journal of American History* vol. 80, no. 1 (June 1993): 75–112.

47. Oliver, "Sources of Afro-American Folk Song 1," 42; "Strut Yo' Stuff," 4.

48. Oliver, "Match Box Blues," 66.

49. Richard Middleton, *Studying Popular Music* (Philadelphia: Open University Press, 1990), 128.

50. Paul Oliver, "Hometown Skiffle," *Music Mirror* vol. 3, no. 11 (February 1956): 9.

51. The term "blues evangelists" is adapted from Schwartz's article subtitle, "Preaching the Gospel of the Blues"; Schwartz, *How Britain Got the Blues*, 40. Oliver stated that "only the American Black . . . can sing the blues" in *Blues Fell This Morning* (1960), 4.

52. Paul Oliver, "Blue-Eyed Blues: The Impact of Blues on European Culture," in C. W. E. Bigsby, ed., *Approaches to Popular Culture* (Bowling Green, OH: Bowling Green University Popular Press, 1977), 230.

53. Paul Oliver, "Introduction to Odetta: An important new folk and blues singer," *Jazz Music Mirror* vol. 5, no. 7 (April 1958): 6.

54. W. E. B. Du Bois, *The Souls of Black Folk* (London: Penguin, 1903); Locke, Alain, *The Negro and His Music* (Port Washington, NY: Kennikat, 1936).

55. Du Bois, 206.

56. Paul Oliver, "Problems of Collecting Race Records," *Music Mirror* vol. 2, no. 9 (September 1955): 13.

57. Oliver, "Match Box Blues," 69.

58. Oliver, "Devil's Son-in-Law," 9.

59. This conception of the blues singer has been challenged by Elijah Wald in his analysis of Robert Johnson.

60. Oliver, "Got the Blues," 8.

61. Rod Gruver, "A Closer Look at the Blues," *Blues World* 26, no. 4 (January 1970): 4–10.

62. Oliver, "Got the Blues," 10.

63. Paul Oliver, "Chocolate to the Bone," *Music Mirror* vol. 1, no. 7 (November 1954): 41.

64. Richard Wright, *Black Boy: A Record of Childhood and Youth* (London: Longman, 1945), 136–37.

65. Richard Wright, *12 Million Black Voices* (1941; rpt. New York: Basic, 2008).

66. Interview with Paul Oliver 26/11/2009.

67. Paul Oliver, "The Folk Blues of Sonny Terry," *Music Mirror* vol. 2, no. 10 (October 1955): 6; "Introduction to Odetta," 6.

68. Richard Wright, *Native Son* (Harmondsworth, UK: Penguin, 1940), 15.

69. Nathan I. Huggins, *Harlem Renaissance* (London: Oxford University Press, 1971), 64.

70. David Levering Lewis, *When Harlem Was in Vogue* (Oxford: Oxford University Press, 1979), 173.

71. Anita Patterson, "Jazz, Realism and the Modernist Lyric: The Poetry of Langston Hughes," in *Modern Language Quarterly* vol. 61, no. 4 (December 2000): 667.

72. Middleton (1990), 127.

73. Oliver, "The Folk Blues of Sonny Terry," 6; Paul Oliver, "Forgotten Men," *Music Mirror* vol. 3, no. 5 (June 1956): 9.

74. Paul Oliver, "Brownie McGhee and Sonny Terry," *Music Mirror* vol. 5, no. 11 (June 1958): 17.

75. Paul Oliver, "Special Agents: How the Blues Got on Record," *Jazz Review* (February 1959), reprinted in *Blues Off the Record*, 48.

76. Paul Oliver, "Big Bill Broonzy on Vogue," *Music Mirror* vol. 3, no. 7 (August 1956): 4.

77. Oliver, "Problems of Collecting Race Records," 14.

78. Paul Oliver, "We're Gonna Rock This Joint: Jimmy Rushing's Early Years," *Jazz Monthly* (December 1957), reprinted in *Blues Off the Record*, 146.

79. Tona Hangen, "Man of the Hour: Walter A. Maier and Religion by Radio on the Lutheran Hour," in Michele Hilmes and Jason Loviglio (eds.), *Radio Reader: Essays in the Cultural History of Radio* (London: Routledge, 2002), 113–34.

80. Oliver, "Forgotten Men," 8.

81. For more on the interpretations of Robert Johnson in blues scholarship, see Wald (2004); Barry Lee Pearson and William McCulloch, *Robert Johnson: Lost and Found* (Chicago: University of Illinois Press, 2003); and Patricia R. Schroeder, *Robert Johnson, Mythmaking and Contemporary American Culture* (Chicago: University of Illinois Press, 2004).

82. Paul Oliver, "Another Man Done Gone," *Music Mirror* vol. 1, no. 4 (August 1954): 27.

83. B. A. Botkin, in the *New York Times Book Review*, quoted on jacket[?] of *The Meaning of the Blues*.

84. See comments by Paul Garon, Bill Ferris, and David Evans in *The Paul Oliver 70th Birthday Tribute*.

4

American Balladry and the Anxiety of Ancestry

—Erich Nunn

Cowboy Songs

In his 1910 *Cowboy Songs and Other Frontier Ballads*, John Lomax writes: "Out in the wild, far-away places of the big and still unpeopled west . . . yet survives the Anglo-Saxon ballad spirit that was active in secluded districts in England and Scotland even after the coming of Tennyson and Browning. This spirit is manifested both in the preservation of the English ballad and in the creation of local songs."[1] Lomax's identification of "the Anglo-Saxon ballad spirit" among his cowboy informants anticipates Cecil Sharp's expeditions into the Appalachian hills in search of survivals of an Anglo-Saxon ballad tradition. Describing the informants from whom he collected the texts and tunes published in his 1917 *English Folk Songs from the Southern Appalachians*, Sharp writes: "these mountain people, albeit unlettered, have . . . one and all entered at birth into the full enjoyment of their racial heritage." Their songs, like other elements of their culture, "are merely racial attributes which have been gradually acquired and accumulated in past centuries and handed down generation by generation."[2] Sharp offers as evidence his having heard sung in Appalachia thirty-seven so-called Child ballads (the texts of which had been recorded in Francis James Child's *The English and Scottish Popular Ballads*, which was published in ten volumes between 1882 and 1898).[3] For ballad collectors like Lomax and Sharp, cultural forms such as the ballad function as the means through which a racial heritage—white Englishness, in this case—is expressed and transmitted. So pervasive was this racialist logic that collectors like Lomax would at times record performances of ballads and other songs by African American singers while simultaneously insisting on the ballads' white racial provenance, eliding or flatly denying any African American contribution to such song traditions. The converse of this understanding of folk music along racially segregated lines—that some musical forms are intrinsically "black" or "Negro," regardless of their immediate provenance—obtains as well.[4] Lomax himself was keenly interested in the music of African Americans, although for him (as for most of his contemporaries) "black" and "white" folk music constituted discrete, mostly non-overlapping areas of interest.

Key examples from Lomax's own work, however, complicate this notion of strictly segregated traditions, and at times he suggests an awareness of these complications. At one point in his introduction to *Cowboy Songs*, for example, he observes that "[t]he range community consisted usually of the boss, the straw-boss, the cowboys proper, and the cook—often a negro." While Lomax acknowledges the presence of the "negro" cook here, he remains apart from "the cowboys proper." A couple of pages later, Lomax goes a step farther, noting that "[i]t was not unusual to find a Negro who, because of his ability to handle wild horses or because of his skill with a lasso, had been promoted from the chuck-wagon to a place in the ranks of the cowboys."[5] In fact, as Lomax recounts in a later edition of *Cowboy Songs*, he collected "Home on the Range," the most famous song in the collection, from an African American informant.[6] He explains: "Some one told me that in San Antonio, Texas, lived a Negro singer and cook, who had first plied the latter art in the rear of a chuck wagon which followed many a herd of long-horned cattle up the trail from Texas to Fort Dodge, Kansas. I found him in 1908 leaning against a stunted mulberry tree at the rear of his place of business, a low drinking dive."[7] While the white cowboys' singing reflects "the freedom and the wildness of the plains,"[8] the "Negro singer" is as debased as his surroundings: "'I'se too drunk to sing today. Come back tomorrow,' he muttered."[9] Lomax perseveres despite this inauspicious initial encounter, extracting "Home on the Range" from the African American inebriate and publishing it in the first edition of *Cowboy Songs* in 1910. In a more detailed account published in 1945, Lomax elaborates on the process through which "Home on the Range" achieved popular currency. Apparently the saloonkeeper kept his word, as Lomax reports that he "spent all the next day under the mesquite with this Negro. Among the songs he sang for me was 'Home on the Range,' the first time I had heard the melody."[10] Lomax recorded the song of "this Negro" onto a cylinder using a portable recording device. "From the record I made that day down in the Negro red-light district," he reports, "Henry Leberman, a blind teacher of music at the State School for the Blind in Austin, a few weeks afterwards set down the music. Leberman used earphones and played the record over and over again until he felt sure that he had captured the music as the Negro saloonkeeper had rendered it."[11] Lomax points out with justified pride that his arrangement of the song, published in *Cowboy Songs*, became popular around the world. "The original cylindrical record of the song has crumbled into dust," he observes, "but the music that Henry Leberman set down from the record I made still survives."[12]

The agents of the song's preservation credited in this final sentence include Lomax, who produces the cylinder recording, and Henry Leberman, who (remarkably, it would seem, given that Lomax describes him as blind) provides the transcription. The "Negro saloonkeeper," who is never named, plays a subordinate role. In the structure of Lomax's narrative, the singer, like Lomax's cylinder recording or Leberman's transcription, plays the role of a passive recording technology that facilitates the song's preservation, rather than an agent actively involved in this project. He serves, in other words, as a conduit between the folk tradition that Lomax sets out to document and the world at large, but not as a contributor to that tradition. Rather, he appears in the narrative as a resource to be mined, with "Home on the Range" as the valuable commodity he possesses and that Lomax wishes to acquire. By the end of the 1945 article, he makes this relationship explicit, as Lomax refers to the singer as "*my* San Antonio Negro saloon-keeper."[13]

"Home on the Range" derives at least in part from Dr. Brewster Higley's 1873 poem, "My Western Home," though its origins had become obscure by the time Lomax encountered it.[14] A 1909 issue of the *Journal of American Folk-Lore* prefaces a version of the song credited to one "Mr. Otis Tye of Yucca, N[orth] Dak[ota]" with the note that "[n]o information could be obtained as to its origin, but after questioning a number of older cowboys it seems that it is almost universally known in the northwest, though most of the men knew but a few verses."[15] That Mr. Tye of North Dakota and Lomax's anonymous informant from San Antonio provide similar versions of the song attests to its popularity; that Tye is named as a participant in the cowboy culture with which the song was identified while Lomax's "Negro singer" is neither named nor given such credit is symptomatic of the racial logic that structures the folklore scholarship of Lomax and many of his contemporaries.

Such a situation obtains in Lomax's 1911 "Cowboy Songs of the Mexican Border," in which he notes that "[a] number of the most interesting songs were obtained from four negroes who have had experience in ranch life."[16] He goes on to conclude that these songs are products of "the ballad instinct of the race, temporarily thrown back to primitive conditions, again actively at work. How much relationship really exists between these songs and the ballads in the great collection of Professor Child of Harvard University, I am not ready to surmise about."[17] The "race" in question here is Anglo-Saxon; despite African American singers' value as sources of interesting songs, they, like Lomax's "Negro San Antonio saloon-keeper," serve as passive conduits, not as active participants in the ballad tradition. The paradox at work in Lomax's assertion illustrates what Werner Sollors has identified as "the conflict between contractual and hereditary, self-made and ancestral, definitions of American identity—between *consent* and *descent*," which Sollors posits as "the central drama in American culture."[18] Approaches to vernacular musical traditions like Lomax's and Sharp's link cultural forms to racial or ethnic identities and articulate what Sollors describes as an ideology of descent, which "emphasizes . . . our hereditary qualities, liabilities, and entitlements."[19]

Such hereditary qualities define Lomax's cowboy informants; they evince "the gallantry, the grace, and the song heritage of their English ancestors."[20] These hereditary traits, in turn, are reflected in the ballads the cowboys sing. "Thrown back on primal resources and for entertainment and for the expression of emotion," they "express themselves through somewhat the same character of songs as did their forefathers of perhaps a thousand years ago."[21] The homology between the hereditary qualities of the singers and the character of their songs emphasizes an ostensibly heritable racial song heritage. The song culture of the cowboys is both transatlantic and transhistorical, spanning two continents and "a thousand years." At the same time, this understanding leaves little room for musical traditions that cross racial lines. In other words, the possibility of a culture of consent—in which the "Negro singer" would count as a full participant—is short-circuited by the logic of descent that structures Lomax's thinking. The "Negro" cannot share the song tradition of the cowboys because he does not share their hereditary qualities. This tautological idea accounts for the seeming paradox that "Home on the Range" represents. Though Lomax collects the song from an African American source, the racial logic that undergirds his project obviates the possibility that this source participates in the song culture being documented. According to this logic,

"Home on the Range," like the other material in *Cowboy Ballads*, expresses a white Anglo-Saxon racial inheritance from which "the Negro singer" is by definition excluded. While the "Negro" may ventriloquize this inheritance, his racial status prevents him from being a part of it.

At the same time, despite Lomax's decision—conscious or otherwise—not to name him or credit him with any degree of agency, without the "Negro singer" there is no "Home on the Range," at least not in the form that Lomax made famous. While it is true that the understanding of folk music that informed Lomax's project held that cowboy songs were the collective product of a folk culture rather than the creations of individuals, it is nevertheless not true that this conception prevented Lomax from naming individual sources. In chapter 3, "Hunting Cowboy Songs," of his 1947 *Adventures of a Ballad Hunter*, for example, Lomax provides another account of his encounter with the source of "Home on the Range," who as in the 1945 article, is referred to by his race and occupation, but never by name (as before, Henry Leberman does receive credit for his transcription).[22] In this same chapter, Lomax gives detailed accounts of named individuals from whom he recorded other songs. He spends two pages, for example, discussing his interactions with a source named Tom Hight: "Tom knew more cowboy melodies than any other person I have ever found."[23]

If the presence of the "Negro singer" poses a problem for Lomax's model of a racially defined ballad tradition that had taken root in the American West, the idea of ancestry provides a solution. Faced with the prospect of acknowledging a multiracial culture of consent being forged among cowboys of diverse ethnic origins, he instead posits a racially homogeneous musical heritage that insulates from the influence of their nonwhite neighbors "many a young Virginia aristocrat; many sons of Alabama, Mississippi, and Georgia planters; many a coon hunter from Kentucky; roving and restless young blades from all over the South." "From such a group, given a taste for killing in the Civil War, in which Southern feeling and sentiments predominated," he continues, "came the Texas cowboy and the cowboy songs."[24] Lomax does not explain precisely what he means by "Southern feeling and sentiments," though the structure of feeling he describes is born of a collective identity that transcends divisions of social class and geography under the sign of a shared racial inheritance. "These boys," who "came mainly from the Southern states," Lomax maintains, "brought the gallantry, the grace, and the song heritage of their English ancestors."[25] While an understanding of folk songs as products of a culture of consent would lead to a consideration of how cowboys of diverse geographic, racial, and ethnic backgrounds might forge a shared musical culture, Lomax's descent model instead seeks continuity with ancestors real and imagined, and proposes a relatively static musical culture whose racial character has remained unchanged for "perhaps a thousand years."

Mountain Ballads

This conception of musical cultures as racially bound depends upon a logic of cultural, social, and often physical segregation; Lomax and other proponents of descent-oriented understandings of ballad and song traditions sought out singers from communities that had supposedly been isolated from members of other racial and ethnic groups and, ideally, from the modern world and its culture industries. Lomax recounts a conversation with Theodore Roosevelt (to whom he dedicated *Cowboy Songs and Other Ballads*), for example, during which the president observed of the cowboy songs that Lomax was collecting that "[t]here is something very curious in the reproduction here on this continent of essentially the conditions of ballad growth which obtained in mediaeval England."[26] Such ideas of ethnic isolation not only inform Lomax's understanding of an English-derived cowboy culture; they also structure dominant conceptions of Appalachian identity in the first decades of the twentieth century. An influential articulation of this idea is William Goodell Frost's "Our Contemporary Ancestors in the Southern Mountains," published in the *Atlantic Monthly* in 1899, which maintained that "the 'mountain whites'" lived "to all intents and purposes in the conditions of the colonial times."[27] Working in part to counter stereotyped depictions of mountain residents as backward "poor white trash," Frost defined "'Appalachian America' . . . as a unique and distinct social and cultural entity" that represented a transplanted English (or "Saxon") culture uncorrupted by industrial American modernity.[28]

Song collector and radio performer Bradley Kincaid, billed as the "Kentucky Mountain Boy," echoes this idea in his popular songbooks, in one of which he maintained that "the mountain folks were isolated from the rest of America for about one hundred years."[29] In Kincaid's self-presentation, the idea of Appalachian isolation serves as a marker of racial and cultural purity. Kincaid was one of the most popular and successful early commercial "hillbilly" singers, though he resisted that label, arguing that his songs were "folk songs," not the degraded dilutions of commercial-minded hillbilly performers. As such, Kincaid serves as an exemplar of the ways in which the concerns about ancestry of folklorists like Lomax and Sharp have influenced understandings of popular music based in vernacular folk traditions.[30] Kincaid's career as a radio and recording artist began in 1927, the same year that Jimmie Rodgers and the Carter Family made their first records, jumpstarting "hillbilly" music as a commercial genre. Though he did not sell records on the scale of the Carters or Rodgers, Kincaid was hugely popular through his radio broadcasts, first on WLS in Chicago and then on a number of other stations, culminating in a stint with WSM's Grand Ole Opry in Nashville in 1944. More so than either the Carters or Rodgers, Kincaid insisted on the folk provenance of his material and denied a pecuniary motivation for his musical activities. Nonetheless, he pioneered the marketing of folk-based music through his radio broadcasts, recordings, and songbooks, twelve volumes of which were eventually published, the first in 1928, the last in 1941. Kincaid undertook yearly collecting trips in rural Kentucky, North Carolina, and Georgia to gather ballads and folk songs, combining the roles of collector, scholar, interpreter, and popularizer of a body of songs that he understood to represent a unified folk tradition. Though his repertoire was diverse—including Child ballads, nineteenth-century parlor songs, novelty tunes, and songs derived from minstrelsy and Tin Pan Alley—Kincaid took pains to distinguish the folk songs of the mountains from the hillbilly songs of his fellow recording artists:

> I have tried earnestly to bring to you a true picture of the people of the mountains as manifested in the songs they sing. To me there is character and dignity to be found in the old mountain ballads: they represent a certain type, and are just as distinctive as the Negro Spirituals. They are truly American Folk Songs, born out of the life and experiences of the mountain people. Therefore, I have tried to bring to the radio audience, only those songs that are truly representative of these people.[31]

Kincaid rooted this folk tradition in a specific locale—the mountains of eastern Kentucky—but he also insisted that it constituted an ancestral racial inheritance. Kincaid maintained that the songs he collected, sang, broadcast, and published embodied an ancestral whiteness that had rooted itself in the Kentucky hills. A promotional piece from 1928 explains: "Bradley Kincaid was born in Garrard County, Kentucky, in the edge of the mountains and very near the Blue Grass. His parents were both native Kentuckians. His great-grandfather was a full-blooded Scotchman, coming to Virginia from Scotland. So Bradley is Scotch, but he says he was born in this country to save transportation."[32] Its attempt at humor aside, the "[g]enerational rhetoric" of this piece, as Werner Sollors explains the phenomenon in general, "confers . . . a sense of kinship and community upon the descendants of heterogeneous ancestors."[33] While the piece's author invokes a legitimate genealogical fact (that Kincaid's great-grandfather emigrated from Scotland), this "supposedly pure descent definition" (the identification of Kincaid as "Scotch") is "far from natural, being largely based on a consent construction."[34] In point of fact, for example, if we consider only the evidence Kincaid presents concerning his Scottish great-grandfather, Kincaid is precisely as Scottish as fellow Kentuckian Muhammad Ali is Irish, as both men are descended from immigrant great-grandfathers. (Ali's maternal great-grandfather, Abe Grady, emigrated from County Clare to Kentucky in 1862.)[35] That in twentieth-century Kentucky Kincaid could self-identify as "Scotch" while Ali could not plausibly self-identify as "Irish" reveals how consent masquerades as descent in such ethnic identifications. In Ali's case, the descent logic of ancestral Irishness is superseded by the binary racial logic of Jim Crow.

The ethnic affiliation by which Kincaid is Scottish by virtue of having a "full-blooded Scotch" grandfather extends to the songs he sings as well. The foreword to the first volume of *Favorite Mountain Ballads and Old Time Songs*, published in Chicago in 1928, for instance, maintains:

> [t]o those who live in the mountains this little booklet will represent a group of familiar songs. To those who live outside of the mountains it will represent the life and spirit of a people in whose veins runs the purest strain of Anglo-Saxon blood to be found anywhere in America. These mountain ballads are songs that grew out of the life and experiences of hardy Scotch, Irish, German, English and Dutch natives. . . . [36]

This passage's conflation of various national and ethnic terms points to an ideological investment in ancestral whiteness that supersedes any intraracial national or ethnic distinctions. According to the then-current racial logic from which this terminology derives, though, of these groups only the English could plausibly be characterized as "Anglo-Saxon." The Scotch and Irish, rather, were Celts, the Germans and Dutch Teutons.[37] Kincaid's emphasis on ancestry echoes the claims of Sharp and Lomax, who held that the ballad tradition in America provided a racial link with English (or Scottish or Anglo-Saxon) forebears.[38]

Kincaid was not alone in doing so. In the preface to the inaugural 1932 issue of the *Cumberland Empire*, a journal whose professed "aim [was] to mirror the mountains so that the world may see and know us, not as the novelist and feature writer pictures us to be, but as we really are," publisher James Taylor Adams wrote:

> For four generations my people were cut off from all intercourse with the rest of the world. During that time they were wrestling with the wilderness. Schools were few and far between. And the art of reading and writing was almost lost. But they had a literature. A beautiful literature, and they preserved it the only way they knew; in the songs they sung [sic] and the tales they told their children.[39]

For Adams, as for Kincaid and Frost, rural isolation is transformed from a handicap into a virtue. Folk song becomes a vehicle for the transmission of a racialized ancestral culture.

The Hound Dog Guitar

In another piece in the same issue of the journal, entitled "Bradley Kincaid and His Houn' Dog Guitar," Adams tells the story of Kincaid's musical education:

> Bradley Kincaid was born in the Point Leavell community of Garrard County, Kentucky, thirty-six years ago. Garrard County is in the Cumberland foothills, and Bradley fell into his first sleep, influenced by the crooning of mountain lullabies. Both his father and mother were gifted with good singing voices and for several months following his advent into the world of men and things, anyone passing their humble home could have heard the "rock, rock" of the cradle, keeping time to a mountain tune....
> Musical instruments were scarce in the hill country at that time. ... But one day something wonderful, almost a miracle happened in the Kincaid home.
> Father brought home a guitar.
> The elder Kincaid was a great hunter; and he had an ear for music. One night as he was returning home from a fox chase he met up with a negro thrumming a guitar. He bartered the Son of Ham for a trade,

and a little later he saw the colored fellow lead away one of his hounds and he was the undisputed owner of the "box," as guitars were called in the hill country at that time.

Because he traded a fox hound for it, Kincaid called the newly acquired musical instrument the "houn' dog guitar," and from that day till this it has been the almost constant companion of Bradley's.[40]

Versions of this story appear in Kincaid's songbooks, in press for his concert performances, in journalistic puff pieces, and in interviews that Kincaid gave almost fifty years after the story first appeared. Almost without exception, such retellings emphasize that the guitar's previous owner was an African American. A 1929 article in the Jackson, Mississippi, *News*, for example, states: "Kincaid senior was following two of his hounds on a hunt when he came across a darky with the dilapidated instrument."[41] The *Washington Post* the next year elaborated: "A farmer in Garrard County, Ky., was fond of fox hunting. Often after a hurried supper he would 'blow up' his hounds and ride away for a few hours of sport. On one such expedition he traded a dog to a Negro for an old guitar."[42] According to a 1931 article in the *Berea Alumnus*, "Mr. Kincaid, the father, was an ardent hunter, and it was on one of his nightly jaunts into the hills to pursue the tricky fox that he located the music box. The father's desire to obtain the guitar was ended when he arranged a trade of a fox hound to an old Negro for it."[43]

This story economically combines a narrative of filiation—young Bradley receives both the "houn' dog guitar" and his song repertoire from his parents—with one of cultural affiliation—the guitar materializes during a fox hunt, a sporting practice that links the working-class Kincaids of rural Kentucky with the British upper classes. This linking of the Kentucky mountain folk with British ancestors neatly complements the Child ballads and other English and Scottish songs in Kincaid's repertoire. "Barbara Allen" (Child 84) was one of his signature pieces, for example. Kincaid claimed these songs—some of which he learned from his mother, others from published folksong collections or from informants he encountered on collecting trips—as a cultural inheritance, evidence of an ancestral British heritage that had crossed the ocean and taken root in the Kentucky hills. The "houn' dog guitar" would serve a similar function in Kincaid's public biography.

The "houn' dog guitar" would become a crucial element in Kincaid's public persona, receiving equal billing with Kincaid himself (see Fig. 4.1). Significantly, Kincaid applied the name to whatever instrument he was

American Balladry and the Anxiety of Ancestry 67

Figure 4.1. Bradley Kincaid and his Hound Dog Guitar. Undated publicity photograph. Photo from the Bradley Kincaid Collection, courtesy of the Southern Appalachian Archives, Hutchins Library, Berea College.

(left) Figure 4.2. The original "Hound Dog Guitar." Photo from the Bradley Kincaid Collection, courtesy of the Southern Appalachian Archives, Hutchins Library, Berea College.

(right) Figure 4.3. 1929 Supertone Bradley Kincaid Houn' Dog Guitar. Photo courtesy of Michael Wright.

currently playing. The original was a mid-nineteenth-century parlor guitar that somehow made its way from France to rural Kentucky (see Fig. 4.2).[44] Publicity photographs show him with fancier steel-string Martins of recent manufacture (see Fig. 4.1), and Sears-Roebuck (who owned WLS, the station on whose Radio Barn Dance Kincaid began his broadcasting career) sold a "Supertone Bradley Kincaid Houn' Dog" guitar mass-produced by Harmony, decorated with a depiction of the eponymous canine (see Fig. 4.3). The cognomen "houn' dog guitar," then, becomes detached from the specific instrument that Bradley receives from his father, and instead becomes an abstracted signifier of authenticity and of a racialized musical inheritance.

What, though, are we to make of the guitar's previous owner, who evidently decides (or is persuaded) that a foxhound is more valuable to him than the instrument is? What is this African American man doing in the middle of this story of transplanted musical Englishness? Is the man's race merely incidental, or is this figure's blackness significant? As with Lomax's story about the origin of "Home on the Range," a black man is at once central to the narrative and yet never fully accounted for. The first article quoted above identifies him within the span of two sentences as "a negro," a "Son of Ham," and a "colored fellow," and such racial designations are echoed in other iterations of the story. More than four decades later, Kincaid would tell an interviewer: "One night my father was on one of these trips with the fox hunters, and there was an old colored feller—they call 'em blacks now, I guess—an old colored feller that had a little ol' guitar, and my father traded one of his foxhounds for that guitar. And he brought it home, and all the kids learned to play chords on it and sing. That was my first introduction to music."[45] In none of these accounts do we learn the man's name, his occupation, or what specific social relationship he might have had with Kincaid's father. The story itself takes the form of a ballad or folk tale, with "the negro" as a mysterious figure outside the social order around whom the narrative circles.

In other words, his appearance in the story represents an instance of what Toni Morrison calls an "Africanist presence" structuring white American self-understandings. Morrison's explanation of "the self-evident ways in which Americans choose to talk about themselves through and within" this Africanist presence, "sometimes allegorical, sometimes metaphorical, always choked," can perhaps help shed some light on Kincaid's story.[46] This "dark and abiding [Africanist] presence," Morrison explains, is "there for the literary imagination as both a visible and invisible mediating force," a "shadow [which] hovers in implication, in sign, in line of demarcation."[47] At a fundamental level, the presence of the descendant of African slaves in this story reminds us of a transatlantic route—from West Africa to the United States—that complicates the one that connects Kincaid with the British Isles. In other words, this Africanist presence in Kincaid's story is not merely incidental to it. Instead, the racial difference highlighted by the repeated invocation of "the negro" facilitates the transhistorical, transatlantic ethnic identification that undergirds Kincaid's self-presentation. The story of ancestry Kincaid tells proposes a "Scotch" identity that comprises both genealogy and cultural inheritance. His self-identification derives both from the "Scotch" identity he inherits from his great-grandfather and from the English ballads he learns from his mother. The story of the "houn' dog guitar" both contributes to this white ethnic self-identification and complicates it by introducing the nonwhite presence of the guitar's original owner.

On one level, the story that Kincaid and others tell concerning his guitar is one of expropriation: Kincaid's father lays claim not only to the material property in question (the guitar), but also, crucially, to the cultural capital it represents. Once it moves from "the negro's" hands to those of the Kincaid family, the guitar serves as a catalyst that eventually enables Kincaid to parlay his English/Scottish/Anglo-Saxon ballad inheritance into commercial success. In this respect, the tale of the "houn' dog guitar" appears to be an iteration of the long history of whites appropriating the property (both literal and figurative) of African Americans for commercial and artistic gain. Lomax's expropriation of "Home on the Range" from his "San Antonio Negro saloon-keeper" is an illustrative instance of this phenomenon, but the history of such appropriations extends well into the previous century. Perhaps the paradigmatic instance of this phenomenon is the (likely apocryphal) story of minstrel pioneer T. D. Rice's donning of the clothes of a black man in order to outfit himself for his first blackface performance in Cincinnati in 1830[48]—or Rice's learning "Jump Jim Crow," as a contemporary account puts it, from "a negro stage-driver, [giving] origin to a school of music designed to excel in popularity all others."[49] Both these stories, as Eric Lott explains, illustrate "the efficient expropriation of the cultural commodity 'blackness.'"[50]

The ways in which Kincaid's story echoes these precedents are not merely fortuitous, as Kincaid, despite his claims to singing "only the typical Folk Songs of the Mountains," in fact performed a number of songs derived from blackface minstrelsy. Significantly, he learned many of these songs from his father. He told an interviewer, "My father used to sing them":

> But when I got into radio, I couldn't use them. They were a reflection on the Negro. In fact, I sang "Kitty Wells" [a minstrel song that was in print by at least the 1850s] one time. The first line is, "You ask me [what makes] this darky weep" and this woman called me up and gave me down the road for it. After that I sang, "You ask me what made the fellow weep." I've got a big repertory of Negro songs that were written back in the 1800's—minstrel-like songs. I couldn't use them.[51]

Kincaid's cultural inheritance, then, includes songs derived from blackface minstrelsy that he learned from his father, in addition to the English ballads his mother taught him. His story about the irate caller suggests that the emphasis of balladry over blackface was motivated in part by audience concerns. In fact, "Negro songs" were part of Kincaid's public repertoire before ballads were. He first came to WLS with a YMCA quartet in Chicago who included "negro" spirituals in their repertoire, and only later sang ballads on the air at the request of the manager of WLS.[52]

The narrative of cultural expropriation manifested in the story of the "houn' dog guitar" is a familiar one, structuring not only the nineteenth-century minstrelsy of T. D. Rice and other blackface performers but also a wide range of twentieth-century popular musical forms and performances, from *The Jazz Singer* to Elvis and beyond. Kincaid's story, however, like Lomax's, is different in that it traffics not in expropriated and commodified *blackness*, but rather in an ancestral *whiteness*, figured variously as Elizabethan, Anglo-Saxon, or "Scotch," and encapsulated in ballad form. But again, what are we to make of the centrality of "the negro" (both as an individual and as a category) to this process? To use Morrison's terms, what is implied, signified, and demarcated by his presence?[53] The story of the "houn' dog guitar" helps illuminate these questions. Kincaid told Dorothy Gable in a 1967 interview at the Country Music Hall of Fame and Museum in Nashville:

> Well, my father used to go out with some of these fox hunters and they'd take their dogs and they'd get up on top of a ridge, and set the dogs off down in the holler chasing the fox, and build—they'd build a fire and sit around and talk and tell stories. And [on] one of these occasions a negro friend of my father's who used to come and fox hunt with them once in a while had this old—this hound dog guitar here. And my father traded him one of his foxhounds for that guitar. And he brought it home and all of the kids learned to play it.[54]

The key difference between this version of the story and its many antecedents lies in the detail that the source of the guitar is not an anonymous "negro," upon whom the hunting party just chances in the woods, but rather "a negro friend of [Kincaid's] father's who used to come and fox hunt with them." This social relationship is elided in the previous accounts. It is possible that Kincaid's acknowledgment in this account that his father and "the negro" were friends is simply a response to the changed circumstances of the late 1960s in which his interview with Gable took place, a liberal gesture. On the other hand, perhaps this seemingly minor detail provides a key to understanding the complex set of social relationships in which Kincaid's father, his "negro friend," and the prosperous landholding whites who ran the foxhunts were enmeshed.

To again take up Morrison's terms, what is being demarcated by the presence of "the negro" in these accounts is the color line between black and white. This imposition of the color line, in turn, facilitates the association of Kincaid's father with the landowners on whose farms he works and whose hunts he and his "negro friend" both join. The presence of "the negro," in other words, allows for what W. J. Cash called the "vastly ego-warming and ego-expanding distinction between the white man and the black."[55] This distinction enforces a transhistorical association that transcends divisions of class and nation through the shared property of whiteness. Paradoxically, it is the figure of "the negro" that enables Kincaid to claim an English racial inheritance that manifests itself in "Anglo-Saxon" blood, in foxhunting, and in balladry.

The class anxiety that underlies this logic of ancestry and cultural inheritance is made even more explicit in later interviews and correspondence. Kincaid wrote to the librarian at Berea College, where he had first become interested in the practice of collecting ballads: "It was at Berea that I first realized that an old country boy like me could be something other than a 'field hand.'"[56] In an elaborate version of the story of the "hound dog guitar," he describes to an interviewer, Loyal Jones, the relationship his father had with his neighbors:

> These farmers around used to go out—they all had foxhounds—old walker hounds, they called 'em. The walkers used to—they were big fox hunters. They were the landowners. They owned two or three or four hundred acres of land, and you could go by their places any time during the day and you'd see fifteen or twenty foxhounds sleeping out in the field and around the house there. They'd been out all night fox

hunting, and they were sleeping during the day. Well my father had two or three foxhounds."[57]

Earlier in this same interview, he tells Jones, "I was raised on a farm, of course. My father was a—he wasn't a sharecropper, he just worked by the day . . . on the farm." "He worked on somebody else's farm?" Jones asks. Kincaid replies, "Mmm hmm."

Kincaid's statements in this interview point to an intraracial class difference. Kincaid's father is not a landowner; nor is he a sharecropper, but rather a day laborer on others' farms. Lomax's *Adventures of a Ballad Hunter* begins with a similar articulation of the liminal class position his family occupied: "My family belonged to the upper crust of the 'po' white trash,' traditionally held in contempt by the aristocracy of the Old South and by their Negro slaves. Father always owned a few acres of land which kept him from being at the bottom of the social scale."[58] Of course, given the presence of "Negro slaves," it is not Lomax's father's land, but rather his whiteness, that insulates him from occupying the bottom rung of Mississippi society. A similar situation obtains for Kincaid's father. He and his "negro friend" occupy similar social roles as agricultural laborers. Jones observes:

> [T]he Kincaids were poor, and the father worked as a tenant or farm worker. . . . It may be that they were little better off than the black tenants and farm workers and thus may have had a camaraderie or even friendship with one another. Certainly blacks and whites played music together and felt a commonality in that endeavor, and also blacks and whites worked together pretty well in the eastern Kentucky coal mines.[59]

Viewed from this perspective, the exchange of the foxhound for the guitar is less an act of expropriation from the weak by the powerful than it is an exchange between individuals occupying similar social positions, albeit on opposite sides of the color line. The language of racial difference—the focus on the racial designations of "Negro," "Scotch," and "Anglo-Saxon"—obscures this social relationship. Kincaid Sr's "two or three foxhounds" provide him entrée into the social world of the fox hunters; exchanging the guitar for a foxhound potentially does the same for "the negro."

Both the foxhound that Kincaid's father trades and the guitar he receives facilitate an economic and cultural exchange across the color line.

As such, they point to a limited process of consent through which new affiliations are potentially formed. A similar possibility manifests itself in John Lomax's encounter with the African American singer of "Home on the Range," and registers in Lomax's own accounts—despite his disavowals of such a possibility. As we trace the transatlantic routes of American roots music, it is important that we not limit our understandings of these routes—as Lomax and Kincaid did—to mapping lines of descent. As the story of Kincaid's "hound dog guitar" and its role in transmitting music from the Old World to the New attests, these routes circulate within the South and across the Atlantic to both Europe and Africa; they are circuitous and surprising. By tracing them carefully, we see not (or at least not only) cultural forms being transmitted via lines of descent from one side of the Atlantic to the other, but rather new cultural forms emerging from the crisscrossing and conjoining of such routes, as ballads and songs are sung by new voices in new places.

Notes

1. John Lomax, *Cowboy Songs and Other Frontier Ballads* (New York: Sturgis & Walton, 1910; New York: Macmillan, 1918). The "Collector's Note" from which this and subsequent citations are drawn is unpaginated.

2. Olive Dame Campbell and Cecil Sharp, *English Folk Songs from the Southern Appalachians* (New York: G. P. Putnam's, 1917), vii.

3. On the significance of the Child canon to later conceptions of American folk music's relationship to English and Scottish antecedents, including those of Sharp and Lomax, see Benjamin Filene, *Romancing the Folk: Public Memory and American Roots Music* (Chapel Hill: University of North Carolina Press, 2000), 9–46.

4. As John Greenway observed in 1957, commercial songs composed and/or recorded by the white singer Jimmie Rodgers (arguably hillbilly music's first superstar) showed up, with no evident intentional irony, for nearly three decades after Rodgers's death in 1933 as examples of "Negro" music in printed collections. For detailed discussions of this phenomenon, see John Greenway, "Jimmie Rodgers—A Folksong Catalyst," *Journal of American Folklore* 70/277 (July–September 1957): 231–34, as well as Tony Russell' 1970 *Blacks, Whites, and Blues* (In *Yonder Come the Blues* [Cambridge: Cambridge University Press, 2001], 143–242). For current rethinkings of the ways in which both folklorists and the recording industry contributed to the racial segregation of American vernacular music, see Karl Hagstrom Miller, *Segregating Sound: Inventing Folk and Pop Music in the Age of Jim Crow* (Durham: Duke University Press, 2010); Erich Nunn, "Country Music and the Souls of White Folk," *Criticism: A Quarterly for Literature and the Arts* 51/4 (Fall 2009): 623–49; Elijah Wald, *Escaping*

the Delta: Robert Johnson and the Invention of the Blues (New York: Amistad, 2004); and Hugh Barker and Yuval Taylor, "Nobody's Dirty Business: Folk, Blues, and the Segregation of Southern Music," in *Faking It: The Quest for Authenticity in Popular Music* (New York: Norton, 2007), 29–99.

5. Lomax, *Cowboy Songs*.

6. John Lomax and Alan Lomax, *Cowboy Songs and Other Frontier Ballads* (Rev. ed., New York: Macmillan, 1938), xviii–xix.

7. *Ibid.*

8. *Ibid.*, xv.

9. *Ibid.*, xix.

10. John Lomax, "Half-Million Dollar Song," *Southwest Review* 31/1 (Fall 1945): 2.

11. *Ibid.*

12. *Ibid.*

13. *Ibid.*, emphasis added.

14. Lomax credits Higley with a single stanza, and argues that the song was current before 1867. See Lomax, "Half-Million," 4.

15. G. F. Will, "Songs of Western Cowboys," *Journal of American Folk-Lore* 22/84 (April–June 1909): 256–57.

16. John Lomax, "Cowboy Songs of the Mexican Border," *Texas Magazine* 3/5 (March 1911): 30.

17. *Ibid.*, 35.

18. Werner Sollors, *Beyond Ethnicity: Consent and Descent in American Culture* (New York: Oxford University Press, 1986), 5–6.

19. *Ibid.*, 6.

20. Lomax and Lomax, xviii.

21. *Ibid.*, xxv.

22. See John Lomax, *Adventures of a Ballad Hunter* (New York: Macmillan, 1947), 61–64.

23. *Ibid.*, 48. Other specifically named sources in this chapter include Harry Stephens (50–53), Garland Hodges (66), "Texas Jack" (72–73), and Stewart Edward White (73).

24. Lomax and Lomax, xviii.

25. *Ibid.*

26. Quoted in Lomax, *Adventures of a Ballad Hunter*, 69.

27. William Goodell Frost, "Our Contemporary Ancestors in the Southern Mountains," *Atlantic Monthly* (March 1899): 311.

28. Anthony Harkin, *Hillbilly: A Cultural History of an American Icon* (New York: Oxford University Press, 2005), 236. See also John Alexander Williams, *Appalachia: A History* (Chapel Hill: University of North Carolina Press, 2002), 11–14. While the boundaries of Appalachia have been defined in different ways since Frost's influential piece was published, the region's core is generally understood to include portions of Kentucky, Tennessee, Virginia, West Virginia, Georgia, and North Carolina. See Williams, 13.

29. Bradley Kincaid, *My Favorite Mountain Ballads and Old Time Songs*, No. 11 (1940), 7.

30. For a detailed overview of the racialist tradition of folksong scholarship in which Lomax and Sharp participate, see Filene, 9–46. On Kincaid's participation in this tradition, see Bill C. Malone, *Singing Cowboys and Musical Mountaineers: Southern Culture and the Roots of Country Music* (Athens: University of Georgia Press, 1993), 82–84, and Malone, *Don't Get Above Your Raisin': Country Music and the Southern Working Class* (Urbana: University of Illinois, 2002), 64–65.

31. Bradley Kincaid, *Favorite Mountain Ballads and Old Time Songs* (Chicago: WLS, 1928), 6.

32. Harold A. Safford, "Bradley Kincaid, A Kentuckian, Became a Noted Singer" (1928), *Kentucky Explorer*, November 1999, 82.

33. Sollors, 234.

34. *Ibid.*

35. Henry McDonald, "Muhammad Ali receives freedom of great-grandfather's Irish home town," *Guardian*, September 2, 2009.

36. Kincaid, *Favorite*, 6.

37. See Matthew Frye Jacobson, *Whiteness of a Different Color: European Immigrants and the Alchemy of Race* (Cambridge, MA: Harvard University Press, 1999). For the putative relationship between "Anglo-Saxon" and "Teuton" races, see especially 46–48.

38. Historian Bill C. Malone, one of the first scholars to examine critically and work to dismantle the romantic racialism that has long structured discussions of country music, observes that the idea of American folk music as English or Anglo-Saxon has largely waned, but thinly veiled claims to an ancestral whiteness infusing vernacular music forms persist. As Malone puts it, "[m]ercifully, no one speaks of 'Anglo-Saxon' roots any longer, but a disquieting attribution of 'celticism'" persists, particularly regarding bluegrass. "As in the days of Bradley Kincaid," he continues, "visions of musical, cultural, and ethnic purity have been revived to distinguish a form of country music from its presumably inferior and more commercial competitors." See Malone, *Singing Cowboys*, 105. Elsewhere he observes that "Appalachian ballad hunters spoke rhapsodically about the Anglo-Saxon or Elizabethan nature of southern mountaineers (without understanding that the two labels were not synonymous)." See Malone, *Don't Get Above Your Raisin',* 21.

39. James Taylor Adams, "Preface," *Cumberland Empire* 1 (January 1932): 5.

40. James Taylor Adams, "Bradley Kincaid and His Houn' Dog Guitar," *Cumberland Empire* 1 (January 1932): 49–50.

41. "Old Ballads Hit on Radio: One-Time Kentucky Mountain Youth Popular Over WLS Station," *News*, Jackson, Mississippi, September 13, 1929.

42. "The Houn' Dog Guitar," *Washington Post*, November 9, 1930.

43. "He Makes a Business of Ballads, as Told to Foster Adams," *Berea Alumnus* (April 1931): 33.

44. Though some accounts erroneously describe the original hound dog guitar as a Martin, when Kincaid's son, Jimmie, took it to George Gruhn's vintage guitar shop in Nashville to have it appraised, he learned that it was in fact a French-made model of mid-nineteenth-century vintage. It is currently on display at the Kentucky Museum Hall of Fame in Renfro Valley. Loyal Jones, e-mail message to author, July 29, 2009.

45. Bradley Kincaid interview by Loyal Jones, Berea, KY, April 24, 1974; audio recording, Bradley Kincaid Collection, Southern Appalachian Archives, Hutchins Library, Berea College.

46. Toni Morrison, *Playing in the Dark: Whiteness and the Literary Imagination* (New York: Vintage, 1992), 17.

47. *Ibid.*, 46–47.

48. See Eric Lott, *Love and Theft: Blackface Minstrelsy and the American Working Class* (New York: Oxford University Press, 1993), 18–19.

49. Quoted in Lott, 56.

50. Lott, 18.

51. Quoted in Loyal Jones, *Radio's "Kentucky Mountain Boy," Bradley Kincaid* (Berea, KY: Berea College Appalachian Center, 1980), 57.

52. *Ibid.*, 57.

53. Morrison, 47.

54. Bradley Kincaid interview with Dorothy Gable, Country Music Hall of Fame, Nashville, November 1967; audio recording, Bradley Kincaid Collection, Southern Appalachian Archives, Hutchins Library, Berea College.

55. Wilbur J. Cash, *The Mind of the South* (New York: Vintage, 1941), 40.

56. Letter to Elizabeth Gilbert, Librarian, Berea College, August 10, 1971; Bradley Kincaid Collection, Southern Appalachian Archives, Hutchins Library, Berea College.

57. Kincaid interview by Loyal Jones, Berea, KY, April 24, 1974.

58. See Lomax, *Adventures*, 1.

59. Jones, e-mail message to the author, July 29, 2009.

5

Woody Guthrie at the Crossroads[1]

—Will Kaufman

The English guitarist Wizz Jones once recalled, not altogether fondly, the London acoustic music scene in the mid to late 1950s: "Skiffle was in at the time and strangulated versions of Woody Guthrie songs appeared in the charts while in the back rooms of smoky pubs Jack Elliott showed us how they should be sung."[2] Woody Guthrie had been in the UK charts? Well, yes, thanks mostly to the self-proclaimed "Skiffle King," Lonnie Donegan, whose takes on Guthrie's "Grand Coolee Dam" and "Sally Don't You Grieve" made it into the UK top twenty in mid-1958.[3] Barring the odd exception such as the Weavers' version of Guthrie's "So Long It's Been Good to Know Yuh," the same could hardly be said for the American charts in the 1950s, which remained impervious to Guthrie's work and all but the most commercially remunerative and apolitical folk forms. Meanwhile, in the UK, a sturdy fellowship of skiffle bands had by 1957 adopted a host of Guthrie songs for their repertoires, bands such as Donegan's Skiffle Group, Chris Barber's Skiffle Group, Ken Colyer's Skiffle Group, Dick Bishop and His Sidekicks, the 44 Skiffle and Folksong Group, the Livewires, the Vipers, and the 2.19 Skiffle Group. Among the Guthrie titles appearing on UK skiffle discs—in addition to "Grand Coolee Dam" and "Sally Don't You Grieve"—were "Gypsy Davy," "New York Town," "Union Maid," and "This Land Is Your Land."[4] Donegan even went so far as to claim co-authorship of the Guthrie songs he recorded.[5]

Guthrie was also working his way into the consciousness of those budding singer-songwriters who would burst onto the British folk scene in the 1960s and 1970s, acolytes such as Ralph McTell, the composer of "Streets of London," who recalled of his youth: "I had become fascinated by the life of Woody and his praise of the workingman and in order to rightly claim my place alongside all working heroes, I felt it necessary to try as many different jobs as I could."[6] It was perhaps inevitable, then, that when Bob Dylan arrived in London in 1962, he was already being called "the new Woody and all that" (as the English guitarist Martin Carthy recollected).[7]

Guthrie himself had been in Britain briefly, during World War II as a merchant seaman on shore leave; he had even made an appearance on BBC radio's *The Children's Hour* in 1944, presented as an American curiosity singing a handful of railroad songs ("Wabash Cannonball" and "Nine Hundred Miles").[8] But in the end, it was never his physical presence that ensured his place in the British musical consciousness; rather, it was—as in America—primarily the work of his protégés and torch-carriers that lodged him in the British imagination. It is, of course, impossible to determine with precision all the reasons for the embracing of a foreign artist in a host country, particularly in such a politically divided society as Britain's. Hence the irritation of the British blues scholar Paul Oliver, who took umbrage at the mildly radical undertones of Jack Elliott's album, *Woody Guthrie's Blues*: "The disc has been issued by the Workers Music Association and one cannot help but feel that there has been a somewhat deliberate use of this feature of Woody's work and Jack's admiration for the man, in the selection that has been made."[9] One can only imagine what Oliver's reaction would have been to the other—more radical—uses to which Guthrie was put in the immediate postwar years in Britain. Indeed, one of his most prominent British champions was John Hasted, founder of the Oxford University Communist Party and, later, musical director of the Campaign for Nuclear Disarmament. Also a passionate devotee and practitioner of skiffle music, Hasted was one of a significant band of players to ensure a link between skiffle music and radical activism; in their hands Guthrie's songs helped to cement that link. Meanwhile, Guthrie's chief U.S. patron, the folklorist Alan Lomax, fled to London in the early 1950s to escape the McCarthyite witch hunts, and from there, through his BBC radio broadcasts, ensured that Guthrie would be a regular feature on the British airwaves.[10]

But it would have to be more than political radicalism that would account for Guthrie's British reception, for there was no shortage of apolitical skiffle players perpetuating his oeuvre through their versions. It is perhaps safest to propose, as a starting point, that Guthrie could be all things to all people. He in fact stood at so many crossroads that it is impossible to address them all within the scope of this chapter. Yet there are three interrelated crossroads at which Guthrie can be found with particular vividness, all helping to explain his attraction to various cross-sections of an international audience. These crossroads are those of the proletarian and the bourgeois, the rural and the urban, and the commercial and the political (not necessarily opposites, but a pairing certainly fraught with tension). All of these crossroads inevitably intersect with one another, complicating even further one of the most complicated personae in American musical history.

(1) Woody Guthrie's Bourgeois Blues

A large audience of Americans—and a smaller British audience—first encountered Woody Guthrie through his *Dust Bowl Ballads* (1940), recorded within months of his relocation to New York from California. They would have seen him including himself, in the first person plural, in the class about which he sang, as he declared in his notes to the album:

> They are "Oakie" songs, "Dust Bowl" songs, "Migratious" songs, about my folks and my relatives, about a jillion of 'em, that got hit by the drouth, the dust, the wind, the banker and the landlord and the police, all at the same time . . . and it was these things all added up that caused us to pack our wife and kids into our little rattletrap jallopies, and light out down the Highway—in every direction, mostly west to California.[11]

Some might have recognized a similarly inclusive tactic of Guthrie's in his review of his friend John Steinbeck's novel *The Grapes of Wrath* (1939), which, he declared, was "about us pullin' out of Oklahoma and Arkansas and down south and driftin' around over the state of California, busted, disgusted, down and out and lookin' for work. Shows you how us got to be that way. Shows the damn bankers, men that broke us and the dust that choked us. . . ."[12]

In his self-identification as a proletarian out of the Dust Bowl, Guthrie set out to construct a persona in which he physically embodied the muse of labor:

> I have always sort of felt
> That this land belonged to me
> And my work belongs to my land
> Because my work is me

And it's all I've got to put into my business
Take my work away from me and I wouldn't amount to much.[13]

Especially in the earliest months of his New York residency, Guthrie tapped into and perpetuated the romanticization of the proletariat in which manual labor was equated with authenticity (a romanticization that would have such a great impact on the young Ralph McTell). As Guthrie wrote to his sister, Mary Jo, in 1940, the Dust Bowl migrants were "Real People, Real Honest To Goodness People, going all over Hell's Half Acre looking for work...."[14] The implication was that people who did not or could not work were of an entirely different, "un-Real" species—an implication to which he returned in the midst of World War II, as he wrote to his future wife, Marjorie:

> [W]ork is the only cure, work is the only medicine now, and work is the only hope, not only for us, but for every other living person, and the only way you or me or anybody else can climb somewhere out of the swamps of financial worry, useless-feeling, out-of-contact feeling, and every other bad mental state, is to work, work, and work. Work to get what we want, what we owe to others, and work to hold our places, and work to get better places. Because I think in the first place that people aint nothing but their work....[15]

But in truth, Guthrie at times felt the need to pull back from equating himself with others in the proletarian sphere. In such cases, he would depict himself as a witness among the proletariat in order to become the eyes, ears, and voice of a class who, without a bardic spokesman, could never represent themselves. In such moments of self-deprecation, he would be simply "just a sort of a clerk and climate tester," operating in a "workshop" which might be variously "the sidewalk, your street, and your field, your highway, and your buildings."[16] Or he would present himself simply as the people's amanuensis: "I hear so many people coming around me and going on about where you get your words and your tunes. Well I get my words and tunes off of the hungry folks and they get the credit for all I pause to scribble down."[17] Sometimes he would share the bardic vision with an unnamed "you" who naturally perceived the same crises between labor and capital as he did. Thus he would present himself as nothing special, an Everyman bearing witness to the proletarian sacrifice (as in the Centralia mining disaster of 1947); but even here, he could not fully resist transforming his act of witnessing into one of outright participation:

> I was there the same as you was there and seen the same things that you did. And you was here the same as I was here and you felt the same things I felt. This is the one trick of human nature that is going to outwit and outfight our owners and their hired bosses, this way, I mean, that we've got of being on the spot at places like Centralia, both in body and in spirit, like being on a manure street in India and seeing the eyes of good folks hungry and starving to death. You see, our landlords and our owners don't make full use of this eye of ours that sees around the world, not like us miners and tongbuckers and shipscalers and riggers do when we risk our lives to get the work done.[18]

It would be too easy to accuse Guthrie of misrepresentation, even mendacity, in his wholesale self-associations with the proletariat. Richard Reuss, among others, has highlighted both the conscious crafting of a myth and the bourgeois reality from which it departs:

> Above all, Woody had "been there"; he had spent most of his life among workers, dust-bowlers, hoboes, and the rural peoples of America, and he was most suffused with their worldview and vernacular.... As a result, he was regarded ... as a model to be emulated.... For his part, Guthrie was sufficiently affected by the ... "proletarian" ethos to deliberately play down his early middle-class upbringing and stress his later years of poverty and cross-country ramblings.[19]

In fairness to Guthrie, he openly acknowledged his middle-class origins in his earliest recordings and writings; his was the story of a small-town land speculator's family fallen into hard times in the Depression.[20] But having absorbed the myth of Guthrie the legendary American hobo, riding the rails or the boxcars with a guitar slung across his back, few Americans would be aware, as biographer Joe Klein discovered, that "Woody only used the trains as a last resort: they were too dangerous and uncomfortable."[21] Few would be aware—as Bess Lomax Hawes, Guthrie's fellow Almanac Singer, told biographer Ed Cray—that Guthrie harbored a secret "'hyper-literacy' carefully hidden in an ill-kempt, often unwashed body."[22] In spite of the litany of "hard work" that Guthrie eulogizes in such songs as "Talking Hard Work" ("I chopped and I weeded forty-eight rows of short cotton, thirteen acres of bad corn, and cut the sticker weeds out of eleven backyards, all on account a' 'cause I wanted to show her that I was a man and I liked to work"),[23] Guy Logsdon and Jeff Place wryly state that Guthrie was "[n]ot known to be a hard worker at manual labor himself"; rather, he listened "to migrants and other laborers and transformed their stories, problems, aspirations, tragedies, loves and work experiences into first-person narratives."[24]

Nonetheless, Guthrie's middle-class origins and background do not, in the end, so far remove him from the reality of the Dust Bowl proletariat with whom he identified himself, and with whom he remains identified. As Peter La Chapelle notes, while Guthrie "may not fit the classic definition of a Dust Bowl migrant" because his family had not "lost a farm to drought or soil erosion," he was nonetheless "fairly representative of the migrant stream" in that he hailed from a "middle- to lower- middle-income" background, had "fallen into the ranks of the working poor," and had sought a better life in California.[25]

Guthrie's personal position at the crossroads of proletarian and bourgeois identity certainly complicates his received image as the Dust Bowl Troubadour. But such a complication is further heightened by developments in American culture at large during the period in which he came to prominence—roughly the mid-1930s to the mid-1940s, the period that Michael Denning refers to as "the Age of the CIO" (Congress of Industrial Organizations)—marked by the cultural activism of the Popular Front and "the laboring of American culture": "First, the laboring of American culture refers to the pervasive use of 'labor' and its synonyms in the rhetoric of the period. . . . Second, it refers to what a more technical usage would call the 'proletarianization' of American culture, the increased influence on and participation of working-class Americans in the world of culture and the arts."[26] As Denning makes clear in his study *The Cultural Front: The Laboring of American Culture in the Twentieth Century*, Guthrie emerged at a time when the very definition of "labor" was undergoing a thorough interrogation: "The Marxist cultural theories that emerged in the era of the Popular Front were attempts to come to grips with the forms of modern mental labor—mass education, industries of culture and entertainment, state cultural bureaucracies, and white-collar employment; and the notion of the 'cultural front' was an attempt to imagine a politics of mental labor."[27]

At the same time, the very communist movement in which Guthrie was immersed (although he was not a card-carrying Party member) was undergoing a significant shift in the interests of the anti-fascist struggle of the 1930s and 1940s. As Reuss notes: "the whole communist movement in the United States was trying to Americanize its appeal. The party now sought to attract the broad middle class to its ranks along with the lower-class 'proletariat.' Nearly all phases of radical life—including terminology, dress, and social deportment—were revised to conform more closely to the routine existence of the average citizen."[28] It was a time when American communist theorists such as Kenneth Burke were arguing for a more expansive vision of the proletariat; as Denning summarizes Burke's position, "the symbol of the 'people' ought to be adopted by the left since it was a more inclusive symbol than that of the 'worker.'"[29] Indeed, the trajectory of middle-class union membership had already been set in motion, as white-collar members began steadily to catch up in numbers with blue-collar workers (finally surpassing them by 1956).[30] Guthrie's own written output indicates that while he put considerable effort into revising his initial perceptions of the American proletariat eventually to include the white-collar ranks, he never fully succeeded in embracing them as members of the working fold. In some respects his difficulties came from his position at the crossroads of the rural and the urban.

(2) An Okie in New York

Woody Guthrie came to New York in the winter of 1940, following at least two years of intense activism on behalf of militant agricultural unions battling against the fruit-crop bosses in the fields of California's San Joaquin Valley. As Denning notes, Guthrie "found his primary audiences in the movement culture of New York's Popular Front and the CIO unions of the Northeast and Midwest."[31] Although Guthrie was fully acclimatized to the rich ethnic makeup of a large American city such as Los Angeles (with its prominent Mexican, Japanese, Chinese, and Filipino communities), in New York he fully immersed himself into the great populace of second-generation immigrants of Eastern European stock, as well as becoming a close associate of African American musicians transplanted from the Piedmont and further south—Leadbelly (Huddie Ledbetter), Josh White, Sonny Terry, and Brownie McGhee among them. Guthrie soon married into a Jewish family (that of Marjorie Mazia, née Greenblatt), had children who were raised as Jews, and came to take a great interest in Jewish culture and traditions (marked, not least, by a considerable output of

Jewish-themed songs).[32] As much as Guthrie was nurtured by the Jewish tradition into which he married, the radical editor Irwin Silber proposed that the nurturing went two ways: "For a New York Left that was primarily Jewish, first or second generation and was desperately trying to get Americanized, I think a figure like Woody was of great, great importance."[33]

Guthrie's immersion into the New York milieu affected him in numerous ways. As Dave Marsh notes, there were periods in which "the bulk of material he wrote . . . came straight out of his leisurely morning readings of the New York *Daily News*, the city's premiere tabloid."[34] Most importantly, Guthrie found himself part of a radical fellowship of urban Popular Front activists including his major patron, the folklorist and collector Alan Lomax. As Reuss argues: "For singers whose political sensibilities and styles were dictated by rural roots and little exposure to urban intellectual exchanges, such as Josh White and Woody Guthrie, Lomax's influence broadened their worldviews considerably."[35] Indeed, at least one acquaintance, the composer Charles Seeger (father of Pete), felt that Guthrie was sometimes in danger of "swamping his native talent in Greenwich Villagese."[36]

The meeting of the rural and the urban threw up other hazards for Guthrie, in terms of the musical activism he and his radical colleagues hoped to achieve. Much of this had to do with the efforts of Lomax and his protégés to inject rural American music into the urban consciousness at the expense of other forms of popular music. R. Serge Denisoff might well argue that, while "not one Guthrie propaganda song was found among the Okies and Arkies who fled the Dustbowl for California," Guthrie's "political material was well accepted predominantly by urban radicals and communists in New York and elsewhere."[37] But this was a far cry from being accepted by the ranks of labor "in New York and elsewhere." Reuss argues that "attempts to superimpose the traditions of the rural American heartlands on a city-oriented labor movement . . . at best had only a limited success and a certain artificiality"; for urban activists, as well as the rank-and-file at large, it was difficult to perceive "what significance rural traditions had for urban industrial life, in particular, the day-to-day mechanics of conducting the people's struggle."[38]

In fact, the "Age of the CIO," as Denning calls it, "witnessed an extraordinary flowering of American musics," from "the transition from swing to bop in jazz, with the work of Duke Ellington, Billie Holiday, Charlie Christian, Count Basie, Dizzy Gillespie, and Charlie Parker," to the "emergence of an American philharmonic music in the compositions of Aaron Copland, Marc Blitzstein, and Virgil Thomson," to the" classic songwriting of Ira and George Gershwin, Harold Arlen, and Yip Harburg."[39] These and other musical forms enjoyed great popularity among the urban proletariat; thus Lomax and his protégés, Guthrie and Pete Seeger among them, faced a continual uphill struggle to reach out to a wider urban audience. In their attempts to meld radical political activism with rural musical forms, they were going against the grain of much of the musical activist tradition that preceded them. Denisoff notes:

> the glorification of a rural musical genre by an urban-based political movement was . . . curious, since social crusaders historically have relied upon songs that were familiar to their potential audiences. Agricultural reformers, the Grangers and Populists, absorbed the musical style and fervor of fundamentalist religious hymns. The syndicalist Industrial Workers of the World utilized hymns and hobo jungle tunes to convert the masses to their One Big Union.[40]

There was thus a grain of truth in the advice of one radical activist for the momentarily disheartened Pete Seeger: "Pete, here in New York hardly anybody knows that kind of music. . . . If you are going to work with the workers of New York City, you should be in the jazz field. Maybe you should play the clarinet."[41] Denning's study of the cultural front confirms this impression: "The latter-day success of the folk music revival— of the music of Woody Guthrie, Huddie Ledbetter, and Pete Seeger—has often led historians and cultural critics to assume that folk music was the soundtrack of the Popular Front. This is not true: the music of the young factory and office workers who made up the social movement was overwhelmingly jazz."[42] Thus the radical folk champions were in for a rough ride—not only from many in their would-be audiences but also from such critics as Irving Howe, who, with Lewis Coser, sneered at "the cult of city-made folk dancing and singing."[43]

Criticism such as this reflected an intensifying debate on musical authenticity that, once again, put Woody Guthrie at a vexing crossroads— that between the commercial and the political, as well as the popular and the "folk." It was here that Guthrie adopted one of his most intransigent stances, possibly misreading the myriad and complex dynamics of folk music, popular music, musical professionalism, and amateurism.

(3) "When it comes to singing, I want to be on the stage and I want them to be in the audience."[44]

Guthrie's endless and strident pronouncements on the authenticity of folk music—as opposed to the "phoniness" of popular music—left little room for compromise. "A folk song," he wrote, "tells a story that really did happen. A pop tune tells a yarn that didn't really take place."[45] Of all musical practitioners, he declared, only folk singers "got sense enough to stay down to earth, to sing hard and rough with the beat of work, and to keep a eye and three ears peeled toward the big shops, mills, mines, railroads, farms, and know what is real American music"; as for "Tin Pan Alley"—the popular music industry—it was, he said, "just about as far from the United States as it can be."[46] He repeatedly advised his folk companions "to stay right in the buggy, because you are dealing with the real old honest to god songs of protest against mean treatment, and that's the highest form of the singing business."[47]

From this presumed moral high ground, he handed down his judgments one after another: "Several million skulls have been cracked while this human race fought its way up. Do the big bands and the orgasm gals sing a word about our real fighting history? Not a croak."[48] He could be wildly off the mark with his dour generalizations about the longevity of popular songs: "Hollywood songs don't last. Broadway songs are sprayed with a few hundreds of thousands of dollars to get them going, and they last, we'll say, a few months at most."[49] He could be positively bitchy in his slandering of popular musicians and songwriters: "The songs have no guts, no strength, no real spirit, and are opium dreams of a few pampered pets who have not yet evolved upward to the plane of a real human being. Could you expect their songs, their whirling dreams to last for long?"[50] For folk-singing colleagues who strayed too far into the popular arena—such as Burl Ives—Guthrie reserved his most scathing attacks, in the process establishing his own incorruptible credentials by way of crude and brutal contrasts: "You see, two folksingers can be terribly big, terribly little, terribly fat, terribly slim, one terribly radical and revolutionary, one terribly inclined to singing for the faces that shine in the ritzy apartments around yonders green park."[51]

To a considerable extent, Guthrie's hostility toward popular music was founded on a perception of "the forces of monopoly" within the commercial industry, whose aim with regard to "all of us progressive singers (folk or not)" was "to hush us up."[52] Hence his celebration of the Library of

Congress and other Federal agencies—particularly during the war—that offered recording alternatives to Tin Pan Alley contracts; thanks to "Uncle Sammy," he crowed, "folk singers ain't no longer at the mercy of agents, royalty thieves and all kinds of commercial robbers that have milked more folk singers than there are prairie dogs in Texas."[53] And hence his wild prediction that for every defection of a Burl Ives into the lap of the industry, there would be a mad rush into the folk camp from the legions of Tin Pan Alley. As he wrote to Moses Asch, his producer at Folkways Records:

> you must not ever fall into the mistake of believing that the big boys can ruin or "hurt" or "wreck" the folk field, because the more outrightly bloody they become the faster their warriors will desert from their side to our side. Most of their fighters are not solidly convinced as you might believe, and the moment it draws to a clear cut battle in words or votes or with bullets, then is the time when (as in all other revolutions), the rich are sadly and sorely surprised to see their hired ones pack up and come over onto the side that every child knows is the right side.[54]

In thus overstating the case, Guthrie seemed to forget the debt he himself owed to the commercial broadcasting sector from the very start of his career, when he and his radio colleague Maxine Crissman together hosted a program on Los Angeles station KFVD. Although it was a progressive station, KFVD was nonetheless commercial. As Peter La Chapelle has pointed out:

> in the late 1930s, commercial radio, at least on the local level, was still an unevenly standardized form of mass communication that allowed a significant amount of political and populist discourse.... [I]n particular locales, regional radio and local country music programming allowed performers such as Guthrie and Crissman to shape content, talk defiantly, and even foment political dissent while simultaneously challenging listeners to become more involved in political affairs.[55]

Moreover, Guthrie was somewhat confused about the place of popular or non-folk culture within the American progressive wing. As Lieberman has noted, within the leadership of the Communist Party of the USA, the "commitment to proletarian culture" had given way by the mid-1930s "to an interest in mass culture, with a focus on Broadway, Hollywood, and big-name writers who endorsed antifascism."[56] Denning points to the central place of Hollywood cultural workers in the activism of the West Coast Popular Front—a radical profile that would turn some of Guthrie's accusations into outright slander:

> Both San Francisco and Los Angeles had . . . a network of avant-garde proletarian artists and writers, but Hollywood studios were without doubt the central cultural apparatus on the West Coast. So it is not surprising that the story of the California cultural front is in large part the story of the links between the left-wing labor movement of [Harry] Bridges's CIO and left-wing artists, writers, and craftspeople in the Hollywood studios.[57]

Guthrie himself was aware that the political songs of his cherished Industrial Workers of the World (I.W.W.) were more often than not parodies of popular songs rather than folk songs—an awareness he implicitly signaled in a letter to his singing colleague, Millard Lampell: "I was thinking that we all ought to keep in mind all the various kinds of songs [of] people here in the U.S.A. & how parodies can be made to all of them. Parodies isn't exactly what I mean, rather, union words. Of course, we know what kind of a music we want—simple, militant straight forward. But I think parodies on popular tunes, marches, hymns, as well as folk songs."[58]

Yet, in spite of such moments of the apparent softening of his position, for Woody Guthrie the battle lines were overwhelmingly drawn between the "progressive" side—the "folk" side—and the popular, "reactionary" side. The reality was much less clear than Guthrie envisioned, the crossroads between "folk" and "popular" much muddier than he thought. As Denning has observed, with reference to Popular Front musicians (such as Josh White) who were much more flexible than Guthrie: "[T]he lines separating folk, gospel, blues, jazz, rhythm and blues, and Broadway musicals were not as absolute for the musicians of the cultural front as they have become for critics and historians."[59]

Moreover, even within the folk field, there was no sure consensus that Guthrie's political activism and philosophies fit the requirements of the genre. Folk purists, as Weissman notes, had their own intransigent positions: "There was . . . the controversy about whether folk music itself should take any political positions at all. Some folklorists thought that trying to make folk songs contemporary by addressing political issues was a violation of folklore itself."[60] Reuss points to the "duty" many folklorists felt "to thwart what they saw as an attempt by radicals to manipulate folk traditions for political ends."[61] Even by preserving his songs on record, some felt, Guthrie would have been violating the very definition of the "folk" process:

> To be traditional in the academic sense, a song . . . must owe at least part of its existence to informal transmission from person to person, often orally, and usually face to face over a period of time. The time may be months or generations, but it must be sufficient to remove conscious adherence to rote reproduction from a fixed original. In other words, the item must live apart from books, newspapers, phonograph records, tapes, or any other frozen form.[62]

Guthrie's pride as a professional recording artist at times put him at odds with one of the most cherished assumptions of the folk genre: that it is a vehicle for the people's expression, otherwise stifled by the censorship and monopoly interests of the popular music industry. In folk music, so conventional wisdom declared, the divine amateur has at least an equal voice with the professional. Guthrie certainly paid a degree of lip service to such a creed:

> The big boss has blasted away at the workers with the most modern kinds of weapons, not only gas bombs, tanks, bayonets, machine guns, and mounted policemen, but with fake radio programs, fake magazines, fake moving pictures that talk at the same time, and fake phonograft records, fake Hollywood, fake Broadway, fake Tin Pan Alley junk and baloney that says, "The reason why we're rich and you're down and out is because the good Lord made us an artist, and we went to schools and colleges to learn big artist words, and talk like artists talk, and you're just an old rough and tumble truck driver, bull-dozer, cat skinner, tractor johnny, powder monkey, hard rock tunneller, steel mill blaster, warehouse heaver, longshore hauler, clodhopper, plow follower, share-cropper, Oakie rambler, and your talent and your art dont amount to a hill of beans; you can't write up no songs, 'cause you aint got the sense to, and you can't make up nothing to go on the stage, 'cause you aint got the brains to, and you caint get together and laugh and sing, 'cause you got to hire us to make you laugh and your voices are too rough and cracked up to sing.[63]

Yet at the same time, Guthrie could express some fairly unforgiving opinions about the place of amateurs in the progressive folk movement. Hence his irritation with the "come-all-ye" ethos of his folk protest group, the Almanac Singers, which, he said, was "bothering" him:

> People who just naturally could not sing, play an instrument, who never had before, and who it would take ten years to teach, I argued that our group should not be governed by the vote of such members, because, not understanding music, nor loving it enough to have already learned, although they may be very sympathetic and very anxious to work with and for and even perform with us, the quality of the performances would not be good enough to win the long lasting respect of trade union audiences, much less white collar workers, or professional people, and much less the moneyed classes.[64]

Guthrie may have been right about the low "quality" of musical performance among the Almanac Singers; he may have been wrong, for he names no names. But he certainly makes no allowance for the possibility that one person's "amateur" is another person's "authentic." Certainly, at the Library of Congress, the shelves of Guthrie's patron, Alan Lomax, were sagging under the weight of tape recordings of singers and musicians who would not have passed muster according to Guthrie's apparent standards.

Thus, we have in Woody Guthrie the classic "bundle of contradictions"—the common Everyman and amateur, "true as the average" (as he would often sign off his letters) and the shrill defender of professionalism; the "Dustiest of th' Dust Bowlers" (as he liked to call himself) most at home on the streets of New York; the bourgeois proletarian never a fully paid-up member of either class; the folk champion whose musical legacy extends far beyond the bounds of folk. In standing at the intersection of so many crossroads, Guthrie embodied the tensions and conflicting currents of both the musical and political cultures of the United States—not only for audiences at home, but also further afield.

Notes

1. I am grateful to the BMI Foundation and the Woody Guthrie Foundation for the award of a BMI-Woody Guthrie Fellowship at the Woody Guthrie Archives, New York, through which much of the research for this chapter was undertaken.

2. Wizz Jones quoted in Hank Reineke, *Ramblin' Jack Elliott: The Never-Ending Highway* (Lanham, MD, and Plymouth: Scarecrow, 2010), 264.

3. Mike Dewe, *The Skiffle Craze* (Aberystwyth: Planet, 1998), 40, 85.

4. Ibid., 40, 42.

5. Pete Frame, *The Restless Generation: How Rock Music Changed the Face of 1950s Britain* (London: Rogan House, 2007), 136, 234, 295.

6. Ralph McTell, *As Far as I Can Tell* (London: Leola Music, 2008), 374.

7. Martin Carthy on *Bob Dylan's Big Freeze*, produced by Katrina Fallon and Patrick Humphries. BBC Radio 2, broadcast November 25, 2008.

8. Guy Logsdon, "Biblio/Discography," in Robert Santelli and Emily Davidson, eds., *Hard Travelin': The Life and Legacy of Woody Guthrie* (Hanover, NH, and London: Wesleyan University Press, 1999), 181–244 (196).

9. Paul Oliver quoted in Reineke, 73.

10. For a more extensive discussion of Guthrie's radicalism and his British reception, see Will Kaufman, *Woody Guthrie, American Radical* (Chicago and Urbana: University of Illinois Press, 2011).

11. Woody Guthrie, *Pastures of Plenty*, ed. Dave Marsh and Harold Leventhal (New York: HarperPerennial, 1990), 41.

12. Guthrie quoted in Ed Robbin, *Woody Guthrie and Me* (Berkeley, CA: Lancaster-Miller, 1979), 31.

13. Guthrie, "Work Is Me," in Guthrie, *Pastures of Plenty*, 117.

14. Guthrie, *Pastures of Plenty*, 31.

15. Guthrie to Marjorie Mazia, n.d. (but between September and December 1942). Woody Guthrie Archives: Woody Guthrie Correspondence, Series 1, Box 1, Folder 44.

16. Woody Guthrie, *Born to Win*, ed. Robert Shelton (New York: Collier, 1967), 18–19.

17. Woody Guthrie to Alan Lomax, September 19, 1940. Woody Guthrie Archives: Woody Guthrie Correspondence, Series 1, Box 1, Folder 39.

18. Guthrie, note to "The Dying Miner," Woody Guthrie Papers: Moses and Frances Asch Collection, Ralph Rinzler Archives, Smithsonian Institution. Song Texts, Box 1, Folder 3.

19. Richard A. Reuss, with JoAnne C. Reuss, *American Folk Music and Left-Wing Politics, 1927–1957* (Lanham, MD, and London: Scarecrow, 2000), 161.

20. See "Beaumont Rag," Woody Guthrie, *Library of Congress Recordings* (Rounder Records, 1988), Disc 1, Track 5; also Woody Guthrie, *Bound for Glory* (London: Penguin, 2004 [1943]).

21. Joe Klein, *Woody Guthrie: A Life* (New York: Delta, 1999 [1980]), 41.

22. Ed Cray, *Ramblin' Man: The Life and Times of Woody Guthrie* (New York: W. W. Norton, 2004), 231.

23. Woody Guthrie, "Talking Hard Work," *This Land Is Your Land: The Asch Recordings*, Vol. 1 (Smithsonian Folkways Records, 1999), Track 20.

24. Guy Logsdon and Jeff Place, "Notes on the Songs," liner notes to Guthrie, *This Land Is Your Land: The Asch Recordings*, Vol. 1.

25. Peter La Chapelle, *Proud to Be an Okie: Cultural Politics, Country Music, and Migration to Southern California* (Berkeley: University of California Press, 2007), 49.

26. Michael Denning, *The Cultural Front: The Laboring of American Culture in the Twentieth Century* (London: Verso, 1998), xvi–xvii.

27. Denning, 97.

28. Reuss and Reuss, 69.

29. Denning, 103.

30. Denning, 37.

31. Denning, 281.

32. See, for instance, The Klezmatics, *Woody Guthrie's Happy Joyous Hanukah* (JMG/Jewish Music Group CD, 2006).

33. Irwin Silber quoted in Cray, 216.

34. Dave Marsh, annotation to Guthrie, *Pastures of Plenty*, 150.

35. Reuss and Reuss, 124–25.

36. Charles Seeger quoted in R. Serge Denisoff, *Great Day Coming: Folk Music and the American Left* (Baltimore: Penguin, 1973), 126.

37. Denisoff, 128.

38. Reuss and Reuss, 107, 140.

39. Denning, 283.

40. Denisoff, 3.

41. Unidentified activist quoted in David K. Dunaway, *How Can I Keep from Singing? The Ballad of Pete Seeger* (New York: Villard, 2008), 135.

42. Denning, 329.

43. Irving Howe and Lewis Coser, *The American Communist Party: A Critical History, 1919–1957* (Boston: Beacon, 1957), 353.

44. Woody Guthrie to Marjorie Mazia, November 17, 1942. Woody Guthrie Archives: Woody Guthrie Correspondence, Series 1, Box 1, Folder 44.

45. Guthrie, *Pastures of Plenty*, 207.

46. Woody Guthrie, "Woody Says," unpublished manuscript, c. 1941, n.p. Woody Guthrie Archives: Manuscripts 1, Box 1, Folder 13.

47. Woody Guthrie to the Almanac Singers, n.d. (but March 1941). Woody Guthrie Archives: Woody Guthrie Correspondence, Series 1, Box 1, Folder 3.

48. Woody Guthrie, "Ten Songs," unpublished manuscript, 4. Woody Guthrie Papers: Moses and Frances Asch Collection, Ralph Rinzler Archives, Center for Folklife and Cultural Heritage, Smithsonian Institution: Typescripts, Woody Guthrie Songs, Box 2, Folder 3.

49. *Ibid.*, 3.

50. *Ibid.*, 4.

51. Woody Guthrie, "Singing High Balladree," unpublished manuscript, January 23, 1947, 4. Woody Guthrie Archives: Manuscripts 1, Box 4, Folder 46.

52. Woody Guthrie, "On Ballad Singers," unpublished manuscript, March 20, 1946, 4. Woody Guthrie Archives: Manuscripts 1, Box 4, Folder 26.

53. Woody Guthrie to Marjorie Mazia, n.d. (but between September and December 1942). Woody Guthrie Archives: Woody Guthrie Correspondence, Series 1, Box, 1, Folder 44.

54. Guthrie to Moses Asch, July 15, 1946. Reprinted in Guthrie, *Pastures of Plenty*, 202.

55. La Chapelle, 47.

56. Lieberman, 34.

57. Denning, 18.

58. Woody Guthrie to Millard Lampell, September 9, 1941. Woody Guthrie Archives: Woody Guthrie Correspondence, Series 1, Box 1, Folder 34.

59. Denning, 360.

60. Dick Weissman, *Which Side Are You On? An Inside History of the Folk Music Revival in America* (New York: Continuum, 2006). 7.

61. Reuss and Reuss, 9.

62. Reuss and Reuss, 19-20.

63. Woody Guthrie, "To a Union Show Troup," unpublished manuscript, c., 1941. Woody Guthrie Archives: Manuscripts 1, Box 1, Folder 12.

64. Woody Guthrie to Marjorie Mazia, November 17, 1942. Woody Guthrie Archives: Woody Guthrie Correspondence, Series 1, Box 1, Folder 44.

6

"It's Not British Music, It's American Music"

Bob Dylan and Britain

—John Hughes

W. H. Auden is rarely identified as an influential figure in the turbulent interactions of American and British folk and popular music in the 1960s. However, in the autumn of 1962 the poet made what can seem a decisive intervention. In his New York apartment, he recommended to the British TV actor-turned-director, Philip Saville, that he visit Tony Pastor's club, a crucible of artistic creativity. There Saville was to see the twenty-one-year-old Bob Dylan perform, and to undertake to bring him to England to act in the BBC play, *The Madhouse on Castle Street*, written by the Jamaican playwright Evan Jones. The play, reputedly flawed but haunting, was set in a lodging house, its tension ratcheted up by the political despair of the unseen, central character who had retreated to his room, seemingly to die. Dylan's spoken participation in the play was to dwindle to one line. However, he sang "Blowin' in the Wind" and several traditional folk songs, more or less reworked by him, for the play. The play went out to mixed reviews on 13 January 1963. Dylan's performances were by all accounts memorable, though the BBC was to wipe the tape in 1968.[1]

A key strand in the argument of what follows is that Dylan's visit to London at the end of 1962 constituted a seminal moment in his development. Ever a figure more prone to visceral critique or apocalyptic visions than to ideological affiliation or constructive political vision, in his encounter with English folk music Dylan found assistance in avoiding what seemed factitious or pious in the programmatic aspects of American folk culture. For all his admiration for Woody Guthrie, Dylan was never one to subscribe unreservedly to the idea that "There's a Better

World a'-Coming" or to promulgate any of the diverse narratives of progress identified by the often competing and overlapping liberal, radical, nostalgic, or anarchic elements in the American folk revival of the late 1950s and early 1960s. Dylan's canny assimilation of English idioms seemingly allowed him productively to channel political indignation into impersonal, balladic modes during most of 1963—when English models held sway—while allowing him to avoid being boxed in as a spokesman pedaling specific pedagogical or political prescriptions bearing on a time to come, beyond current conflicts.

Nonetheless, Dylan's temperamental aversion to offering salving visions for the future did not prevent him tapping, with undeviating directness, into the one unifying cause that galvanized him, along with everyone in the U.S. folk revival at the time, whether of a nationalist or internationalist persuasion: the civil rights struggle. Racial injustice was to be the abiding theme of many of the songs he wrote in the year following his visit to England. It was here that the British influence was vital, if short lived, allowing the songs, as we shall see, to sound at once contemporarily engaged—narrowly focused on situation—yet also of the ages. Questions of influence are complex, but many of the songs of 1962–63 are evidently indebted, in musical structure and unsparing tragic focus, to British folk songs, such as those English and Scottish ballads collected, numbered, and published by Francis James Child during the late nineteenth century. The following section sets out to describe the creative alchemy that resulted throughout 1963, as Dylan melded this more anonymous tone with the more native influences of Woody Guthrie or Harry Smith's 1952 *Anthology of American Folk Music*.[2]

Of course, beyond the issue of the influence of British folk music on Bob Dylan's writing, this book's larger focus on transatlantic cultural and musical traffic during the twentieth century raises other questions that ramify in every direction. A central one is the influence on Dylan of other British music during the sixties and, reciprocally, the breadth of the effect of his work on British music. Though this complex dialogue is too wide a topic to deal with adequately here, it is necessary briefly to signpost some of the most compelling points of interest. For instance, the intricacies of Dylan's influence both on and by the Beatles is clearly a study in itself, though it is important in this discussion to mention how Dylan himself identified his turn to rock and roll with their success, in April 1964, in occupying the top five slots in the U.S. hit parade. His "4th Time Around" and "I Wanna Be Your Lover" are, as has often been noted, clearly responses to Beatles songs "Norwegian Wood" and "I Wanna Be Your Man," respectively (much as Lennon's "You've Got to Hide Your Love Away" is a response to Dylan's "I Don't Believe You"). And so one could pursue, similarly, how Dylan was a major influence on an enormous number of other British groups and artists emerging in the 1960s—not just Donovan but the Animals, Fairport Convention, Manfred Mann, Joe Cocker, John Mayall, John Martyn, Rod Stewart, David Bowie, and so on, ad infinitum. If such questions and contexts are beyond the scope of this discussion, then, it is because my prime focus is more closely on Dylan's developing sensibility as an artist through the 1960s, and on the complex and overlapping cultural, musical, and national contexts of Britain and the United States, whose interactions proved so formative for it.

I

As a songwriter, Dylan's major period of engagement with British music can be given a useful kind of narrative arc by referring it to two celebrated, possibly mythical, moments in his career, one in England, one in the United States. In each case, musical performance, or at least the possibility of it, came into conjunction with someone wielding an axe. The first moment involved Martin Carthy, the folk singer, guitarist, and folk music historian, and only a week older than Dylan himself. Dylan spent some nights during his stay sleeping on Carthy's sofa or floor in London, in a winter locked up by frost, and by snows that lasted in much of England until March 1963.[3] On 18 December, his second night in London, Dylan was introduced to Carthy, who remembers him playing at the Troubadour. On 29 December he played there again, before moving on to the Roundhouse with Carthy. This was the night before the first day of filming of *The Madhouse on Castle Street*, and on this day and the next a blizzard blew across the country, leaving—I quote from the Met Office—"drifts six metres deep which blocked roads and rail routes, left villages cut off and brought down power lines."[4] The story is that Dylan and Carthy kept warm by chopping up the house piano.[5] Whatever the precise truth, the story is a useful metaphor for Dylan's voracious, not to say ruthless, consumption and transmutation of English musical material at this point in his career.[6] And part of what he did was to consign Carthy's "Scarborough Fair" and "Lord Franklin" to his creative fires, whence they rose, phoenix-like, as "Girl from the North Country," "Boots of Spanish Leather," and "Bob Dylan's Dream."

In London, Dylan met up with Eric Von Schmidt, illustrator and singer, and the two were to fly back to the United States together on 15 January 1963.[7] And when he sang "Masters of War" at Gerde's in New York less than a week later, it was the distinctive melodic delivery of a version of "Nottamun Town" by Jackie Washington—a close friend of Von Schmidt's—that Dylan adopted.[8] Though this performance has often been taken to be the premiere of the song, Carthy (not someone likely to get his facts wrong) remembers Dylan singing it at the Troubadour on the night they met.[9] Certainly Anthea Joseph, manager of the Troubadour, claims he sang it, along with "The Ballad of Hollis Brown," at the Singers' Club run by Ewan MacColl, just before Christmas—presumably December 22. This club in High Holborn was steeped in a traditionalist ethos that harked back ten years to its earlier manifestation as the Ballads and Blues Club, where Alan Lomax, MacColl, Bert Lloyd, Peggy Seeger, and many others regularly performed.[10] The club's code was strictly traditional music, and MacColl had looked askance at Dylan arriving with his guitar. In response to the crowd's mounting clamor for him to sing, Dylan, ever the provocateur, drank more beer during the interval before eventually succumbing, presumably with a maximum of exasperating pantomime. He went on to sing four times the allowed period of five minutes, which did two things: it brought the house down, and it fomented a lifetime of righteous resentment on the part of MacColl, who was enraged at Dylan's trampling on the club's defining protocols.

If "Masters of War" was performed in London, it is clear that it must have been something of a work in progress, since there is little doubt that the first version was written in New York City, at a time when the papers were still full of the Cuban crisis. Heylin refers to the singer's prefatory remarks to the song, on a recording made when he sung it to Alan Lomax on his return to New York: "I wrote it in London [. . .] I kept seeing in the papers every day [them] putting down MacMillan, [saying] Kennedy's gonna screw him, on these missiles . . . They got headlines in the papers, underneath MacMillan's face saying, 'Don't mistrust me, don't mistrust me, how can you treat a poor maiden so?'"[11]

In 1991 Carthy said, "I've read a lot of books about him and not one talks in any detail about his time in England. As far as I can hear, by listening to his records, his time in England was actually crucial to his development."[12] By now, the research of writers like Matthew Zuckerman and Clinton Heylin have demonstrated the truth of Carthy's remarks, and it is possible to see clearly how traditional British, as well as Irish, songs provided early

Dylan with a considerable, even crucial, resource, as he raided their melodies, their anonymous, immemorial, modes of address, and deliberate, foursquare verses and structures for his own songs.[13]

Another facet of British folk songs that can seem to have passed into Dylan's work of the time, is the wide-ranging presence of weather-related imagery within them, and it is plausible that motifs of rain and snow merged in his imagination with the actual conditions he experienced in London that December and January. Aside from "Scarborough Fair," one can take as representative the openings of well-known songs—like Child Ballads 78 and 98, "The Unquiet Grave" and "Brown Adam", respectively—where weather functions both as scene-setting and as metaphor for the feelings that the song will unfold:

> The wind doth blow today, my love,
> And a few small drops of rain;
> I never had but one true-love,
> In cold grave she was lain.[14]

> O WHA woud wish the win to blaw,
> Or the green leaves fa therewith?
> Or wha wad wish a leeler love
> Than Brown Adam the Smith?[15]

An interesting song of Dylan's in this connection would be the mysterious song "Liverpool Gal" (possibly written in December 1962, though more likely developed around May 1963), which uses the weather to frame the song's depiction of the transitory affair between the singer and the Liverpool girl of the title one London night. So, initially he meets her by the Thames with "the wind blowing through my hair," sleeps with her in a night of "drizzling rain" when they confide by the fire, before waking as the rain "had turned to snow." He leaves her for reasons that the song does not explain, their parting apparently as unaccountable and inevitable to both of them as the changes in the weather.

> I gazed all up at her window
> where the snowy snow-flakes blowed
> I put my hands in my pockets
> And I walked 'long down the road.[16]

The song's obscurity is fascinating in itself, and manifold. There are the elliptical aspects of situation and motive, these alternating with careful registering of mundane detail (her blue eyes, the worn-out rug, the fire). The one recording in existence of it has apparently been guarded by Tony Glover and never surfaced since it was recorded, apparently, in Minneapolis in July 1963. One can speculate if the song was too autobiographical for Dylan to acknowledge in 1963.[17]

Whether based on fact or imagination, it remains possible to connect this "Liverpool Gal" with that other northern girl from that winter visit, and left behind across the border where the snows fall, in "Girl from the North Country."[18] What also appears indisputable, in terms of transatlantic connections, is that "Liverpool Gal" is closely modeled, both musically and narratively, on "The Lakes of Pontchartrain," a song of migration and travel fiercely claimed, like so many, by competing Irish and Appalachian factions. A traveler is taken in by a girl whose kindness and hospitality he celebrates, and whose image and memory, at the close of the song, he still holds within his mind, as he returns to his travels.

Of course, long before December 1962, Dylan had sung and drawn on many English songs. In *Chronicles*, he memorably describes the riveting effect of traditional British folk, introduced to him in Minneapolis by a literature professor named Harry Webber:

Webber was an English literary professor, a tweed-wearing, old-fashioned intellectual. And he did know plenty of songs, mostly roving ballads—stern ballads, ones that meant cruel business [. . .] I loved all these ballads right away. They were romantic as all hell and high above all the popular love songs I'd ever heard. Lyrically they worked on some kind of supernatural level and they made their own sense [. . .] I was beginning to feel like a character from within these songs, even beginning to think like one.[19]

In August 1963 Dylan began writing "Tomorrow Is a Long Time," a song based on the fifteenth-century lyric, "Westron Wind."[20] Two months or so before the London visit, too, during September in New York, he had reworked a Carthy favorite, Child Ballad 12, "Lord Randall," as "A Hard Rain's a-Gonna Fall," at the Gaslight, a club on MacDougal Street in Greenwich Village. In October he was performing his song of a returning veteran, "John Brown," a song loosely based on the Irish song

"Mrs. McGrath."[21] However, the London visit was a watershed, marking a decisive turn to English songs that was to last until the end of 1963, and that corresponded to his working on his third album. So "Who Killed Cock Robin" underpins "Who Killed Davey Moore," and Child Ballad 173, "Mary Hamilton," provides the basis for "The Lonesome Death of Hattie Carroll." As Heylin shows, elements of an anthologized folk song, "The Everlasting Circle," provided inspiration for "Eternal Circle," while a Scottish ballad, "The Road and Miles to Dundee," provided the melodic structure for "Walls of Red Wing" (Heylin, *Revolution in the Air*, 147). Further, Dylan himself identified the source of "Lay Down Your Weary Tune" as being an unnamed Scottish ballad.[22] Finally, it has long been well known that particularly rich sources from this period were the songs that he would have heard in New York by the celebrated Irish band the Clancy Brothers: "The Leaving of Liverpool" and "The Patriot Game," respectively, became reworked as "Farewell" and "With God on Our Side."

Ironically or fittingly, it was the conversion of another Clancy Brothers song, "The Parting Glass" into "Restless Farewell," that was to mark the next turning point in Dylan's career—a turning from English folk models. The song's title, and restrained valedictory fervor, indicate Dylan's desire to move away from what the third album represented, not least that dependence on English music that the song itself both exemplified and relinquished. The third verse indicates the ironic torsions whereby identification with political causes and emancipation can itself constitute a trap, and forestall possibilities of self-exploration:

> Oh ev'ry foe that ever I faced
> The cause was there before we came
> And ev'ry cause that ever I fought
> I fought it full without regret or shame

The "farewell" of the final line in the verse indicates a decisive value shift, from political vision, from the dedication to causes and new dawns, to a pursuit of more unknown, personal dimensions.

> And if I see the day
> I'd only have to stay
> So I'll bid farewell in the night and be gone[23]

Written at the end of October 1963, it seems it was the last song he would write until the new year, which would begin with "Chimes of Freedom," and "Mr. Tambourine Man," songs that in theme, idiom, and sentiment were suddenly scoping a wholly different sort of visionary mode and inspiration, and new routes of personal freedom.[24] The next album, *Another Side of Bob Dylan*, is, in this respect, as much a renunciation of the old direction as announcement of a new one. There is a nice symmetry in the fact that, when Dylan returned to London in May 1964, he would debut "Mr. Tambourine Man" at the Royal Festival Hall. As before, Carthy was to be the first to hear the new song: "Almost as soon as he landed [. . .] he was on the phone to Martin Carthy. As Carthy recalls, 'He came around. And he sang . . . "Mr Tambourine Man" and it was [like], "Where [the hell] is this man going?"'" (Heylin, *Revolution in the Air*, 184). Whatever the places that Dylan had been coming from, what was to be important from now on, as Carthy suggests, was that he was now going somewhere else altogether.

II

This brings me to the second bit of axe-wielding. I take this as marking a decisive shift in the use of English music, and I refer, of course, to the axe associated with Pete Seeger at the Newport Folk Festival on 25 July 1965. At this notorious concert, Dylan went electric to a scandalized folk community, by playing a raucous short-lived set accompanied by Mike Bloomfield, Al Kooper, et al. The three songs were accompanied further by a cacophony of audience noise, the members either booing at Dylan's betrayal of his folk mission, or calling for the sound to be turned down, depending on whose version you adopt. Insightfully, Mark Polizzotti wrote of the album that Dylan was recording—both before and after the Newport performance—that "What Dylan has abandoned in *Highway 61 Revisited* is not his sense of outrage or protest, but the illusion of community."[25] And certainly, the incidents of the Newport concert bear that out. Though Seeger himself, like everyone else, has offered different accounts of the events of that evening (not least the axe-wielding), the definitive truth seems to be as follows: Seeger either did or did not find his axe, and then either did or did not threaten, and either did or did not attempt to cut the cable, which was itself either a microphone cable or power cable. It is an incident clouded, like most of that day, by claim and counter-claim, facts shrouded in collective cultural fantasy.

However, indisputably, things had turned graphically physical earlier that day, between Alan Lomax and Albert Grossman, Dylan's manager, after Lomax's disparaging introduction of the Paul Butterfield Blues Band, another member of Grossman's stable of artists. James Brewer describes the resulting *contretemps*: Lomax had "described their music as 'purely imitative' and basically asked for the forbearance of the audience. The pair of middle-aged men ended up rolling around in the dirt of the festival grounds."[26] Whether Grossman's motivation was in defense of the artistic integrity of his clients or his royalties is not recorded. To return to the later incident, Greil Marcus actually has Lomax, as well as Seeger, both laying their hands on the axe during Dylan's electric set: "Backstage Pete Seeger and the great ethnomusicologist Alan Lomax attempted to cut the band's power cables. Pete Yarrow and singer Theodore Bikel blocked them until a full guard could be rounded up."[27]

One can only ponder what turn history might have taken had Lomax managed to locate Seeger's axe for the earlier confrontation with Grossman. Certainly all this was a shift from the onstage communal linking of arms, between Dylan, Baez, Bikel, Yarrow, Seeger, and the others in Newport two years earlier as they sang "We Shall Overcome." By 1965 all that linked most of the stars was that they contributed 25 percent of their income to Albert Grossman.

After the high water mark of early 1963, Dylan's use of, even dependence on, English songs as raw material for his own compositions petered out, as his American heritage, always the dominant factor, asserted itself more univocally in his work through the rest of the sixties. As the album titles *Bringing It All Back Home* and *Highway 61 Revisited* suggest, the returning and revisiting involved predominantly American sources, in particular rock and blues structures and arrangements. In the passage from *Chronicles* above, where Dylan references his assimilation of English folk songs, he indicates also how the transporting effects of this music could not elbow aside the rural and country blues music that had shaped his musical imagination as a youth. The passage that refers to this reads less as description than as homage to formative influences so deep that they demand evocation, as if the purpose of the prose were to summon the presiding spirits of self, past, place:

But there was a lot more to it than that . . . a lot more. Beneath it I was into the rural blues as well; it was a counterpart of myself. It was connected to early rock and roll and I liked it because it was older than Muddy and Wolf, Highway 61, the main thoroughfare of the country blues, begins where I came from . . . Duluth to be exact. I always felt like I'd started on it, always been on it and could go anywhere from it, even down into the deep Delta country. It was the same road, full of the same contradictions, the same one-horse towns, the same spiritual ancestors. The Mississippi River, the bloodstream of the blues, also starts up from my neck of the woods. I was never too far away from any of it. It was my place in the universe, always felt like it was in my blood. (Dylan, *Chronicles, Volume One*, 240–41)

If the turn to electricity at Newport indicated that Dylan was returning to his musical home, then, in an important way this was the Hibbing of his youth, and pre-eminently the various rock and roll ensembles that practiced in his parents' garage and house—the Jokers, the Shadow Blasters, and the Golden Chords.[28] The names of these bands are intriguing, echoing DC Comics as much as CBS Records, so that for all the self-protective humor, they perhaps hint at the tie-in of music with identity changes and the taking on of new powers.[29] One performance of the Golden Chords was certainly a callow anticipation of the shape-shifting and power-play of the mid-sixties, of the controversies and bombardments of Newport, the Free Trade Hall, or Forest Hills. On 6 February 1958, Dylan, the cherubic agitator, fronted the Chords in a rambunctious, deafening set at his Hibbing School. According to one account at least, there was hooting and booing involved, and Michael Gray has it that Dylan broke the pedal on the school Steinway grand during the second song, and English teacher Boniface J. Rolfzen had to intervene. On the principal's say-so, Rolfzen was successful where Seeger later was to fail, and "cut the power to the house mikes" (Gray, *Bob Dylan Encyclopaedia*, 314).[30]

For Dylan in 1965, the route back to these times, Highway 61, was clearly not an accidental reference, as we have seen. It was the road that linked his home town of Duluth with the University of Minnesota, with the radio stations of his youth, and "folk clubs of Minneapolis and St Paul."[31] So too it was the route that linked the Mississippi, the home of blues and jazz, with the North:

It passes by the birthplaces and homes of Muddy Waters, Charley Patton, Son House, and Elvis Presley. The crossroads at which Robert Johnson made his supposed pact with the devil is said to have been the intersection of Highways 61 and 49, today his grave rests off Highway

61 in Greenwood, Mississippi [. . .] The stretch of Highway 61 near Clarksdale, Mississippi, is the road on which Bessie Smith [. . .] was fatally injured in 1937 [. . .]. (Polizzotti, *Highway 61 Revisited*, 24–25)

What took place by 1965, most essentially, was a shift that had little to do with English folk music, which is to say that it was a shift within the kind of American subjectivity projected during and after the period in which he was most influenced by Woody Guthrie.[32] As shall be argued, where Guthrie had offered a politically viable persona, by *Blonde on Blonde* in 1966, Dylan's inspiration took him, in ways both liberating and risky, into the uncovering of more intimate and opaque psychological areas. However, prior to this, and most likely in summer 1960, Dylan underwent his early, epiphanic, encounter with Guthrie, and came to write of it that "[I]t was like I had been in the dark and someone had turned on the main switch of a lightening conductor [. . .]" (Dylan, *Chronicles, Volume One*, 245). Leaving aside the adolescent dimension of Dylan's turning himself, as he put it, into a walking "Woody Guthrie jukebox,"[33] the decisive and important, if obvious, feature here is that this influence was to convert singing into a matter of vocation, of individuality or identity, even of a kind of transfiguring power. As an aspect of this, Guthrie was not merely an example for Dylan but an exemplar, someone whose songs conveyed a code, a vision, a critique, a personal ethic and political attitude, "the poet of hard crust sod and gumbo mud" (Dylan, *Chronicles, Volume One*, 245). Guthrie's persona and political vision invited both intimacy and identification, the sense that one both knew him and could become like him: righteous as well as powerful, the hard-travelin' man with the six-string machine that could kill fascists. . . . As a young man, Dylan even attempted to get people to call him Woody, and Ramblin' Jack Elliott (formerly Elliot Charles Adnopoz, a surgeon's son from Brooklyn) predicated his whole career on a similar modeling and association.

This all brings me to an elaboration of the main point. English and Irish folk songs, and their American counterparts (themselves often reworkings like "Gypsy Davey"), sung by Guthrie and the young Dylan, granted Dylan the means to inhabit or narrate seemingly timeless themes, injustices, and yearnings. Their appropriation gave Dylan's songs the broadest, most impersonal kind of scope, an aura of the immutable. Songs like "A Hard Rain's a-Gonna Fall" or "Masters of War," for instance, conveyed in their artfully unadorned, rough-hewn, yet effective fabric the authority of something that had survived, whose reference was seemingly universal. At the same time, the interpolation of a critical vision modeled on Guthrie gave the songs their political dynamism, their undeflectable drive toward change. The vision was from the mountaintops, but it scanned the horizon. It was this particularly American element that Dylan took from Guthrie, an individual angle and payoff that he combined with the time-honored dimension common to American and English folk music. The themes of Dylan's early songs might be predictable and sound old, but the precise topics and angles of approach were subtly unpredictable, as in "A Pawn in their Game," "The Ballad of Hollis Brown," or "The Lonesome Death of Hattie Carroll."

This is where Guthrie's example seems so important, and the combination of anonymous folk framework and individuating viewpoint so crucial. After all, what is the main effect of these songs? They tell you something you already know, while also insisting on a change of viewpoint, similar to that enacted by the speaker whose approach to the material involves looking again with new eyes. The aim is to jolt you out of your political torpor, and in the process summon and anticipate a new community, new interpersonal realities such as those modeled in the response and connection the songs demand. Political change and self-change are inseparable. Guthrie's songs too incorporated this crucial connectivity of viewpoint in their tone, wit, and intelligence as much as in their content, conveying the sense of a speaker in the world but not of it. He is without a home, passing through, anticipating in hope a world to come, while describing, with an outsider's sharpness, a truth clouded by everyday custom, greed, and compromise. Dylan's knowingness in the use of this transformative persona shaded at times into mischievously affectionate parody, as when he sought to win the farmer's trust in the 1964 song "Motorpsycho Nitemare" ("Well, by the dirt 'neath my nails / I guess he knew I wouldn't lie" [Dylan, *Lyrics*, 123]).

So, the bracing, arresting, effect of Dylan's early songs, as with Guthrie's, is to refuse to allow you to say you were not told, that you had not seen. Political dedication and change, they insist, are a matter of vision, and seeing remains accordingly an important trope, as well as the ultimate means of critical power. For example, when Dylan sings "But I see through your eyes" in "Masters of War" (Dylan, *Lyrics*, 55), the listener first wonders what he means. Is this just lazy cliché backfiring, creating the idea that Dylan sympathizes with these profiteers, sees things their way? For an instant, the song courts aesthetic disaster, the listener's comprehension stalling. Then one realizes that the line echoes the earlier line "But I see through your masks" (Dylan, *Lyrics*, 55), and that this later line implies a deeper psychological uncovering—of the deceits these men practice to themselves, as well as to the world. They wear a mask in public, but also in private: self-justification is necessarily both *of* the self (to others), but also *to* the self. It is a matter of the lies and distortions necessary to continue doing "what you do." Moreover, at the same time that the listener's mind is provoked into a subtler comprehension of the situation, so he or she comes to see through the eyes of the singer, the song invoking the politicized community it implies.

By such enactments, expansions, of vision, as well by content, Dylan's early songs offer themselves not merely as interpretations of the world but as ways of interpreting it, "road maps for the soul,"[34] small verbal anticipations of other revolutions and revisions. Like Guthrie's, too, the songs tap into humor or anger as the motors of personal as well as political change, bringing about shifts in sensibility, conversions in attitude. Response entails an ethical change, and indissolubly links the personal and the political. The impetus toward change is based not on the supposed perfections of the speaker, but on the very American orientation toward perfectibility, a shared future yet to be made. I would suggest that this sense of honesty outside the law, of nonconformity and autonomy, is the decisive, essential, American, Emersonian element in Dylan's work throughout his career.

III

This Emersonian ethic of self-reliance (the need to "Trust Yourself," as Dylan put it in his 1985 song), indeed, appears a constant throughout his career. However, its co-ordinates and form changed post-1963, as Dylan's work moved from the public to the private sphere, a move that also involved the shift back to American musical frameworks. Before 1965, for instance, there had been the sense that Dylan was no more responsible for the predicaments he found himself in than he was for the weather. The victimizing, romantic, poetic staples often found in English folk song—the snow that drifts, the wind that blows, the rain that falls—had been suitable accompaniments of this, as I have said. By 1966, in *Blonde on Blonde*, though, these become internalized in the unstable scenarios, of songs where wind, rain, snow, cold, and so on figure an urban, subjective drama of disorientation and entrapment, of vertiginous personal dissociations of the self from itself and from others. The singer, for instance, variously inhabits cryptic scenarios where he can no longer tell what effect his words will have, or even what he can see or say. The songs persistently turn on, and refer to, impairments of vision, misunderstandings, deafness, intoxication, lameness, disorientation, confusion, repetition and imprisonment. In this world, one is divided from oneself, and from others, the self is hanging off its hinges, or stuck in unavailing cycles of confusion, desire, loss, or frustration.

In "One of Us Must Know," for instance, misrecognition is the main trope in the song. Dylan sings four times the phrase "I couldn't see" (what you could show me / how you could know me / when it started snowin' / where we were goin') and voices over and again the entwinements of his failing understanding ("I didn't realize just what I did hear / I didn't realize how young you were"), with his failed desire for a face-to-face ("you said you knew me and I believed you did"). The song is a testament to desire as failed intention ("I never really meant to do you any harm"), and to the renewed hope that "[s]ooner or later one of us must know / That I really did try to get close to you." In the closing lines, the song's sense of a vulnerable "I" fighting for self-integrity amid the violent fall out of a baffling romance condenses on the final image of his vulnerable "eyes," his failing capacity to see:

And then you told me later as I apologized
That you were just kiddin' me, you weren't really from the farm
And I told you, as you clawed out my eyes
That I never really meant to do you any harm (Dylan, *Lyrics*, 195)

The girl who "clawed out" his eyes, reveals that (unlike the girl in "Motorpsycho Nitemare," from two years before) "she wasn't really from the farm." In "One of Us Must Know" intentions cannot be distinguished from misunderstandings, facts from illusions. In this world of missed chances, desire and love—the attempt to connect—have fateful consequences. As for Oedipus, for the singer desire is oblivious to the facts, and eventual knowledge, seeing the truth, entails a deeper form of suffering—of blindness and mutilation. At the end of the verse, he ineffectually sings, "That I never really meant to do you any harm." Understanding, if it comes at all, is ironically belated, and registers self-destruction. On *The Basement Tapes*, too, the causes of disintegration and the inability to read the signs of the times are perhaps even more personal, as in the irrepressible "Million Dollar Bash": "I looked at my watch, / I looked at my wrist, / I punched myself in the face / With my fist." When he continues, "I took my potatoes down to be mashed," the sense of self-mutilation uneasily, comically, works beneath the imagery of the farm (Dylan, *Lyrics*, 279).

Nonetheless, it is necessary to emphasize how important English and Irish music has remained for Dylan throughout his life and career, even if sidelined as an influence on his own self-projections and writing after the end of 1963 (occasional songs, like 'Highlands" on the 1997 album *Time Out of Mind*, aside). To briefly emphasize here Dylan's continued performance of British songs is also to point to an important, often unacknowledged, aspect of his talent as a lifelong interpreter of British traditional music. Toward the beginning of Martin Scorsese's biographical film, *No Direction Home*, Dylan says that his first childhood musical memory was listening to "Drifting Too Far from the Shore," an experience he loved, because it made him feel he was "someone else." Crossing the Atlantic has always had a similar and emancipating effect upon him as a singer. Michael Gray's comment on the Appalachian ballad "Copper Kettle" on *Self Portrait* applies, I think, to the most important feature of Dylan's performance of English songs—"As with all the music he touches on in this collection, he brings back to life the spirit of the age the song is all about and does it immeasurably better than the purists to whom his version (it has violins and women on it) is anathema."[35]—though it also needs saying that the origin of the song itself is subject to some debate.[36] Earlier I mentioned that Dylan used English and Irish folk models in his own compositions to counterbalance the individuating ethic first identifiable with Guthrie's influence. By this combination, the singer could be identified with the ethical viewpoint transmitted through the song while it also appeared timeless, even anonymous.

Contrarily, Dylan's singing of actual British and Irish songs bears out Gray's suggestion, since they are wholly detached from any trace of his personality presiding over them. The strength of these performances is inseparable from his capacity to extinguish, in the singing of them, any sense of his own identity. In his own songs, Dylan's famous lack of a stable personality often takes the forms of refusal or leave-taking: of a speaker who is evasive, retaliatory, obscure, or antagonistic, or who is in motion, "keeping on keeping on." Rather differently, English songs enable him both to lose himself in the song and to find the song in the process. He disappears into them, becoming a kind of revealing agent through which the songs' human drama and protagonists can be unfolded in a dynamic way.[37] In contrast, these performances show also how much folk singing is prey to becoming co-opted by singers who appropriate it for the purposes of their moralistic self-presentation or pedagogical antiquarianism.

A list of English or Irish songs memorably performed by Dylan, and many of them revisited, might include, for instance, "A Long Time a' Growing" or "Young but Daily Growing," "Wild Mountain Thyme," "House Carpenter," 'When a Man's in Love,' "The Cuckoo Is a Pretty Bird," "Pretty Peggy-O," "Come All You Fair and Tender Ladies," "The Water is Wide," "Polly Vaughan," "Arthur MacBride," "Froggie Went a Courtin'," "Mary of the Wild Moor," "Barbara Allan," "Eileen Aroon." To this one can add songs like "The Bells of Rhymney" and "That Old Triangle," which are rooted in the UK or Ireland though not, properly speaking, folk songs. One would need to make the case, also, for two further wonderful songs of emigration, "Canadee-I-O" and "Jim Jones," from his two early-nineties albums of public-domain songs—and even more contentiously, perhaps, since its origin is so debated, "The Lakes of Ponchartrain." In these performances of migration, he does indeed appear to leave his native shores behind, to become someone else. However, it is nearer to the truth to say, as suggested, of these performances themselves, that they constitute a kind of debt repaid, and show an unremarked, but remarkable and very English, capacity for what Keats termed negative capability, for bringing to life songs in which his own personality plays the role merely of a catalyst, invisible in what it brings to view.

A further aspect of this larger topic would be Dylan's later visits to England in 1965 and, in particular, 1966 (not to mention 1981). Can we identify the gladiatorial intensity, the exhilarating hostility of the 1966 tour, for instance, in terms of a collision of English and American musical culture? Greil Marcus has written memorably that the source of the audience anger was that Dylan suggested that the whole folk movement had been a pose, and that his standing on stage tricked out in Carnaby Street motley and drainpipes, Cuban heels and the rest, bobbing and bopping, gyrating and tripping across the stage, was the final straw, signifying the deflation of the collective political hope and aspiration, not to say the *armour propre*, of his folk audience, who felt that the Hawks were taking a wrecking ball to their moral self-projections.[38] In the 1965 San Francisco conference, Dylan quips, "they must have a lot of money, to be able to go some place and boo," but what better index of their perceived connection to Dylan than the belief that they could win him back by protest?[39]

The question is, though, how far can this iconic shootout be read in terms of the differences between American and British culture? Certainly, much of D. A. Pennebaker's handheld-camera films made of Dylan's 1965 and 1966 tours (*Dont Look Back* and *Eat the Document*, respectively) brings out the obvious differences. One thinks of the miscomprehension—by turns touching, exasperating, comic, embarrassing, or idiotic—that surfaces in so much of *Dont Look Back*, or in the tinny, truncated recording of "God Save the Queen" that provided C. P. Lee and everyone else at the Free Trade Hall with their final musical experience of the night. It is hard, too, not to miss the transatlantic needle at the beginning of that celebrated electric set, as Hudson's organ comically doodles Grainger's "In an English Country Garden" prior to the sledgehammer intro that set the tone for "Tell Me Momma." And, after all, it is easy, and a large part of the point, to scoff at the "science student" in *Dont Look Back* or the fulminating moralists spitting at Dylan's betrayals to Bob Neuwirth or Pennebaker in the lobby of the Free Trade Hall in *Eat the Document*. There is, indeed, a telling kind of cultural divide, exploited by Dylan, in the hostility that surfaces in outtakes from that film, and that show the full inchoate horror of the verbal jousting between Dylan and John Lennon as they shared a taxi ride around London on the day of the Albert Hall concert where he was to speak the words that I take as the title of this piece, in a mock-pedagogical drawl.[40]

All in all, though, Dylan's attitude in Pennebaker's films appears, contrarily, totally without hostility—it is more one of bemusement, amusement, detachment, or indifference. It is as if Britain offered him, I would suggest, not so much a competitive domain, literally and figuratively, as a theatre for playing out and amplifying—provocatively, no doubt—conflicts internal to American culture, for rehearsing what being American, and in particular, being an outlaw or alienated, might mean more clearly than might be possible back home. Dylan in England in 1965 and 1966 cultivates and relishes how the backdrop of England accentuates the sense of himself as alien, as a Martian, as unknowable, or incomprehensible. For all its failings, Todd Haynes's casting of Cate Blanchett in *I'm Not There* registers this exotic allure, at least, as well as the way in which Dylan in 1966 preserved, among other indices of cool and control, something of the inscrutable hauteur and fascination of a screen goddess.

IV

This brings me to the closing topic: post-Newport Dylan and America. A useful reference here is Alfred Kazin's comment in 1982 that the greatest single fact about modern American writers was their "absorption in every last detail of their American world together with their deep and subtle alienation from it."[41] What better epitome of this equivocal cultural attitude than the Dylan of 1966 who toured with a gigantic, enigmatic stars and stripes behind him? or the hapless deadbeat persona, at once commonplace, surreal, and unfathomable, that Dylan would adopt on the Basement Tapes, in songs like "Clothes Line Saga," "Yea, Heavy and a Bottle of Bread," "Please Mrs. Henry," or "Lo and Behold"? To this one can add his equally enigmatic silence (one cryptic verse in "Tombstone Blues" and another wisecrack in the same press conference notwithstanding) concerning the possibility he might be conscripted into the Vietnam War.[42]

There is his avoidance of the Woodstock festival on his doorstep, or the shunnings of the post-1966 counterculture that were *John Wesley Harding*, *Nashville Skyline*, and *Self-Portrait*. The yearning and anger that had attached to his apostasy in 1966 were never far from the surface in the late sixties, though they were now ironically directed at a new apostasy—his refusal any longer to be the Telecaster-toting renegade of those very 1966 shows. As his audience caught up, Dylan moved on. So, throughout the late sixties he was to mime the beatific, hat-tipping, backwoods patriarch of Elliott Landy's *Nashville Skyline* cover photo. The crowds that braved the cold, and the insanitary conditions of the Isle of Wight festival on September 1, 1969, for instance, waiting for hours into the night for the brief set by Dylan and the Band, were repaid by a confounding, dismissive, emollience. The opening words, "It's nice to be here, sure is," were so uncharacteristic as to seem rehearsed, willfully perverse, an index of how the performance would resist the audience's wishes by its weird old New England courtesies, and its very mellifluousness.[43] It would not be until the best of the Christian shows of 1980 and 1981, not least those at Fox Warfield and Earls Court, that Dylan would find his gifts for antagonism and nonconformity raised again in sustained fashion to a concentrated and concerted intensity of focus comparable to that which surfaced in the folk clubs of 1962–63 or the theatres of 1966.[44]

So far as that antagonism is an artistic and cultural matter, however, one finds its American provenance described in Emerson's account of the poet, who is more ourselves than we are because he anticipates what we want to say but are too afraid, too oblivious, or inarticulate to express. The poet, for Emerson, is, as this might imply, the enemy of convention. Turning away from those who censure him, "[h]e unlocks our chains, and admits us to a new scene."[45] Toward the end of his essay "The Poet," Emerson gives a description of the poet that, as Mark Ford has pointed out in an essay on

Dylan and Emerson,[46] speaks perfectly and uncannily of the Dylan of the Free Trade Hall"

> Doubt not, O poet, but persist. Say "It is in me, and shall out." Stand there, balked and dumb, stuttering and stammering, hissed and hooted, stand and strive, until at last rage draw out of thee that *dream-power* which every night shows thee is thine own; a power transcending all limit and privacy, and by virtue of which a man is the conductor of the whole river of electricity. (Emerson, *The Portable Emerson*, 263)

Interestingly, the imagery echoes Dylan's reference to Guthrie's influence as being like a "lightening conductor." Emerson's poet is a conductor of vision and unspoken truths, one whose words contest the constraints of social identity.

More broadly, for Stanley Cavell, Emerson's work inaugurates American philosophical subjectivity as precisely an "aversive thinking," where self-reliance, one's private war of independence, depends on the turning away from the received script of social consciousness.[47] Perhaps the essential connection between Emerson and Dylan, which Cavell's reading of the Emersonian schema allows us to see, is that the antagonism is always with the self. Ford, for instance, has pointed out that the coruscating singer and the victim of "Like a Rolling Stone" can be seen as intimately connected, so that, appearances aside, the song can seem a soliloquy by other means. The song soars in celebration of the discarded presumptions of a defunct self. However, whether the self is identified as one's own or as that of one's scapegoat is a distinction less interesting than the idea that the tension between the two can be identified with our own self-betrayals and self-blindness. Only by the uncertain transitions from former modes of being can the American mind make progress to what Emerson calls in *History* the "unattained but attainable self" (Emerson, *The Portable Emerson*, 117).

Let us draw together the threads of this discussion, then. As Mike Marqusee wrote, it would be "impossible to imagine the evolution of either British or American popular music, or the dissident cultures that sprouted in both countries," without the 'constant and complex" interchange of English and American culture and music throughout the 1960s and after (Marqusee, *Wicked Messenger*, 74). This chapter has sought to explore some of the key ways in which Bob Dylan, from his first visit to London as a young, relatively unknown singer, was affected by these exchanges, as well as describing how through this decade particularly, he would increasingly contribute to these accelerating transatlantic cross-currents, as an often iconoclastic and divisive figure of growing worldwide fame. The discussion has traced Dylan's lifelong and enduring uses of English music, even if the argument has been that the high-water mark of the creative influence of English traditional folk music upon him as a songwriter was reached by the end of 1963, before the return to rock and roll of an essentially, consciously American kind. Finally, in acknowledging also that Dylan's significance has always been as someone who resists purely musical categorization, the closing part of the chapter has all too briefly alluded to what can be called a characteristically Emersonian component in Dylan's subjectivity and sensibility, a feature of his American heritage that became decisively evident as that legacy reasserted itself in the mid-1960s.

Notes

1. Dylan was also to sing and rework two American folk songs, "Hang Me, O Hang Me" and "Cuckoo Bird," and to alter, in performance apparently, the lyrics furnished by Jones for another song, "Ballad of the Gliding Swan." Caspar Llewellyn Smith's highly readable and informative *Observer* article, "Flash-Back," from 18 September 2005, and available online, is my source for the Auden connection: guardian.co.uk/music/2005/sep/18/folk.popandrock.

2. As Marqusee has also noted, this latter collection was clearly rooted in the music, times, places, and performers of the late 1920s and 1930s: "these were 'race' and 'hillbilly' records, released on commercial labels, and recorded between 1927, when new technology boosted the quality of musical reproduction, and 1932, when the depression finished off the regional markets. The performers were anonymous members of a folk tribe: they included a host of distinctive stylists—Clarence Ashley, Buell Kazee, Blind Lemon Jefferson, Charlie Patton (disguised as the Masked Marvel), the Carter Family, Mississippi John Hurt, Dock Boggs, Blind Willie Johnson." Mike Marqusee, *Wicked Messenger: Bob Dylan and the 1960s* (New York: Seven Stories, 2005), 34.

3. Richard Williams, *Dylan: A Man Called Alias* (London: Bloomsbury, 1992), 46; Tim Cumming, "Talking Bob Dylan's Blues," *Independent Online*, 28 September 2005.

4. The link is to the Met Office web site: metoffice.gov.uk/corporate/pressoffice/anniversary/winter1962-63 html.

5. Smith's "Flash-Back" follows the alternative tradition, identical in other respects, that the axe was, in fact, a samurai sword.

6. In an interview with Dave Brazier for Dylan fanzine the *Telegraph* in the early nineties, Carthy spoke of how while Dylan sat

in all those folk clubs in '62, he was just *soaking stuff up all the time*. He heard Louis Killen, he heard Nigel Denver, he heard Bob Davenport, he heard me, he heard The Thameside Four, dozens of people. Anybody who came into The Troubadour, or came into The King & Queen, or the Singers' Club, and he listened and he *just gobbled stuff up*. Huge, huge, huge difference. His coming to England had an enormous impact on his music, and yet nobody's ever said it properly. He came and he learned. (Dave Brazier, "A Conversation with . . . Martin Carthy" [26 September 1991], *The Telegraph*, 42 [Summer 1992]: 96)

Selections from the interview, and interviews with other prominent figures, are available on: www.bobdylanroots.com/carthy.html.

7. A multi-talented and exuberant figure, Von Schmidt had been a friend since the two of them had attempted a game of croquet in Cambridge, Massachusetts, under the influence of red wine and cannabis. My source for this anecdote is Von Schmidt's fascinating 1996 interview with Elijah Wald: elijahwald.com/vonschmidt.html.

8. According to Eric Von Schmidt and Jim Rooney, Dylan had pestered Jackie Washington over and again to perform his minor-key version of this extraordinary, surreal old English folk song. See their book, *"Baby Let Me Follow You Down": The Illustrated History of the Cambridge Folk Years* (Amherst: University of Massachusetts, 1979), 219. "Nottamun Town" was also somewhat bizarrely branded as family property by Jean Ritchie, who was to become litigious with Dylan over his appropriation of her version of the song. Ritchie referred to it as "the Ritchie Family [Kentucky version]" ibiblio.org/jimmy/folkden-wp/?p=6932. An out-of-court settlement of $5,000 was even reached, according to Howard Sounes, *Down the Highway* (London: Doubleday, 2001), 132. Finally, David Hajdu has Carthy's friend Bob Davenport as the person from whom Dylan learned "Nottamun Town" and "The Miner's Lament" on this first London visit: David Hajdu, *Positively 4th Street* (London: Bloomsbury, 2001), 126. This is less than persuasive, not least as Washington's version had even made it onto his first LP, *Jackie Washington*, for Vanguard Records in December 1962.

9. Though there is the obvious inconsistency between this and Dylan's following remarks that he wrote the song, apparently over several days, during his stay in England in response to the daily papers' coverage of the missile crisis.

10. Clinton Heylin, *Behind the Shades* (London: Viking, 1991), 64.

11. Clinton Heylin, *Revolution in the Air: The Songs of Bob Dylan*, Vol. I: 1957–73 (London: Constable, 2009), 117.

12. Carthy, *The Telegraph* 42 (1992): 96.

13. An expanded version of Zuckerman's article, "'If There's An Original Thought Out There, I Could Use It Right Now': The Folk Roots of Bob Dylan" is available at expectingrain.com/dok/div/influences.

14. traditionalmusic.co.uk/child-ballads/ch078.htm.

15. traditionalmusic.co.uk/child-ballads/ch098.htm.

16. No text is given in the lists on bobdylan.com or in *Bob Dylan 1962-63: Lyrics* (New York: Simon & Shuster, 2004), so I follow the version cited on Eyof Oestrem's site: dylanchords.info/00_misc/liverpool_gal.htm.

17. As Clinton Heylin noted, the song was finished in Woodstock in May 1963, when Suze Rotolo would have been in close attendance. I agree with Heylin that the song might refer to one "with whom the singer spent the night" but whom he "had not quite resolved to forget," since it has an aura of actual recollection; but all is speculation (Heylin, *Revolution in the Air*, 143).

18. The full text for "Liverpool Gal" can be found at: dylanchords.info/00_misc/liverpool_gal.htm.

19. Bob Dylan, *Chronicles, Volume One* (New York: Simon & Shuster, 2004), 239–41.

20. This has long been recognized, though Clinton Heylin usefully cites the lyric with the original spelling (Heylin, *Revolution in the Air*, 87):

O westron wynde when wyll thow blow
The small rayne downe can rayne
Cryst yf my love wer in my armys
and I yn my bed agayne.

21. Clinton Heylin, *A Life in Stolen Moments: Bob Dylan Day by Day, 1941–1995* (London: Omnibus, 1996), 32.

22. This was presumably a version of "The Water is Wide" that he would revisit so unforgettably in 1975 with Joan Baez with the Rolling Thunder Revue. A version is available on the CBS anthology from the tour, *The Bootleg Series Vol.5: Bob Dylan Live 1975*.

23. Bob Dylan, *Lyrics: 1962–2001* (New York: Simon & Schuster, 2004), 97.

24. Mike Marqusee's book offers a highly nuanced and detailed account of the complex and intolerable position Dylan found himself in the 1960s, writing "both within the historical tide and against it," in so far as he sought to protect his autonomy and privacy amid the ever-shifting configurations and imbrications of the personal and political (Mike Marqusee, 120). Marqusee's account of Dylan's reactions to these shifting currents in many ways parallels the one given here, in so far as Dylan's desire to opt out becomes the increasingly personal reaction against those who attempted to co-opt him, whether for commercial, ideological, or radical purposes.

25. Mark Polizzotti, *Highway 61 Revisited* (London: Continuum, 2006), 12.

26. James Brewer, "Beyond the Roots of American Popular Music: Examining the Legacy of Alan Lomax," 13 June 2003, World Socialist Web Site: wsws.org/articles/2003/jun2003/lom-j13.shtml.

27. Greil Marcus, *Invisible Republic* (London: Picador, 1997), 12.

28. Michael Gray, *Bob Dylan Encyclopaedia* (London: Continuum, 2006), 313–14.

29. Perhaps there is an echo between this and Dylan's boyhood heroes, "Robin Hood and St. George the Dragon Slayer," as he confessed to Archibald McLeish (Dylan, *Chronicles*, 113).

30. Of course the dust of rumor circulates around this story too; in an earlier book, Richard Williams has the janitor as the one cutting the cable, and the event taking place in 1956, the Golden Chords apparently having already disbanded. See Richard Williams, *Dylan: A Man Called Alias* (London: Bloomsbury, 1992), 18.

31. Polizzotti, 22.

32. In an interview with Studs Terkel in May 1963, Dylan invented a boyhood encounter with Guthrie. Terkel asked him what stuck in his mind, and Dylan replied: "It stuck in my mind that he was Woody, and everybody else I could see around me was just everybody else." Terkel replied that in his view Dylan was also "unique" in that "It's hard to separate you from the songs you sing." Jonathan Cott, ed., *Dylan on Dylan* (London: Hodder & Stoughton, 2006), 6.

33. See woodyguthrie.org/merchandise/oklahomagazette.

34. The phrase is from the 1965 song "Tombstone Blues." Dylan, *Lyrics*, 170.

35. Michael Gray, *Song and Dance Man III: The Art of Bob Dylan* (London: Continuum, 2008), 26.

36. Pete Seeger claimed that he came across "Copper Kettle" in 1946, one of several songs of brought to him by a man calling himself Frank O. who had mimeographed them for inclusion in Seeger's quarterly, *People's Songs Bulletin*, as folk songs (though he also claimed to have partly rewritten some of them). See Pete Seeger, *The Incompleat Folksinger* (New York: Simon & Schuster, 1972), 278–79. Subsequently, E. F. Beddoe would claim, in a letter to *Time* on 30 November 1962, that he wrote the song for his 1953 musical *Go Lightly, Stranger*.

37. If I had to find a formula for describing this, it would be that Dylan's strength in performing folk songs is to extinguish any sense of his own identity. Contrarily, his own writing, while it might artfully incorporate the impersonal elements of folk music, blues, or country, is a vehicle for the extension of individuality, for experiencing individuality as temporal, as discontinuous, in ways that are particularly American.

38. Writes Marcus:

> Dylan's performance now seemed to mean that he had never truly been where he had appeared to be only a year before, reaching for that democratic oasis of the heart—and that if he had never been there, those who had felt themselves there with him had not been there. If his heart was not pure, one had to doubt one's own. It was as if it had all been a trick—a trick he had played on them and that they had played on themselves. That was the source of the betrayal felt when Bob Dylan turned to his band, and he along with Danko and Robertson turned to face the drummer, who raised his drumstick, the three guitarists now leaping into the air and twisting to face the crowd as the drummer brought the stick down for the first

beat. That was the source of the rage. (Greil Marcus, *Invisible Republic* [London: Picador, 1997], 31)

39. Bootleg videos of this and other press conferences have recently surfaced on YouTube, but Chrome Dreams has packaged the San Francisco conference, along with the Los Angeles 1965 conference and a 1966 Montreal interview, on a CD, *Bob Dylan: The Classic Interviews*.

40. In a long outtake from *Eat the Document* that goes some way to explaining John Lennon's ambivalence, and sporadic hostility, toward Bob Dylan, one sees the two of them sharing a long taxi ride on the night of the Royal Albert Hall concert. Stoked by drugs or alcohol, the concealed hostility and defensive aggression of both curdles at the point when Dylan, fighting nausea, reduces Lennon to stony stupefaction by reminding him of his ignorance of America, and Texas. It is worth pondering briefly, though, that Dylan scarcely seemed an artist animated by an animosity to things British, given his obvious affection for British music, and his lifelong love of London.

41. Alfred Kazin, *On Native Grounds* (New York: Harcourt Brace Jovanovich, 1982), xv.

42. In San Francisco he laconically drawls, when asked what response he would make to the draft, "I would just do what had to be done [. . .]" I have always taken the following verse from "Tombstone Blues" as his single coded reference to the war while it was taking place:

The king of the Philistines his soldiers to save
Puts jawbones on their tombstones and flatters their graves
Puts the pied pipers in prison and fattens the slaves
Then sends them out to the jungle

43. By a further nice ironic twist, also, while the Dylan of *Highway 61 Revisited* remained the prince across the water for his late 1960s audience, his finest, most intensely engaged, inspired performances of 1968 and 1969 were surely of songs associated with Guthrie, such as those performed with the Band at the Woody Guthrie Memorial Concerts at Carnegie Hall in January 1968, and the singing of 'East Virginia Blues" with Earl Scruggs and Family for American TV in 1969.

44. In contrast, the bizarrely overrated glitz of Earls Court and Blackbushe in 1978 were an exceptional case of Dylan's desire to please his audience being met by their desire to be pleased, by their desire (truth notwithstanding) to be present at a great Dylan show.

45. Ralph Waldo Emerson, *The Portable Emerson*, ed. Carl Bode, in collaboration with Malcolm Cowley (London: Penguin, 1981), 259.

46. Mark Ford, "Dylan and Emerson," in *Do You, Mr Jones: Dylan with the Poets and the Professors* (London: Chatto & Windus, 2002), 127–42.

47. Stanley Cavell, "Aversive Thinking: Emersonian Representations," in David Justin Hodge, ed., *Emerson's Transcendental Etudes* (Stanford: Stanford University Press, 2003), 141–70. He suggests as well, ironically enough, that Emerson's thought underpins the Nietzschean vision that predominates in what is seen as the alternative tradition of contemporary Continental thought.

7

Alan Lomax

An American Ballad Hunter in Great Britain[1]

—Ronald D. Cohen

In Great Britain during the 1950s, various styles of folk music merged to form a swelling popular movement, known as the second revival. Collectors such as Peter Kennedy (England), Seamus Ennis (Ireland), and Hamish Henderson (Scotland) joined with the political/musical activists Ewan MacColl and A. L. "Bert" Lloyd, along with many others, to stimulate the study of traditional tunes. The English Folk Dance and Song Society (EFDSS), founded before World War I by the collector Cecil Sharp, became a vital part of the revival, along with the Communist Party–affiliated Workers' Music Association (WMA), established in 1936, and its folk magazine *Sing*, beginning in 1954. The WMA began issuing records under the Topic Records label in 1939. Folk clubs appeared by the early 1950s. Out of this mix of traditional and left-wing folk movements emerged by mid-decade a popular style known as skiffle, which was heavily influenced by folk, blues, and jazz coming from the United States. This transatlantic connection also included numerous American performers and collectors who found a temporary but welcoming home in England, in particular Alan Lomax.[2]

Lomax (1915–2002) was one of the most significant figures in the study and appreciation of folk music in the twentieth century. He was a traditional music collector, writer, ethnomusicologist, radio personality, political activist, performer, and musical impresario. He began his field research in the United States in the mid-1930s, which lasted over many years, but he also traveled to the Bahamas, Haiti, and Mexico, then to Great Britain, Italy, and Spain in search of folk music and musicians. He was a prominent radio broadcaster and producer, first in the United States and then in Great Britain. While Lomax was not the only American promoting folk music in the British Isles during the 1950s, he was among the most creative, active, and influential.[3]

Lomax was born in Texas, attended Harvard College and the University of Texas, and began working with his father, John, during a collecting trip through the South in 1933. Three years later he joined the Archive of American Folk Song at the Library of Congress, where he would remain until late 1942. His numerous book collaborations with his father, particularly *American Ballads and Folk Songs* (1934), *Negro Folk Songs as Sung by Lead Belly* (1936), *Our Singing Country* (1941), and *Folk Song USA* (1947), vividly demonstrated his extensive knowledge of folk songs and their histories. His radio career began in 1939 with a series of children's shows, *American Folk Songs*, as part of the CBS *American School of the Air*, which was quickly followed by *Wellsprings of Music*. Simultaneously, he produced and starred in CBS's 1940–41 evening show *Back Where I Come From*, which featured such musicians as Woody Guthrie, Pete Seeger, Burl Ives, and the Golden Gate Quartet. These programs were strictly for domestic consumption, but with the outbreak of war for the United States in late 1941, Lomax's attention partly shifted across the Atlantic, as the United Kingdom became the country's vital ally. American folk songs had already reached the British Isles as early as 1938 through the BBC broadcasts of Alistair Cooke; with Lomax's assistance, Cooke had borrowed a number of recordings from the Library of Congress.[4]

Beginning in late 1942 Lomax, working for the federal government's Bureau of Special Operations of the Office of War Information (OWI), launched *Transatlantic Call: People to People*, a collaboration between the British Broadcasting Company (BBC) and CBS. The first program, "Savannah: A City of the South," broadcast on April 11, 1943, illustrated the series' style, connecting the wartime experiences of average people in the United States and Britain. It was soon followed by "San Antonio: Heart of Texas," "Duluth, Minnesota," and "July 4, 1943: The Story of War Time Philadelphia." Lomax traveled through the States eliciting stories from a variety of people, a technique he had perfected over the past decade. The series lasted into 1945, although Lomax's role diminished once he joined the Army in April 1944, where he remained until early 1946.

Lomax also managed to produce three ballad operas in 1944, beginning with *The Man Who Went to War*. Using text by the African American poet Langston Hughes and music selected by Lomax, the all-black cast included Paul Robeson, Josh White, Ethel Waters, Sonny Terry, and Brownie McGhee. While this program was meant for domestic consumption, the next two, *The Martins and the Coys* and *The Chisholm Trail*, were only broadcast over the BBC home service. For those in war-torn England lucky enough to listen, they were introduced to Woody Guthrie, the Coon Creek Girls, Sonny Terry and Brownie McGhee, Burl Ives, Cisco Houston, Wade Mainer, Pete Seeger, and Hally Wood. *The Martins and the Coys* was broadcast in June 1944, while *The Chisholm Trail* followed in February 1945; the former was also released as a five-disc 78-rpm record album.[5]

While in the Army, Lomax produced various programs for the Armed Forces Radio Service in 1945, including *Bound for Glory, Let's Go to Town*, and *Singing Country*. Although intended for military audiences throughout the world, these programs, heavily musical, may have reached a wider market. Following the war he had a domestic show, *Your Ballad Man*, on the Mutual Broadcasting System in 1948. Unlike his previous musical programs, which had exclusively featured live performances, these included commercial recordings of folk, jazz, pop, blues, country/western, and even international musicians. But the shows did not cross the Atlantic.

Lomax moved to Great Britain in late 1950, fleeing an accelerating domestic anticommunist witch hunt, while planning on recording the world's folk music for Columbia Records during his stay abroad. Although never a member of the Communist Party, he had long identified with such left-wing causes as civil rights, labor unions, socialism, and world peace. In 1948, he had headed the music desk of the Henry Wallace/Progressive Party presidential campaign, and was active in People's Songs, the radical musical movement launched by Pete Seeger in early 1946. In 1950 Lomax was listed as a suspected subversive in the right-wing publication *Red Channels: The Report of Communist Influence in Radio and Television*, which certainly encouraged his decision to take off across the Atlantic.

In England he initiated an energetic broadcasting career that lasted through most of the decade. Accompanied by the singer and actress Robin Roberts, Lomax first arrived in Paris. "Perhaps you have heard this or that about my departure [from the United States]," he quickly wrote to friends. "Fact is, I just couldn't stand the possibility of being cut off from Robin by the worsening political atmosphere." His reasons were certainly more complex, however, while his future remained unclear: "I'm buying a car . . . and I'm going to see as much of the world as I can. London before Xmas, Scotland for New Year, Ireland for 2 weeks—then South for a long time—Africa,

Egypt—. Then home to starve." Before Christmas they did move to London, where Lomax immediately connected with Douglas Kennedy at Cecil Sharp House, the home for that bastion of traditional songs EFDSS, as well as Geoffrey Bridson and others at Broadcasting House, the BBC headquarters. "Robin & I just saw Bartholomew Fair at the Old Vic," he soon wrote. "We are going on BBC together & then go to Ireland to record folk songs & fairy tales." Although he had come to collect vernacular music throughout Great Britain (and on the continent), his connections with the BBC quickly landed him a program, *Adventure in Folksong*.[6]

According to the historian David Gregory, "the three-part series combined a coast-to-coast survey of the wealth and variety of American folk song with an account of Alan's experiences collecting for the Library of Congress in the 1930s. Although Lomax slipped in an occasional recording, such as Leadbelly's 'Goodnight Irene,' the majority of songs were performed by himself (usually with guitar accompaniment) or by the American performer Robin Roberts." Actually there were four airings. The untitled first half-hour of Adventure in Folksong" aired February 13, 1951, 9:30–10:00 PM. Next was the three-part *Patterns in American Folksong*, recorded in late May, subtitled "Violence," "Work," and "Love." They mixed traditional English, Scottish, and Irish ballads with American (mostly African American) folk songs. For example, in "Violence" Roberts performed "Who Killed Cock Robin," "Molly Bawn," and "Matty Groves," while Lomax did "Sam Bass," "Pretty Polly," and "Po Lazarus." For "Work" Roberts did "Cape Cod Girls," "West Virginia Boys," and "Moonshiners" and Lomax included "Git Along Little Dogies," "Brave Wolf," "The Buffalo Skinners," and "Take This Hammer." Lomax, always the educator, was particularly interested in introducing a British audience to mostly unfamiliar American folk songs.[7]

As an example of Lomax's style and thinking, he introduced "Love" this way, after quoting two lines from "On Top of Old Smokey":

> But I hardly need to continue. By now most of you must have heard this American folk song, recently twisted into a popular song hit, a few too many times. But still there may be some of you who wonder if there is any such thing as American folk music. Robin Roberts and I will sing a couple of dozen and you may draw your own conclusions, but I'll give you my opinion. Yes, there is an American folk song in precisely the same sense as there is an English or a French folk song— only Americans have more varieties than most countries.

He was particularly concerned about not only spreading his love for American ballads and folk songs to his new audience, but also making an intellectual argument that they were as legitimate for scholarly study as British ballads, which he also cherished. He began the "Violence" episode by introducing "Who Killed Cock Robin": "This California version of the old English rhyme suitably introduces the subject of this second recital of American ballads . . . the bad man ballads. I suppose if there is any taste that links the British Isles with the United States it is our fondness for tales, novels, films, radio programs and folk ballads dealing with mayhem and bloody murder." Cultural styles in the United States drew upon the British background, but also much more.[8]

American folk songs were not unknown in England, but the audience had been quite restricted. In addition to Alistair Cooke's prewar broadcasts, during the war American soldiers stationed in the country shared their blues, jazz, and country records. "When, after the Second World War, American recordings became more readily available in Britain, the influence of the transatlantic folk singers spread rapidly," A. L. Lloyd explained in his influential *Folk Song in England*. While Lloyd's chronology is vague, his point is well taken; by the early 1950s American blues and jazz recordings had stimulated a trad jazz movement which included the band leader Chris Barber and the musicians Alexis Korner, Lonnie Donegan, and others. They were particularly influenced by the American blues musicians Leadbelly, Big Bill Broonzy, Scrapper Blackwell, Blind Boy Fuller, and jazz greats King Oliver and Louis Armstrong.[9]

The *London Times* correspondent was intrigued by Lomax's radio programs but somewhat less than enthusiastic:

> Most of our popular music is based ultimately on American folk songs, many of them Negro songs, and when we hear the originals we often find we like them better than the commercialised versions Tin Pan Alley turns out. The chief source of genuine American songs is the Lomax collection in Washington, and veteran listeners like me remember with pleasure the series of broadcasts of them that Alistair Cooke gave before the war. Now we have Alan Lomax here in person, giving us gems from his discoveries on Tuesdays in the Home Service. I found his first broadcast disappointing. His dialogue with his girl singer, Robin Roberts, was as wooden as the worst in "In Town Tonight," and used as we are to American accents on our air, his Texan seemed to me very hard to understand.

Yet, despite Lomax's seeming failings as a singer, "this week's installment conquered me. The mixed white-and-Negro songs of the chain gangs, steel gangs, and dynamite gangs did something to the singers, and Robin Roberts sang the blues like one inspired."[10]

Lomax's next BBC series, *The Art of the Negro*, which aired during October and November 1951, was strictly concerned with American music, with programs entitled "Mr. Jelly Roll [Morton] from New Orleans," "Trumpets of the Lord," and "Blues in the Mississippi Night." He drew on his earlier original recordings of Jelly Roll Morton, Vera Hall, Big Bill Broonzy, and other African American performers (although a recording of Woody Guthrie singing "Talking Columbia Blues" appeared during "Blues in the Mississippi Night"). While Morton was one of the most influential commercial jazz musicians, Hall and Broonzy were traditional performers, although the latter had also a vibrant career as an urban, commercial bluesman. "At once an enthusiastic championing of the music of ordinary black Americans and a damning indictment of Southern racism," Gregory explains, "The Art of the Negro was an extraordinarily powerful documentary feature that won Lomax many admirers and, no doubt, not a few enemies too." This was among the last of Lomax's radio programs for the next four years that dealt with the Western Hemisphere, since he would subsequently focus on *World Folk Songs*, *Spanish Folk Music*, and *Folk Music of Italy*. In late 1956, however, as part of his series *Reminiscences of a Folk Song Collector*, one show dealt with "America." Late the next year he introduced a new program, *A Ballad Hunter Looks at Britain*, with music only from the British Isles.[11]

Since his listing in *Red Channels* and his political activities would have precluded his getting another radio program in the United States, Lomax appreciated the BBC's welcoming tolerance, at least initially. As he later wrote:

> In the days before the hostility of the tabloid press and the Conservative Party had combined to denature the BBC's *Third Programme*, it was probably the freest and most influential cultural forum in the Western world. If you had something interesting to say, if the music you had composed or discovered was fresh and original, you got a hearing on the "Third." . . . My broadcast audience in Britain was around a million, not large by American buckshot standards, but one really worth talking to.[12]

By the early 1950s Lomax was not alone in introducing a British audience to American folk music and musicians. In addition to his companion Robin Roberts, he welcomed Big Bill Broonzy to London in late 1951 (Broonzy would return twice in 1952 and again in 1955, before making his final visit in 1957). Lomax's friends Burl Ives, the popular performer and actor, and Jean Ritchie, a traditional musician from the South, arrived and soon had their own BBC shows. In late 1952 Ives's *Historical America in Song* was aired, and in 1953 *Jean Ritchie in Kentucky* was heard on the BBC Third Programme. Other American folk performers would come and go, such as Sandy and Caroline Paton, popular singers from Chicago, who arrived in 1957. In a piece in the New York folk fanzine *Caravan*, Paton, while critical of skiffle, appreciated the more traditional stylings: "Here in London, a few weeks ago, Caroline and I attended a 'Ballads and Blues' concert on British Industrial Songs. Ewan MacColl, A. L. Lloyd, Seamus Ennis and Dominic Behan made up the program." He concluded, "this was a damned exciting evening of real folkmusic and there were less than 75 people in the audience." By "real" Paton meant from traditional sources, rather than the hybrid skiffle. He was soon performing in local clubs and coffeehouses.[13]

Born Jimmy Miller in Lancashire, Ewan MacColl (1915–1989) had an active career as an actor and playwright before turning to folk music in the late 1940s. His left-wing political commitments began early, when he joined the Young Communist League as a teenager, and would continue throughout his life with a firm commitment to the Communist Party. He began to popularize older folk songs, particularly sea shanties and industrial songs, as well as the ballads collected by Francis James Child. In 1953, he initiated *Ballads and Blues* as a BBC radio series, which

> consisted of six half-hour programmes, each dealing with a different theme such as war and peace, love, the sea, railways, work, the city. Each of the programmes featured seven or eight British and American songs about these subjects, recorded by American singers Big Bill Broonzy, Jean Ritchie, Ma Rainey and Alan Lomax. Bert Lloyd, Isla Cameron and Ewan MacColl sang the British songs.... The main objective of the series was to demonstrate that Britain possessed a body of songs that were found in the United States.

Mixing both live and recorded performances, the programs resembled in style and substance Lomax's earlier radio shows in the United States. "At that time, the only singers we could really draw upon, that could handle scripted material, were Bert [Lloyd] and myself and Isla Cameron, and that was about it on the English side," MacColl would recall to Fred Woods. "On the American side we brought in Jean Ritchie, Big Bill Broonzy, [Alan] Lomax himself and one or two other American traditional singers who were known and who happened to be in England or Europe at the time." A loose coalition of performers, including MacColl, Lloyd, and Cameron, soon emerged also under the name "Ballads and Blues," which raised funds for the *Daily Worker* into 1954. Around this same time the Scottish traveling singer Jeannie Robertson appeared along with MacColl and Ken Colyer's Jazzmen at the Royal Festival Hall, with the latter performing the chain-gang song "Another Man Done Gone."[14]

Lomax met MacColl in early February 1951 at the BBC, igniting a lasting friendship, since they had a musical and political affinity. "He is big, but not gigantic," MacColl later enthused. "The illusion of size is the result of his expansiveness and of the warmth he generates.... Everything in his world is big. Words like 'English,' 'French,' 'Italian,' 'American,' don't come readily to his tongue. He sees human beings in anthropological categories, as groups and sub-groups, as representatives of this or that culture or subculture, this or that linguistic area. His one conversational lack is small talk." MacColl had much to learn from Lomax: "In the course of the next year or so I spent more and more time listening to Alan's enormous collection of tapes, to songs from the Americas, Africa, India, Italy, Spain and Britain, arguing, discussing, learning and trying to acquire Alan's worldview of this extraordinary corpus of songs and stories." "Alan has amazing energy," he continued. "Everything is done at breakneck speed. No sooner is a task completed than he is hurrying to begin the next one."[15]

In December 1953 Lomax shared the stage with MacColl, Lloyd, and others as part of the Ballads and Blues "Songs of the Iron Road" program at St. Pancras Town Hall. The initial "Ballads and Blues" concerts, mostly at the drafty Theatre Royal, Stratford East, were followed in late 1957 by a new series with Lomax, jazzmen Jim Bray and Bruce Turner, the American performers Guy Carawan and Ralph Rinzler, the traditional musician Margaret Barry, and Seamus Ennis. Drawing less than a full house, MacColl soon moved to the more friendly Princess Louise pub on High Holborn in London, where he, Lloyd, and Ennis, along with Lomax, initiated the Ballads and Blues Club (later renamed the Singers' Club). The American musical influence was certainly pronounced, partly due to Lomax's presence. "That development was also reflected in the early English folk club scene, which was dominated by an American repertoire and by skiffle," Britta Sweers contends. "This was true, for example, of Ewan MacColl and the Ballads and Blues Club, where more American than British music could be heard." MacColl would later restrict musicians to perform only songs from their national background, but initially he welcomed the mix of song styles and types. Moreover, he had been highly influenced by the topical songs included in *The People's Song Book*, issued by People's Songs in New York in 1948 (for which Lomax had written the foreword), a book influenced by the Workers' Music Association and quickly imported by Collet's bookshop in London.[16]

MacColl believed the Ballads and Blues Club initiated the stimulating, expanding club movement in late decade: "Every Sunday evening, the large upstairs room of the pub would fill with young people, many of whom carried guitars.... Resident performers in the club included Bert [Lloyd], Seamus Ennis, Fitzroy [Coleman], Peggy [Seeger] (after 1956) and myself." Although MacColl did not mention Lomax, surely the variety of songs would have appealed to him:

> While the greater part of our programmes consisted of the kind of songs which even the most strict traditionalists would class as folk material, that is, country songs, versions of the English and Scots popular ballads, sea shanties and forebitters (another form of shanty), we were also attempting to extend the national repertory by introducing children's street songs, industrial songs and ballads, epigrammatic squibs, popular parodies, broadside ballads and new songs written in the folk idiom.

Tradition mixed with contemporary songs and left-wing politics was the order of the day, for MacColl and Lomax alike, at least initially.[17]

In late 1953 and early 1954 Lomax also had an eight-part BBC television series, *Song Hunter*, and one show featured Theodore Bikel. Born in Austria, Bikel had moved to Palestine at the outbreak of World War II; a budding actor, he moved to London in 1946 to study at the Royal Academy of Dramatic Art. Within a few years he also began to sing and play the guitar, learning American folk songs while becoming involved in the expatriate community. Bikel remembered "the time Lomax brought Margaret Barry to my apartment. She was an Irish Gypsy with swarthy, leathery skin and a mouth that seemed lopsided because quite a few of her teeth were missing."[18]

This was typical Lomax, making introductions and stimulating musical exchanges. As he wrote to his sister Shirley in early 1954, "here I've become sort of the American singer in England. Without wanting to, you know. But this afternoon I was able to turn down an offer for a concert in a London suburb, because I know that in a few months I won't have to accept less than the biggest hall in London. All very silly because I don't sing particularly well, or even like to very much." And he continued, "I've always hated radio performing and concerts, and I suddenly found myself liking TV. It took me a long time to figure out why. It was because after they'd had the lights on me for half an hour, I got warm for the only time I have ever been warm in England. . . . Most of the time I had no prepared script but just worked out what I had to say on the air." The TV series proved to be a success.[19]

Lomax's work with the BBC impressed and influenced MacColl, who later wrote:

> Both Bert [Lloyd] and I, quite independently, were writing scripts dealing with various aspects of folk-song for the BBC Home Service and the Third Programme. Alan, much more perceptive than either of us about the future of television, presented three one-hour programmes on the BBC, in which singers and instrumentalists from all over the British Isles demonstrated the magnificent riches of our traditional music and song. The programmes were produced by David Attenborough and, though they delighted the hearts of the small band of folk enthusiasts who witnessed them, they were not popular with the general public.

Mutually influencing, Lomax, MacColl, Lloyd, and their friends, by the mid-1950s, were walking a fine line between traditional and commercial, American and British music, but always with some sort of left-wing tilt. While the British Communist Party was wary of foreign cultural influences, particularly from the United States—the party even supported a ban on comic books from across the Atlantic—it seemingly had no problem with Lomax's promotion of American folk songs, since they were perceived as having working-class and African American origins. At least this was MacColl and Lloyd's approach.[20]

Lomax had spent seven months recording in Spain in 1952–53, and after playing excerpts from this field trip, the BBC sent him off to Italy for more recordings during 1954–55; when he returned he soon met Shirley Collins.

Born in 1935, two decades after Lomax, she early began her study of traditional songs at the English Folk Dance and Song Society's Cecil Sharp House, then traveled to perform in Moscow. "On my return to London from Moscow, I accepted an invitation from Ewan MacColl to a party he was throwing for Alan Lomax, who was coming back to England after two years collecting folk sings in Spain and Italy," Collins has written. She felt that Lomax was "an affable, tall, solid Texan with a big head of shaggy dark hair, and he put me in mind of an American bison. I blurted out that one of my ambitions was to go to the Library of Congress to hear his field recordings, and he said he was amazed that I even knew about it. He had great warmth and an irresistible chuckle." They connected professionally and emotionally, and Collins quickly found herself working with Lomax on his Columbia World Folk Music recordings series as well as his massive book compilation, *The Folksongs of North America* (1960). Living with him, she found "the house often full of visiting American bluesmen—Sonny Terry and Brownie McGhee, Memphis Slim and Muddy Waters, for whom Alan cooked a special Southern dinner of fried chicken and smothered greens to make him feel at home." Collins joined Lomax when he returned to the United States in 1958, where they embarked on a collecting trip into the South; she would soon return to England and a stellar musical career performing electric folk.[21]

By mid-decade skiffle music, which Lomax had helped stimulate through his promotion of Leadbelly, Woody Guthrie, Josh White, and Burl Ives, was in full bloom. "For at least two years, 1956–57, skiffle equaled rock 'n' roll as the music of English youth," David Gregory has explained. Lomax was quick to hop on the bandwagon. His group, the Ramblers, included Shirley Collins, MacColl, Bruce Turner, and Peggy Seeger. Anxious to add the banjo-playing Peggy to the group, Lomax had contacted her father, Charles Seeger, to track her down in Europe and invite her to move to England. MacColl quickly met her in Lomax's basement flat in Chelsea. Supplemented by various other musicians, they made fourteen one-hour programs, *The Ramblers*, for Granada TV in the summer of 1956. The next year their songbook *The Skiffle Album* was published, including mostly British songs. The Ramblers were briefly joined by Ralph Rinzler, a mandolin-playing folk music promoter from New York, who would soon play a major role in the folk revival in the United States.[22]

Lomax played a vital role in the short-lived skiffle movement. His earlier recordings of Lead Belly, Josh White, and Burl Ives proved highly influential. In early 1957, during the first of what would later become a series of tours with African American artists including Sister Rosetta Tharpe and Sonny Terry and Brownie McGhee, Chris Barber appeared in numerous venues in England and Scotland with Big Bill Broonzy and the gospel/blues performer Brother John Sellers. Just before leaving the country in March, Broonzy appeared on the *Six-Five Special* TV program, joined by the Vipers skiffle group and the pop singer Tommy Steele. The following year, Lomax served as one of the MCs at a benefit concert for Broonzy, then gravely ill in Chicago. The event drew some of Britain's biggest skiffle and jazz stars to the London Coliseum, including Charles McDevitt, Johnny Duncan, and Humphrey Lyttelton.[23]

Despite his involvement, Lomax was somewhat disappointed in the skiffle movement, but he still had hope: "The first songs to become popular among the young skifflers were the American Negro prison songs. There they showed fine taste, because these are the best and most powerful of our folk songs," he wrote in 1957. Since he preferred traditional tunes, however, he continued:

> At first it seemed very strange to me to hear these songs, which I had recorded from convicts in the prisons of the South, coming out of the mouths of young men who had suffered, comparatively speaking, so little. But I soon realized that these young people *felt* themselves to be in a prison—composed of class-and-caste lines, the shrinking British Empire, the dull job, the lack of money—things like these. They were shouting at these prison walls, like so many Joshuas at the walls of Jericho.

As they learn more about their musical heritage, "the skifflers have already considerably Anglicized our American versions of British songs. And I suspect that this process will go on, and that soon more regional British songs will be skiffled. . . . Then, the people of this island may—with the stimulus of skiffle music—go on to create their own national amalgam of regional folk-song styles."[24]

Lomax had always mixed his love of traditional songs with his interest in commercial products and developments. While considered the most influential promoter of traditional American musicians, black and white, he nonetheless recorded and encouraged vernacular musicians in whatever country he visited. John Hasted, the skiffle performer and left-wing music journalist, while barely mentioning Lomax in his autobiography, duly followed up: "Very soon the American songs were supplemented by British folksongs sung in the skiffle style."[25]

Ramblin' Jack Elliott and his wife, June, arrived in England in September 1955. Born Elliot Adnopoz in Brooklyn in 1931, Ramblin' Jack had become fast friends with Woody Guthrie but had developed his own distinctive performance personality, a combination of Guthrie and a cowboy singer. "We quickly fell in with the burgeoning group of British folk performers just then on the verge of making it big with 'skiffle,'" June recalled. "Jack became well known almost immediately in this world, being offered all the work he could handle in pubs and folk music clubs." They quickly made the rounds: "We met some very interesting people, such as Bert Lloyd, a famous folklorist and singer who collected all the songs of the old whalers, and Ewan MacColl, the Scottish [sic] folklorist, writer and playwright. Jack also renewed his friendship with Alan Lomax." The Elliotts were limited to a three-month stay on their tourist visas and Jack was not allowed to work, "but luckily, our singing in the pubs and clubs, went undetected," June remarks. Lomax also helped Jack record his first Topic record album, *Woody Guthrie's Blues*, in October. Elliott was soon joined by another American, the banjo player Derroll Adams, and they became a popular hit.[26]

In December 1955 Joan Littlewood's Theatre Workshop produced *The Big Rock Candy Mountain*, written by Lomax and Yola Miller, featuring both Jack and June Elliott. "'It will be their version of a Christmas Pantomime,'" June recalls Lomax as saying, "'which is a very popular institution in England. Jack, we want you to star in it as the narrator and chorus.'" Littlewood, an activist theatre director, and earlier married to MacColl, had met Lomax in early 1951. She had this initial reaction: "He was a big, slommocky man, dark-haired, with a small, straight nose. He sang us a song about molasses, then explained the background and thrummed into a ballad which sounded Scottish." A few years later, "We were putting on *The Big Rock Candy Mountain*, by Alan Lomax, for Christmas and he came along to join in the fun, the nicest Alan this time, with a sackful of catchy tunes and 'Rambling Jack Elliott, the Singing Cowboy' in tow." The musical ran for two weeks and generated positive reviews. Lomax's directions for the opening act set the fanciful scene:

AS THE LIGHTS GO DOWN, THE BALLAD SINGER [Elliott] EDGES ON STAGE. AS HE BEGINS TO TALK, VARIOUS

RAUCOUS ANIMAL NOISES COME FROM SEVERAL PARTS OF THE PIT. FINALLY HE GROWS EXASPERATED AND JUMPS DOWN FROM THE STAGE, CHASES THE ANIMALS THROUGH THE AUDIENCE, LASSOS THE LION AND DRIVES AND DRAGS THEM ONTO THE STAGE. TWO OR THREE OF THESE ANIMALS SHOULD BE THE MUSICIANS AND THEY SHOULD FORM AN ORCHESTRA.

And so it went, folk songs interspersed with dialogue and physical action, all pulled together by the inventive Lomax.[27]

For the historian Georgina Boyes, *The Big Rock Candy Mountain* was

> the most comprehensively "folk" and almost completely American musical by Alan Lomax. It was recognised that there was "a wonderful world of music and song, of gaiety and humour, of sharp satire and sheerest fantasy" in Lomax's play and in American music in general. The contribution to the development of the English Revival of American performers like Pete Seeger, Peggy Seeger or Lomax, the creator of the role of media celebrity collector, was welcomed.

Indeed, Boyes argues, "Specifically 'folk' material became increasingly available particularly through performances on radio and television. But common interest in 'authentic' American music meant that audiences for folk and jazz were often identical, or brought together by appreciation of the 'country blues' repertoire of Huddie Leadbetter [sic] and Big Bill Broonzy and the work of itinerant songmakers such Woody Guthrie." Lomax was surely responsible for much of this, the overlapping musical styles and all.[28]

Lomax was regularly praised for his role in promoting folk music, old and new. For example, in a 1957 article on the nineteenth-century ballad collector Francis J. Child in the left-wing magazine *Sing*, Fred Dallas remarked:

> In all the excitement and the bawling of the skiffle movement, we are apt to forget the diligent folk who have made the whole thing possible. ... Three names probably predominate, in chronological order: Child, [Cecil] Sharp, Lomax. The last is probably the most famous, John and his son Alan, who have probably been responsible for more of the

sort of material the skifflers sing than the best-selling Mr. [Lonnie] Donegan could ever know.

A subsequent issue of *Sing* readily noted: "The world of folk song and skiffle owes an immeasurable debt to people like Leadbelly, Woody Guthrie, and Pete Seeger," and it was well known that Lomax had boosted the careers of all three. Moreover, an overview of Guthrie's life in *Jazz Music*, published in London, while passing over Lomax's crucial role in the singer-songwriter's career, does note that Woody was "also recorded for the Library of Congress in Washington where Alan Lomax had started the Folksong Archives." While Lomax did record hours of Guthrie talking and singing, he did not initiate the archives, but was its head from 1937–42.[29]

Lomax's stay in England seemed to serve him well, as he wrote to his brother Johnny in late 1955: "This period of being abroad and completely on my own efforts and my own name has been awfully good for me. I've at last almost emerged completely from father's shadow, which I now realize always hung over me in America." MacColl, himself a powerful and prominent force in the surge of interest in British folk music, later credited Lomax as an important catalyst: "Right from the early days of the revival, Alan Lomax, then Bert (Lloyd) and I and then Peggy [Seeger] had been stressing the fact that our traditional music was not only valuable in itself, but could also serve as a model for contemporary popular music."[30]

While living in London, Lomax kept busy with numerous projects, for example writing the illustrated story and songbook *Harriet and Her Harmonium* (Faber and Faber) in 1955. "Harriet Foster was born and raised about a hundred years ago in Mugridge, Middlewhistle, a place you can't find on the map. In fact M. was long ago swallowed up in a smokey London suburb," he begins. Twelve-year-old Harriet sets off across the Atlantic to join her father, "Fiddling" Foster, in San Francisco, and after landing in Boston travels across the country. Lomax tells of her adventures, quoting from her journal, interspersed with thirteen folk songs, including "Tinmaker-Man," "Springfield Mountain," "Runaway Train," and "Jesse James." *Sing* magazine quickly published a glowing review, concluding: "Tell your Dad it's got lots of social history and commendable ideas about freedom and tolerance too."[31]

Lomax had hoped that by leaving the United States he could escape the mounting anticommunist hysteria, but instead it followed him overseas. In late December 1951 a representative of the BBC contacted the Home

Office regarding their inquiry: "In reply to your letter of 13th December, I attach such particulars as we have for Alan Lomax. It appears from the papers that he was brought to this country on Ministry of Labour Permit to take part in several programmes based on his specialised knowledge of international folk music and songs." Lomax was shadowed by the Special Branch, the government's domestic monitoring agency, through 1956, with the American Embassy kept informed of his whereabouts. For example, a 1953 report noted:

> An American citizen named Alan LOMAX is reported to be a convinced Communist, who stands well with the Communist Party. He is a man whose profession is to collect, record and re-play or broadcast folk songs. He is in partnership in this business with a Scotsman named Ian McCAUL [Ewan MacColl] who lives in Manchester and seems to have some influence with the Midlands Regional Broadcasting Authority. Both these men are over 40 and they are supposed to advertise themselves as "folklorists."

In early 1955 the Home Office concluded: "Although LOMAX has been reported on a number of occasions to be a Communist, we have no evidence in our records to prove this information. He is known to associate with other Communists, and by the choice of his material he would appear to be sympathetic towards the extreme left wing."[32]

As the political climate cooled in the United States, and his work in Europe seemed to wind down, Lomax re-crossed the Atlantic in June 1958. During his eight-year stay he had definitely made his mark on British popular music and culture, which would never be the same. His influential role in introducing American folk music and musicians has been somewhat overlooked, but certainly not forgotten, by historians. Lomax consistently adhered to the potent mixture of left-wing politics and his love of folk music, both traditional and contemporary, which found a welcoming audience. He benefited greatly from his friendships with Ewan MacColl and A. L. Lloyd, who shared his musical and left-wing enthusiasms, and who introduced him to the wider world of British folk song and radical politics. They easily connected traditional songs, from the United States and Great Britain, with their contemporary political and cultural transatlantic ties, using the BBC, Topic Records, *Sing* magazine, and other outlets in the process. The British folk music scene would have been quite different without the presence of Alan Lomax and his many American friends, who helped to introduce American roots music, particularly from African American sources, and which would soon serve as a major influence on the native rock and blues explosion of the 1960s.

Notes

1. I want to thank Ben Harker, Bob Riesman, and E. David Gregory for their editorial assistance.

2. For background information, Britta Sweers, *Electric Folk: The Changing Face of English Traditional Music* (Oxford: Oxford University Press, 2005); Georgina Boyes, *The Imagined Village: Culture, Ideology and the English Folk Revival* (Manchester, UK: Manchester University Press, 1993); Michael Brocken, *The British Folk Revival, 1944–2002* (Aldershot, UK: Ashgate, 2003); Ronald D. Cohen, *Folk Music: The Basics* (London: Routledge, 2006).

3. John Szwed, *Alan Lomax: The Man Who Recorded the World* (New York: Random House, 2010); Ronald D. Cohen, ed., *Alan Lomax: Selected Writings, 1934–1997* (New York: Routledge, 2003); Ronald D. Cohen, ed., *Alan Lomax, Assistant in Charge: The Library of Congress Letters, 1935–1945* (Jackson: University Press of Mississippi, 2011).

4. Andrea Lynn Woody, "*American School of the Air:* An Experiment in Music Education and Radio Broadcasting," unpub. MA thesis, University of Texas, 2003; Stephen Winnick, "Alistair Cooke: A Radio and TV Icon in the Archive of Folk Culture," *Folklife Center News* 27, nos. 1–2 (Winter/Spring 2005): 6–8.

5. *The Ballad Operas: The Martins and the Coys*, Rounder 11661-1819-2, 2000, with liner notes by Dave Samuelson. Information on *The Chisholm Trail* is very sketchy.

6. Tony Judt, "On Being Austere and Being Jewish," *New York Review of Books*, LXVII, no. 8 (May 13, 2010): 20; Lomax to unknown, from Paris (n.d.); Lomax to unknown, first page missing, manuscripts in the collection of Barry Ollman, Denver, Colorado. For Lomax in Britain, see Szwed, *Alan Lomax*, 251–305.

7. E. David Gregory, "Lomax in London: Alan Lomax, the BBC and the Folk-Song Revival in England, 1950–1958," *Folk Music Journal* 8, no. 2 (2002): 140 and 136–69 in general.

8. *Patterns in American Folksong*, No. 1, "Love," and *Patterns in American Folksong*, No. 2, "Violence," copies in the Alan Lomax Collection, American Folklife Center, Library of Congress.

9. A. L. Lloyd, *Folk Song in England* (London: Lawrence & Wishart, 1975), 373. Oddly, Lloyd makes no mention of Lomax. See also, Bob Brunning, *Blues: The British Connection* (London, 1995).

10. Undated clipping from *London Times*, courtesy of Robin Roberts.

11. Gregory, "Lomax in London," 140.

12. Cohen, ed., *Alan Lomax: Selected Writings*, 182–83.

13. Sandy Paton, "A Letter from London," *Caravan* 6 (1958): 7.

14. Ewan MacColl, *Journeyman: An Autobiography* (London: Sidgwick & Jackson, 1990), 275; Ben Harker, *Class Act: The Cultural and Political Life of Ewan MacColl* (London: Pluto Press, 2007), 111, 126–27; Fred Woods, *Folk Revival: The Rediscovery of a national Music* (Poole, UK: Blandford Press, 1979), 56; Michael Verrier, "Folk Club or Epic Theatre: Brecht's Influence on the Performance Practice of Ewan MacColl," in Ian Russel and David Atkinson (eds.), *Folk Song: Tradition, Revival, and Re-Creation* (Aberdeen, UK: University of Aberdeen, 2004), 112.

15. MacColl, *Journeyman*, 269–71; Harker, *Class Act*, 95–96; Gregory, "Lomax in London," 149.

16. Britta Sweers, "Ghosts of voices: English Folk(-rock) Musicians and the Transmission of Traditional Music," in Russel and Atkinson, *Folk Song*, 132.

17. MacColl, *Journeyman*, 286.

18. *Theo: The Autobiography of Theodore Bikel* (New York: HarperCollins, 1994), 89.

19. Alan Lomax to Shirley and family, January 2, 1954, Lomax Papers, 3D222, folder 6, Center for American History, University of Texas, Austin, Texas; Bob Groom, *The Blues Revival* (London: Studio Vista, 1971), 12–13 (including a photo of Lomax with Broonzy in 1951).

20. MacColl, *Journeyman*, 277.

21. Shirley Collins, *America Over the Water* (London: SAF, 2005), 19–20 and *passim*.

22. Alan Lomax, "Skiffle: Why Is It So Popular? and Where Is It Going," in Cohen, ed., *Alan Lomax: Selected Writings*, 135–38; Chas McDevitt, *Skiffle: The Definitive Inside Story* (London: Robson, 1997).

23. Brian Bird, *Skiffle: The Story of Folk-Song with a Jazz Beat* (London: Robert Hale, 1958), 18; McDevitt, *Skiffle*, 93–95.

24. Lomax, "Skiffle: Why Is It So Popular? and Where Is It Going," 136–37.

25. John Hasted, *Alternative Memoirs* (Itchenor, UK: Greengate, 1992), 131.

26. June Shelly, *Even When It Was Bad... It Was Good* (USA: Xlibris, 2000), 50–51; Hank Reineke, *Ramblin' Jack Elliott: The Never-Ending Highway* (Lanham, MD: Scarecrow, 2010), 63–110.

27. Shelly, *Even When It Was Bad*, 55; *Joan's Book: Joan Littlewood's Peculiar History As She Tells It* (London: Minerva, 1995), 409, 466; "The Big Rock Candy Mountain: An American Ballad Opera," manuscript, in author's possession.

28. Boyes, *The Imagined Village*, 230, 214–15. See Reineke, *Ramblin' Jack Elliott*, for a full discussion of the Elliotts' stay in England.

29. Fred Dallas, "Francis J. Child: and the 'Ballads,'" *Sing* 4/1 (1957), 5; John Hasted, "a singer's notebook," *Sing* 4/2 (1957), 22; Bill Stamm, "Woody Guthrie—The Man and the Music," *Jazz Music* 8/5 (1957): 3.

30. Alan Lomax to Johnny Lomax, November 13, 1955, Lomax Papers, 3D222, folder 6, Center for American History, University of Texas, Austin; MacColl, *Journeyman*, 338.

31. Alan Lomax, *Harriet and Her Harmonium* (New York, n.d. [1955]); "Uncle Sing," "Music hath charms," *Sing* 2/5 (1956): 76.

32. N. E. Wadsley to Miss Dabell, December 17, 1951, REPORT, July 1, 1953; Report, February 10, 1955, Lomax file FKV2/2701, Special Branch, in Records of Security Services, Personal Files, National Archives, Kew, UK.

8

Putting the Blues in British Blues Rock

—Roberta Freund Schwartz

British blues rock is a fusion initially created by young musicians raised on rock 'n' roll playing urban blues standards of the 1940s and 1950s. Over time it evolved into a distinct style of rock music that adopted the riff-based structures, improvisatory focus, instrumental virtuosity, vocal approach, and instrumental timbres of blues. Blues rock arguably reached its apex in 1970, but it influenced many of the stylistic developments in rock music in the 1960s and 1970s: psychedelic rock, heavy metal, and hard rock are widely accepted as its descendants, as are many of the conventions of "classic" rock.

During its heyday blues rock was widely criticized as inept and emotionally sterile by blues critics, and its musicians accused of unfairly appropriating black American folk music. Thus, little consideration has been given to the evolution of blues rock itself. Though it was quickly embraced by blues lovers in other countries, the style emerged most forcefully and successfully in England, and British bands dominated blues rock during the 1960s. Therefore, England provides the most fruitful ground for a study of the music's stylistic development.[1]

Between 1962 and 1970, blues rock, which in England was also called "British blues" and "R&B," developed in three phases, each shaped by a particular blues style and group of artists. The way that British devotees interpreted, performed, and adapted American blues evolved as well. An analysis of the core stylistic influences and resulting output of British bands reveals that as they became increasingly familiar with the root idiom they made more significant alterations to their models, ultimately creating original blues-based material and incorporating the most accessible characteristics into a new approach to rock music.

Blues records began arriving in England in the 1930s, but very few discs were available. Occasionally, records by female singers performing popular, composed blues with jazz bands appeared in Hot Jazz or Rhythm-Style series; the earliest was perhaps Bessie Smith's "Gimme a Pigfoot" (Okeh 8949), recorded especially for British release in 1933.[2] However, blues recordings were quite scarce until the late 1940s, when a segment of Britain's jazz intelligentsia opined that understanding the blues was crucial to true jazz appreciation. Through their advocacy—and on their recommendations—record companies began releasing greater numbers of blues discs in England.[3] After a successful tour by Josh White in 1950, American blues singers like Big Bill Broonzy, Lonnie Johnson, and Muddy Waters toured the country, and articles on the blues appeared in musical publications like *Jazz Journal*, *Jazz Monthly*, and *Melody Maker*. Though still very much a niche genre, the audience for the blues continued to grow. In the late 1950s young Britons began to embrace the music as an alternative to the perceived artificiality of pop music and the commercialization of rock 'n' roll; others were drawn to the blues through trad jazz or the skiffle craze of 1956–58.

By 1962 the blues had a large enough constituency that native—mostly young—rock 'n' roll and skiffle musicians who endeavored to try playing the music themselves found receptive audiences, kicking off Britain's "R&B Boom."[4] The first British bands to perform blues on electric instruments in the late 1950s—Blues Incorporated and Cyril Davies and the R&B All-Stars, as well as Alexis Korner's Breakdown Group featuring Cyril Davies—were older jazz and skiffle musicians who drew their material from blues available on record in England at that time. The Breakdown Group recorded mostly blues that had become jazz standards and traditional songs drawn from Leadbelly recordings.[5] The Blues Incorporated album *R&B Live at the Marquee* (Ace of Clubs ACL1130, 1960) includes a quartet of Muddy Waters's tunes, blues standards like "How Long, How Long Blues," and jazz-oriented originals.

The Rolling Stones, arguably the first blues rock band, was made up of young blues enthusiasts who sat in with Blues Incorporated during their earliest Thursday night gigs at the Marquee Club in London in 1962.[6] They formed their own group because they wanted to focus more closely on the Chicago (a.k.a. urban) blues: strongly rhythmic blues played on amplified instruments, generally by a quartet (lead singer, lead guitar, rhythm guitar, bass, and drums) or quintet (adding harmonica, piano, or saxophone), with forms and lyric themes drawn from earlier styles of blues.

The Chicago blues entered Britain when the Pye and Decca labels realized that their leasing arrangement with the Chess label in Chicago gave them access to blues artists that occasionally crossed over to the American pop and R&B charts, like Muddy Waters, John Lee Hooker, Chuck Berry, and Bo Diddley.

The Stones' early repertoire[7] was dominated by Chess recording artists and by Jimmy Reed.[8] The group eagerly pursued new material by Reed, as is evident from an extant letter by Brian Jones to blues and soul enthusiast Dave Godin in 1962:

> Herewith the tape on which you kindly agreed to stick some Reed gear. Couldn't out [sic] the blank side on the outside, as I didn't have a spare reel. The one side has Bo Diddley on most of it—it is an Extra Play tape, so you should easily be able to stick *Rockin' With Reed, I Can't Hold Out* and flip (Elmore) and your Reed singles (only ones which aren't duplicated on LPs) on it.
>
> Also, Dave, if you possibly could grab hold of one, could you tape *Just Jimmy*, the latest Reed LP over Bo Diddly. But please don't record over Bo unless it is *Just Jimmy*. This is really good of you mate—if there's anything we can do for you—let us know. Cheers, Brian Jones.[9]

In 1963–64 Stones set lists included the Reed songs "Bright Lights, Big City," "Shame, Shame, Shame," "Big Boss Man," "The Moon Is Rising," "Honey What's Wrong" (also known as "Baby What's Wrong"), and Reed's version of Clarence Carter's "I Ain't Got You." Most were part of the common repertoire of many early British R&B bands: the Downliners Sect and the Yardbirds[10] did "Baby What's Wrong"; "Big Boss Man" was recorded by Graham Bond and the Pretty Things, who also covered "The Moon Is Rising."

Bo Diddley was another early favorite of the Stones, who covered "Road Runner," "Hey Craw-dad" (as "Hey Crawdaddy"), "Mona," "Bo Diddley," and "Pretty Thing." The Pretty Things, named after that song, naturally included a version on their first album, along with three more Diddley covers. The Yardbirds recorded his "I'm A Man," and "Here 'Tis," and "You Can't Judge a Book by Looking at the Cover" was a popular live feature also performed by the Stones.

Many groups performed songs by John Lee Hooker, whose talking blues style and hypnotic boogie patterns were both appealing and accessible: the Stones covered "Crawling King Snake," and "Dimples," the first single issued by the Spencer Davis Group. The Yardbirds recorded "Louise" and "Boom Boom," the latter the first hit record by the Animals. Many groups lacked the vocal firepower to cover songs by Howlin' Wolf, the most aggressive and edgy of the Chicago blues artists, though the Stones recorded "Little Red Rooster" and the Yardbirds performed "Smokestack Lightning" until the group broke up in 1968. But the most influential Chicago blues artist for early British blues rock bands was Muddy Waters; virtually every group (save for the Yardbirds) played "Hoochie Coochie Man," "I've Got My Brand on You," and "I've Got My Mojo Working"; the last was so ubiquitous George Melly dubbed it the "Saints [Go Marching In]" of the R&B Boom.[11] Revered blues guitarist Elmore James would prove to be more influential in the next phase of blues rock, though "Dust My Broom" was already on the set list of many bands, as were the Slim Harpo songs "Got Love If You Want It" and "I'm a King Bee."

Though originally more plentiful in the marketplace and in live performance, country blues did not form a part of the core repertoire of early blues rock bands. It is possible that this music seemed less accessible, but the most likely reason is that the Chicago blues was rougher, wilder, and more aggressive; in short, when compared to Sonny Terry and Big Bill Broonzy, it sounded and felt more like rock 'n' roll. Most bands played unadorned cover versions of these songs and tried, to the best of their ability, to replicate the sound of the Chicago blues they heard on records. Learning songs "was almost a religious experience for the pious Stones, copying the old blues standards as if they were scripture."[12] Phil May likewise observed, "it was like a church. You couldn't be disrespectful. The harmonica was learned note-for-note."[13] A good example is the Yardbirds' cover (UK Columbia DB7283, 1964) of "I Wish You Would" by Billy Boy Arnold.[14] Save for an added two-bar introduction that foregrounds the bass riff[15] of the original, the band copies their model as closely as possible, down to the amount of reverb on the harmonica. An extant live version, recorded at the Crawdaddy Club in December 1963, contains sectional repetition and several extended solo breaks, but is substantively the same.

In truth, most cover versions were not identical to the American original; due to the inexperience of the musicians, nearly all lack the nuances and emotional intensity of the original recordings. But other, deliberate alterations were made. The most evident is tempo. Nearly all British blues covers from this time period are significantly faster than the originals. Subtle lyric alterations are also prevalent. Most seem to be the result of imperfect recollection or spontaneous reordering of verse elements, but at times these changes serve to make the lyrics more immediately relevant; for example, the Yardbirds changed the first line of "I Ain't Got You" (as recorded by Jimmy Reed) from "I got an El Dorado Cadillac / with a spare tire on the back" to "I got a Maserati GT / with snakeskin upholstery," presumably a more familiar luxury car to young British audiences.[16] The most significant changes, however, were rhythmic. In most cover versions of the period, the relaxed, jazz-like shuffle rhythms of the original were transmuted into the even eighth notes that are typical of early rock 'n' roll. In strictly musical terms, this changes blues models into blues rock.

The cover version of John Lee Hooker's hit "Dimples" (Vee-Jay 205, 1956) by the Spencer Davis Group (Fontana TF 471, 1964) demonstrates many of these alterations. The latter is thirty-six beats per minute faster than the original, and a double-time figure in the rhythm guitar creates a consistent feeling of eight beats to the bar. The lyrics have been reconfigured as well; the first and third strophes are rewritten to break the aaab rhyme scheme of Hooker's version, and the second (which provides the title phrase) is substituted for the fourth verse of the original. The Spencer Davis group also inserts harmonica solos after the second and fourth strophes, and rearranges the accompaniment into a series of stop-time breaks. This device—a characteristic of early jazz featured in a number of Chicago blues hits of the 1950s, most famously in Muddy Waters's "Hoochie Coochie Man"—was occasionally adopted by British blues rock groups as a recognizable touchstone to the root idiom.

By 1965 the so-called "R&B boom" had burst. Many of the young bands that had enthusiastically performed the Chicago blues moved on to new styles like beat, folk, and American soul. Even the groups that remained devoted to the blues began to abandon the Chicago sound of the 1950s in favor of more contemporary electric blues artists like Otis Rush, the three Kings—Freddie, Albert, and B.B.—and most significantly, in terms of his ultimate impact on rock guitar style, Buddy Guy. The young musician's club tour in February 1965, in the words of *Blues Unlimited* editor Simon Napier, "brought the real modern blues to Europe."[17]

The inner circle of British blues guitarists had already discovered Guy through the 1964 album *Folk Festival of the Blues* (Pye NPL 28033); according to Jimmy Page, "everybody got tuned into [him] . . . in the early days. [Guy] just astounded everybody." However, his full impact seems to have emerged after his live appearances. According to Eric Clapton, "He was the epitome of it all . . . he gave us something to strive for—the way he dressed, the way he moved, the way he expressed himself."[18] His long, developed solos and exploitation of new technologies and tone colors were revelations to young guitarists who were just beginning to grasp their inherent possibilities. Shortly thereafter there was a general shift among blues rock guitarists from mostly strumming chords to "utilizing finger vibrato, string bending, distortion, clipped phrases and fluid soloing."[19] These new influences are evident in the 1966 album *Blues Breakers: John Mayall with Eric Clapton* (Decca LK 4804), widely regarded as the seminal testament of blues rock. Clapton's extended solos on Freddie King's "Hideaway" and "Double Crossing Time" (a reworking of the Little Esther and Johnny Otis collaboration "Double Crossing Blues") were unprecedented in their facility and duration, launching the guitar into a new and featured role as a solo instrument in rock music.

Even the sound was revolutionary. Clapton was the first British player to adopt the heavy Gibson Les Paul with humbucker pickups,[20] the preferred model of Freddie King and Hubert Sumlin. When run through the reverb-inducing Marshall amplifier preferred by English bands, the Les Paul created a loud, aggressive sound with a substantial bottom end. Attempting to replicate Buddy Guy's sound, Clapton insisted on turning his amplifier up all the way to create maximum distortion and sustain and then allowing the sound to bleed into the microphones, a decision supported by then–session musician Jimmy Page. The resulting color and presence led many other blues rock guitarists in the country to adopt a similar setup, and overdriven distortion and the Marshall stack—two or more speakers connected to a single amp—became enduring parts of the rock lexicon as the characteristic timbre of psychedelic rock, hard rock, heavy metal, and punk.

Though no longer central influences, songs by Howlin' Wolf, Muddy Waters, and John Lee Hooker remained part of the blues rock canon. Elmore James, previously a minor influence on British blues rock, became more prominent as more of his recordings were released in Britain and his raw, distorted sound was more fully appreciated. Though not a modern blues artist, Robert Johnson, often cited by guitarists of the period as a key source of inspiration, began to appear on set lists; though a handful of copies leaked out in 1962, a contract dispute with Columbia Records delayed the full release of Philips' *Robert Johnson: King of the Delta Blues Singers* (BBL 7539) for two years. However, it was his songs, rather than his performance style, that captured the attention of blues rock bands.

Though most bands continued to play primarily cover versions of American blues, they began to create arrangements that altered or recontextualized their models. Guitarist Ian Anderson commented, "What we are all doing is taking traditional material and rewriting it in our own way—which is exactly what the old country blues men did themselves."[21]

To a certain extent, this resulted from greater familiarity with the conventions of the idiom, derived from repeated performances and playing with visiting American blues artists, which often produced less than spectacular results.[22] Reflecting on his experience playing behind Sonny Boy Williamson as a member of the Yardbirds, Eric Clapton stated: "At that point in time it hadn't occurred to me that to know a song was different to [sic] being familiar with it. I thought it would be in a key, and it would have a tempo; I didn't realize that the detail was important. It didn't occur to me that there would be a strict adherence to a guitar line, to an intro, to a solo. And that's what I learned very quickly."[23] The exact meaning of this comment is not immediately clear, as during the early years of his career Clapton primarily did adhere strictly to the various elements of recorded models. A later comment in the same interview, "I thought we could get away with just busking it," suggests that he is referring to the balance between the stable and improvisatory elements of blues performances. Recordings from this period demonstrate that British blues rock musicians had a nascent understanding of the various elements that make up a blues song—the introduction, riff-based accompaniment, fills, solos, melody, lyrics, form, and chord changes—and how they function as individual components of the whole. Bands frequently isolated several of these elements from a recorded model and employed them as a framework for an arrangement or a "new" song.

Phil Cohen relates that, by 1966, the Yardbirds commonly wrote new material by "playing someone else's song, and when the arrangement and melody grow substantially away from the source tune, add an original Yardbirds lyric, and you will have a song which is 75% (if not totally) original." An example is "The Nazz Are Blue," a retrofit, so to speak, of the blues standard "Dust My Broom."[24] Elmore James's signature slide riff serves as an introduction, but it is not used continuously as a fill, as it is on the original recording. The Yardbirds lifted the supporting riff played by the bass and rhythm guitar, but the descending bass figure that concludes each chorus of "Dust My Broom" is reworked into a dramatic and prominent transition; heard only once in the original, in "Nazz Are Blue" it is repeated three times and pushed to the foreground of the mix. The melody is based on the original, but it is significantly altered with vocal gestures from American soul music.[25]

Such retrofits were common. The 1966 album *The Yardbirds/Roger the Engineer* alone contains three more reworked Chicago blues. After several different arrangements, "Someone to Love Me" by Snooky Pryor was transformed into "Lost Woman."[26] "Rack My Mind" is based on Slim Harpo's "Baby Scratch My Back," a song the Yardbirds performed live on BBC radio in February 1966, just a month before they began working on the album. The main riff of Harpo's original serves as the foundation, though the tempo is increased and the shuffle rhythms are replaced by a driving, solid rock beat. Drummer Jim McCarty emphasizes this change by carefully articulating the last three eighth notes of each bar on the hi-hat. The Yardbirds discard Harpo's introduction, a free meter evocation of a train, in favor of an upbeat leading directly into the main riff and harmonica solo. The harmonica parts are similar, but there is no borrowing; this can be attributed to the fact that both are solos over standard blues changes. The original is a talking blues—the lyrics are recited, rather than sung—so the Yardbirds use Harpo's harmonica solo as "guide," or melodic prototype, for the vocal line, with adjustments made to create a more directionally balanced melody with antecedent-consequent phrases. Jeff Beck's guitar lines are original, but his fills in the second verse may be in homage to the "chicken scratch" solo of the original, which is also aped in the melody of the refrain. The third retrofit on the album, "What Do You Want," is a version of Bo Diddley's "Who Do You Love," its similarities disguised by a flood of echo, delay, and wah-wah pedal.

In an interview Mick Clarke of the band Killing Floor related that sometimes these alterations were made out of necessity. When the group went into the studio to record their eponymous debut album (Spark [S]RLP 102, 1969) they were informed that

> all the material had to be original, for publishing reasons. This was a little awkward, as we had a complete set of Chicago blues standards which we'd been rehearsing and playing for the last six months. Consequently Bill went and sat in the toilets at Pye Studios and reluctantly rewrote all the lyrics. Classic blues songs suddenly became originals ... Actually the songs had all been re-arranged to such an extent that they were already halfway to becoming originals.[27]

The degree of rearrangement varies. "Sunday Morning" is clearly the blues standard "Stormy Monday" with new lyrics; likewise, "Bedtime Blues" obviously began life as Elmore James's "The Sky is Crying." On the other hand, "My Mind Can Rest Easy" is an uptempo arrangement of the gospel blues "Jesus Gonna Make Up My Dying Bed," based on Josh White's 1956 recording.[28] White's introduction, a single-string version of the tune interspersed with strummed chords, is discarded in favor of bongo and woodblock. The concluding line of the refrain, "Jesus Gonna Make Up My Dyin' Bed" is stated once in the original, followed by an echo of the phrase on guitar. Killing Floor repeats the first part of the line ("Jesus gonna make up") three times, with the second and third iterations entering half a beat late to create a syncopated swagger more akin to Stax soul than the blues; a horn section plus harmonica repeats the phrase instead of concluding the line. "Try to Understand" is based on the rhythm section riff from "Everything's Gonna Be Alright" by Buddy Guy and Junior Wells (possibly by way of Cream's "Lawdy Mama"); the group adds new lyrics, as well as some fine boogie-woogie piano by Lou Martin.

Cover versions of American records were still plentiful during this period, but more significant alterations were made than in the earliest phase of British blues rock. Eric Clapton explained that his approach was to "take the most obvious things and simplify them. Like my way of doing 'Crossroads' was to take that one musical figure"—the fill that Robert Johnson used to conclude each verse—"and make that the point, the focal point. Just trying to focus on what the essence of the song was—keeping it simple."[29] Cream extended the short fill into a propulsive riff that gives their version a relentless drive.

Fleetwood Mac reworked "You Got to Move" twice. Played live at the BBC in 1967, it was transformed to a sly shuffle by changing its rhythmic emphasis and introducing melodic variations that allowed Jeremy Spencer to shadow, and then expand, the bottleneck statements derived from Mississippi Fred McDowell's version. On their 1968 eponymous debut album, the song becomes a Chicago blues, perhaps modeled more closely on Elmore James's "It Hurts Me Too," which utilizes the same melody derived from the Mississippi Sheiks' "Sitting on Top of the World."

By 1967 American blues had a sizeable fan base in the United Kingdom,[30] and blues from across the entire historical spectrum was widely available. Recordings and live set lists of British blues rock groups from this period contain material by a stylistically diverse range of artists. For example, in Cream's recorded output between September 1966 and August 1967,[31] Howlin' Wolf's "Spoonful" stands alongside the traditional "Cat's Squirrel" (based on the version by Dr. Isaiah Ross), the Robert Johnson songs "Four Until Late" and "Crossroad Blues" (re-titled "Crossroads"), "Rollin' and Tumblin'" (Muddy Waters), "I'm So Glad" (Skip James), "Sitting on Top of the World" (credited to Howlin' Wolf), "Born Under a Bad Sign" (Albert King), and "Outside Woman Blues" (Blind Joe Reynolds).

The haphazard nature in which recordings of different blues styles had reached the country meant they were often encountered non-chronologically, and thus were conceptualized and combined in new ways. Charles Shaar Murray has argued that

> the spiritual and geographical distance which separated the Brit bands from their sources ultimately proved to be their greatest asset. Lacking firsthand knowledge of and access to their role models, they were forced to reinvent the music, to juxtapose styles and idioms which rarely mixed on their native soil, to join up the dots with their own ideas. "If I'm building a solo," Eric Clapton explained . . . "I'll start with a line that is definitely Freddie King . . . and then I'll go onto a B.B. King line. I'll do something to join them up, so that'll be me. . . ." Out of their creative misunderstandings of the distant worlds of the South Side and the Delta, Clapton and his kind accidentally-on-purpose invented something uniquely their own . . .[32]

Songs constructed in this way—combining elements from various songs and styles—are pastiches that often bear little resemblance to any particular blues. As Murray observes, this is different from the way that American blues artists reconfigure and adapt material, as older material was usually updated to match the conventions of his or her time. British musicians freely pulled elements from the entire historical spectrum and reassembled them in ways that obscured, rather than reflected, their source material. For example, Cream's "Strange Brew" (*Disraeli Gears*, 1967) is based on the group's earlier arrangement of the traditional blues "Oh Lawdy Mama," which uses the bass and rhythm guitar riff of the Buddy Guy and Junior Wells recording "Everything's Gonna Be Alright" and a lead guitar lick from Albert King's "Crosscut Saw." The lyrics and melody are entirely new, but Clapton's solo interlude in "Strange Brew" is lifted in large measure from King's "Personal Manager."

Sometimes a single borrowed element might provide the framework for an ostensibly new composition, with other elements drawn from the increasingly familiar American blues tradition. As Mick Clarke noted, "We borrowed ideas quite liberally from other blues and rock albums of the time, but the way the ideas were woven into our own created an end product that was certainly unique."[33] For example, Led Zeppelin's version of "How Many More Times" (*Led Zeppelin*, Atlantic 19126, 1969) is modeled after "How Many More Years" by Howlin' Wolf, but borrows only the melodic outline. The lyrics and most of the melody are phrases and couplets drawn from half a dozen blues in various styles, including "It Ain't Right" by Little Walter (1952), either B.B. King's "It's My Own Fault" or Lightnin' Hopkins's "Your Own Fault Baby, To Treat Me the Way You Do" (1960), Albert King's "The Hunter" (1965), and the African American folk songs "O Rosie" and "Steal Away."[34] Those present at the session unanimously recall that the last three were spontaneously added during the recording process. Live recordings from 1968–69 affirm that Robert Plant, who spent his teen years singing blues covers in folk clubs and spent a brief period under the tutelage of Alexis Korner, had already developed the ability to improvise lyrically within the blues idiom —in the words of George Case, he "knew the blues like a fire-and-brimstone preacher knew the Bible: quoting a line here, a verse there, and a chorus from somewhere else . . ."[35] The bass line is based on a single chord riff wedded to a standard blues progression, also heard in Cream originals like "Sunshine of Your Love" and "NSU," and ultimately inspired by models like Howlin' Wolf's "Spoonful." Dave Headlam notes that this derivative technique represents the "culmination of the British adaptation of blues into rock . . . where this type of blues-based motivic riff and harmonic motions like A-C-G or E-G-A . . . serve as the basis for a seemingly endless number of songs"; it also served as a flexible platform for extended improvisation.[36]

Even new compositions were often inspired by older models. While writing *Beggar's Banquet* (London PS539, 1968) Mick Jagger and Keith Richards played old blues numbers until a core idea emerged. Richards would "monotonously strum a refrain over and over again, sometimes wailing incomprehensible sounds that only Jagger could translate, until—often after many hours or days—they were singing 'Stray Cat Blues' or 'Salt of the Earth.'"[37]

As is inevitably true, these stages of blues rock development are not absolute. Many bands moved through each stage with varying degrees of speed; some bypassed one or more. However, by 1967 most blues rock acts followed a similar trajectory: a first album jammed with blues covers; a follow-up that contained retrofitted versions of American blues and more divergent arrangements; and subsequent releases composed of originals that were pastiches or rooted in the blues by either form or feeling.

By 1970, the majority of British blues rock artists adopted a "new, original and personal approach to the blues with relevance to our time and generation . . . into fields which are blues feel rather than blues form . . . so many people on the British scene, after years of copying records and styles, are at last beginning to move their music on. . . ."[38] John Mayall noted that for many British musicians, the blues "was a starting point. . . . They had to find their own way of expression. That kind of led them into other areas that just happened to make them very popular on the rock and roll pop scene."[39] Some, like Mayall and Alexis Korner, pursued jazz-based explorations of the blues, drawing inspiration and ideas from a variety of blues-based styles. Fleetwood Mac, Ten Years After, the Aynsley Dunbar Retaliation, and the Taste extended the improvisatory approach to blues into sprawling, open-ended structures that came to define the "arena rock" of the 1970s. Led Zeppelin's emotionally intense, psychedelic-influenced approach to the blues was soon labeled "hard rock"; bands that added blues influences to acid rock created "heavy metal."

Whatever their new style, most British bands of the blues rock tradition retained influences from the blues. The guitar, previously an accompanying instrument occasionally used for brief solos, became the defining instrument of the genre. The blues inspired the extended guitar solo, which soon became a standard element of blues-influenced genres and "a musical laboratory for counter-culture experiments in spontaneity, free expression and self-development."[40] The influence of the blues is particularly prominent in what Michael Hicks dubs the "blues rock" voice, a grinding, raspy quality that remains part of the vocal arsenal of British vocalists like David Bowie, Elton John, and David Gilmore, who sang with blues bands in their early years.[41] The blues has also been cited as the source of male rebelliousness and "narcissistic egocentrism" that emerged in British rock bands of the 1960s, and the "socially provocative stage and public persona" of these acts "marked an important breaking away from the traditions that ruled pop and popular music in general."[42] More plainly stated, the American blues, transmitted in new ways by British blues rock bands, helped rock mature into a style that, while often overlapping with popular music, had its own musical identity.

Notes

1. The blues influenced nearly every popular musical style in Britain during the 1960s, and many musicians knew a great deal about the music and performed, drew inspiration from, or referenced the blues at least occasionally. Please see Roberta Freund Schwartz, *How Britain Got the Blues: The Transmission and Reception of American Blues Styles in the British Isles* (Aldershot, UK: Ashgate, 2007) for details on how folk, British pop, Northern soul, and Scottish R&B performers understood and incorporated the blues into styles rooted in other American musics.

2. Paul Oliver, "Taking the Measure of the Blues," in Neil A. Wynn, ed., *Cross the Water Blues* (Jackson: University Press of Mississippi, 2007), 27.

3. For a detailed discussion of blues records released in Britain prior to 1953 see Schwartz, *How Britain Got the Blues*, 29–38.

4. At the time the musical press called almost all bands drawing influences and material from black American music, from folk blues to Motown, "R&B groups," to the great confusion and ire of many fans.

5. On both *Blues at the Roundhouse*, vol. 1 (Tempo EXA 76, 1957) and vol. 2 (Tempo EXA 102, 1958), the group is listed as Alexis Korner's Skiffle Group.

6. At this date the band included keyboardist Ian Stewart, Pretty Things founder Dick Taylor, and future Kinks drummer Mick Avory.

7. Rolling Stones set lists from 1962–2001 are available at "Rolling Stones' Set Lists," *Frayed.org*, n.d. www.frayed.org/stones/index.html (8 August 2009); and Nico Zentgraf, "The Complete Works of the Rolling Stones, 1962–2009," *The Complete Works Website: The Rolling Stones Database* www.nzentgraf.de/books/tcw/works1.htm (16 August 2009).

8. Reed recorded primarily for Vee-Jay Records. In Britain his works were released on a number of labels, including Columbia, Stateside, Fontana, and Sue.

9. Mark Paytress, *The Rolling Stones—Off the Record* (New York: Omnibus, 2003), 15.

10. Chrome Oxide Music Collectors Pages, 16 November 2007 www.chromeoxide.com/chrome.htm (12 August 2009).

11. George Melly, *Revolt into Style: The Pop Arts in Britain* (London: Penguin, 1970), 53.

12. Steve Appleford, *The Rolling Stones: It's Only Rock and Roll: Song by Song* (New York: Schirmer, 1997), 9.

13. Richie Unterberger, *Urban Spacemen and Wayfaring Strangers: Overlooked Innovators and Eccentric Visionaries of '60s Rock* (San Francisco: Backbeat, 2000), 15.

14. Discographic information is included to uniquely identify the version considered in this study, as live recordings, alternate masters, and later versions may be notably different.

15. A riff is a repeating rhythmic pattern, or ostinato, that also has a distinctive melodic identity; the opening material of "Louie, Louie" is a serviceable example. In the Chicago blues riffs generally serve as the harmonic and rhythmic foundation of a song.

16. From the album *For Your Love* (Epic LN 24167/BN-26167, USA only, 1965).

17. Simon Napier, "Editorial," *Blues Unlimited* 21 (April 1965): 2.

18. Eric Clapton, foreword to Buddy Guy and Donald E. Wilcock, *Damn Right I've Got the Blues: Buddy Guy and the Blues Roots of Rock and Roll* (San Francisco: Woodford, 1993), 1.

19. Martin Celmins, "Mayall, John," in Summer McStravick and John Roos, eds., *Blues Rock Explosion* (Mission Viejo, CA: Old Goat, 2001), 178; Harry Shapiro, *Alexis Korner: The Biography*, discography and additional research by Mark Troster (London: Bloomsbury, 1996), 55. In a 1977 interview Jimmy Page credited Don Peek, the guitarist on the Everly Brothers' tour of England with introducing finger vibrato to England, and claimed, "Clapton picked up on it straight away, and others followed soon after." Dave Schulps, "Jimmy Page Interview," *Roberto's Led Zeppelin Home Page*, 30 April 2009 www.iem.ac.ru/zeppelin/docs/interviews/page_77.trp (15 October 2009).

20. Humbucker pickups are a pair of electro-magnetic coils (the "microphones" that convert the vibration of the strings into an electrical signal) arranged in such a way that they do not pick up interference from other electronic devices in the vicinity. The result is a heavier, more focused sound.

21. Bob Dawbarn, "The Two Ians," *Melody Maker*, 13 July 1968: 6.

22. Not only did young British musicians have little sense of the subtleties of timing, pitch variance, modulation, and phrasing that are central to well-performed blues, but rehearsals were also perfunctory (or nonexistent).

23. Peter Guralnick, "Eric Clapton at the Passion Threshold," *Musician* 136 (1990): 45. The album *Sonny Boy Williamson and the Yardbirds* (Fontana TL5277), originally released in 1966, documents their performance at the Crawdaddy Club on 8 December 1963.

24. "The Nazz Are Blue" appeared on the group's eponymous 1966 album, colloquially known as *Roger the Engineer* (Columbia SCX6063 [stereo]/SX6063 [mono], 1966).

25. "Dust My Broom" is also the model for an Eric Clapton and Jimmy Page jam, entitled "Tribute to Elmore" (1965), and the near cover by John Mayall and the Bluesbreakers, entitled "Dust My Blues." The Clapton/Page track, now available on several anthologies, is the first documented example of Clapton's influential combination of the Gibson Les Paul and Marshall amp. The Bluesbreakers' "Dust My Broom" is on the 1967 album *A Hard Road* (Decca LK [mono]/SKL [stereo] 4853).

26. The transformation is documented in ten tracks on the compilation *The Yardbirds Story* by Giorgio Gomelsky (Charley SNAB 905, 2002).

27. "Mick Clarke," *Killing Floor.org* www.marshalamp.com/killingfloorcom.htm (9 August 2009).

28. The most likely source in Britain was the album *Josh at Midnight* (Bounty 6001, 1956). "In My Time of Dying" by Led Zeppelin is a more extensive reworking of the same song.

29. Guralnick, "Eric Clapton," 54.

30. A *Melody Maker* poll taken in 1965 revealed that 41 out of 100 people who bought pop records also purchased American blues records, at least occasionally. Bob Dawbarn, "What Makes you Buy Records and Why?" *Melody Maker* (6 March 1965): 11.

31. This includes the albums *Fresh Cream* (Reaction 59300, 1966), *Disraeli Gears* (Reaction 594003, 1967), and the studio tracks for *Wheels of Fire* (Polydor 583003, 1968).

32. Charles Shaar Murray, *Boogie Man: The Adventures of John Lee Hooker in the American Twentieth Century* (New York: St. Martin's, 2000), 270.

33. Clarke, www.marshalamp.com/killingfloorcom.htm.

34. "It Ain't Right," recorded in 1952, is a Chicago blues; "Your Own Fault Baby..." is a style of electric blues commonly categorized as Texas blues; "My Own Fault, Baby" and "The Hunter" are examples of the mid-1960s soul blues style; and "O Rosie" and "Steal Away" are folk songs first collected in 1867 in Lucy McKim, William Francis Allen, and Charles Pickard Ware in *Slave Songs of the United States* (New York: Simpson and Co., 1867). Robert Plant quoted the same portion of "Steal Away" in "Operator," a track recorded with Korner in the same year but not released until 1972 on Alexis Korner, *Bootleg Him* (Warner Brothers 2XS-1966); it is not known where he first encountered the song.

35. George Case, *Jimmy Page: Magus, Musician, Man: An Unauthorized Biography* (New York: Hal Leonard, 2007), 67.

36. Dave Headlam, "Blues Transformations in the Music of Cream," in John Covach and Graeme M. Boone, eds., *Understanding Rock: Essays in Musical Analysis* (New York: Oxford University Press, 1997), 85.

37. Victor Bockris, *Keith Richards: The Biography* (New York: Da Capo, 2003), 143.

38. "Back to Square 1 with 'R&B' Korner," *Melody Maker* (19 March 1966): 15.

39. Chris Welch, "Mayall's 'Bare Wires'—a Progression in Attitude," *Melody Maker* (13 July 1968): 7; Appleford, *Stones*, 35.

40. Elijah Wald, *Josh White: Society Blues* (Amherst: University of Massachusetts Press, 2000), 246; Iain Chambers, *Urban Rhythms: Pop Music and Popular Culture* (London: Macmillan, 1985), 101.

41. Michael Hicks, *Sixties Rock: Garage, Psychedelic, and Other Satisfactions* (Urbana: University of Illinois Press, 1999), 2–3.

42. Chambers, *Urban Rhythms*, 67–68.

9

That White Man, Burdon

The Animals, Race, and the American South in the British Blues Boom

—Brian Ward

Introduction: From Georgia to Walker

In February 1964 Newcastle-upon-Tyne's foremost rhythm and blues hopefuls the Animals recorded a fairly obscure tune of African American origin. The song offered a cautionary tale about the misfortunes that might befall a small-town innocent corrupted by the bright lights of the big city and appeared as the B-side of the band's first single "Baby Let Me Take You Home." "Gonna Send You Back to Walker" was a spirited reinterpretation of a song originally called "Gonna Send You Back to Georgia" which was a minor national hit for soul-bluesman Timmy Shaw in early 1963. In the Animals' version, lead singer Eric Burdon simply substituted Walker, his birthplace in the North East of England for the southern state of Georgia.[1]

The Animals' debut appeared as the British blues boom approached its commercial zenith. During 1964 the estimated number of broadly blues-based groups in England soared from 300 to more than 2,000 and enthusiasm for the blues and its derivatives spread far beyond the esoteric world of specialist magazines and a small, passionate coterie of aficionados to intersect with the beat group boom that dominated British popular music after the emergence of the Beatles.[2] This was a period when musical nomenclature became increasingly unstable. As Chris Roberts wrote in *Melody Maker*, "you'll have a job drawing the line between rhythm and blues and plain old rock and roll on the London scene today. Or between rhythm and blues and hard bop. Or soul. Or any of several other borderline combinations."[3] In an era when relatively casual blues appreciation coexisted with what *Guardian* music critic Geoffrey Cannon described as the "hysterical sincerity" of hardcore white blues cognoscenti, the cheerfully populist *Record Mail* hailed the Animals' recording as "a raw, chunky number with more than a flavour of that Deep South sound, which has hallmarked so many of the great coloured performers of this music."[4] No accolade could have pleased Eric Burdon and his bandmates more, since it mobilized racial and regional indices of quality and yoked them to a common set of British aesthetic preferences that tended to favor certain blues sounds ("raw, chunky") over others within the idiom.

One of the main purposes of this essay is to explore how and why definitions of musical excellence, sincerity, and authenticity became so intimately connected to British ideas about the regional, as well as the more frequently noted racial roots of the blues. The objective here is not to deny the paramount significance of race, especially assumptions and misassumptions about African Americans and their culture, in shaping white British enthusiasm for blues-based styles. Countless histories, memoirs, and interviews attest to how the racial provenance of the music, particularly its swaggering enactment of black masculinity, accounted for much of its appeal to whites on both sides of the Atlantic.[5] Consequently, a major theme of this essay concerns how the Animals, and Eric Burdon in particular, negotiated the tension between the universal qualities that British fans found in the blues ("There's no black, no white," insisted Van Morrison. "The blues is truth") and the music's racially specific roots.[6] Yet, it also posits a secondary set of related tensions in the British blues boom that involved recognition of the blues' global currency and appreciation of their regionally specific origins and associations. For the Animals—here meaning the various incarnations of the group prior to 1967—as for many other British blues performers, critics, and fans, invocations of an imagined American South, often suspended temporally in a pre-industrial, interwar past as well as spatially in rural locations below the Mason-Dixon Line, served as a kind of shorthand for ideas about musical integrity, emotional honesty, and freedom from the corrupting influence of the commercial recording industry and modern mass media. Exploring the special place of the South in British narratives of blues authenticity can deepen our understanding of what fans found exciting and of value in the music at a particular historic moment.

Black and White Suns of the Atlantic World

"Gonna Send You Back To Walker" prefigured some of the lyrical themes of the Animals' better-known cover of a much older tune, the global smash hit "The House of the Rising Sun."[7] Both songs, however, suggest something of the complex process of transatlantic musical exchange, theft, borrowing, parody, and homage, as well as the myriad connections, real and imagined, between British and southern music. "The House of the Rising Sun" has a particularly contentious and complex genealogy, spawning numerous myths about its origins that are variously the product of serious research, rumor, memory, imagination, and wishful thinking. As Marybeth Hamilton noted in her study of how white American collectors, critics, and record producers decisively shaped the dominant canon of "authentic" blues styles, "Stories of musical origins are always social and political fables."[8] This, alongside Joseph Roach's observation that "improvised narratives of authenticity and priority may congeal into full-blown myths of legitimacy and origin," offers a useful framework for thinking about what was at stake when Eric Burdon and his bandmates tried to describe the lineage of their most famous recording.[9] Alan Price, the Animals' original keyboard player whose name contentiously appeared on the band's version as "Arranger" of this "traditional" tune—thereby earning him a fortune in royalties and the lifelong resentment of his former bandmates—believed the song was originally a Jacobean ballad about a Soho brothel that was transplanted to the southeastern United States.[10] Eric Burdon similarly described "The House of the Rising Sun" as a song with "roots in a seventeenth century British folk melody" but like Price emphasized that the song only "became what it is today after circulating among Southern American musicians."[11]

As Ted Anthony has explained in a painstaking investigation of the musical and lyrical provenance of "The House of the Rising Sun," it is actually very difficult to establish any concrete connections back to British folksong. True, "The House of the Rising Sun" belongs to a venerable tradition of don't-do-as-I-have-done British ballads such as "The Unfortunate Rake," which usually end with a wretched narrator awash with sin, guilt, and regret. And the melody does bear a passing resemblance to the old British folk tune "Matty Groves." Nonetheless, efforts to source "The House of the Rising Sun" to a single song on either side of the Atlantic are ultimately fruitless. It is more productive to think of the song's evolution in terms of a vast Atlantic reservoir of recurring musical and lyrical themes, with hundreds of fragments of melodies, verses, stock characters, scenes, and locations that could be endlessly tapped and reassembled into new compositions. Anthony does insist, however, that it was in the American South, more specifically in what he calls the "Golden Triangle where Kentucky, Tennessee, Virginia, and North Carolina meet" sometime after the Civil War, that the disparate musical and lyrical strands that would become "The House of the Rising Sun" were woven together. This collective enterprise produced, not a single definitive version, but rather a variety of laments for lost virtue and a grim accounting of the wages of sin, all of which were set in an establishment called the Rising Sun—sometimes a brothel, sometimes a bar, sometimes gambling den—that was located in New Orleans, a city whose transatlantic reputation as "the decadent city of our wildest dreams" was already well-established.[12]

In broad terms, then, the vague arguments that Price and Burdon made for the British roots of the Animals' biggest hit are less compelling than their insistence that the song grew into recognizable shape in the postbellum American South, thereby offering an alternative point of origin and source of legitimacy for the song. And for Burdon it was also crucial to stress that this process was largely accomplished by African American musicians in the region. The song "was first recorded, in fact, by black bluesman Texas Alexander in 1928," he stated categorically, thereby revealing far more about the ways in which ideas about race, region, and authenticity fused in the British blues imagination than it does about the history of "The House of the Rising Sun."[13]

In fact, Alger "Texas" Alexander's 1928 recording of "The Rising Sun" has no lyrical or musical link to the song later reworked by the Animals.[14] Rather, the first recording of a true progenitor was made in 1933, not by a black bluesman but by Clarence "Tom" Ashley, a "white songster and balladeer" born in Bristol, Virginia, on the Tennessee border.[15] Ashley learned the song from his maternal grandparents at a time when there were many orally transmitted versions of the song circulating in the "Golden Triangle."[16] Once Clarence Ashley had committed his version to shellac, other commercial recordings by white southerners quickly followed, including Homer Callahan's "Rounder's Luck" and Roy Acuff's "The Rising Sun," many offering couplets and lyrical sub-themes that would eventually wind up in the Animals' version. Meanwhile, on September 15, 1937, in Middlesboro, Kentucky, folklorist Alan Lomax captured white teenager Georgia Turner's quintessential a cappella lament for a poor country girl who goes to New Orleans, is swept up by the vice and corruption of the Crescent City, and ends up ruined and alone in the Rising Sun bordello.[17]

This was, then, a song in a constant state of production, refinement, and reproduction—less a fixed cultural entity than a work permanently in the throes of creation and re-creation in studios, parlors, fields, porches, concert halls, and bars around the United States, but particularly in the rural South. Contrary to Eric Burdon's claims, however, no African Americans appear to have recorded the song (though some may have sung it) until the early 1940s, when Leadbelly and Josh White each cut several versions.[18] Thus Burdon unwittingly misrepresented the race of those southern artists who first brought some kind of order to the unruly collection of tales and song fragments that coalesced as "The House of the Rising Sun." Inverting a much more common phenomenon, whereby African American contributions to American musical culture were frequently un- or under-acknowledged, Burdon was so keen to give black artists their due that he neglected the role of white southerners in the evolution of the song.

Initially, this was probably more a function of ignorance than design or willful deception. In the early 1960s Burdon may simply not have known about the pre-eminence of southern whites in the early recording and performance history of "House of the Rising Sun," whereas versions by Leadbelly and Josh White were more easily available. Nonetheless, it is striking how doggedly he stuck to the notion that the song was really of black southern origin even as countervailing evidence mounted. Certainly by the time the Animals recorded the song in May 1964 there were dozens of white versions available, including those by Woody Guthrie, Esco Hankins, Ramblin' Jack Elliott, Frankie Laine, The Sundowners, Andy Griffith, and Britain's own Lonnie Donegan, alongside relatively few black versions by the likes of White, Leadbelly, Odetta, and Nina Simone. With so many potential templates around, it is fascinating to consider how the Animals chose to recount the genesis of their own iconic version.[19]

Aside from Eric Burdon, the Animals claimed that their inspiration was Bob Dylan's rendition on his 1962 debut album—itself filched from Greenwich Village folksinger Dave Van Ronk, who had in turn been influenced by hearing Alan Lomax's protégé Hally Wood sing the song.[20] Guitarist Hilton Valentine was adamant that "it was the Bob Dylan version that we took the chord sequence from." He replaced Dylan's strummed acoustic guitar figures with the mesmerizing electric guitar arpeggios that underpin the Animals' recording. Burdon, however, has always maintained that it was a much older version by black South Carolina bluesman-cum-folk balladeer Josh White that the Animals copied. Valentine conceded that Burdon had known the song before the others heard it and it is plausible that White's was the first version he heard. Although he would only have been five years old in 1946 when the British Brunswick label issued White's 1942 recording as a single, it was regularly re-packaged. Bill Wyman of the Rolling Stones remembered hearing a version by White on Harry Parry's Friday night Radio Rhythm Club in the late 1950s. Perhaps significantly, just weeks before the Animals recorded "The House of the Rising Sun" it had reappeared in Britain on a new White compilation called *Singer Supreme*.[21]

What really matters here, however, is the significance of Eric Burdon's determination, for the best part of fifty years, when narrating the story of "The House of the Rising Sun" to emphasize southern black musical progenitors rather to admit any whiter influences. John Steel, the band's original drummer, interpreted this as part of an ongoing effort to try to establish the integrity, the authenticity, and ultimately the value of the band's Anglo-pop-blues. "No matter what you hear about Josh White," Steel explained, that "was another fairy tale from Eric because we didn't want it to be thought that we were just copying from somebody as 'weakened' as Dylan. It had to come from somebody more obscure."[22]

For Burdon in 1964, "weakened" might just as well have been "whitened." Josh White's race primarily, but also his southern-ness and his relative obscurity outside of the blues and folk fraternity in Britain, combined to make him a much more appropriate inspiration for a bunch of Tyneside blues enthusiasts than an increasingly successful white New York–based folksinger from Minnesota. This racially and regionally inflected valorization of obscurity, the veneration of little or unknown southern blues performers, ideally country-based singers who had cut their teeth between the wars, coupled with a principled disdain for just about anyone who enjoyed mainstream commercial success, was typical of the more zealous British blues fans. As Steel recalled, Burdon "was very committed to black American blues, and R&B was a passion with him, it wasn't just a passing interest or a fad."[23] In this atmosphere, Steel admitted that "It wasn't cool to say that we'd pinched the song from [Dylan's] album. We'd much prefer it to be thought that we were delving into some really obscure stuff."[24] Even when Eric Burdon subsequently remembered that a local folk singer called Johnny Handle had been singing "The House of the Rising Sun"—and apparently vouchsafing its Elizabethan British roots—in the Tyneside clubs the Animals frequented in the late 1950s, he still insisted that he had always assumed it must really be a much older blues song. Only many years later did Burdon admit, somewhat sheepishly, perhaps even disappointedly, "Well it certainly isn't a black chord sequence. It's a European chord sequence."[25]

The South in the British Blues Imagination

There was a certain irony in Burdon's choice of Josh White as a touchstone of authenticity, because White's credentials as a "genuine" bluesman were the subject of great debate among white blues aficionados on both sides of the Atlantic, where he actually enjoyed a fair amount of popular acclaim. Some purists felt that the sheer eclecticism of White's repertoire, which spanned folk, spirituals, blues, and pop, coupled with his relatively smooth, somewhat jazzy vocal and instrumental stylings, and his solid biracial commercial success both on record and in major concert venues placed him beyond the realm of a "real" bluesman.[26] Nonetheless, in the wider context of British popular music in the early 1960s, White remained a fairly exotic influence to cite. Even more crucially for this essay, arguments over White's credibility had helped to shape British understandings of the relationship between the blues' southern roots and notions of worth and authenticity, as well as of genesis. The southernization of the British blues imagination had intensified in the late 1950s in part thanks to the mischievous promptings of Big Bill Broonzy, who cast his downhome blues as the southern antithesis to White's cosmopolitan artifice. When the self-declared "last of the Mississippi blues singers" spotted White in the audience at one of his London shows, he harangued the younger singer from the stage. "He cain't sing the blues! He's from the North—ain't never heard anyone from the North sing the blues."[27] To play authentic blues, Broonzy assured readers of *Melody Maker* meant being "born a Negro in Mississippi, and you got to grow up poor and on the land," adding that the blues were at heart, "field hollers.... Go to the city and you get jazz, not blues."[28]

In Europe Broonzy favored a much earthier sound than did White—or than was apparent in much of Broonzy's own recorded repertoire. He also liked to introduce songs with folksy recollections of growing up in the rural South, thereby turning such stylistic differences into measures of authenticity. It mattered little that Broonzy's own claims to be the living embodiment of a vanishing Mississippi country blues tradition were rather dubious. Although he was born in Mississippi (he claimed in 1893, but recent research suggests 1903)[29] and grew up in Pine Bluff, Arkansas, by the time of his first visit to Europe, Broonzy had not lived in the South for decades. In Chicago's decidedly modern and metropolitan setting he had pioneered an innovative and commercially successful contemporary urban blues, a blend of blues, jazz, and pop far removed from the primitive retro-blues stylings he presented to British audiences only after hastily reacquainting himself with a rural blues repertoire to cater to their expectations.[30] By 1958, when Rex Harris and Brian Rust's influential *Recorded Jazz: A Critical Guide* appeared, Broonzy was safely ensconced in British minds as "one of the last Mississippi blues singers and guitarists," a man whose stature was inextricably linked to his fidelity to old rural southern stylings. "Many modern blues singers are surrounded by 'gimmicks' and echo chambers and special effects," Harris and Rust complained, "but Broonzy likes to sing the way he has always sung."[31]

As British journalist and photographer Val Wilmer recalled, sophisticated artists like Broonzy and to some extent even White, as well as countless electric bluesmen, "were forced to adopt a 'country boy' persona in order to deliver the fantasy version of the Deep South that listeners apparently craved."[32] If commercial considerations meant that these artists were sometimes complicit in projecting such images in order to maximize their appeal, the whole rustication enterprise nonetheless reflected the power of the stereotypes linked to race, region, and musical style. Muddy Waters and John Lee Hooker were among the others who initially struggled to please British audiences, who were broadly divided between purists who wanted the commercially unsullied southern country blues of their imaginations, and others who, with varying degrees of grace and enthusiasm, conceded that the blues was a protean music that had flourished and been refreshed in many settings beyond the rural and small-town South. After a mixed reception for his highly amplified Chicago blues sets in 1958, Waters admitted that he had misunderstood British blues tastes, which seemed anchored in the sounds of the interwar South. "Now I know people in England like soft guitar and the old blues," he explained to *Melody Maker* journalist and blues booster Max Jones. "Next time I come, I'll learn some old songs first."[33]

Even among the most avid British blues fans there were some who rejected such rustic fetishization of the blues. Paul Oliver, the most respected of all British blues authorities, warned against the prevailing "myth . . . of a scale of authenticity which relates to a singer's proximity to the country," describing it as "a fallacious and unworthy argument which can do great harm to the recognition that many city artists rightly deserve."[34] Despite such warnings—the very existence of which testified to a British tendency to privilege and romanticize southern rural blues over other blues styles in the early 1960s—schisms developed, some of them largely generational, between those who were happy to let Muddy Waters, John Lee Hooker, and B.B. King plug in and blast out their modern blues much as they did when playing to black audiences at home, and others who were appalled at such departures from the acoustic and rural traditions that they felt constituted the real blues.

These fissures within the blues fraternity were by no means absolute. A young Eric Clapton, for example, could admire and borrow from electric blues guitarists like Hooker, Waters, B.B. King, Otis Rush, and Buddy Guy and hail Chicago and its blues scene as his "spiritual home" while still enjoying Big Bill Broonzy's acoustic work. As Clapton explained, he "sort of worked backwards into country blues" without feeling the need to disavow his original enthusiasm for more urban and electric styles. Nevertheless, Clapton came to reserve special reverence for the country blues of Broonzy and interwar Delta legend Robert Johnson, insisting that "all rock 'n' roll, and pop music too, for that matter had sprung from this root" and declaring Johnson "the master."[35]

It is not hard to discern where Clapton, Burdon, and their peers acquired their sense of the South's importance as a point of blues origin and as the permanent wellspring of its musical integrity—nor is there much to quibble with in their appreciation that the blues was, indeed, rooted in and saturated by southern black influences. Earnest discussions of the authenticity of visitors to Britain such as White, Broonzy, and Waters; the high proportion of southern performers among the first wave of blues recordings issued in the UK; the pre-eminence of southern artists and topics in radio broadcasts on the blues; the dominance of southern-born performers on the influential American Folk Blues and Gospel tours that traversed Britain in the early 1960s and drew impressionable young fans such as Jimmy Page, Keith Richard, Mick Jagger, and Brian Jones; the emphasis on the South in key works of ethnography and blues scholarship by the likes of Frederic Ramsey, Samuel Charters, and Paul Oliver; and the reverence for southern blues originators in specialist blues magazines and columns all affirmed the region's centrality to the history of the blues. Consequently, when the British blues boom took off in the early 1960s, cognoscenti and casual fans alike were well aware that the blues were played by black performers throughout the entire United States, but they tended to agree that the music's racial and regional roots offered the most important touchstones of its authenticity, no matter how far the music and its practitioners had roamed geographically, or how much they had embraced the electrified sounds of the city and succumbed to the temptations of the modern commercial entertainment and media industries.[36]

As the blues boom leaked out into the more mainstream world of beat music and pop, the more avid British guardians of blues purity worked even harder to depict the best, most authentic blues as either located in the South or as part of a southern black diaspora, even when profiling artists who had long left the region. "Like many another good blues artist, J.B. [Lenoir] was born in Mississippi," John Broven assured readers of the British magazine *Blues Unlimited* who may have worried about the credibility of a flamboyant Chicago-based artist who favored a boogie electric guitar style, bold horn sections, and zebra-patterned suits. Nobody reading Broven's 1964 interview with Lenoir would have been in any doubt that Lenoir's Chicago blues were forged by his southern experiences of poverty and disadvantage. "I have picked cotton, I have plowed, I have sawed logs, I have worked on railroads; out of all that I would go home and create my blues at night," Lenoir explained. "It is amazing to work alongside people and hear them moan and groan the blues. Nobody can sing the blues if he has never been 'blued'; nothing can come out of you unless it's in you; sometimes, when you've been mistreated and work like a slave, the only way to relieve it is to sing or moan the blues." Broven told his readers that "Besides being a neat chronicle of the terrible lot of the Southern Negro," Lenoir's testimony offered "an apt commentary on the true meaning of the blues." Once again the rural southern black experience was cast as the touchstone of blues authenticity, but at least here it was coupled to a more realistic, de-romanticized vision of that region.[37]

The southernization of the British blues imagination was further advanced by the intrepid bluesologists from both sides of the Atlantic who took to the back roads of the South hunting the rarest, most isolated (and, therefore, according to one index of value, the most authentic) blues. In a rather typical article, Karl Michael Wolfe reported for the British magazine *Blues World* from Woodville, Mississippi, where he had tracked down an aging bluesman named Scott Dunbar. Dunbar was a modestly gifted performer with a rather jaunty style that, as Wolfe acknowledged, revealed the proximity of black blues and white country forms in the region. Yet, in his report this racial hybridity evaporated in the face of Wolfe's desire to affirm Dunbar's racial and therefore musical purity, an agenda supported by fixing the singer in a remote and archaic southern milieu. Born on Deer Park Plantation near Woodville, from whence he seldom roamed, Dunbar was uneducated ("I've never been to school in my life") and musically self-tutored: a natural, raw talent, whose isolation and very physiology seemed testament to his and his music's purity. "Scott has very dark skin and nothing Caucasoid in his features," Wolfe explained. He seemed almost delighted that "Scott's shack only received electricity through REA (Rural Electrification Act) a few years ago," thereby ensuring there would be no electronic gimmickry to sully the unvarnished beauty of his music.[38]

European blues fans tended, much like their white American counterparts, to romanticize the vanishing pastoral South, not unreasonably privileging the Delta as the historic home of the blues, but also solipsizing it as the place where it endured in its purest form. They focused on the region's supposedly organic nature, its powerful sense of community, and a reverence for place and tradition that was literally rooted in the soil and kinship ties, and largely uncorrupted by the forces of modern life. Consequently, they underplayed the fact that, since at least the turn of the century, mass culture, indeed modernity in all its forms—cultural, economic, social, intellectual, technological, and psychological—had been steadily encroaching on the South. This was certainly true in major cities like New Orleans, Memphis, Houston, Atlanta, and Charlotte. But it was also apparent in smaller towns and cities in the region's rural hinterlands, not least in the bustling commercial city of Clarksdale, Mississippi, which was carefully re-imagined by blues fans and commentators, and later by the local tourist trade, as a rural backwater so that it could fit more neatly into a conventional southern blues image. In fact, the blues as it emerged in the South and spread, transformed and transforming, around the nation in the early twentieth century was a response to black experiences within a rapidly modernizing world, not the sound of a fossilized past. It was the generally white collectors, fans, critics, and practitioners at the heart of the post–World War II blues revival who promoted the idea that the most powerful and authentic blues were direct expressions of some kind of pre-modern, primitive black consciousness best heard in the backwoods of the South.[39]

When writers did alight upon genuinely isolated southern communities, many underestimated or misunderstood the sheer virulence of racism and the attendant power structures that sustained white power and restricted black opportunities, thereby neglecting the social, economic, and racial contexts that shaped the blues culture for black performers and their primary audiences. Wolfe's article on Scott Dunbar, for example, acknowledged that "White supremism and prejudice certainly exists in Wilkinson County . . . but as far as I can see it is much more subtle and delicate than anyone who lives in a city ever suspects. . . . I never observed any white person in any overtly prejudiced act, attitude, or remark and several whites showed me that they were rather proud of old Scott. . . . The whites like him but I found plenty of evidence to show that they respect him too."[40]

Doubtless this was true at some level, but the image of paternalistic southern whites admiring the musical prowess of an unschooled African American who appeared to know his place at the bottom of southern society exemplified the kind of racial myopia and rural idyllicism that permeated a good deal of specialist British blues writing and fandom.

An even more telling illustration of this tendency was an article in *Blues Unlimited* by the magazine's co-founder, the influential blues writer and discographer Mike Leadbitter, on J. D. (Jay) Miller, a white record store owner who also recorded blues, alongside hillbilly, rock and roll, and Cajun music. Leadbitter was hardly ignorant of the racial oppression in which southern blues music was rooted and his blues interests extended far beyond the rural South. Yet his 1967 piece on Miller was saturated with evidence of romantic assumptions about the region, about its race relations, and about the nature of the blues and the local recording industry that serviced it. Miller immediately confounded Leadbitter's purist expectations by explaining how he used the same white musicians on all his recording sessions, regardless of genre. "It is still startling to think that the music on the best of Jay's blues recordings was provided by a white trio . . . a trio who would also play on French, hillbilly and rock 'n' roll sessions in turn," Leadbitter wrote. Equally troubling was Miller's indifference to notions of musical authenticity and cultural purism. He cut and issued records, any records, not to preserve vanishing folk art forms, but "because someone thinks he can sell enough to make money."[41]

Most troubling of all was the fact that among Miller's most popular releases were poisonous pro-segregation songs on his Reb Rebel imprint, with twin Confederate flags printed on the label. Country/Cajun singer Clifford Joseph Trahan, recording under the pseudonym Johnny Rebel, was the major attraction, offering material such as "Stay Away from Dixie," "Nigger Hatin' Me," "Some Niggers Never Die (They Just Smell that Way)," and "Kajun Klu [sic] Klux Klan," which depicted African Americans as congenitally lazy, dishonest, and ignorant, ridiculed the civil rights movement, and generally endorsed segregation and white supremacy as God-ordained virtues. In 1966 Reb Rebel's biggest hit, Son of Mississippi's "Flight NAACP 105"—a skit about how a white air-traffic controller duped a black pilot and his planeload of civil rights activists away from their intended destination in Mississippi and ultimately to their deaths—sold a quarter of a million copies.[42]

Leadbitter tried to understand, rather than merely condemn, Miller's racial attitudes. But in so doing, he disingenuously merged his own authorial voice with that of his subject in ways that made him seem like an apologist for Miller and the old, recalcitrant white South. "Jay is not a racist, but he believes in segregation and this is what he was raised to believe in. Segregation records sell in huge quantities and the only personal motive involved is the one about much-needed money," Leadbitter wrote. "You can blame anything or everything onto social conditions or lack of education, but you cannot overlook the fact that the average bluesman in the Deep South is not dependable, is not too keen on furthering himself, and is sometimes pretty simple. Just like everyone, he wants money and drink a-plenty, and this and the results thereof often see him in The Pen . . ."[43]

Leadbitter's article on Miller brought a stinging rebuke from one reader. Frank Scott denounced Leadbitter's mix of condescension and naivety: "just because many of the white southerners that you met were very pleasant people doesn't prevent the fact that most are infected by a totally irrational prejudice against people of black skin—you cannot seperate [sic] segregation from racism; the former is simply the practical aspect of the latter." Crucially, Scott couched his outrage in terms of his own understanding of contemporary southern society. "To try and shrug off segregation records as pure money making concerns is an abject piece of nonsense, "Scott wrote. "These records are weapons of hatred whose aim is to promulgate a system which denies the essence of humanity to other human beings and which lives in hatred and mistrust." Scott concluded his broadside by invoking the modern civil rights movement: "Your comments disgusted me and show little concern for all the noble beings who have laid out their lives to produce freedom in that part of the USA."[44]

The Leadbitter–Scott exchange in *Blues Unlimited* was symptomatic of a growing tension within the British blues boom. Knowledge of the southern freedom struggle and of the massive, often violent white resistance that greeted it steadily eroded the bucolic romanticism about the South that suffused the British blues imagination in the early 1960s. The argument here is not so much that British blues fans and writers had once been wholly ignorant of, or indifferent to, racial oppression in the South and the role it played in shaping blues history, but rather that as the decade progressed it became increasingly difficult to reconcile recognition of the region's racial inequalities with nostalgic visions of an enviably unsullied, pre-modern South.

The Animals Encounter the South

There were, however, countervailing forces from within and beyond the world of the British blues boom that could moderate excessively romantic views of the South and its race relations. Eric Burdon always maintained that it was black music itself that initially encouraged his fascination with the region and sensitized him to its racial problems. Writing in 1966 for the African American magazine *Ebony,* Burdon explained how "People like [Chuck] Berry, [Ray] Charles and [Bo] Diddley did more for the Negro race outside the United States than anybody." Just a few years previously "we were either too young or didn't want to know about the Negroes' troubles in America," but now he was one of those who "think(s) about the race situation in America." Adding Sonny Boy Williamson, Nina Simone, B.B. King, and John Lee Hooker—all of them southern-born—to his list of inspirational artists, Burdon believed that "If it hadn't been for them I wouldn't have been interested in this country in the first place. I started collecting things—photographs newspaper articles, magazine clippings— to find out why Negroes were being mistreated and often brutally so."[45]

A *Melody Maker* feature, published as "House of the Rising Sun" sat on top of the British charts in the summer of 1964, noted that Burdon was "Intensely interested in America's Negro Civil Rights Bill, and keeps a scrapbook of cuttings on the subject." He had actually started a scrapbook on the civil rights movement years before, about the same time that he wrote the word *Blues* across an art journal in his own blood.[46] A similar music-inspired interest in the freedom struggle also explains why Burdon, Price, and bassist Chas Chandler, all of whom grew up in a city with a tiny nonwhite population, chose "bigotry" as one of their major dislikes in a *New Musical Express* profile.[47]

News reports from the frontlines of the civil rights struggle in the South and personal contacts with southerners, black and white, on both sides of the Atlantic intensified the sense that something was deeply wrong in a region whose musical culture continued to have enormous allure. The

Animals' first national British tour was in the company of Jerry Lee Lewis and Chuck Berry. The tour bus, Burdon recalled, "was a four-wheeled microcosm of America's biggest social problems. . . . The two of them were at each other's throat constantly." Jerry Lee and his roadies even tried to enforce southern-style segregation: when Berry got on the bus, Lewis "would always sneer under his breath something like 'Yeah, get to the back of the bus, nigger, where you belong.'"[48]

On their 1965 U.S. tour, the Animals encountered a Ku Klux Klan parade in Memphis. Earlier that day Burdon had visited Otis Redding at the Stax studios, where the integrated house band Booker T and the MGs seemed to augur well for the birth of a new, more egalitarian South. "My idea that I was in the 'New South' lasted for only those hours I met Otis in the recording studio," he lamented, his optimism shattered by the sight of Klansmen "gathered under the trees in a public park, a massive cross burning, and a ring of cops protecting them."[49] In New Orleans, Burdon watched white bouncers prevent a black GI entering a club in the French Quarter where black musicians provided the entertainment. "I was amazed that this could happen in New Orleans, the place where jazz was born," he later wrote. "Even on that hallowed, almost sacred ground, people had to face that shit, that Southern scourge: racial prejudice. My feelings were so intense, it was actually beginning to hurt me."[50] Burdon accompanied the soldier to Professor Longhair's bar, where he was invited to sing with the band, only for the invitation to be withdrawn because a city ordinance forbade interracial performances.[51]

When the Animals played in Mobile, Burdon also got a sharp reminder that there was no necessary or simple correlation between white love of black music and progressive racial attitudes on either side of the Atlantic. Otis Redding had played the same venue the previous evening and Burdon struck up a conversation with a young fan who agreed that Redding's version of "My Girl" was the hottest record of the moment. When Burdon asked if the girl had seen Redding's show, she was incredulous. "Did I see him?" she replied, "You got to be joking, man, the place was full of niggers."[52]

It is impossible to verify these stories or the dozens of similar tales that punctuate Burdon's interviews and memoirs. Yet the literal accuracy seems less important in understanding Burdon's relationship to the blues, or to the South and its racial history, than does his compulsion to narrate these kinds of incidents over and over. With their messy blend of truth, imagination, and faulty memory, most of these anecdotes end the same way. "I felt a twinge of shame running through me simply for being a white man," he admitted after seeing the black soldier humiliated in New Orleans. Remembering how he had been denied the chance to sing at Professor Longhair's club, he flirted with a glib analogy between his temporary frustrations and the exclusions faced daily by African Americans like his GI pal in the 1960s. "I had experienced . . . pain created by the same prejudices that had affected him. I thought I was really seeing the real thing in Mississippi when I had seen the segregated toilets for coloured and white folks but now, I saw what he had really been through."[53]

For the most part, though, Burdon steered well clear of this kind of simplification, recognizing the huge gulf between the plight of moderately disgruntled young white Brits and the systematic racial oppression against which African Americans struggled. If anything, Burdon and his bandmates tended to draw imaginative analogies based on region, not race, to explain the transatlantic appeal of the blues. For example, Burdon met John Lee Hooker when the Animals, then still known as the Alan Price Rhythm and Blues Combo, supported him at Newcastle's Club A-Go-Go in 1963, and again in Detroit in 1964. According to Burdon, Hooker "told me we had a bond thicker than white or black because of where we had been born—him from Clarksdale, Mississippi, and me from Newcastle, a gritty, working-class city he always said could have been situated right in the heart of the deep American South."[54] Here Burdon explicitly linked his own geographic and class roots to John Lee Hooker's southern origins, neatly bypassing the bluesman's relocation to Detroit—on the face of it a more promising comparison with Newcastle—in order to locate common ground with the U.S. South.

John Steel also found several points of literal, as well as metaphysical and emotional contact between Tyneside and the Delta. Miners and shipbuilders on the Tyne and sharecroppers and day laborers in the fields of Mississippi were all, in Steel's mind, commensurate laboring classes, doing "the big dirty jobs." Moreover, the South since the Civil War had an ambiguous status within the nation. It was both emphatically part of and yet in many ways still palpably different from the rest of the nation in terms of social organization, religious and cultural predilections, economic basis, and historic memory. Newcastle also experienced its own sense of social and cultural marginalization within England, due to its distance from the main center of national political, economic, and cultural power in London. "The North East corner where we come from is a bit isolated from the rest of England," explained Steel, arguing that it was this sense of embattled isolation, of outsiderness, that helped to nurture a powerful attachment to place, community, and local cultures, but also an emphasis on individualism and self-reliance—precisely the kinds of qualities associated with the blues, the South, and its African American practitioners.[55]

Conclusion: Where the Blues Is From

By the late 1960s the British blues boom had entered a new phase. Groups like Cream, Ten Years After, Fleetwood Mac, and Led Zeppelin, as well as veterans such as the Rolling Stones, were using the blues as points of musical departure but rarely seeking to replicate the sound of their African American idols in quite the way that the vanguard groups of 1964 had tried to do. Burdon joined this trend. He launched a new group, Eric Burdon and the Animals, and experimented with a psychedelic progressive rock-soul-folk fusion that peeled further away from the Animals' original blues template. As he headed off in new musical directions he reflected on what he had actually done for a living in the early 1960s when he quite deliberately tried to sing like a black man: "I was trying to express myself in the past, but I was also trying to escape. I wasn't being myself. It wasn't me that was singing. It was somebody trying to be an American Negro."[56]

It is commonly held that Burdon and the Animals executed this mimicry better than any of their contemporaries. Much was made at the time and even more has been written subsequently about whether whites can really sing or play the blues. Paul Oliver stated the conventional wisdom among blues cognoscenti in 1960 when he stated: "Only the American Black, whether purple-black or so light skinned as to be indistinguishable from his sun-tanned white neighbour, can sing the blues."[57] There was some agreement that exceptionally sensitive and gifted white musicians might excel at instrumental blues: "I thought that white boys couldn't play the blues, but they were playing the hell out of the music," Little Walter told *Melody Maker* in 1964. But the consensus was that whites rarely mastered the blues vocal idiom. "A lot of these white boys play the blues real good," admitted Honeyboy Edwards, but "most can't sing a thing."[58] With his cavernous bellow and an enunciation that Geoffrey Cannon, looking back at the British acts who had spent the 1960s "playing at Negroes," characterized as "simultaneously Newcastle and Southern," Burdon was generally held to be among the best, as in the blackest-sounding, of British blues vocalists, while "The Animals played the solidest and purest rhythm'n'blues."[59] Burdon "has richly deserved his reputation as an astonishingly authentic rhythm and blues singer," claimed Bob Brunning, briefly bassist with Fleetwood Mac and the Savoy Brown Blues Band and an early chronicler of the British blues boom.[60] Animals biographer Sean Egan agreed: "The Animals clung to their roots with the determination of purists—sounding more uncompromisingly black than any of the countless bands who saw chart action in the wake of the Beatles, including the Rolling Stones."[61]

By 1967, however, it troubled Burdon that the roots to which the Animals clung so tenaciously really belonged to somebody else. Distressed by what he thought of as an almost existential act of bad faith by performing in black voice, his dilemma revolved less around how well he could sing the blues than around whether white British artists should ever try to express themselves using the music of a community of which they were not members, grounded in historical experiences they would never fully understand, let alone share. "I'm white, English. I have my own brand of feeling and soul . . . every country has its own soul and there's a terribly wrong conception of what soul means," he explained. "As soon as you mention the word soul, everybody thinks of American Negroes and it's entirely wrong. Even the Germans have got their own brand of Nordic soulfulness."[62] He had stopped imitating his African American heroes and finally found his own voice: "Now I am singing blues of my own mind, 1967 blues, my own blues."[63]

In the late 1960s, then, Eric Burdon was gamely trying to reconcile, or at least juggle, two modes of analysis that have dominated scholarly and popular commentaries on the meaning and appeal of the blues. In crude terms, one model has privileged the music's transcendent qualities: "Blues is a universal language," claimed Michael Bane.[64] The other model has interpreted the core meanings of the blues primarily in terms of their connections to the experiences of African Americans. In 1967, Eric Burdon mobilized both models. On one hand, he recognized the geographic, national, and racial specificity of particular musical forms and the uniqueness of their animating spirit. There was, he argued, something inimitable about African American blues styles because they were grounded in socio-historic experiences with which white Englishmen might empathize, or draw comparisons, but that they ultimately did not share. Burdon had suggested as much in 1964 when he imagined Bo Diddley comically dismissing the Animals as "the biggest load of rubbish I ever heard in my life" at the climax of the Animals recording "The Story of Bo Diddley." In a similar vein, the Rolling Stones had cautioned "those who listen to groups like ours, and think we are originators . . . Don't listen to us. Listen to the men who inspire us. Buy their records."[65] Here was a sanguine recognition that, in so far as young white blues pretenders initially strove to reproduce faithfully the sounds and affective power of their idols, they knew they were doomed to fail. Those "failures," thanks to an inscrutable mixture of chance, inspiration, technical ineptitude (and technical brilliance), and the confluence of diverse musical influences from far beyond the blues, could generate important new musical hybrids.

On the other hand, Eric Burdon also embraced the universal qualities frequently associated with the blues. On "It's All Meat," a track from the 1967 album *Winds of Change*, he speculated on "Where the blues is from" and concluded "The blues is from the whole wide world / Deep within the souls of men."[66] Here Burdon was closer to the majority of his British peers whose efforts to define the blues and explain its attractions routinely emphasized truth and honesty, the sheer corporeal and emotional power of the music over its formal characteristics or the racial and regional circumstances of its production. "The blues is definitely not simply playing 12-bar themes with a specific series of chord changes . . . it's a feeling," insisted British blues musician and impresario Alexis Korner.[67]

Paradoxically, however, even when privileging what Leighton Grist has called "the emotive and the ineffable" aspects of the blues, British admirers like Korner still unwittingly recycled venerable white stereotypes about the essence of African American—especially male—identity and culture.[68] In most white British imaginations "real" blues music was routinely celebrated as instinctive not calculated, visceral not cerebral, raw not refined, natural not manufactured, sexually explicit not coy. While such associations were not exactly unfounded, they aligned the blues into preconceived racial stereotypes and encouraged a very restricted view of what constituted "real" black music. These racial stereotypes dovetailed neatly with regional stereotypes that held up the South as a permanent, largely primitive, and somewhat dangerous "other." The region was the focus of a host of "projective fantasies" in which it appeared as a repository of archaic and anarchic, yet also highly seductive and enviably uninhibited habits and practices.[69] At a historic moment when there was palpable frustration among young Brits—in 1956 five million of them, including the Animals, were aged between 15 and 24, sharing a disposable income of £1.5 billion that provided the economic fuel for the blues boom—with what

Grist described as the "increasing bureaucratization and rationalization" of British life, images of a rowdy, rebellious, and hedonistic South, with its stoic, individualistic, and sexually prodigious blues heroes, were particularly appealing.[70]

The real point here is that British preoccupations with the kinetic and emotional coordinates of the blues could encourage a disingenuous and potentially racist disavowal of the music's unique relationship to the black experience and a romanticized view of the South, miraculously emptied of white racism. Eric Clapton, for example, recalled that the blues went "straight to [his] nervous system," contending that "The blues is actually more of an emotional experience than one exclusive to black or white, or related to poverty."[71] In seeking to master the idiom, Clapton had tried to imagine the minutiae of a bluesman's life, "what kind of car he drove," but extraordinarily did so with "no idea there was a racial thing involved."[72] Unable or unwilling to recognize the material circumstances from which the blues emerged, Clapton preferred to invoke the universal qualities he found in the music. He even insinuated that his indifference to the blues' racial provenance reflected his own racial enlightenment. In a rather defensive passage in his autobiography, written to counter enduring criticisms of drunken remarks he had made on stage in Birmingham in 1976 in support of Enoch Powell's scheme to repatriate immigrants from Britain's new, as in colored, Commonwealth, Clapton admitted that he "had never really understood or been directly affected by racial conflict; I suppose being a musician helped me to transcend the physical side of that issue. When I listened to music I was fairly disinterested in where the players came from, or what colour their skin was."[73]

By contrast, as this essay has shown, Eric Burdon and his fellow Animals were always interested in the racial and regional roots of the blues. Like most British blues fans in the 1960s, they were hardly immune to the visceral pull and honesty of the music. "We just had an instinctive emotional identification with black American blues," remembered John Steel.[74] Similarly, in a 1964 interview marked by the earnestness and respect with which the group discussed the meanings of the blues, Eric Burdon explained that "Negro music is very deep." But Burdon and his bandmates had always located the source of that profundity in a very specific sociohistorical reality. "It all stems from feelings of deprivation and is about the world of the negro," Burdon argued, thereby grounding the aesthetics of the blues, and their global, trans-racial appeal in the concrete realities of African American life and the music it spawned.[75] For Eric Burdon and the

Animals, averring the universal qualities and shared humanistic impulses in the blues did not diminish their ability to recognize the racism that profoundly affected the black worlds where the music originated.

Coda: The South Will Rise Again

This essay has focused principally on Eric Burdon's career prior to his relocation to the United States, but it is worth noting briefly that his interest in the blues, the South, the African American experience, and race relations did not vanish. Even his 1967 move to the West Coast, with the Haight-Ashbury district of San Francisco briefly assuming a quasi-utopian status in Burdon's imagination, was in part due to a belief that some combination of drugs and counterworld living might cure the racial malaise he felt was engulfing the nation. "I don't want to see race hatred flaring into a full scale war—it's happening," he explained in September 1967.[76] These concerns punctuated his recordings for the next few years. The 1968 album *Every One of Us* was saturated with songs about race relations, including "White Houses" (bitingly contrasted with the "tumbled down black shacks over the tracks") and "New York 1963—America 1968," which featured an unaccompanied monologue about American racism by a black sound engineer. "The Immigrant Lad" offered a scrambled but sincere meditation on racial attitudes within Burdon's own white Tyneside community by depicting a young Geordie, newly transplanted to London, who is unnerved by the racial diversity of the capital.[77]

At the turn of the 1970s, a short-lived but prolific collaboration with the multiracial group War yielded a major hit single ("Spill the Wine") and a couple of successful albums including *The Black Man's Burdon*.[78] Burdon spent much of his time with War trying to coax his young black musical collaborators—the only other white member of the band was Danish harmonica player Lee Oskar—toward the blues, when their own tastes veered far more towards funk and rock. "They didn't listen to the blues and didn't want to play it," Burdon later recalled, appreciating that "American blues meant one thing to a group of black guys from Long Beach and quite another to people like me, Eric Clapton, Jimmy Page, and Keith Richards."[79] There was, of course, a certain irony in the fact that Burdon and his British peers were figured here as guardians of the blues tradition, working hard to encourage indifferent young African American musicians to take more interest in that part of their musical heritage.

By 1971 Burdon was recharging his own blues batteries by cutting *Guilty!* with one of his heroes, veteran Jimmy Witherspoon.[80] Although the album title might suggest lingering doubts about the ethics of his own performance style, in the years following his 1967 public crisis of conscience and consciousness, Burdon agonized rather less over whether his enthusiastic recasting of black blues and rhythm and blues vocal styles really constituted a disingenuous or even disrespectful form of modern minstrelsy. Instead, as he continued to record and tour, he preferred to stress the universal human appeal at the heart of all great music, seeing it all as available for pleasure and reinterpretation. He did, however, continue to ponder, to borrow the title track of his 2006 album, what constitutes the "Soul of a Man" and, more specifically, how best to express his own soul through music. And it was clear that the blues remained the touchstone for his art and expression of selfhood. The title track was recorded by Blind Willie Johnson and the album included a version of Howlin' Wolf's "Forty Four" to which, as Burdon painstakingly explained in the liner notes, he had humbly added new lyrics "to express the artist's feelings. No disrespect to the original version by the great Howlin' Wolf." Just as in his commercial heyday, Burdon reworked these old blues to find his own voice and meet his own emotional and artistic needs. Yet he remained fully aware that socio-historical factors meant that his needs were quite different from those of the songs' originators, even as he recognized a common bond of humanity with blues performers across time, space, and race. Burdon also retained the zeal of the hardcore enthusiast and collector of rare recordings, eager to parade his arcane knowledge, but also to evangelize about the music he had uncovered. In the same liner notes he explained how "Red Cross Store" had also been updated, noting that his rendition drew on three different versions of the song, all by southern-born bluesmen: Leadbelly, Walter Roland, and Mississippi Fred McDowell. Indeed, his affection for the South and for the New Orleans that had featured so prominently in "The House of the Rising Sun" remained undiminished. *Soul of a Man* is a post–Hurricane Katrina album poignantly dedicated to the battered "Crescent City": it proudly bears the legend "The South will rise again."[81]

Notes

1. The Animals, "Baby Let Me Take You Home"/"Gonna Send You Back to Walker," Columbia DB7427, 1964; Timmy Shaw, "Gonna Send You Back to Georgia," Wand 146, 1963. Sean Egan, *Animal Tracks: The Story of the Animals: Newcastle's Rising Sons* (London: Helter Skelter, 2001), 41.

2. Roberta Freund Schwartz, *How Britain Got the Blues: The Transmission and Reception of American Blues Styles in the United Kingdom* (Aldershot, UK: Ashgate, 2007), 135.

3. Chris Roberts, "Trend or Tripe," *Melody Maker* (January 5, 1963): 5. See also Schwartz, *How Britain Got the Blues*, 106–13; 137–39.

4. Geoffrey Cannon, "Transcending the Blues," *Guardian* 11 February 1969: 7. John Castle, "On the Record," *Record Mail* (April 1964): 2.

5. See, for example, Ulrich Adelt, *Blues Music in the Sixties* (New Brunswick: Rutgers University Press, 2010); Marybeth Hamilton, *In Search of the Blues: Black Voices, White Visions* (London: Jonathan Cape, 2007); Schwartz, *How Britain Got the Blues*, especially 231–37.

6. Van Morrison, quoted in *Red, White & Blues*, Dir. Mike Figgis (Reverse Angle International DVD, 2003).

7. The Animals, "The House of the Rising Sun," Columbia DB 7301, 1964.

8. Hamilton, *In Search of the Blues*, 151.

9. Joseph Roach, *Cities of the Dead: Circum-Atlantic Performance* (New York: Columbia University Press, 1996), 3.

10. Michael Heatley and Spencer Leigh, *Behind the Song: The Stories of 100 Great Pop and Rock Classics* (London: Blandford, 1998), 90. See also Ted Anthony, *Chasing the Rising Sun: The Journey of an American Song* (New York: Simon & Schuster, 2007), 145.

11. Eric Burdon with J. Marshall Craig, *Don't Let Me Be Misunderstood* (New York: Thunder's Mouth, 2001), 22.

12. Anthony, *Chasing the Rising Sun*, 20–21, 27; Helen Taylor, *Circling Dixie: Contemporary Southern Culture Through a Transatlantic Lens* (New Brunswick: Rutgers University Press, 2001), 92.

13. Burdon, *Don't Let Me Be Misunderstood*, 22.

14. Texas Alexander, "The Risin' Sun," Okeh 8673, 1928.

15. Tom Ashley and Gwen Foster, "Rising Sun Blues," Vocalion 02576-B, 1933.

16. Anthony, *Chasing the Rising Sun*, 29–30.

17. *Ibid.*, 56–57.

18. *Ibid.*, 75–83; Josh White, "House of the Rising Sun," *Strange Fruit* (set of 3 EPs), Keynote 125, 1942. Leadbelly cut at least three versions of the song: "In New Orleans" (1944), available on *Leadbelly: Absolutely the Best*, Fuel 2000 Records, 2000; "New Orleans (Rising Sun Blues)" (ca. 1947), available on *Where Did You Sleep Last Night?: Lead Belly Legacy, Vol. 1*, Smithsonian Folkways CD-40044, 1996; and "House of the

Rising Sun" (1948), on *Leadbelly's Last Sessions*, available on Smithsonian Folkways SF CD-40068/71, 1994.

19. Nina Simone, "House of the Rising Sun," *Nina Simone at the Village Gate*, Colpix CP-421, 1962; Odetta, "House of the Rising Sun," *Sometimes I Feel Like Cryin'*, RCA LSP 2573, 1962.

20. Bob Dylan, "House of the Risin' Sun," *Bob Dylan* Columbia 08579, 1962; Hally Wood, "House of the Rising Sun," *The Folk Box*, Elektra EKL-9001, 1964; Egan, *Animal Tracks*, 42–44; Anthony, *Chasing the Rising Sun*, 133–55.

21. Hilton Valentine, quoted in Egan, *Animal Tracks*, 42; Josh White, "House of The Rising Sun," Brunswick 03749, 1946. The song also appeared in the UK on *Josh White Stories* (HMV CLP 1150, 1956) and *Singer Supreme* (World Record Club T298, 1964). Bill Wyman, *Blues Odyssey* (New York: Dorling Kindersley, 2001), 315.

22. John Steel, quoted in Egan, *Animal Tracks*, 42.

23. John Steel, quoted in Chris Phipps, John Tobler, and Sid Smith, eds., *Northstars* (Newcastle upon Tyne: Zymurgy, 2005), 159.

24. John Steel, quoted in *ibid.*, 42.

25. Anthony, *Chasing the Rising Sun*, 142–43 (Burdon quote, 143). Eric Burdon, interview with Brian Ward, 15 February 2006.

26. See Elijah Wald, *Josh White: Society Blues* (Amherst: University of Massachusetts Press, 2000), 172–76, 210–16, 218–21, 243–46, 275–76; Schwartz, *How Britain Got the Blues*, 35–39.

27. Humphrey Lyttelton, *Best of Jazz: Basin Street to Harlem* (London: Penguin, 1980), 72–73. For more on Broonzy's impact in the UK, see Schwartz, *How Britain Got the Blues*, 39–42; 100; 102–3; Wald, *Josh White*, 220–21.

28. Big Bill Broonzy, quoted in Ernest Borneman, "Big Bill Talking," *Melody Maker* (29 September 1951): 2.

29. Bob Reisman, *I Feel So Good: The Life and Times of Big Bill Broonzy* (Chicago and London: University of Chicago Press, 2011), 7 & facing, 166.

30. Lyttelton, *Best of Jazz*, 72–73; Wald, *Josh White*, 221.

31. Rex Harris and Brian Rust, *Recorded Jazz: A Critical Guide* (Harmondsworth, UK: Penguin, 1958), 44.

32. Val Wilmer, *Mama Said There'd Be Days Like These* (London: Women's Press, 1989), 33.

33. Muddy Waters, quoted in Harry Shapiro, *Alexis Korner: The Biography* (London: Bloomsbury, 1996), 44.

34. Paul Oliver, "Crossroads Blues," *Jazz Beat* (February 1965): 20–21.

35. Eric Clapton, quoted in Ray Coleman, *Clapton!* (1985; Warner Books, 1986), 26. Eric Clapton, *Eric Clapton: The Autobiography* (London: Random House, 2007), 40, 34.

36. See Schwartz, *How Britain Got the Blues*, especially, 17–128; Hamilton, *In Search of the Blues*, especially 125–97.

37. John Broven, "J.B. Lenoir," *Blues Unlimited* 15 (September 1964): 5.

38. Karl Michael Wolfe, "Scott Dunbar: Sing 'Em Everywhere I Go," *Blues World* 39 (Summer 1971): 3–7.

39. Hamilton, *In Search of the Blues*, especially 153–97. For blues and modernity, see also LeRoi Jones, *Blues People* (New York: William Morrow, 1963), 50–80; Leighton Grist, "The Blues is the Truth: The Blues, Modernity, and the British Blues Boom," in Neil Wynn, ed., *Cross the Water Blues: African American Music in Europe* (Jackson: University of Mississippi Press, 2006), 202–13.

40. Wolfe, "Scott Dunbar," 6.

41. Mike Leadbitter, "J. D. Miller," *Blues Unlimited* 47 (October 1967): 4–7.

42. *Ibid*. See also John Broven, *South to Louisiana: The Music of the Cajun Bayous* (Gretna, LA: Pelican, 1983), 252–53.

43. Leadbitter, "J. D. Miller."

44. Frank Scott, Letter, *Blues Unlimited* 49 (January 1968): 11.

45. Eric Burdon, "An 'Animal' Views America," *Ebony* 22 (December 1966): 166–71 (first quote, 166; second quote, 168).

46. *Melody Maker* (4 July 1964): 8; Burdon, "An Animal Views America," 168; Egan, *Animal Tracks*, 133; Burdon-Ward interview.

47. *New Musical Express* (24 July 1964): 14.

48. Burdon, *Don't Let Me Be Misunderstood*, 19.

49. *Ibid.*, 57. See also Eric Burdon, *I Used to Be an Animal, But I'm Alright Now* (London: Faber and Faber, 1986), 89–93.

50. Burdon, *I Used to Be an Animal, But I'm Alright Now*, 100.

51. *Ibid.*, 102.

52. Burdon, "An Animal Views America," 168.

53. Burdon, *Used to Be an Animal*, 102.

54. Burdon, *Don't Let Me Be Misunderstood*, 53.

55. John Steel, quoted in Egan, *Animal Tracks*, 11.

56. *Melody Maker* (15 August 1967): 5.

57. Paul Oliver, *Blues Fell This Morning: Meaning in the Blues* (1960; Cambridge: Cambridge University Press, 1990), 4. See also, Paul Garon, *Blues and the Poetic Spirit* (New York: Eddison, 1978), 61.

58. Little Walter, quoted in *Melody Maker* (26 September 1964): 8. David "Honeyboy" Edwards, Janis Martinson, and Michael Robert Frank, "*The World Don't Owe Me Nothing: The Life and Times of Delta Bluesman Honeyboy Edwards* (Chicago: Chicago Review Press, 1997), 196.

59. Geoffrey Cannon, "Playing at Negroes," *Guardian* (11 November 1969): 8.

60. Bob Brunning, *Blues: The British Connection* (1986; London: Helter Skelter, 2002), 68.

61. Egan, *Animal Tracks*, 60.

62. *Record Mirror* (26 August 1967): 12.

63. Eric Burdon, quoted in Bob Dawbarn, "The Ultimate Burdon," *Melody Maker* (7 October 1967): 5.

64. Michael Bane, *White Boy Singing the Blues: The Black Roots of Rock and Roll* (Harmondsworth, UK: Penguin, 1982), 160.

65. The Animals, "The Story of Bo Diddley," *The Animals* (Columbia 33SX 1669, 1964); "The Rolling Stones Write for Melody Maker," *Melody Maker* (2 May 1964): 3.

66. Eric Burdon and the Animals, "It's All Meat," *Winds of Change* (MGM 665084, 1967).

67. Alexis Korner, quoted in Bob Dawbarn, "You Don't Have to Be in Chains to Play Blues," *Melody Maker* (13 July 1968): 6.

68. Grist, "The Blues is the Truth," 203.

69. See, Leigh Anne Duck, *The Nation's Region: Southern Modernism, Segregation and U.S. Nationalism* (Athens: University of Georgia Press, 2006), 3.

70. Grist, "Blues is the Truth," 203; Peter Hennessy, *Having It So Good: Britain in the Fifties* (London: Penguin, 2006), 492.

71. Clapton, *Eric Clapton*, 33; Eric Clapton, quoted in Coleman, *Clapton!*, 28.

72. Eric Clapton, quoted in Harry Shapiro, "Wall of Sound," *Mojo* 53 (April 1998): 91.

73. Clapton, *Eric Clapton*, 99–100.

74. John Steel, quoted in Egan, *Animal Tracks*, 11.

75. Eric Burdon, quoted in *Record Mail* (July 1964): 7.

76. Eric Burdon, quoted in *New Musical Express* (30 September 1967): 11.

77. Eric Burdon & the Animals, "White Houses," "New York 1963—America 1968," and "The Immigrant Lad," *Every One of Us* (MGM SE 4553, 1968).

78. Eric Burdon and War, "Spill the Wine," *Eric Burdon Declares "War"* (MGM SE 4663, 1970); *The Black Man's Burdon* (MGM SE 4710-2, 1970).

79. Burdon, *Don't Let Me Be Misunderstood*, 107.

80. Eric Burdon and Jimmy Witherspoon, *Guilty!* (MGM SE 4791, 1971).

81. Eric Burdon, "Soul of a Man," "Forty Four," "Red Cross Store," and liner notes, *Soul of a Man* (SPV 78412, 2006).

10

Born in Chicago

The Impact of the Paul Butterfield Blues Band
on the British Blues "Network," 1964–1970

—Andrew Kellett

Many of the young British men who spearheaded the "blues revival" in the early 1960s came to coalesce around the London area and to form an interpersonal social network—a group of more or less like-minded young enthusiasts-cum-performers who were of a broadly defined generation and socio-economic class and who knew each other socially (or at least had mutual acquaintances). These young men appraised each other's work and relied on each other for the kind of inspiration, discussion, and criticism that has, historically speaking, often impelled cultural creativity. They were certainly not all friends, but generally regarded each other as peers, steeped in the same cultural inheritance and devoted to the same obscure musical idiom: African American blues and rhythm and blues (or R&B). Generally speaking, they fulfilled the role of what blues historian Francis Davis has called "hands-on preservationists"—that is, young devotees who strove, by performing and publicizing the blues, to spread what they felt was the gospel of the blues to an outside world that seemed not to know or care much about the music, its messages, or its most important practitioners.[1] Their efforts not only created a viable blues "scene" in Britain, but they also positioned themselves to bring their blues "gospel" to the music's homeland—the United States—as part of the so-called British Invasion in 1964–65.

To these British blues enthusiasts-cum-performers, who became convinced that white Americans knew little to nothing of the blues, the emergence of Chicago's Paul Butterfield Blues Band in 1964–65 presented an interesting riposte: the existence of white American "hands-on preservationists." Singer/harmonica player Butterfield and guitarist Michael Bloomfield were aspiring white bluesmen who received their musical education direct from the source—the blues clubs of Chicago, where they sat in and socialized with the likes of Muddy Waters and Howlin' Wolf. This was a kind of education that British blues enthusiasts could not initially hope to match. For the most part, the British worshipped the blues from afar, having first learned about the blues, and then learned to play it, from record albums, radio broadcasts, and fleeting personal encounters with their heroes. As I will demonstrate, Eric Clapton, Mick Jagger, Steve Winwood, and their compatriots on the British blues scene looked up to African American blues musicians as a coterie of adopted "fathers," and tried to portray themselves as their white "sons"—that is, as younger men who looked to their heroes for formative guidance, however ludicrous the geographic and economic distance between fathers and sons might have made that seem, and who vowed to carry on their heroes' musical legacy.

Butterfield and Bloomfield aspired to fill the twin roles of African American bluesmen's white "sons" and "hands-on preservationists" as well—and as they had grown up and learned to play the blues in Chicago they could be seen to have forged a much stronger personal rapport with their "father figures" than the British. This stronger personal affinity resulted in the British perception that the Butterfield band's music, especially on their eponymous debut album (1965), was also more technically proficient—that is, in the idea that personal closeness had led to closeness to the sounds, the structure and the "feel" of blues music that the British were unable to achieve. Whether or not this was actually the case, British musicians perceived that it was. Thus, the example of Paul Butterfield and Michael Bloomfield can provide an interesting counterpoint to the British musicians' sense of themselves, their relationship with their self-selected black blues "fathers," and their understandings of the effect of proximity and distance—that is, of being "born in Chicago" rather than in what jazz historian George Melly puckishly called "the Thames Valley cotton fields"—on ideas of musical "authenticity."[2]

Butterfield and Bloomfield's perceived successes in the role of black bluesmen's other white "sons" can be seen to have provided a spur to the British scene's continued musical development. By 1966, partly in response to the example of Butterfield and Bloomfield, numerous British groups tended to move away from blues "orthodoxy" and playing note-for-note homages to their beloved blues. Instead, they adopted a much looser approach to the blues—experimenting with its structure, combining it with other musical idioms and, by 1968, expanding on the blues' tropic and musical vocabulary and making longer, louder, and more aggressive "cover" versions.

The white American blues "scene" cannot, of course, be reduced simply to Butterfield and Bloomfield. There were numerous white blues groups (among them, the Blues Project, Canned Heat, and the Steve Miller Band) who became just as adept at recombining and innovating blues structures and tropes as the British. However, these bands largely entered the mainstream after Butterfield and Bloomfield, and though well-known, they did not exert the same influence as Butterfield during that crucial period (early 1966 to mid-1967) in which the British "scene" moved toward experimentation.

Most British rock bands did not abandon their love of the blues, as has sometimes been argued; nor did they stop believing that it was, in singer/keyboardist Steve Winwood's estimation, "an interesting, wonderful form" that needed to be brought to "people's attention." However, the tendency to do this by playing the blues exactly as it was played by Chicago and Mississippi's masters seems to have become less important, and the desire to use the blues as a "chair . . . to sit on" (in John Lennon's famous metaphor) more important.[3] This gradual paradigm shift was one of the socio-cultural factors that spurred the development of such varied musical idioms as hard rock, psychedelic rock, and—in the early 1970s—glam rock and heavy metal.

The "Thames Valley Cotton Fields": British Blues Enthusiasts

Beginning in the late 1950s and continuing into the early 1960s, a subset of mostly young, middle-class British men chose to embrace and appropriate for themselves aspects of both a musical style and a culture that—on the surface, at least—might have seemed diametrically opposed to their own: African American masculine blues culture. Growing up during the era of the Cold War and of British withdrawal from its global empire, dissatisfied with certain aspects of their white, middle-class inheritance, and in many cases in thrall to ideas of "America" and its mass consumer culture, these young men "affiliated" themselves (to borrow a concept from Edward Said) with this culture in preference to the culture they had grown up with. As consumed and interpreted by British enthusiasts, the blues seemed to provide an "authentic" alternative to the banal sentiments that were currently being offered by the pop music establishment in the late 1950s and early 1960s.[4] The blues seemed to speak directly and honestly, and with a hint of menace and danger, about classic tropes like sexuality, freedom, violence, and power.[5] The archetypal African American bluesman was perceived by his British acolytes as offering an alternative masculine ideal to which these young men could aspire—in short, a blueprint on how to be a man.

Finally, since the blues was part of the larger American culture (however oppressed and marginalized the form and its practitioners may have been), it provided a sort of back way in to America and its culture, vividly depicting American landscapes, structures, ways of life, and consumer goods. Like *films noir* and Western movies before it, the blues was seen as another point of entry for young Europeans yearning for some kind of interaction with American culture. In keeping with Said's concept, by consuming blues music, by forming their own ideas about what it meant (and what it could mean for their own lives), and then by forming fledgling blues bands to emulate it, these young Britons self-identified as the young, middle-class white "sons" of faraway, often much older African American "fathers" (most of whom had only the vaguest of ideas, at best, that they had been so adopted, and then not until much later).

British enthusiasts' education in blues music and culture was pieced together from three key types of media, acquired and consumed via various, often haphazard methods: record albums, radio broadcasts, and published material about the blues and the society that had spawned it. To these three were added sporadic live performances given by a few African American blues "fathers" in Britain during these years. Without access to all of the sources they might have had had they lived in the United States, and without a great deal of information as to how African American blues performers actually lived and worked, British enthusiasts came to develop their own peculiar understandings of the music they were worshipping from afar. For example, many of the young fans who became Britain's first transatlantic rock stars acquired a strongly held belief that blues lyrics were a form of autobiography—that is, that bluesmen actually lived the lives they sang about on their records, instead of merely speaking through an invented persona. So, to a young Eric Clapton or Jeff Beck, to be truly "authentic" as blues musicians would have meant actually having firsthand knowledge of the unique socio-economic environment of black America—feeling the kind of deprivation and heartbreak, and living the sort of rootless, wandering, devil-may-care lifestyle that they thought they heard Muddy Waters or Howlin' Wolf singing about. Said Clapton long after he had had the opportunity to replace idol-worship with actual flesh-and-blood friendships with men like Waters and Wolf, "I enjoyed the mythology surrounding the lives of the great jazz musicians, like Charlie Parker and Ray Charles, and bluesmen like Robert Johnson, and I had a romantic notion of living *the kind of life that had led them to create their music*" (emphasis added).[6]

Likewise, Keith Richards justified becoming re-addicted to heroin during the recording of the Rolling Stones' blues-soaked 1972 double album, *Exile on Main St.*, by telling his friends and bandmates that "the work required that level of decadence . . . that fantastic self-confidence to create that incredible work."[7] The British believed that knowing how black bluesmen lived, and then emulating that lifestyle themselves, was the only way to be true to that particular art form. And with that in mind, one can see how they might believe that their blues education, as eye-opening and electrifying as it had been, was somehow incomplete because they did not actually come from that social stratum, had not actually developed a close personal relationship with their tutors. It was as if they had taken correspondence courses as opposed to earning a post-graduate degree with a respected scholar.

This vaguely pessimistic self-assessment seemed to be periodically confirmed for them by interviews with actual African American blues performers in the British blues magazines they read. Interviewed by Geoffrey Smith as part of blues magazine *Crawdaddy*'s coverage of the 1965 American Folk Blues Festival, drummer Fred Below gave his opinion on the matter: "Before white men attempt to sing the blues, they must mix with the real Negro blues singers. They can't do it by just listening to records." Guitarist George "Buddy" Guy, who was at that point just starting to make himself a hero to Eric Clapton and Jeff Beck, agreed: "For white audiences to really appreciate the blues they would have to live for a while in a Negro neighbourhood."[8] This, then, formed part of the British performers' fundamental idea about their (in)adequacy and (in)authenticity vis-à-vis the blues, and can help explain why they reacted to the emergence of Butterfield and Bloomfield—two young white men who had "mix[ed]" and continued to "mix with the real Negro blues singers . . . in a Negro neighbourhood"—the ways they did.

Direct personal relationship with the blues or not, however, the approach of many British blues enthusiasts fits in with the concept of hands-on preservation, and it was in contrast to the prevailing ethos amongst folklorists and folk music revivalists on both sides of the Atlantic. In Great Britain this movement was led by, among others, Ewan MacColl and Bert Lloyd, whose overall goal was to resuscitate and preserve what they thought of as authentic folk traditions.[9] These revivalists felt that these traditions should be kept in the natural, authentic state in which they had rediscovered it, not corrupted by commercial influences or by people who did not come from the original cultural milieu that had produced the music in the first place. For example, only people of Irish descent could properly play Irish jigs or reels, or—more relevant to the current study—only African Americans could properly play the blues.[10]

The hands-on preservationists were of a younger generation than those they dubbed "the moldy figs," and shared their elders' desire that blues music be preserved, based on their perception that contemporary popular music had become, at least to Rolling Stones guitarist Brian Jones, "watered down." Where they differed from the moldy figs was in their ideas of who could or should play blues music, and for what reasons. These younger British enthusiasts, especially self-appointed evangelists like Eric Clapton and John Mayall, made the transition from avid listeners and amateur researchers to performers—a transition of which the older revivalists were openly contemptuous—because, very simply, they wanted to hear more of it, and if that meant playing it themselves in an unpolished, less-than-virtuosic manner, then so be it.[11] Furthermore, they felt the best way to preserve the blues was to expose more people to it than their own already enlightened network of *cognoscenti*. Keith Richards echoed Steve Winwood's earlier-quoted opinion with his own: the purpose of the Rolling Stones, he said, was "to turn other people on to Muddy Waters . . . to get a few [more] people interested in listening to the shit we thought they ought to listen to." In fact, even after 1964, when many British blues bands were enlisted and deployed as tuneful, polite purveyors of pop music by the British Invasion, many of them continued trying to spread the gospel of the blues in America even as they climbed the pop charts. To this end, the Rolling Stones and the Yardbirds made pilgrimages to record at Chess Studios, and the Stones refused to perform on the American TV program *Shindig!* unless Howlin' Wolf could perform as well.[12] Even the Beatles, who were not as directly influenced by Chicago blues as some of their countrymen, did what they could to raise awareness of the music. At the band's first Stateside press conference in February 1964, Paul McCartney said he wanted to see Muddy Waters, and reacted with befuddlement when a reporter asked him, "Where's that?"[13]

However, such an evangelizing mission was only possible so long as there existed an "authenticity gap" in the dominant culture. When the mainstream popular music of the day was perceived as banal, saccharine, and without much in the way of deep lyrical meaning, then the novelty of young, more-or-less educated Englishmen belting out impassioned note-for-note homages to the Chess and Atlantic catalogues had a certain resonance that was unavailable anywhere else. Thirty years later, R&B producer and entrepreneur Quincy Jones said that the British were so immediately successful because "they were students of American music, much more so than any American musicians were. And they gave everybody a run for their money."[14]

"Grown Up in It": Paul Butterfield and Michael Bloomfield

Although the British perceived white Americans as either completely ignorant of or hostile to blues music (and thus in need of the hands-on preservationists' evangelical mission), this was not entirely true. There were growing pockets of young white Americans who had heard and become enthralled with blues music, and who wanted to become students of it as well. Two of the most influential—in terms both of injecting more blues music into the American mainstream, and of acting as an indirect spur on the British blues-based bands—were Chicago's Paul Butterfield and Michael Bloomfield.

There were actually quite a few parallels in the early experiences of the white British and Chicagoan hands-on preservationists. It is hard to generalize the entire British scene, as opposed to only two white Chicagoans, but both sides grew up in comfortable socio-economic circumstances that firmly separated them from the African Americans who played and listened to the blues and R&B at that time. If anything, Butterfield and Bloomfield (the former the son of a lawyer, the latter the son of a wealthy entrepreneur) were at least a half-step up in economic class from the British blues enthusiasts, most of whom were lower middle class.[15] And both were introduced to the blues and R&B in much the same ways—by hearing it on records and on the radio. An important early divergence is in how each side supplemented their initial, non-live relationship with the blues.

Whereas British enthusiasts were restricted to sporadic live performances, during the course of which they were able to see Muddy Waters or "Big Bill" Broonzy a few times at most, Butterfield and Bloomfield were able, by virtue of living a train ride away, to forge a much stronger personal rapport with their idols. The two young blues fans (who were not as of yet aware of each other's existence) began to frequent the nightclubs and bars of Chicago's South Side, where many of the biggest names in the electric urban blues plied their trade every night.[16] Even entering an otherwise all-black club in the evening would without a doubt have taken a great deal of nerve, but Butterfield and Bloomfield eventually went beyond this; they would actually approach the bandleaders—whether Muddy Waters, Howlin' Wolf, "Sunnyland" Slim, or "Big Joe" Williams—and ask to sit in and play with their bands.[17]

Over time, they began to learn they were not the only whites sitting in on the South Side. Guitarist Elvin Bishop, a native Oklahoman who was studying physics at the University of Chicago, would come by to sit in, as would harmonica player Charlie Musselwhite, a transplant from Memphis.[18] Gradually, the newcomers earned the respect of the older musicians with their confidence and proficiency, and became more or less accepted as a fixture on the Chicago club scene. Of Butterfield, Bloomfield said, "If you wanted to play with some authority, you had to go down and prove yourself. You had to burn. [And Paul] wouldn't take no jive from nobody. And he held his own. God, did he hold his own."[19] When one of the white bluesmen entered the club, Waters or Wolf would smile at them—the precise moment where the displeasure of the bandleaders could have gotten the interloper ejected or worse—and announce their presence to the audiences.[20] In time, Waters began inviting Butterfield, Bloomfield, Bishop, and Musselwhite to his home—where, incidentally, about half his band also lived—for some of his wife Geneva's "down-home" cooking.[21] Waters, whose extreme graciousness was noted by many, and who admittedly may have been unique among black bluesmen in his regard for the young white players in their midst, frequently referred to another white harmonica player from Chicago, Paul Oscher, as his "white son."[22]

Sonny Boy Williamson II and the British

This was a level of intimate rapport that the British had not yet achieved, although some had, by 1964, met and performed with some of their idols on occasion. Appreciative of the warm reception they were accorded by British audiences as part of the wildly successful American Folk and Blues Festival tour packages of 1964–65, American bluesmen like John Lee Hooker, Howlin' Wolf, and Sonny Boy Williamson II decided to stay behind after the festival and tour around Britain. This added touring was organized off-the-cuff and carried out on a shoestring budget—which meant that Chess Records, for instance, could not afford to retain their studio band in Britain to back up their bluesmen.[23] In stepped an inexpensive and easy-to-move talent source, practically begging to be tapped—young British blues bands. Of the numerous peculiar pairings that resulted, the most noteworthy, the most contentious—and arguably the most telling—was the shotgun marriage between Sonny Boy Williamson II and, in succession, the Yardbirds, the T-Bones, and the Animals.

By 1964, when he joined forces with his young acolytes, Williamson II was in his early fifties, had lost most of his teeth, and was drinking several bottles of whiskey a day.[24] Based on these facts alone, one might guess that his relationship with his young white acolytes would be uneven at best. Williamson II did seem to harbor a genuine respect and affection for Great Britain. He was touched by the fervent applause he received all over Britain and the relative lack of racism he encountered; he certainly enjoyed the paycheck, which was several times more money than he was used to getting playing the so-called "chitlin' circuit" in the American South.[25] Fond of Britain though he may have been, however, Williamson II seemed far less affectionate toward his backing bands. He came off to the Animals and Yardbirds as a condescending, mean-spirited drunk who berated them for their onstage failings (which, it should be noted, were as often his fault as they were theirs) and, on one occasion, pulled a knife on them in the dressing room.[26]

The final indignity came after Williamson II got back to Arkansas, when he confided in another band of young white admirers, the Hawks, that "these British kids, they want to play the blues so bad . . . and they play the blues *so bad!*"[27] The British tried to put a brave face on it; Clapton told blues chronicler Peter Guralnick in the 1980s that he allowed himself the comforting thought that, by doing their best and letting their very heartfelt sincerity show through, the Yardbirds and the Animals did in the end manage to earn Williamson II's grudging approval.[28] But the point remains: at this formative stage in their creative development, British blues enthusiasts' "affiliated" father figures seemed to have bestowed their approval on their other, closer-to-home white "sons"—Butterfield and Bloomfield.

Blues "Sibling Rivalry": Differences in British and American Experiences

It is clear that both British and white Chicagoan blues enthusiasts viewed Waters, Wolf, Hooker and Williamson II as their adoptive father figures, and wanted the African Americans to view them as adoptive sons. Reflecting before his death in 1981, Bloomfield said:

> A lot of those cats were old enough to be my father. And . . . several guys took to me almost like I was their son—Big Joe Williams, Sunnyland Slim and Otis Spann. They took me to be like their kid, man; they just showed me from the heart. They took me aside and said, "You can play, man. Don't be shy. Get up there and play." What I learned from them was invaluable. A way of life, a way of thinking . . .[29]

On the British end, we have, among numerous similar testimonies, that of Andy McKechnie, guitarist of a London blues group called the T-Bones, who served as Howlin' Wolf's backing band at a dozen or so performances on Wolf's 1964 British tour. McKechnie attested that "what [Wolf] had to offer to a very young bunch of boys was so very touching—not just in the music field, but [also] heart-to-heart father-like instructions for a good life."[30] Giorgio Gomelsky, onetime manager of both the Rolling Stones and the Yardbirds, illustrates how that same attitude was shared by others on the British scene by relating an event that occurred in his living room in 1964: Howlin' Wolf, Willie Dixon, and Sonny Boy Williamson II sitting on his sofa, imparting wisdom to a small knot of young British acolytes including Jimmy Page and Eric Clapton, seated respectfully at their feet.[31]

So both sides wanted to view their relationship with African American bluesmen as paternal/filial, and certainly both sides did have the chance to forge such relationships, however uneven the results. There are, however, major differences between the experiences of Butterfield and Bloomfield and, say, Clapton and Burdon. For one, the British relationship with African American bluesmen was, at this early stage at least, not nearly as sustained. For those Britons not fortunate enough to be able to barnstorm the country backing up Wolf or Williamson II, there were only brief encounters backstage, in hotel rooms, and at nightclubs. The visiting bluesmen were usually only in Britain for a few weeks at the very most, and only ever came across the ocean a precious few times. Conversely, Butterfield and Bloomfield were able to perform and socialize with their heroes much more easily and frequently, since they all lived in the same city.

It was not only the frequency of the encounters, however, that made it difficult to develop a really intimate rapport between African American "fathers" and aspiring British "sons"; it was also where they took place. None of the aforementioned venues were anything even close to the bluesmen's "home turf," as would have been the South Side blues clubs with which they were more familiar—to say nothing of Muddy Waters's own kitchen. On the road, African American bluesmen were sometimes uncomfortable with their accommodations, and definitely uncomfortable with their unfamiliar surroundings—as are many first-time and infrequent travelers abroad. Thus, British tours might have provided less opportunity for the bluesmen to truly accept their young white acolytes, open up to them, and invite them into a more intimate relationship, than they were able to do with Butterfield and Bloomfield. Over time and the course of dozens of trips back and forth across the ocean, quite a few British blues musicians would develop the close personal relationship for which they hungered. Eric Burdon became close friends with John Lee Hooker, as did Clapton with Howlin' Wolf and Buddy Guy.[32] But it is crucial to note that, as of 1965, the time of the Paul Butterfield Blues Band's seismic emergence on the transatlantic blues scene, the British had not yet reached this level.

It is also crucial to recall, as mentioned earlier, that we are talking about British perceptions—and how those perceptions influenced what they thought, did, and said, not necessarily how things existed in reality. British blues enthusiasts had no real way of knowing whether or not "growing up in it" (as Howlin' Wolf said) would have resulted in greater blues authenticity (or even greater technical skill). And they had no real idea what their blues "fathers" honestly thought about a bunch of young, middle-class white men from either side of the Atlantic claiming to pay homage to their music, and whether or not they could or should do this. For example, it is not clear that Sonny Boy Williamson II actually had no respect for his British backing bands, or even if he did, what combination of factors led him to hold those views. Nor is it clear what Muddy Waters actually thought of Butterfield and Bloomfield coming and sitting in with his band. He tolerated them graciously, of course, but getting at why he did so would require getting at a knot of racial and personal motivators that Waters himself may not even have been able to unravel. It could very well be that, as white guitarist/singer Nick Gravenites asserted, African American performers and patrons humored their white guests, realizing that if they did not (and especially if things escalated), the repercussions from the police or local government could be worse for them than for the white interlopers.[33]

Finally, there is the flipside of having close personal contact with one's idols—the opportunity it might provide for one to be directly discouraged by those idols. British enthusiasts may have longed for the ability to get to know Muddy Waters on a day-to-day basis; but isolated in Britain, they would have had no way of knowing, for instance, that Muddy Waters had at one point in the early going warned Paul Butterfield that the latter was "not yet man enough to sing the blues."[34] Conversely, Mick Jagger, not having had this man-to-man chat with his idol, was free to develop a vocal style that might not have qualified as authentic, but which has certainly proved compelling enough to help keep Jagger, and his band, a going concern for almost fifty years.[35] In reality, there might not be much truth to the claim that learning the blues the way Butterfield did (through a direct personal rapport with African American musicians) was superior to the way the British enthusiasts did (from radio broadcasts and record albums).[36] However, the British *thought* that their way had been inferior, and they spoke and acted accordingly.

The Paul Butterfield Blues Band

If Butterfield and Bloomfield had stuck to merely performing with their idols, of course, the British never would have been troubled by their example—just as if the British had stuck to collecting obscure records and jamming together at art school, fifty years of popular culture would have been vastly different. But on both sides of the Atlantic, young white blues enthusiasts took the crucial steps of becoming hands-on preservationists—that is, of forming their own bands and making their own records. Encouraged by their successes sitting in with Waters and Wolf, Bloomfield and Butterfield formed their own bands, playing residencies at Chicago clubs such as the Fickle Pickle (which Bloomfield also operated), Big John's, and Magoo's. Butterfield scored an initial coup when he convinced Howlin' Wolf's rhythm section—bassist Jerome Arnold and drummer Sam Lay—to join his own outfit.[37] This lent Butterfield yet another perceived layer of credibility, as it made his the first racially integrated blues band outside of Memphis, where Booker T. and the MGs served as Stax Records' house band (and scored a nationwide hit with the instrumental "Green Onions" in 1962).[38] With the exception of the Ram Jam Band (featuring an African American ex-GI named Geno Washington on vocals) and the Savoy

Brown Blues Band, there were no top-flight British blues bands in the mid-1960s who could boast any nonwhite musicians in their lineups.[39]

As a condition of their recording contract with Elektra Records, Butterfield added Bloomfield as his lead guitarist, and the solidified six-piece band—Butterfield, Bishop, Bloomfield, Lay, Arnold, and pianist Mark Naftalin—recorded and released their eponymous debut album in 1965. The year before, Muddy Waters had told Bloomfield, who was interviewing him for *Down Beat* magazine: "I have a feeling a white is gonna get it and really put over the blues. . . . I know they can feel it, but I don't know if they can deliver the message."[40] The general impression on both sides of the Atlantic was that Butterfield's outfit might have done both—"felt it" and "delivered the message." The music on the album is powerful, capturing the energy and exuberance of the classic Chess sides that both American and British enthusiasts had listened to, spellbound, as adolescents.

Part of the revelatory nature of Butterfield's music was simply that it was electric; before this, white American musicians had rarely attempted to play the urban electric style of blues. Generally speaking, when blues was played by white Americans in the late 1950s and early 1960s, it was of the acoustic Delta variety, with a lone singer accompanying himself on an acoustic guitar: shades of the folk revival movement, quiet and properly reverential. It is important to stress that the British contingent was just starting to emerge from its first wave, where groups paid eternal lip service to their blues and R&B influences. So, in 1965, a band featuring young white men plugging in and playing forceful, up-tempo electric blues was a revelation.

However, *The Paul Butterfield Blues Band* was a challenge to the British not simply because it was electric, but also because it was so staggeringly well done. Critics were nearly unanimous in praising Butterfield and company for their instrumental skill and their proficiency in preserving and duplicating the classic Chicago blues sound. Perhaps this was to be expected; after all, two of their members had been part of Howlin' Wolf's band only a year ago, and the rest had sat in with Wolf and Waters frequently enough to pick up a few things. Butterfield's British counterparts were quick to contribute their favorable, if awestruck, assessments—sometimes at their own expense. Years after the fact, Eric Clapton told Peter Guralnick: "I had the first Butterfield album right after it came out. . . . I thought it was great. . . . I thought Butterfield was the first one that I heard who could come anywhere near it. My singing doesn't stand up to the test, 'cause I don't consider myself a singer. I still consider myself a guitar player, and I always did."[41]

Clapton's statement is interesting because it points to a distinction sometimes made between white guitar virtuosity and black vocal authenticity, a distinction that Waters himself made, and that Bloomfield subconsciously confirmed elsewhere. When asked by *Crawdaddy*'s Paul Williams in 1966 which blues guitarists he liked, Bloomfield named Clapton, Beck, and Alexis Korner along with a few Americans. However, when asked about singers, he did not mention a single Briton.[42] Thus, although both Butterfield's band and some of the British bands had virtuoso guitarists, only Butterfield's (at least in Clapton's opinion) also boasted a white singer who could "come anywhere near" an authentic sound.

In November 1966 the Paul Butterfield Blues Band traveled to Britain for a package tour that also included British R&B stalwarts Georgie Fame and Chris Farlowe. After the tour ended, the Chicagoans stayed on, like Sonny Boy Williamson II before them, to play two more weeks of club dates.[43] Fresh off the release of his much-acclaimed album, *Bluesbreakers with Eric Clapton*, John Mayall invited Butterfield into the studio to record an extended-play (EP) record with him.[44] Butterfield's band and the British blues network finally got to meet, and continued a social trend that started with Bob Dylan's first meetings with the Beatles and the Rolling Stones: when American and British blues or blues-influenced musicians met, no matter how much they felt intimidated or threatened by each other musically, they invariably came to like—or at least respect—each other, and were excited to get the chance to socialize, trade ideas, and jam together. Bloomfield, Beck, and Clapton had nothing but praise for each other's guitar work, and both sides enjoyed swapping stories about their experiences with their mutual idols.[45]

The example of the Paul Butterfield Blues Band helped to contribute to a kind of blues renaissance in the United States—or rather, it is more accurate to say, as Ulrich Adelt has, that it helped to contribute to a realignment of the blues-consuming market in this country along racial lines.[46] That is, white Americans became the major consumers for blues—whether white- or black-produced—while African Americans continued turning away from the blues toward other musical styles, such as soul. The popularity of the Paul Butterfield Blues Band and the British Invasion groups led audiences and record companies to accord greater attention to white American electric blues groups. Of the few that approached the Butterfield Band or the Invasion groups in terms of combining proficiency and mainstream popularity were New York's Blues Project, Boston's J. Geils Band, San Francisco's Steve Miller Band, and Los Angeles' Canned Heat.[47]

All of these bands were made up of committed young white men who initially had the same hands-on preservationist approach of Butterfield, Bloomfield, and the British bands. Danny Kalb, the guitarist of the Blues Project, was featured on a 1964 Elektra compilation of white acoustic blues players whose purpose was to showcase the blues and hopefully interest more white record buyers in the style. What is more, these young white Americans actively sought out and became personally acquainted with blues legends. Peter Wolf of the J. Geils Band developed a personal rapport with Muddy Waters and his band in the early 1960s by offering his services as an "impromptu valet," and his apartment as a hangout whenever the band was in Boston.[48]

These bands joined Butterfield's in becoming popular in the late 1960s (although J. Geils's first album was not released until 1970). Through their advocacy, they helped to introduce younger white audiences to blues masters like John Lee Hooker and B.B. King.[49] However, it would be too simplistic to argue the case that white American bands stood for being authentic and "getting it right," while the British side chose creativity and innovation instead. What actually happened was that the white Americans did not stay hands-on preservationists for very long, but instead mirrored their British counterparts and began to branch out from blues orthodoxy within months of their debuts. For example, the Blues Project expanded on, sped up, and retooled blues classics like Willie Dixon's "Spoonful" and constructed long psychedelic blues rock jams (one of which featured heavy use of the flute). Likewise, Canned Heat also began to stretch out, just as other psychedelic bands on both sides of the Atlantic were doing, and expand the blues' structural boundaries. Perhaps the best example of this is the eleven-minute psychedelic jam "Fried Hockey Boogie" (1968), which is a "cover" of John Lee Hooker's "Boogie Chillen" only in that it derives its main riff from Hooker's.[50] Finally, as will be discussed below, even the Paul Butterfield Blues Band made only one "orthodox" blues album—their debut—before embracing jazz and Indian musical influences.

Can't Be Satisfied: The British Move Toward Experimentation

Even if a sharp dichotomy should not be drawn between orthodox white Americans and innovative Britons, it is true that (with the exception of

Butterfield) the aforementioned American groups either had not yet released their debut albums or had not embarked upon the kind of experimentation just discussed until 1966 or after—by which time many notable British blues rock stars had already started moving in that direction. In the aftermath of *The Paul Butterfield Band*'s 1965 release and its impact on the British scene, there seemed to be very little chance of British bands being able to match the kind of close personal tutelage that, in the minds of the British, Butterfield and his band had already enjoyed to great result. Thus, there seemed little point in trying to match the Butterfield Band's technical proficiency or fidelity to blues structures and tropes.[51] In response, the British bands took the bold step of abandoning hands-on preservationism and aiming instead to reconstruct and innovate the blues. Thus, they turned what might have been perceived as an inadequacy into a virtue.

The seeds for an anti-purist strain of British blues were sown with the very methods by which the blues and other forms of American music were transmitted to Britain in the first place. The British were separated from the social circumstances that had produced varying types of American music, and absorbed it at will, without worrying whether it was defined as jazz, blues, R&B, or soul. Admittedly, in the beginning, authenticity and orthodoxy were qualities for which both sides strove, because the mission of spreading the blues "gospel" was so important. But there was always the impulse among the most creative British performers to regard straight purism as somewhat limiting, and to think beyond it. This impulse comes out in Eric Burdon's discussion of the genesis of their first major hit, "House of the Rising Sun." The idea to remake the old folk chestnut in the particular way in which they did came on an early American tour in support of Chuck Berry. Burdon said, "I realized that if you tried to out-rock Chuck Berry, you're wasting your time. So I was looking for a song that . . . would have a different feel to it, but that would [instead] be very erotic, very atmospheric."[52]

The impulse to experiment, however, was often reined in by British bands that felt that the blues originals needed to be treated with respect. In 1968, thinking back on the early days of the band, Mick Jagger told *Rolling Stone*'s Jonathan Cott: "We were blues purists who liked ever so commercial things but never did them on stage because we were so horrible and so aware of being blues purists."[53] In a way, the counterpoint provided by Butterfield was creatively liberating; if Butterfield and Bloomfield provided greater orthodoxy from a pair of white enthusiasts, then that meant British blues enthusiasts could indulge their more creative and commercial impulses.

Evidence that the British were beginning to tread a different musical path from the orthodoxy they thought they heard in Butterfield's work can be seen in a 1966 blues rock anthology released by Elektra Records, *What's Shakin'.* The anthology was conceived by Elektra producer Joe Boyd as an attempt to offer listeners a sampler of offerings from various blues- and folk-rock bands on both sides of the Atlantic. The first half of the anthology features tracks from American groups the Lovin' Spoonful, the Blues Project, and the Paul Butterfield Blues Band. For the second half, Boyd enlisted Eric Clapton to help him put together an all-star British blues band, which included Clapton, Paul Jones and Jack Bruce (of Manfred Mann), and Steve Winwood (of the Spencer Davis Group). The group called itself the Powerhouse, and Clapton saw the project as a sterling opportunity to match his talents, and those of his countrymen, up against those of the Butterfield Band, especially seeing as Butterfield's band had contributed a version of "Good Morning Little Schoolgirl" to the anthology. Clapton and his first band, the Yardbirds, had released their own version of the blues classic as their second single in 1964.[54]

In many ways the Powerhouse's three contributions to the Elektra anthology are indicative both of the ways in which British blues had already developed, and of the ways in which it would continue to develop in response to the seemingly more orthodox Butterfield and Bloomfield. "I Want to Know" was an original composition (written by Paul Jones's wife, Sheila MacLeod) that bore enough similarities to the Chicago style that Boyd mistakenly thought it was by bluesman Otis Rush. "Stepping Out" was an instrumental piece, originally by Memphis Slim, but was reworked by the Powerhouse into an extended jam that fused elements of jazz to the original blues format. For the third and final track, Boyd and Clapton wanted something that would showcase Clapton's guitar proficiency. Boyd suggested Robert Johnson's "Cross Road Blues"; Clapton countered with Johnson's "Travelling Riverside Blues." Rather than choose, they simply fused deconstructed portions of both songs together, calling the resulting mélange "Crossroads." None of these is a faithful re-creation, but they retain enough of the originals to serve as a basis for the British penchant for reconstruction and experimentation. The *What's Shakin'* anthology, though perhaps not as well-known as other recordings from this popular era, remains important from a music history perspective, as it points to trends in British rock music that would intensify as the 1960s wore on.[55]

Partly spurred on by the electric orthodoxy of the Butterfield Band, and partly by other developments on the music scene (for example, Bob

Dylan's "plugging in" at the Newport Folk Festival in July 1965), British rock musicians built on their existing tendencies, continuing to fiddle with the structure of the blues, and blending in as many outside musical and artistic influences as they could think of. The differences between the more orthodox approach of the Butterfield Band on their first album, and the looser, more experimental approach of the British blues bands, can be gauged by listening to British blues-based rock as it developed during the crucial nine-month period from March (when *What's Shakin'* was recorded) to December 1966 (when Cream's debut album, *Fresh Cream*, was released). In April, the Rolling Stones released the album *Aftermath*, the first to be composed solely of songs written by the Jagger/Richards songwriting team.[56] This continued a trend the band had begun the previous year, of including more of their own songs and less covers of blues and soul favorites.

However, it is not simply the fact that there are no covers on *Aftermath* that demonstrates the developing British approach; it is also the kinds of songs they included, and what sounds the band combined to make them. "Paint It, Black" combined Jagger's growing fascination with Bob Dylan's complicated songwriting and Brian Jones's interest in Indian sitar music (and in Eastern music more generally). Jagger and Richards reached back into Britain's Elizabethan past for the delicate love ballad "Lady Jane" (and reached across the ocean yet again for the Appalachian dulcimer that features in the background). Furthermore, the band attempted to cement their growing reputation as the "anti-Beatles" with the borderline-misogynistic "Under My Thumb"—but also pushed musical boundaries by having the multi-instrumentalist Jones play African marimbas on the track.[57]

That summer, Eric Clapton stunned the British blues rock scene for a second time by quitting John Mayall's Bluesbreakers and forming (with Jack Bruce and Ginger Baker) Cream. It has been suggested that the germ of this "experimental blues group" grew out of the *What's Shakin'* sessions, where Clapton paired with Bruce (and was supposed to have paired with Baker, who bowed out at the last moment). Clapton has recalled that "the initial agenda was that Cream was going to be a dada group," with "all these weird things" and "mad props" onstage.[58] This agenda never fully materialized, but the band's music, especially on their second album, 1967's *Disraeli Gears*, is far more experimental and given to deconstructing blues structures and themes than anything Clapton would have ever thought to do with Mayall in 1965. It had only been fifteen months since Clapton— a self-proclaimed "apostle of the blues"—had quit his previous band, the

Yardbirds, because he did not feel they were authentic enough, and now he was forming a group whose members claimed they wanted to bring a giant stuffed teddy bear onstage with them every night.[59] This is indicative of the sea change British blues rock was undergoing in 1966. (The Yardbirds, for their part, also embraced the swift move toward experimentation, releasing an album—late 1966's *Over, Under, Sideways, Down*—that includes guitarist Jeff Beck's heavy use of "fuzz box" for distortion, as well as his attempts to make his guitar sound like a sitar.)[60]

One can also identify the looser, more experimental approach of the British blues bands by comparing later recordings where white "sons"—whether Butterfield and Bloomfield, or the British—backed up their blues "fathers" on retreads of the latter's old hits. *Fathers and Sons* (1969) paired Muddy Waters (along with some of his band) with Butterfield and Bloomfield, who reunited for these sessions, while *London Sessions* (1972) saw Waters backed by a constellation of British rock stars (including guitarist Rory Gallagher, keyboardist Steve Winwood, and drummer Mitch Mitchell).[61] Both albums, along with the enormously controversial 1968 psychedelic offering *Electric Mud*, were attempts by Chess Records to sell Waters to younger, predominantly white audiences.[62] Of the three, *Fathers and Sons* is the most straightforward. Although Butterfield and Bloomfield had long since branched out from their former blues orthodoxy, there is still a great deal of faithfulness to the old Chicago style that readily suits Waters, who had seemed somewhat lost when attempting to front an "acid" jazz band the year before.[63]

On the other hand, *London Sessions*, in the words of Waters's biographer Robert Gordon, "brings a modern sensibility to Muddy's blues, updating his updated blues."[64] Listeners familiar with the classic Chess sides are more likely to immediately recognize the workouts given to them by Waters, Butterfield, and Bloomfield on *Fathers and Sons*. The differences were apparent not just to listeners, but also the blues "fathers" themselves. After the sessions were finished, Waters, gracious as always, praised his British acolytes to interviewer Peter Guralnick as "top musicians . . . [who] can play with me." However, "that ain't what I need to sell my people; *that ain't the Muddy Waters sound*" (emphasis added).[65]

Howlin' Wolf, who also recorded a *London Sessions* album in 1971, with similar backing from his British "sons," was a bit more direct when it came to what was and was not the "Howlin' Wolf sound," growing irritable during the sessions at the British propensity to take liberties with the blues. Said Eric Clapton, who played guitar on the record: "His attitude was the same as Sonny Boy's. You know, like, 'We're going to do "Little Red Rooster" and it goes like *this*. And it doesn't go like anything *you* think it goes like.' . . . You see, I was already going along a different path. I was a rock musician. *And it's not that I'd left my blues roots behind* [emphasis added]; it's just that I'd forgotten a lot of the ways things [actually] went."[66] In the end, at least according to Clapton, Wolf relented, and although he did take the time to walk the band through "Little Red Rooster," how he felt it *actually* went, the resulting album still mostly contains reconstructed and impressionistic takes on Wolf's hits.[67]

It can be argued that the British approach to, and treatment of, the blues is the one that ultimately won out in the end. Blues inflections and improvisations form the backbone not only of much of the rock music of the late 1960s and early 1970s, but also of such seemingly unconnected popular subgenres as heavy metal and glam rock. Even Butterfield and Bloomfield, as mentioned, began to stray from strict twelve-bar orthodoxy. On 1966's *East-West*, the follow-up to their eponymous debut, the Butterfield Band began blending their Chicago blues with jazz and Indian influences (primarily through the use of modal scales and "raga" rhythms). It is not unreasonable to posit that they were helped along in this direction by the British musicians, several of whom—Ray Davies of the Kinks, Jeff Beck of the Yardbirds, and George Harrison of the Beatles chief among them—had already started to incorporate these non-European influences in their work.[68] Almost immediately after *East-West* was released, Bloomfield left Butterfield to set up his own band, the Electric Flag. This band was an attempt by Bloomfield to realize "the music he heard in his head"—which encompassed the entire vast spectrum of American music "from Stax to Phil Spector to Motown."[69] Although short-lived (Bloomfield quit his own band after only a few months), the Electric Flag was a strong statement of where blues rock was going—away from twelve-bar purism and toward a vast array of other influences.

Conclusions

The Paul Butterfield Blues Band provide an interesting point of comparison: that is, how white musicians on both sides of the Atlantic responded to and "affiliated" themselves with African American blues music in the early to mid-1960s. Both were young white men of a markedly higher social class than most African American blues performers, and both aspired to fulfill the role of these bluesmen's white "sons"—with one set of sons coming to the blues from the other side of town, and another from across the Atlantic Ocean. The difference was that the prospective British "sons," who had to content themselves mostly with recorded and printed substitutes and only sporadic in-the-flesh encounters, could not initially develop a very close relationship with their adopted "fathers." Butterfield and Bloomfield, meanwhile, by virtue of having been born in Chicago, were much better able to meet and play alongside their idols in person, and—as Howlin' Wolf put it—"grow up in it." British blues enthusiasts were aware of the dichotomy between themselves and their potential "blues brothers" in Chicago. They developed an understanding of the blues as something that needed to be experienced firsthand, by living near, socializing, and performing with actual black blues musicians; and so, taking Butterfield's band as a foil, Britain's hands-on preservationists took some interesting and innovative steps.

The general direction of these bands was a deviation away from the purism and orthodoxy to which they had self-consciously adhered during the first years of the British blues boom. In undertaking this change in direction, British musicians showed themselves adaptable enough to be able to meet a musical challenge that might well have discouraged them from continuing to make the kind of music they wanted to make. In many ways, the example of Paul Butterfield and Michael Bloomfield, and the British responses to it, set a precedent for British blues-based rock music. When challenged by seemingly more authentic or orthodox American acts, the British responded on their own terms—with recombination, experimentation, and innovation—and not by trying to "out-authentic" them. It was neither so much that the British would stop borrowing, nor that they would stop using American influences as a foundation. If anything, the music produced by British bands in the 1970s is marked by an even greater amount of bricolage than that of the earlier decade.

What the transatlantic call-and-response between white Americans like Paul Butterfield and Michael Bloomfield and Britons like Eric Clapton and Steve Winwood really did for rock music was to help set the parameters for its continued evolution. As they felt they had been outflanked by Butterfield with regard to proximity to the blues—and thus to technical proficiency—British musicians opted instead to indulge their developing tendencies toward experimentation, to search for common ground between the blues and broader-based popular and folk idioms, and then to integrate them all to create music that was not technically blues, but could not be said *not* to be blues, either. It was during that crucial period between 1965 and 1967, when British musicians stopped worrying so much about their personal and musical proximity to, and distance from, the blues (to say nothing of whether or not they "sounded black"), and chose instead to recombine and innovate, using the blues as a foundation, that popular music became more of a two-way transatlantic dialogue.

Notes

1. Francis Davis, *The History of the Blues: The Roots, the Music, the People: From Robert Johnson to Robert Cray* (New York: Hyperion, 1995), 221.

2. George Melly, *Revolt Into Style: The Pop Arts in Britain* (London: Penguin, 1970), 88.

3. Steve Winwood, interview in *Red, White and Blues*, dir. Mike Figgis (2003); John Lennon, interview with Jann Wenner, in Wenner, *Lennon Remembers: The Rolling Stone Interviews* (New York: Straight Arrow, 1971), 66.

4. Edward Said, *The World, the Text and the Critic* (Cambridge, MA: Harvard University Press, 1983). I am grateful to Professor Adam Gussow, at the University of Mississippi at Oxford, for explaining this theory to me.

5. John W. Hellmann Jr., "'I'm a Monkey': The Influence of the Black American Blues Argot on the Rolling Stones," *Journal of American Folklore* 86, no. 342 (October–December 1973): 370.

6. Eric Clapton, *Clapton: The Autobiography* (New York: Broadway, 2007), 134.

7. Keith Richards, quoted in Robert Greenfield, *Exile on Main St.: A Season in Hell with the Rolling Stones* (New York: Da Capo, 2006), 99. This seems to have been a self-fulfilling prophecy: according to Greenfield, who lived in close proximity to the band while the album was recorded, nothing much of value was recorded or even written until Richard went back on the drug, from which he had been "clean" since the year before.

8. Fred Below Jr., and George "Buddy" Guy, interview with Geoffrey Smith, "The American Folk Blues Festival—1965," *Crawdaddy!* 6 (January 1966): 20–21.

9. Benjamin Filene, *Romancing the Folk: Public Memory and Roots Music* (Chapel Hill: University of North Carolina Press, 2000), 58.

10. Martin Carthy, quoted in Colin Harper, *Dazzling Stranger: Bert Jansch and the British Folk and Blues Revival* (London: Bloomsbury, 2000), 31.

11. Davis, *The Blues*, 222.

12. Stephen Davis, *Old Gods Almost Dead: The 40-Year Odyssey of the Rolling Stones* (New York: Broadway, 2001), 125–26.

13. Keith Richards, interview by Jas Obrecht, "Muddy, Wolf and Me," *Guitar Player* 27, no. 9 (September 1993): 90; McCartney's exchange with journalist quoted in Filene, *Romancing the Folk*, 123.

14. Quincy Jones interview in *Britain Invades, America Fights Back*, dir. Andrew Solt, episode 3 of *The History of Rock 'n' Roll*, prod. Quincy Jones, Bob Meyrowitz, and David Salzman (1995).

15. Jan Mark Wolkin and Bill Keenom, eds., *Michael Bloomfield: If You Love These Blues* (San Francisco: Miller Freeman, 2000), 12.

16. Mike Rowe, *Chicago Blues: The City and the Music* (New York: Da Capo, 1975), 212.

17. Ed Ward, *Michael Bloomfield: The Rise and Fall of an American Guitar Hero* (New York: Cherry Lane, 1983), 23.

18. Robert Santelli, "A Century of the Blues," in Peter Guralnick et al., eds., *Martin Scorsese Presents the Blues: A Musical Journey* (New York: Amistad, 2003), 45.

19. Bloomfield, quoted in Wolkin and Keenom, *If You Love These Blues*, 36.

20. Wolkin and Keenom, *If You Love These Blues*, 49; Howlin' Wolf (Chester Burnett), interview with Paul Williams, "Blues '66, Part One," *Crawdaddy!* (November 1966): 12–13.

21. Robert Gordon, *Can't Be Satisfied: The Life and Times of Muddy Waters* (Boston: Little, Brown, 2002), 187.

22. Peter Wolf, "Muddy, Wolf and Me: Adventures in the Blues Trade," in Guralnick et al., *The Blues*, 190–93; Paul Oscher, "The Gift," in *ibid.*, 224.

23. Ulrich Adelt, *Blues Music in the Sixties: A Story in Black and White* (New Brunswick, NJ: Rutgers University Press, 2009), 63; Charles Shaar Murray, *Boogie Man: The Adventures of John Lee Hooker in the American Twentieth Century* (New York: St. Martin's, 2000), 269.

24. Bob Brunning, *The British Connection* (New York: Blandford, 1986), 175. Williamson II's age has been verified since the mid-1960s, but, like so many other aspects of his character and back story, it was periodically subject to change, depending on Williamson II's audience and mood.

25. Horst Lippmann, quoted in liner notes accompanying CD box set, *American Folk Blues Festival 'Sixty Two to 'Sixty Five* (Evidence, 1995). The "chitlin' circuit" was a loose network of bars, nightclubs, and jook joints in the Deep South, which featured black performers for the entertainment of predominantly black audiences in the 1950s and 1960s.

26. Sean Egan, *Animal Tracks: The Story of the Animals, Newcastle's Rising Sons* (London: Helter Skelter, 2001), 37; Eric Clapton, *Clapton: The Autobiography* (New York: Broadway, 2007), 48.

27. Robbie Robertson, quoted in Robert Palmer, *Deep Blues* (New York: Penguin, 1981), 263. It is quite possible that the British heard this negative assessment directly from the Hawks, who, after becoming the Band, would forge their own personal relationship, with the Beatles, the Rolling Stones, Clapton, and Van Morrison later in the 1960s and 1970s.

28. Eric Clapton interview with Peter Guralnick, in "Eric Clapton at the Passion Threshold," *Musician* 136 (February 1990): 48.

29. Michael Bloomfield, quoted in Wolkin and Keenom, *If You Love These Blues*, 27–28.

30. James Segrest and Mark Hoffmann, *Moanin' at Midnight: The Life of Howlin' Wolf* (New York: Pantheon, 2004), 218.

31. Giorgio Gomelsky, quoted in Willie Dixon with Don Snowden, *I Am the Blues* (New York: Da Capo, 1989), 135.

32. Eric Burdon with J. Marshall Craig, *Don't Let Me Be Misunderstood* (New York: Thunder's Mouth, 2001), 52–53. One way to measure Clapton's closeness to Wolf is to note that, when the latter died in 1976, Clapton purchased his headstone. Clapton's rapport with Guy is demonstrated via a 2010 television commercial for the T-Mobile cellular phone company; when Clapton's custom "Fender Android" phone rings, it is a call from Guy, which Clapton answers with friendly enthusiasm.

33. As Gravenites put it, "[T]he blacks knew that whitey was crazy. Whitey couldn't take that kind of upfront shouting and screaming. Whitey'll pull a gun and kill ya. . . . The blacks were well aware of what would happen if the morning's headlines read, 'White student killed in bar brawl.' Somebody black would do time, hard time. Once you get used to what was happening, you realized that we were a whole lot more dangerous to them than they were to us." Quoted in Michael Bane, *White Boy Singin' the Blues: The Black Roots of White Rock* (New York: Da Capo, 1991), 187.

34. Davis, *Old Gods Almost Dead*, 91.

35. Robert Christgau, "The Rolling Stones," in Anthony DeCurtis, James Henke, and Holly George-Warren, eds., *The Rolling Stone Illustrated History of Rock & Roll* (New York: Straight Arrow, 1992), 240.

36. The example of '70s proto-punk rocker Iggy Pop serves as a good counterexample. In the late 1960s, when he was a middle-class white kid named Jim Osterberg, Pop also made a pilgrimage from his native Detroit to sit in with black Chicago blues bands. Yet there are probably not many who would consider what Iggy Pop did as a member of the Stooges (or later, in collaboration with David Bowie) to be "authentic" blues.

37. Not surprisingly, Butterfield was able to do this because he was offering substantially more money than Wolf. See Sam Lay, quoted in Wolkin and Keenom, *If You Love These Blues*, 86.

38. Robert M. J. Bowman, *Soulsville, U.S.A.: The Story of Stax Records* (New York: Schirmer, 1997), 67.

39. Martin "Jet" Celmins and Jeff Wat, "The History of Savoy Brown," The Savoy Brown and Kim Simmonds Official Website www.savoybrown.com/band4/html (accessed May 31, 2010).

40. Muddy Waters interview with Michael Bloomfield, *Down Beat* (February 1964), quoted in Gordon, *Can't Be Satisfied*, 187.

41. Eric Clapton interview with Peter Guralnick, in Guralnick, "Eric Clapton at the Passion Threshold," 48.

42. Muddy Waters interview with Robert Palmer, in Palmer, *Deep Blues*, 260; Michael Bloomfield interview with Paul Williams, in "Blues '66, Part Two," *Crawdaddy!* (November 1966): 10.

43. Christopher Hjort, *Strange Brew: Eric Clapton and the British Blues Boom, 1965–1970* (London: Jawbone, 2007), 63.

44. *Ibid.*, 78.

45. Michael Bloomfield interview with *Melody Maker* (October 17, 1966): 17; Clapton, quoted in "Blind Date," *Melody Maker* (December 24, 1966): 8.

46. Adelt, *Blues Music in the Sixties*, 18.

47. Ed Ward, "The Blues Revival," in DeCurtis et al., *The Rolling Stone Illustrated History* 343.

48. Wolf, "Muddy, Wolf and Me," in Guralnick et al., *The Blues*, 190.

49. Charles Keil, *Urban Blues* (Chicago: University of Chicago Press, 1991), 282.

50. The Blues Project, "Goin' Down Louisiana" (an updated Muddy Waters song) and "Spoonful" (a sped-up Howlin' Wolf song), both on *Live at the Café Au Go-Go* (Verve/Folkways, 1966); The Blues Project, "Flute Thing," *Projections* (Verve/Folkways, 1966); Canned Heat, "Fried Hockey Boogie," *Boogie With Canned Heat* (Liberty, 1968).

51. Howlin' Wolf (Chester Burnett) interview with Paul Williams, in "Blues '66, Part One," *Crawdaddy!* (November 1966): 7.

52. Eric Burdon, interview in *Britain Invades, America Fights Back*.

53. Mick Jagger, interview with Jonathan Cott, reprinted in Peter Herbst, ed., *The Rolling Stone Interviews: Talking with the Legends of Rock, 1967–1980* (New York: St. Martin's, 1981), 46.

54. Dave Thompson, *Cream: The World's First Supergroup* (London: Virgin, 2005), 81; Joe Boyd, *White Bicycles: Making Music in the 1960s* (London: Serpent's Tail, 2006), 112. Baker bowed out at the last moment and was replaced by Pete York of the Spencer Davis Group.

55. Hjort, *Strange Brew*, 41; Boyd, *White Bicycles*, 112; Thompson, *Cream*, 82. Clapton would play yet a third version of this song during his tenure with Cream (1966–68).

56. Mick Jagger, quoted in Davis, *Old Gods Almost Dead*, 163.

57. The Rolling Stones, "Paint It Black," "Lady Jane," and "Under My Thumb," *Aftermath* (ABKCO, 1966).

58. Eric Clapton, quoted in Thompson, *Cream*, 80.

59. Eric Clapton, interview in *Red, White and Blues*; Adelt, *Blues Music in the Sixties*, 65.

60. The Yardbirds, *The Yardbirds* (released in US as *Over, Under, Sideways, Down*) (U.S. release: Epic Records, 1966).

61. Muddy Waters, featuring Michael Bloomfield and Paul Butterfield, *Fathers and Sons* (Chess, 1969); Muddy Waters, *London Sessions* (Chess, 1972). *Fathers and Sons* also featured Donald "Duck" Dunn of Booker T. and the MGs on bass guitar.

62. Muddy Waters, *Electric Mud* (Chess, 1968). Although rock stars like Jimi Hendrix, Mick Jagger, and Jimmy Page loved the album, Waters himself dismissed it, calling it "dogshit"; quoted in Rich Cohen, *Machers and Rockers: Chess Records and the Business of Rock 'n' Roll* (New York: W.W. Norton, 2004), 176.

63. Gordon, *Can't Be Satisfied*, 206.

64. *Ibid.*, 294.

65. Waters, quoted in Peter Guralnick, *Feel Like Going Home: Portraits in Blues and Rock 'n' Roll*, 2nd ed. (Boston: Back Bay, 1999), 81.

66. Clapton, interview with Guralnick, "Eric Clapton at the Passion Threshold," 36.

67. Studio patter between Howlin' Wolf and session band [Clapton audible], "Little Red Rooster, Take 2," on Howlin' Wolf, *London Sessions* (Chess, 1971).

68. The Paul Butterfield Band, *East-West* (Elektra, 1966); Sandy Pearlman, "Patterns and Sounds: The Uses of Raga in Rock," *Crawdaddy!* 18 (January 1967): 5.

69. Bloomfield, quoted in Wolkin and Keenom, *If You Love These Blues*, 139.

11

"When Somebody Take Your Number and Use It"

The 1960s, British Blues, and America's Racial Crossroads

—Robert H. Cataliotti

In September 2008, the B.B. King Museum and Delta Interpretive Center opened in Indianola, Mississippi. The museum is built on the site of and connected to the only standing brick cotton gin in the state of Mississippi. In fact, King worked in this cotton gin as a young man prior to embarking on his now legendary blues career. It is no wonder that one of themes trumpeted in the museum is: "From Indianola to Icon." He embodies the self-made man that is so integral to the mythos of America as a land of opportunity. King's is a triumphant and genuine American rags-to-riches story. For the past forty years, a key component in that story has consistently credited the bluesman's interaction with British blues rock artists of the 1960s with reviving his career and facilitating his crossover from the diminishing realm of the African American rhythm and blues circuit to world icon status.

About three quarters of the way through the museum, which chronologically follows King's life along with the evolution of the blues and the cultural, economic, and social life of the Delta, the exhibits arrive at the era of the 1960s. There are displays that chronicle King's recognition of the credit and exposure he received from Eric Clapton, the Rolling Stones, and the Beatles, among others. The section also features a series of interactive panels that draw lines of descent and ascent between King and other major black blues guitarists and their white rock acolytes, apparently aimed at creating symbiotic stylistic relationships between generations and races.

Clapton is featured prominently in the museum's opening and closing films, testifying to King's mastery, Clapton's personal debt to King's innovations, their friendship, and the pervasive influence King has had worldwide. The story that King and other black American bluesmen tell is that this music that was forged in the flames of segregation, oppression, and exploitation during the first half of the twentieth century ironically emerged as a racial crossroads during the 1960s. American music exported to Britain and then re-imported to America played a significant role in the formation of this racial nexus.

Testimony to a cross-Atlantic blues exchange—both from black bluesmen and reciprocally from white blues rockers—has been stock in trade for blues histories since the 1960s. King claims in his memoir, *The B.B. King Treasures* (2005): "The black blues singers didn't make a big impact on society until the British groups, for example, the Rolling Stones, Cream, the Who, when these groups started to play the blues in the United States then it started to really become a very popular type of music. And it opened the door for a lot of the black blues singers and blues musicians like myself."[1] Although this might be an exaggeration, King found this interaction with British musicians so important to his career that one of the chapters of his autobiography, *Blues All Around Me* (1996), is entitled, "Did You Read What John Lennon Said?" referencing a *Rolling Stone* magazine interview in which Lennon evaluated his own guitar playing, stating, "Well, I wish I could just do it like B.B. King."[2] Coming from one of the sixties' most prominent rock stars, this remark has tremendous resonance for King. The bluesman's autobiography also points out the recognition American blues artists received from the Stones: "The Rolling Stones, for example, wouldn't stop talking about the bluesmen who inspired them. Keith Richards and Mick Jagger were scholars of black music. I think they felt the same way I did—that bluesmen deserved a wider audience. Through sheer conviction on their part, they helped introduce that audience to B.B. King."[3]

Clapton's influence in helping King and other bluesmen bridge America's racial divide is lauded as well: "Because this country is so predominantly white, it's only logical that white boys have had the most impact in keeping twelve-bar blues alive. Englishman Eric Clapton is devoted to the blues and never stops paying tribute to his masters. For that, I pay tribute to him. Eric is the number-one rock guitarist in the world and plays blues as well as anyone and better than most."[4] In addition to acknowledging the contribution that Clapton and other British blues artists made to his career, King characterizes Clapton, as the premier "rock guitarist," asserting that, regardless of commercial success or popularity, in the realm of the blues B.B. King is "the master," and that speaks volumes about his conception of his journey from that Indianola cotton gin to international icon.

Young British blues rockers initiated this mutual admiration society with a crusading fervor when they emerged in the early 1960s fired by radio broadcasts and, eventually, the collecting of imported blues records, along with a developing London club scene rooted in earlier traditional jazz and skiffle crazes. Also, increasingly through the 1950s, American bluesmen—Big Bill Broonzy, Josh White, Sonny Terry and Brownie McGhee, Muddy Waters with Otis Spann, Memphis Slim, Willie Dixon, Champion Jack Dupree, and John Lee Hooker—began to make their way to England for live performances. For aspiring British blues musicians, efforts to find blues sounds and information became a kind of search for a holy grail. The records they tracked down presented them with remarkably diverse approaches to the form, and these sounds opened up new worlds for them. Keith Richards of the Rolling Stones describes discovering the music of an artist like Muddy Waters as if it was a blues Rosetta Stone: "When I heard him, I realized the connection between all the music I'd heard. He made it all explainable. He was like a codebook."[5] The recollections of initial encounters with recorded sounds of black American bluesmen for Richards, Clapton, and other British musicians from this era are cast as a kind of mystical experience. It was serious, it was life-transforming, and it was totally unpredictable that sounds produced by black artists from the Mississippi Delta or the Southside of Chicago would have this impact on British youth.

The focus on recordings as the primary exposure to the blues for British initiates affected the reception of the blues because to some extent it minimized racial distinctions. Richards explains: "For example, nobody knew that Jerry Lee Lewis was white for ages; we only heard about it through the grapevine; nobody realized he was a blond Welshman from Louisiana. You'd go to a record store and there would be a picture of Chuck Berry, and then you knew."[6] The racial distinctions that seemed indelibly written into American society were an ocean away from the world where Richards and his contemporaries were immersing themselves in the sounds of Chicago, Memphis, New Orleans, and the Mississippi Delta. It is a perspective on the United States that, even today, is hard for Americans to grasp. People from outside the States often view artists like Chuck Berry and Jerry Lee Lewis as *American* artists, not black or white American artists.

This lesson is strikingly illustrated by James Baldwin in his essay, "Equal in Paris" (1955). Arrested at the same time as a white American, Baldwin, based on his experiences in New York, expects unequal treatment, only to find that French police have a different perspective on the two men: "For them, I was an American. And here it was they who had the advantage, for that word *Americain*, gave them some idea, far from inaccurate, of what to expect from me."[7] The young British musicians in pursuit of the blues during the early 1960s followed their blues crusade, like Baldwin's Parisian police magistrate, primarily from the perspective that the artists they were emulating were first and foremost Americans. In a way, the British blues rockers' reintroduction of the blues to a U.S. audience contributed to a redefinition of Americanness.

With increased opportunities to hear and perform with touring American blues artists, the young British musicians made considerable progress with their forays into the blues, but the ultimate challenge they faced was across the Atlantic. The impulse to spread the word, to preach the blues gospel, both in Britain and eventually—and maybe even more passionately—in America, was part of the agenda for many of these British bands. They were on a mission. Richards explains: "When we started the Rolling Stones, our aim was to turn other people on to Muddy Waters."[8] The incredible sensation caused by the Beatles and the ensuing British Invasion set the stage for British bands to bring the blues back home. Although they were more rock and roll/rockabilly/R&B than blues oriented, the Beatles insisted on giving credit to the black American artists who had inspired them. One of the most oft-repeated anecdotes from the Beatles' early American press conferences is an exchange between a reporter and McCartney, in which he said that he hoped to see Muddy Waters and Bo Diddley while in the States. The puzzled reporter responded, "Muddy Waters? Where's that?" The incredulous McCartney replied, "Don't you know who your most famous people are here?"[9] Clearly, to be hip to black music was one of the badges that these young musicians would wear. The blossoming youth rebellion of the 1960s had found its soundtrack. Of course, an association between rebellious white teenagers and black music, especially black music performed by white musicians, was nothing new.

The significant difference between British bands of the 1960s and white rock and rollers of the 1950s was their insistence that the original African American innovators get the recognition that was their due. Probably the most high profile example of this impulse to give credit to blues originators was the Stones' insistence that they would appear on the ABC television show *Shindig* to perform their smash hit "(I Can't Get No) Satisfaction" only if the network booked Howlin' Wolf along with them. Richards recalled: "The idea of working with the guy that brought you 'Smokestack Lightnin'—whoa! You're in awe. . . . Howlin' Wolf was a large guy with a very large heart. He didn't say a lot, but he didn't have to. . . . We were just surprised to be in America, let alone doing a TV show in L.A. with Howlin' Wolf."[10] On May 20, 1965, Howlin' Wolf made his American network television debut. He sang "How Many More Years" with the Stones sitting worshipfully at his feet and surrounded by dancing, young, go-go booted white girls. Stanley Booth, a music writer who eventually befriended the Stones and wrote *The True Adventures of the Rolling Stones* (1984) with their cooperation, watched the *Shindig* broadcast:

> The first time I saw the Rolling Stones, they were on television: five funny-looking boys on *Shindig*, one of the rock and roll shows that sprang up like mushrooms (and faded just as fast) in the wake of the Beatles 1964 invasion. I had seen the Beatles, but I thought Chuck Berry did his songs better. The Stones, though, got my attention because they had brought Howlin' Wolf. Whoever these guys are, I thought, if they with Wolf, they somebody.[11]

The blues credibility of the *Shindig* event received a further boost when the rediscovered Son House, along with his manager Dick Waterman, appeared on the set and was reunited with Howlin' Wolf. In his collection of blues photography, Dick Waterman relates that Stones lead guitarist Brian Jones approached and asked, "Who's the old man that Wolf is so happy to see?" When Waterman replied, "That's Son House," Jones replied, "Ahh, the one who taught Robert Johnson and Muddy Waters."[12] Clearly, this young Englishman had been doing his homework, for that kind of insider blues knowledge was not widely available in 1965.

Network television and *Shindig*, however, definitely were widely available, and thousands of young American popular music fans were able to witness the relationship that the Stones were setting up between themselves and older black bluesmen like Howlin' Wolf. It was a very clear and very public message: these people that have been invisible to you throughout the history of your country not only deserve to be seen, but they deserve respect and reward because they have produced something that is a towering artistic achievement, something that people from outside your culture have recognized, and something that you need to recognize. Howlin' Wolf had a number of singles which were hits on the American R&B charts in the early 1960s and would have been known to white blues enthusiasts like Stanley Booth, but the appearance on *Shindig* with the Stones brought Howlin' Wolf right into living rooms in middle-class American homes that were far removed—physically and culturally—from the sounds of the Mississippi Delta and the Southside of Chicago.

By 1966, a second wave of British blues influence on the United States took place with Cream leading the way. A new generation of hard-edged British blues rock bands such as Fleetwood Mac, Savoy Brown, and Ten Years After were regularly featured on the same bill as American blues rock artists and African American blues originators. For many black bluesmen these mixed bill concerts became the first venues where they could reach white listeners. In 1969 the Stones, encouraged that rock audiences were listening rather than screaming as in the days of the British Invasion, embarked on an American tour for which they handpicked black blues and R&B acts to open the shows: B.B. King, Chuck Berry, and Ike & Tina Turner. From King's perspective, the Stones' tour opened the door to a world from which he and his music had been largely excluded:

> When [the Rolling Stones and I] played Baltimore, there was a white lady that came up with her children and she said, "You're B.B. King." I said, "Yes ma'am." She said, "Have you ever made any records?" I said, "Yes ma'am." She said, "Well, my kids and I like what you did. Can you tell me where I can get one?" I mean, she wasn't joshing me at all, she was serious. And I'm thinking, "I've been making records since '49."[13]

Many black bluesmen acknowledged that the British musicians had opened the door for crossover success with white American audiences during the late 1960s; however, as militancy grew in the African American community, that was not necessarily viewed as a good thing. The British Invasion took place when the primary focus of the American civil rights movement was on Martin Luther King Jr.'s "Freedom Now" push for integration. So, when the Beatles and Stones arrived in the United States talking about their creative debt to African American artists, the message they were sending could be viewed as an opportunity to build another bridge between the races. During the later years of the decade, however, many young African Americans, increasingly impatient with the slow response to the movement's call for integration, rejected "Freedom Now" and embraced the concept of "Black Power," characterized by a separatist black nationalism, an Afro-centric cultural pride, and a sense of rage. The Black Arts Movement was, according to Larry Neal, "the aesthetic and spiritual sister of the Black Power concept," calling for the construction of a "black aesthetic . . . the destruction of the white thing, the destruction of white ideas, and white ways of looking at the world."[14] For African Americans who adopted this perspective, white musicians making money performing black music was a big, straight-up ripoff.

Writer LeRoi Jones (Amiri Baraka) was one of the architects of the Black Arts Movement, and the shifts in his perspective on white musicians playing blues-based music reflect a progression toward black nationalism. In his 1963 sociological history of black music, *Blues People,* Jones considered blues-influenced rock and roll: "It is still raw enough to stand the dilution and in some cases, to even be made attractive by the very fact of its commercialization. Rock 'n' roll is the blues form of the classes of Americans who lack the 'sophistication' to be middle brows."[15] Jones seems to grudgingly accept blues-based rock and roll because it implicitly rejects mainstream American values, and the attraction of its "commercialization" seemingly lies in the fact that its widespread dissemination confronts "middle brows" with its "raw" and "alien" nature. In a 1965 *Down Beat* column, Jones directly addresses the British Invasion's success with commercializing blues music: "These English boys are literally 'hipper' than their white counterparts, hipper because as it is readily seen they have actually made a contemporary form, unlike most white U.S. 'folk singers' who are content to imitate 'ancient' blues forms and older singers.... As one young poet said, 'At least The Rolling Stones come on like English crooks.'"[16] Once again, Jones seems to appreciate the black music rendered by white musicians because it represents a rejection of mainstream white America. Although the British bands might be crooks, at least they are straightforward about it and not *American* crooks.

In 1966 Jones called for the formation of the Black Arts Movement, and his take on British bands performing blues-based music radically altered. In his essay, "The Changing Same (R&B and New Black Music)," he charges: "Actually, the more intelligent the white, the more the realization he has to steal from niggers. They take from us all the way up to the line. Finally, what difference between Beatles, Stones, etc., and Minstrelsey [sic]. Minstrels never convinced anybody they were Black either."[17] The separatism that was fundamental to the black power and Black Arts movements precludes an equitable cultural exchange between blacks and whites. Music from black culture served a unique function exclusively within the culture. In his 1971 essay "The Ethos of the Blues," Larry Neal declares: "The ethos of the blues, then, is the musical manifestation of one's individual cultural experiences in Afro-America with which members of the black community can identify."[18]

Unfortunately for African American blues artists trying to keep their music and careers viable during the 1960s, interest among black record buyers and live audiences, for the most part, had declined. The blues often was seen as vestige of an exploitative and oppressive past. As Neal suggests: "The blues are the ideology of the field slave—the ideology of a new 'proletariat' searching for a means of judging the world."[19] Although critics like Neal and Jones understood the full range of history and styles encompassed in the blues/jazz continuum, most black nationalists looked to uplifting, nationalistic soul anthems like James Brown's "Say It Loud, I'm Black and I'm Proud," Nina Simone's "To Be Young, Gifted and Black," or Curtis Mayfield's "This Is My Country" or the free-ranging jazz improvisations of John Coltrane, Archie Shepp, Charles Mingus, or Miles Davis for their "means of judging the world."

B.B. King recognized the shift in African American tastes away from the blues and the rise of soul music as their predominant popular musical form. He found himself moving down on bills at concerts as soul artists took over the headliner spots that he had once occupied. He comments on this shift in musical preference by black audiences in his autobiography:

> The sixties were filled with beautiful soul because black people were more vocal about the respect we wanted and the good feelings we had about ourselves. The politics seeped into the music, and the politics were about life-affirming change. I liked all that.
>
> But I didn't like being booed. That cut me to the quick.
>
> Most critics would probably say that B.B. King has soul, but B.B. King wasn't really part of the soul movement. Sure, I played bills with Marvin Gaye and Jackie Wilson and just about everyone else you can name—dozens of bills all over the country—but I was the outside, the bluesman, just like I'd been the outside bluesman in the rock 'n' roll shows of the fifties. I felt like a sheep among cows. Marvin and Jackie didn't see me that way—the artists treated me with respect—but on this particular night in this particular city, the audience booed me bad. I cried. Never had been booed before. Didn't know what it felt like

until the boos hit me in the face. Coming from my own people—especially coming from young people—made it worse.[20]

Certainly blues artists, including Bobby "Blue" Bland, Albert King, Jimmy Reed, Little Milton, Slim Harpo, Rufus Thomas, and even B.B. King scored over 20 hits on the R&B charts throughout the 1960s, but clearly a change had come.

The migration of African Americans from the blues during the early 1960s put black bluesmen in a bind. Up until this point, their careers had functioned solely with their own communities; there was no way for them to direct their music toward a different audience. The popular and commercial success of the British bands in bringing the blues back home to America, as Paul Oliver theorizes in his essay "Blue-eyed Blues: The Impact of Blues on European Popular Culture" (1976), may have contributed to the alienation of African American audiences from the form: "When it was over it was the rock stars who had the Rolls Royces, the film contracts, the big houses with swimming pools, and profiles in *Vogue*; not the blues singers. It was no coincidence that the black audiences quit the blues like it had never been, when the Beatles and Stones topped the charts."[21] While resentment over perceived white exploitation of the blues may have been a factor in African Americans deserting the music, the diminishing support had begun long before the British Invasion. Waters and other black bluesmen had seen the writing on the wall in terms of black support for their blues, and decided to cross the Atlantic to try and connect with a British audience beginning in the late 1950s.

Whatever the motivations might be for the African American audiences and record buyers to shift their allegiance to other musical forms during the 1960s, a great many black bluesmen from that era have consistently recognized the role of British blues rock artists in introducing their music to a white American audience. The interaction with these musicians from across the Atlantic is a part of the story that they tell of their careers. The challenge, by participants in the Black Arts Movement, to the value of the blues creating a link between African American and white British musicians represented a distinct perspective on artistic expression and its function within black culture and was very much in tune with the tenor of the times. The indisputable reality is that the overwhelming majority of the blues audience in America since that time is white. In the decades since the 1960s, however, it has not been uncommon for critics and commentators, a vast majority of them white, to challenge the assumptions of that story. Even during the 1960s, British blues magazines, such as *Blues Unlimited* and *Blues World*, either totally ignored or viciously disparaged the efforts of homegrown artists performing the blues. First published in 1963, *Blues Unlimited* did not even mention the Rolling Stones until its eighty-third issue in 1971, when two lines appeared: "ROLLING STONES TO PAY FRED McDOWELL for a title on the latest million-seller. Nice example to others we hope."[22] If one had to depend solely on these periodicals for the story of cross-Atlantic reception of the blues, it would certainly be different from the one told by the musicians.

One of the challenges to the story of the beneficial role British blues rockers played in the careers of African American bluesmen is the disparity of economic rewards. This is also indisputable, and not all African American blues artists told a story of cross-Atlantic bonhomie. The money that artists like Clapton and the Stones have made over the past five decades dwarfs what these bluesmen ever received. And, of course, there are plenty of instances where British blues rockers did not give credit—for riffs, for grooves, for whole songs—where it was due; some of them were sued and money finally made it to the originator. Very few African American bluesmen have ever received their just rewards in relation to white artists performing in a blues-based idiom.

Yet African American bluesmen frequently focus on the music, rather than on how much more money a blues rocker is paid. In the first issue of *Living Blues* in 1970, Howlin' Wolf was told that Jeff Beck covered one of his records; his response is marked by a sense of professional pride and a veteran's savvy understanding of the record business: "But I don't feel bad about it because when somebody take your number and use it, why that's lettin' 'em know that they really appreciate your sound, you know. I wished a lot of 'em would take 'em."[23] In July 1975, the Stones invited Howlin' Wolf to attend their concert in Chicago Stadium. His wife Lillie Burnett described the scene: "You should have seen Wolf. It was wonderful. We went to the concert, and Bill Wyman must have arranged something, because when Wolf walked into the stadium a spotlight went on him and the whole place stood up and cheered. It was so good for him. I watched that from the side of the stage and I was so proud."[24] What was the significance of that walk through the crowd of Stones fans for Howlin' Wolf? Here he was receiving a standing ovation in a massive stadium in his hometown where he had worked in Southside clubs for over twenty years.

His wife indicates such recognition provided Wolf with a sense of personal satisfaction; however, it probably had little benefit for him financially. The Stones were signaling their admiration for Wolf and acknowledging his influence on their music, yet, for many of the Stones fans in that audience, the black bluesman's innovative artistry is validated as a source rather than on its own terms, testifying to the racial disparity that is ingrained in the American experience.

Another line of criticism leveled at the story of British blues rockers contributing to the revival of the careers of African American blues artists is that their testimonials establish a connection to the "real" thing, and this connection ultimately serves to validate their own music. In other words, if a white musician wants to establish his blues credentials, all he has to do is drop the right names, and he becomes a faithful acolyte keeping the blues flame burning. Bruce Cook articulates this position in *Listen to the Blues*: "There is no real point, however, in overemphasizing these tributes in print by some young rock superstar or other to certain fairly obscure black bluesmen. For let's face it, it's hip for some fugitive from the middle-class to say, 'All that I am or hope to be I owe to Howlin' Wolf.' It lends a certain legitimacy to his efforts and suggests an authenticity that—who knows?—his music may lack."[25]

In the decades since the 1960s, it may have become *de rigueur* for an up-and-coming white musician working in a blues-derived style to name-drop his black antecedents, but when the Stones and Clapton were first lauding Muddy Waters or Howlin' Wolf or Freddie King or Otis Rush, how could there have been any legitimatizing payoff for themselves? As McCartney found out at that press conference, most Americans did not know who their "most famous people" were. If audiences did not know the original music, then how could white musicians gain credibility, since there was no point of comparison? Similarly, it has been suggested that the recognition of black artists as creative influences or the inclusion of black artists as opening acts for rock stars assigns them to the status of, as Brian Ward has said, "perpetual 'forerunners' in the minds of white rock fans."[26] Criticism of these testimonials to African American originators or the employment of them as opening acts sets up the white artist in a can't-win-for-losing situation. White American rock and roll artists who covered black music without giving credit to black artists in the 1950s were condemned for taking credit for something they did not create. Yet the British blues rockers gave the credit to black musicians and included them on their tours, and they are accused of a manipulative self-authentication or the reduction of African American originators to sources that serve to lionize white creativity.

Maybe both British and American white blues rockers could have been more assertive in their promotion of their blues heroes; however, they may not have always had the last word in such matters. A case in point is the Rolling Stones' 1969 American tour that featured B.B. King and Ike & Tina Turner as opening acts. The tour was recorded, and Mick Jagger originally conceived of the live album that was released, *Get Yer Ya-Ya's Out!*, as a double album that would include the blues/R&B guests. Ultimately, the record label rejected the idea of including King and the Turners. As Jagger recalled, "Decca weren't interested. They went, 'Who are these people?'"[27] The Stones finally reissued the album as a triple compact disc in 2009 with a disc devoted to the live sets of King and Ike & Tina.

The mutual admiration society established between African American and British blues artists during the 1960s led to a succession of collaborative recordings that prominently trumpeted London as the site of the sessions. This crossover strategy has also been critiqued. For the contemporary British blues purist press, the joining together of black American bluesmen and British rockers was an intolerable bastardization. A *Blues Unlimited* review of *B.B. King in London* begins: "Where will it all end? Howlin' Wolf in London and now B.B. King, complete with cover photo outside No. 10 Downing Street. One can only assume the next thing will be for Chess to release Edward Heath blowing amplified harmonica at Smithy's Corner."[28] The objection to these types of albums seems to be that black bluesmen are overshadowed and should be acknowledged on their own terms, not because of the self-validating endorsements of white blues rockers. However, it seems just as likely that a blues album purchased because it featured a Clapton or a Stone served as a gateway to exploring the blues artist's career.

Perhaps the single concept most bandied about among blues critics is the notion of authenticity—a somewhat nebulous touchstone that seems to involve both race and folk, as opposed to commercial, transmission. One side of the issue that levels criticism at the music made by British blues rockers from the 1960s is that their music is too imitative. Bob Groom's *The Blues Revival* (1971) was one of the first critical analyses to articulate the imitative critique: "On the whole, white blues has been content to re-create rather than renew.... The valid objection to most white blues is that it is imitative and ephemeral, and lacks the emotional substance that has made the great negro blues timeless."[29] British covers of black American blues records, especially early efforts such as the Stones' version of "I Just Want to Make Love to You," the Yardbirds' version of "Smokestack Lightning," or the Animals' version of "Boom Boom" literally sound like pale imitations of the originals by Muddy Waters, Howlin' Wolf, and John Lee Hooker because that is what they were—young English musicians learning how to create the sounds and construct grooves that are deeply rooted in the African American oral tradition. Something else they needed to figure was how to use a studio to emulate the sound of the original recordings; it is no wonder bands like the Stones and Yardbirds made a beeline for the Chess and Sun Studios when they got to America. British artists eventually were able to achieve fluency in the idiom's instrumental techniques; however, criticism of their vocals persisted. As Robert Palmer asserts in *Rock & Roll: An Unruly History* (1995): "But good blues *singing* involves subtleties that are deeply imbedded in the blues culture's spoken idiom. Suffering for your art has nothing to do with it; if you didn't grow up in that culture, your singing is going to sound like what it is: an imitation."[30] It is unlikely that most of the sixties British blues rockers would claim to be able to equal or surpass the vocal artistry of the American originals.

Black blues musicians recognize the differences in white blues vocal facility but certainly do not preclude their white counterparts from participation in the genre because of it. As Muddy Waters commented: "They got all these white kids now. Some of them can play *good* blues. They play so much, run a ring around you playin' guitar, but they cannot vocal like the black man."[31] There is a video of Waters jamming with Buddy Guy, Junior Wells, and members of the Stones recorded in 1981 at the Checkerboard Lounge on Chicago's Southside (Waters' last known recordings). On stage side by side, Waters and Jagger duet on classics such as "Hootchie Cootchie Man" and "Mannish Boy." There is no question of who is the originator and who is the imitator; however, what is striking about the performance is the sense of play between these two men who have come from such different worlds. They exhibit knowledge of the music and each other and the differences between each other and a willingness, even a delight, to play with that knowledge and those differences.

The imitation critique turns insidious in terms of race when critics charge that British blues rock performers are latter-day minstrels. It is one thing for LeRoi Jones, immersed in the social turmoil, rage, and nationalist redefinition of the Black Arts Movement, to call music of the Beatles and Stones minstrelsy, but contemporary, largely white critics who throw this term about exhibit a cynical, faux hipness and a profoundly inaccurate historical understanding of minstrelsy. In *Blues-Rock Explosion* (2001), Summer McStravick and John Roos report a number of these criticisms: Charles Shaar Murray calls Jagger's dance moves "updated Al Jolson routines"; Albert Goldman asserts that the singing of Steve Winwood or Janis Joplin is "vocal blackface"; McStravick and Roos themselves suggest that Jagger "works on imitating a black American's singing style so that when he sings a Robert Johnson tune it sounds every bit as phony as Jolson singing 'My Mammy,'" and that the Elmore James tributes of Fleetwood Mac's Jeremy Spencer are "blues vaudeville."[32] Leveling this line of criticism at the British blues rockers of the 1960s is mean-spirited, racially divisive, and historically uninformed. As Eileen Southern states in *The Music of Black Americans* (1997), one theme common to minstrel performances was "to disparage the black man and life style."[33] Even Eric Lott's *Love and Theft* (1993), which explores the complexities and ambiguities of minstrelsy, asserts:

> Minstrel performers often attempted to repress through ridicule the real interest in black cultural practices they nonetheless betrayed.... It was cross-racial desire that coupled a nearly insupportable fascination and a self-protective derision with respect to black people and their cultural practices, and that made blackface minstrelsy less a sign of absolute white power and control than of panic, anxiety, terror, and pleasure.[34]

There is a signature difference between the British blues acolytes of the 1960s and the legacy of the American minstrel show in that the intent to "disparage" and to "ridicule," the element of "derision," was not present, so when a contemporary critic tries to soften the blow and characterizes sixties blues rock as "respectful minstrelsy,"[35] there is a fundamental contradiction; by its very nature minstrelsy cannot be respectful. There certainly were attempts by British musicians to imitate the performance styles and techniques of black American blues artists that were poorly executed or lacking in an understanding of idiomatic nuances, but they were undertaken in a spirit of proselytizing admiration that possibly led to a respect for African American culture that was deepened when white audiences recognized the disparity between the imitators and the originals.

The other side of the imitative critique is that in attempting to be innovative, British blues-inspired musicians lost their connection to the source, particularly by placing too much emphasis on technical innovation. Groom's *Blues Revival* (1971) was one of the earliest articulations of this position: "That is not to say that there is no value in the 'progressive blues' of artists like John Mayall, but their 'progressiveness' has taken them a long way from the indefinable essence of the real blues."[36] In *The Land Where Blues Began* (1993), Alan Lomax echoes this complaint about the British blues rockers' focus on flashy technical innovations:

> The young English intellectuals and artists, moving into rock, fell in love with this music, and through them, and in the hands of the likes of Eric Clapton, the slide guitar style became a main orchestral ornament of the international rock movement. Unfortunately, in spite of displays of mass hysteria at their every appearance on stage, these urban translations of Mississippi slide guitar have gone aesthetically and emotionally flat. Today's rock guitarist slides out the notes of his music with unmatched virtuosity, but succeeds only moderately in having his guitar intone or cry out the poetry, or, if it does, these passages are inexpressive and the effect is mechanical and dull, even though delivered passionately and triple forte.[37]

The innovative critique, with its emphasis on technical facility, raises the essentialist question of whether it is possible for a white musician, let alone a white British musician, to grasp the idiomatic cultural nuances and context in which the music is rooted and really play the blues. One thing is certain: black American bluesmen, while they may have had doubts about the quality of some of the music British players were making, had no problem recognizing that what they were playing was the blues.

Michael Bane's *White Boy Singin' the Blues* (1982) takes the racial implications of the innovative critique even further:

> The central question changed from Can a white man sing the blues? to Can a *black* man sing the blues? because after Cream the whites had the terminology all sewed up. With the skills of a surgeon, popular culture removed "black" from "blues" leaving the term free to become almost synonymous with British groups in the Mayall cast. It was the triumph of the British contention that music was without color and the American dis-ease of coming to terms with rock and roll.[38]

Bane may see this reversal as a clever rhetorical flourish, but it is puzzling how the British blues rockers of the 1960s, with their unrelenting efforts to gain recognition for African American originators, can be charged with the responsibility for removing the black connection in the popular culture's conception of the blues. In *Escaping the Delta* (2004), Elijah Wald suggests that "for most modern listeners, the history, aesthetic, and sound of blues as a whole was formed by the Stones and a handful of their white, mostly English contemporaries."[39] This amazing assertion quite possibly says more about the influence of the mass media than it does about the Stones or the blues, but ultimately these types of critiques overemphasize the impact of British blues rockers on acceptance of the blues. Like the countless commentaries that ascribe the evolution of the blues as a genre to the influence of white romantic notions of authenticity, this perspective reduces the long line of black artists who created and extended the blues tradition to creative clay to be shaped by the hands of paternalistic outsiders. No wonder the Stones asked in "Street Fighting Man": "Well, what can a poor boy do except to sing for a rock 'n' roll band?"[40]

No one would argue that there was any kind of parity in terms of financial rewards between blues originators like B.B. King or Muddy Waters and blues rockers like Eric Clapton or the Rolling Stones. But the interest of white record buyers and concertgoers generated by British blues certainly enabled African American blues artists to make more money than working solely for a dwindling black audience. Yet fifty years later, how do we ultimately evaluate this cross-Atlantic blues exchange? Its significance goes beyond financial concerns. It was an interaction that tapped into the core of American identity. Muddy Waters bluntly assessed the contribution that the Stones and other British blues rockers had in breaking down racial barriers on the American music scene:

> Before the Rolling Stones people didn't know nothing and didn't *want* to know nothing about me. I was making race records, and I'm gonna tell it to you the way the older people told it to the kids. If they'd buy my records, their parents would say, "What the hell is this? Get this nigger record out of my house." But then the Rolling Stones and those other groups come over here from England, playing this music, and now, today, the kids buy a record of mine, and they listen to it.[41]

And the result of that listening led to a reconception of this music that had for so many years been associated with the low-down and funky, the back-in-the-alley, the down-the-dirt-road.

Today the blues lies before us majestic in the breadth of its creativity, the richness of its tradition, and its resiliency and inventiveness in response to a mean old world. The blues has been recognized as a testimony to triumph over adversity, an unyielding endurance, and a spirit that reaches people from all cultures with its message that you do have to laugh to keep from crying. The pervasive influence of and interest in the blues during the 1960s, including the contributions of British blues enthusiasts, had direct influence on that reconception. In many ways the blues *became* a musical genre in the 1960s. Artists like B.B. King and Buddy Guy have often asserted that during the 1950s they considered their music R&B and that somehow in the sixties the "R" was gone, and now it was classified as blues. Many stylistically distinct artists were gathered together under the umbrella of the blues, at the least sharing roughly twelve bars, three chords, a series of "blue" notes, and a remarkably durable, existential worldview. In 1971 Peter Guralnick reflected on the impact of bands like the Stones on the blues tradition in *Feel Like Going Home*:

> On their 1969 American tour they did the *Ed Sullivan Show* in somewhat muted form except for a blues that featured acoustic and slide guitar.
> *The blue light was my blues*
> *And the red light was my mind.*
> It was Robert Johnson's "All My Love in Vain," thirty years after Johnson himself had died, resurrected on national TV in front of fifty million viewers. I thought to myself, what if Johnson himself were around to see this, and I could fantasize that he was alive somewhere in Mississippi or out in L.A. watching a TV he still owed payments on, thinking—what? The only consolation must be that the music had been preserved.[42]

Almost four decades later, that preservation is more than just a consolation. Today, part of the majesty of the blues is that this amazingly diverse tradition lies before us to listen to, to grapple with, and to use to create new music. The blues-based music produced by British artists in the sixties made it clear that the form could still be a springboard to creative possibility.

The adaptability of the blues form has played a significant role in universalizing what for so many years played a role exclusively within African American culture. For Eric Burdon of the Animals, the form of the blues is its essence: "It's simple. Anybody can play it. It has the magical structure of three chords, which you can tie into earth, moon, man, woman, God."[43] Yet, for many critics the question remains as to whether blues can be, to use the ultimate buzzword, *authentic*, if it is not connected directly to its black roots. Interestingly, Toni Morrison's essay "Rootedness: The Ancestor as Foundation" (1984), in which she argues for the adoption of the novel as a tool for black cultural survival, asserts: "For a long time, the art form that was healing for Black people was music. That music is no longer *exclusively* ours; we don't have exclusive rights to it. Other people sing it and play it; it is the mode of contemporary music everywhere."[44] Her comment seems to be both a lamentation and a declaration of cultural pride. In many ways this is similar to the stories that African American bluesmen such as B.B. King and Muddy Waters have told about the 1960s and their interaction with British blues rockers like the Rolling Stones and Eric Clapton. They lament the desertion from the blues of the black audience and, at the same time, celebrate the breaking down of the barriers to white American, British, and ultimately international audiences.

There are certainly many white Americans who were first turned on to the blues by the Robert Johnson or McKinley Morganfield or Skip James or Fred McDowell songwriting credits in tiny print underneath song titles on Rolling Stones or Cream or John Mayall or Fleetwood Mac record labels. Others had their initiation into the blues world through seeing B.B. King or Albert King or Freddie King on the bills with their favorite rock bands. Many of those initiates went on to become devotees and students of the black blues originators. They not only pursued the music but came to understand both the humanity of black folks with whom their lives in America had little direct contact and how essential black people have been and continue to be in the definition of the American character. Individual lives may have been transformed, but overall much work still needs to be done to achieve a systemic or societal transformation of the country. Economic disparity still exists between white and black musicians, and the music of blues artists is still appropriated without recognition or recompense. Yet the 1960s British blues rockers helped bring about a fundamental change in understanding of and appreciation for the blues. They did their part. Since the 1960s, the blues purist critics have also done a tremendous job in preserving and delineating and nurturing the black blues tradition. Ironically, their efforts worked together with the efforts of the Stones, Clapton, and others to ensure that the story of the blues was told, remembered, and carried on. Many of the critical responses to this story of mutual admiration and musical desegregation told by African American bluesmen and British blues rockers can lead to a cynicism that makes one wonder if there really was any progress in breaking down racial barriers. As Toni Morrison recognized, black music has transcended its origins and allows for creative expression throughout the world, but that does not deny the fundamentally African American nature of the expression.[45]

Many of the rare African American musicians of subsequent generations who turned their talents to the blues say that they found their way to the source through listening to the music of Clapton and the Stones and other British blues rockers from the 1960s. Singer/guitarist Michael Hill followed a similar path into the blues as many white fans during the 1960s thanks to a succession of bands led by Clapton: "I saw Cream's last tour at the Fillmore. I saw Blind Faith, and Derek and the Dominos. And it was interesting: they would always talk about their heroes—B.B. King, Buddy Guy, Albert King—so we got into them."[46] Singer Shemekia Copeland, daughter of singer/guitarist Johnny Copeland, acknowledges the British blues influence: "It's strange but I like a lot of rock 'n' rollers. The Rolling Stones and the Beatles I loved. Led Zeppelin I just got into—when I first heard Robert Plant I thought Led Zeppelin was a big black gospel singer."[47] The racial nexus the British blues helped to form in the 1960s continues to resonate in the twenty-first century with this ironic reversal in which African American artists are introduced to music from their own cultural heritage through a cross-Atlantic exchange.

In August 2009, B.B. King's summer tour stopped at Wolftrap Park outside of Washington, D.C. Prior to the show, the Stones played over the amphitheater's public address system. An octogenarian, King introduces each of his songs with long monologues that often include bits and pieces of his remarkable life story. About halfway through the show, King began a discourse on all the great musicians with whom he has played over the years, relating that he often hears from fans who ask him what it is like to play with "Eric." He said that he quickly turns this around: "I like to think Eric played on my record." He continued his story with details about meeting Clapton in New York in the mid-1960s and how when they first jammed together, the younger musician's technical facility took him by surprise. He went on to describe the "Eric Is God" graffiti he encountered when he first went to England and how this time he was ready when they jammed, and he "cut" Eric. He added that when they work together, and he gets peeved at Clapton, he jokes, "Okay, God, what's next?" At the conclusion of this monologue, he launched into "Key to the Highway" from his collaboration with Clapton, *Riding with the King* (2000). Clearly, King is comfortable with the cultural exchange that took place with the 1960s British blues rockers, and it remains an important part of the story that King tells of his life as a bluesman. Five decades later, the interaction that took place between African American and British blues artists during the 1960s continues to create a racial crossroads where we can examine the nature of what it means to be American.

Notes

1. B.B. King with Dick Waterman, *The B.B. King Treasures* (New York: Bullfinch, 2005), 92.

2. Jann S. Wenner, *Lennon Remembers* (1971; London: Verso, 2000), 21.

3. B.B. King with David Ritz, *Blues All Around Me: The Autobiography of B.B. King* (New York: Avon, 1996), 230.

4. *Ibid.*, 293.

5. Robert Palmer, "Muddy Waters: 1915–1983," *Rolling Stone* (June 23, 1983): 42.

6. Dora Loewenstein and Phillip Dodd, eds., *According to the Rolling Stones* (San Francisco: Chronicle, 2003), 16.

7. James Baldwin, "Equal in Paris," in *Notes of a Native Son*, (1955; New York: Beacon, 1984), 146.

8. Sandra B. Tooze, *Muddy Waters: The Mojo Man* (Toronto: ECW Press, 1997), 202.

9. Bruce Cook, *Listen to the Blues* (New York: Scribner's, 1973), 181.

10. James Segrest and Mark Hoffman, *Moanin' at Midnight: The Life and Times of Howlin' Wolf* (New York: Thunder's Mouth, 2005), 222–23.

11. Stanley Booth, *Rythm Oil: A Journey Through the Music of the American South* (New York: Pantheon, 1991), 180.

12. Dick Waterman, *Between Midnight and Day: The Last Unpublished Blues Archive* (New York: Thunder's Mouth, 2003), 42.

13. King with Waterman, *The B.B. King Treasures*, 49.

14. Larry Neal, "The Black Arts Movement," in Patricia Hill, ed., *Call and Response* (Boston: Houghton Mifflin, 1998), 1450–51.

15. LeRoi Jones (Amiri Baraka), *Blues People* (New York: William Morrow, 1963), 222–23.

16. LeRoi Jones (Amiri Baraka), *Black Music* (New York: William Morrow, 1967), 123–24.

17. *Ibid.*, 205–6.

18. Larry Neal, "The Ethos of the Blues" (1971), in *Visions of a Liberated Future: Black Arts Movement Writings* (New York: Thunder's Mouth, 1989), 117.

19. *Ibid.*, 113.

20. King with Ritz, *Blues All Around Me*, 210–11.

21. Paul Oliver, "Blue-eyed Blues: The Impact of Blues on European Popular Culture," in C. W. E. Bigsby, ed., *Approaches to Popular Culture* (Bowling Green, OH: Bowling Green University Press, 1976), 239.

22. "ROLLING STONES TO PAY FRED McDOWELL," *Blues Unlimited* 83 (July 1971): 23.

23. "Living Blues Interview: Howling Wolf," *Living Blues* 1 (1970): 16.

24. Bill Wyman with Richard Havers, *Bill Wyman's Blues Odyssey: A Journey to Music's Heart and Soul* (London: DK, 2001), 297.

25. Cook, *Listen to the Blues*, 179.

26. Brian Ward, *Just My Soul Responding: Rhythm and Blues, Black Consciousness, and Race Relations* (Berkeley: University of California Press, 1998), 175.

27. Neil Spencer, Review, "The Rolling Stones: Get Yer Ya-Ya's Out! Deluxe Edition," *Uncut*, Web, n.d.

28. Dave Ward, Review, *B.B. King in London*, *Blues Unlimited* 89 (February/March 1972) 30.

29. Bob Groom, *The Blues Revival* (London: Studio Vista, 1971), 102.

30. Robert Palmer, *Rock and Roll: An Unruly History* (New York: Harmony, 1995), 125–26.

31. *Ibid.*, 125.

32. Summer McStravick and John Roos, *Blues-Rock Explosion* (Mission Viejo, CA: Old Goat, 2001), xv, xxi.

33. Eileen Southern, *The Music of Black Americans: A History*, 3rd ed. (New York: W. W. Norton, 1997), 91.

34. Eric Lott, *Love and Theft: Blackface Minstrelsy and the American Working Class* (New York: Oxford University Press, 1993), 6.

35. McStravick and Roos, *Blues-Rock Explosion*, xv.

36. Groom, *The Blues Revival*, 102.

37. Alan Lomax, *The Land Where Blues Began* (New York: Delta, 1993), 355.

38. Michael Bane, *White Boy Singin' the Blues: The Black Roots of White Rock* (New York: Penguin, 1982), 159.

39. Elijah Wald, *Escaping the Delta: Robert Johnson and the Invention of the Blues* (New York: Amistad, 2004), 220–21.

40. Rolling Stones, "Street Fighting Man," (1968; ABKCO, 1986).

41. Robert Palmer, *Deep Blues* (New York: Penguin, 1981): 259–60.

42. Peter Guralnick, *Feel Like Going Home: Portraits in Blues and Rock 'N' Roll* (1971; Boston: Little, Brown, 1999), 35.

43. Mike Figgis, Dir., *Red, White & Blues* (Vulcan Productions/Road Movies, 2003).

44. Toni Morrison, "Rootedness: The Ancestor as Foundation," in Mari Evans, ed., *Black Women Writers 1950–1980* (New York: Anchor, 1984), 340.

45. *Ibid.*, 340.

46. Adam Gussow, "Interview with Michael Hill," *Living Blues* 35, no. 4 (July-August 2004): 18–27.

47. Dan Aykroyd and Ben Manilla, *Elwood's Blues: Interviews with Blues Legends and Stars* (San Francisco: Backbeat, 2004).

12

Groove Me

Dancing to the Discs of Northern Soul

—David Sanjek

> I think we have to be very cautious about interpreting those moments of connection. We know what that language articulates because we know about the intensity of pleasure that we discover. But I think sometimes that language of an essential particularity, which we use to explain those moments of affiliation and linkage, represents a kind of shortcut to the more obviously political work involved in explaining how solidarity happens and how culture, technology, and language mediate that solidarity. I think if we could be just a little harder on ourselves before we start celebrating, we might have something more worthwhile—a more politically coherent understanding of what those fragile solidarities add up to.
> —Paul Gilroy[1]

Common sense would seem to dictate that infatuation constitutes a relatively uncomplicated phenomenon. In the most rudimentary terms, a person temporarily succumbs, in one manner or another, to an overwhelming interruption of their ordinary equilibrium. However long they remain in the presence of the agent of this disorientation, their center of gravity, so to speak, collapses. One might draw upon a romantic vocabulary in order to provide the most appropriate characterization of this sensation: a swoon— or, perhaps just as accurately, employ that vivid English colloquialism: "gobsmacked." Whatever the precipitating phenomenon, whether it be the most elevated or altogether down to earth, the end result remains the same. The architecture of our interior topography undergoes a tectonic shift. We consequently feel compelled to inspect each and every step we take, as through the inclination to trip over ourselves was almost unavoidable.

If the experience of infatuation can be recounted in a more or less universal manner, the various trajectories that the emotions are able to traverse remain uncountable. The human heart may well contain a finite set of chambers, but the affections are able to attach themselves to an infinite number of targets. Perhaps the most persuasive argument against the purported monogamous nature of human beings might well be the fickle behavior of our consciousness. We flit from perception to perception, leapfrog from one position to another as though we rarely exceed, whatever our age, the conceptual overload experienced by infants that William James famously characterized in *The Principles of Psychology* as "one great blooming, buzzing confusion."[2] We exist in a continuous state of potential intrigue, promiscuously attracted to any number of divergent avenues of infatuation.

Making sense of that oversaturated set of circumstances can be somewhat less oppressive if we harness our attention to one of those occasions when a set of individuals become mutually absorbed by an identical target, engage in a kind of collective embrace, and thereby become classified as fans. Fascination with what have been determined to be specifically demarcated communities of fans has consumed many an academic and average person alike. This takes place not simply due to a kind of analytic shorthand but also because these conglomerations might be thought of as the institutionalization of infatuation. It is possible to think of fan communities as what occurs when what would otherwise appear to be random acts of solitary rapture achieve a kind of critical mass. Lawrence Grossberg has frequently and eloquently written of the "affective alliances" that arise when two or more individuals recognize and act upon their mutual investment of time, consciousness, and cash in a common object. He recognizes as well that the act of being consumed by popular music in particular cannot be separated from whatever other activities might potentially take up a portion of our lives. Consequently, "The meaning and effect of specific music always depends on its place within both the broad context of everyday life and the potentially multiple, often specific contexts and alliances of other texts, cultural practices (including fashion, dance, film), social relationships, emotional investments, and so forth."[3]

Understanding any specific act of infatuation requires that we distinguish and dissect those "contexts and alliances"; make sense of how we attach ourselves to a particular form of music; why we do so; and what the consequences, intended and potentially inadvertent, might be. As Paul Gilroy points out in the epigraph with which we began, "moments of connection" that result in a demonstrable "intensity of pleasure" will remain perennially fragile constructions until or unless we unpack and interrogate the impulses that give rise to those routinely overpowering sensations. And when we find ourselves seized by song, dominated by rhythms on the dance floor, or flummoxed by the fabulous vocal arabesques of an inspired singer, a good deal of unpacking will have to be done. Invariably, the baggage that accompanies the experience of popular music challenges our capacity for juggling disparate discourses, intersecting ideologies, colliding forms of consciousness. In the process, we might well find that intertwined with pleasure is some form of polemic, even if that construction of consciousness does not emerge overtly or even coherently in the rapturous experience from which it originates.

To that end, let us take a specific fan community and a time-honored attachment by several generations of aficionados to a particular form of music—African American rhythm & blues—and the resulting alliance that has come to be known now for some forty years as Northern Soul. Its parameters as a mass audience phenomenon can be described quite simply. Starting in the early 1970s, a group of working-class English men and women developed a mutual embrace of a specific repertoire. They came together to listen and dance to that playlist at clubs by and large located in the North of England, hence the topographic determination of the group's name. At the same time, if the culture that bred the music these individuals favored was urban, their place of residence tended not to be overtly cosmopolitan. As Katie Milestone observes, most Northern Soul communities occur in small towns in the Northwest of England, like Wigan, Blackburn, Morecambe, Cleethorpes, and Tunstall, places on the margin that remain "peripheral to the concentration of economic and cultural power in city centres."[4] Nothing terribly complicated brings them together, simply a common passion for a specific form of popular culture and the desire to join a community of fellow fanatics.

However, the more one investigates the phenomenon of Northern Soul, the less simple it appears. Several questions about geography, race, and ideology arise. First, there is the matter of the transatlantic migration of the material, the fact that one national culture embraced the performances of a portion of another. In this case, something led these individuals to seek out meaning and identity in the recordings not of their country, but that of America. Why were they drawn across the Atlantic and how did they characterize their fascination with a foreign culture? Second, there is the issue of the cross-racial element of the process: for the most part, fans of Northern Soul were and are white while the recordings they sought out were created and marketed by African Americans. What led them to cross racial barriers that often exclude rather than include outsiders? Finally, what conscious and unconscious ideological claims can be said to attach themselves to what might otherwise seem nothing more than a spirited engagement with recorded commercial music? The fans of Northern Soul do not appear to have promoted any explicitly polemical positions regarding either the material they admire or the individuals who create it; yet simply by seeking it out, and drawing the public's attention often to recordings that were obscure if not completely unknown, this group appears to have engaged in work that possesses ideological dimensions.

In the remainder of this essay, I will examine four issues that arise from these vexing questions. First, what is the composition of the discography they constituted, and how does it demarcate a particular portion of the rhythm & blues repertoire as innately superior to better-known and publicly popular recordings? It needs to be stressed that at the present time, when cultural canons routinely are overturned, the advocates of Northern Soul constructed just such a hierarchy of validated sounds. They identified and advocated for a very specific body of recordings that in their minds stand out by virtue of being, by and large, drawn from the least commercially successful and in some cases altogether unreleased portion of the rhythm and blues repertoire. What cultural capital is amassed by such a set of choices, and what positions are thereby issued about commercialism? Second, what relationship is projected between the two nations of the United States and England, and how is the geography from which the music originated imagined? Is there any implicit desire on the part of the Northern Soul community to engage with the tangible topography and the citizenry of another society, or has the actual territory given way to a landscape of the emotions and the imagination? Third, how has the Northern Soul community integrated issues of race, and what determination might be made about the kinds of bonds that elude and perhaps eradicate lines of potential hostility that can originate through the acquisition and acclimation of commercial products? Finally, what specific ideological statements might be intertwined within particular acts of pleasure, and might something be emancipated on the dance floor other than the inhibitions of the audience? The hope is that asking such questions will allow us to be a bit harder on ourselves in the manner that Paul Gilroy invites, and allow Northern Soul to be understood as the complex and consequential phenomenon that it has been and continues to be for a number of people.

Before continuing, some further details about the phenomenon itself are required. Northern Soul has been said to have originated in Manchester at the Twisted Wheel venue (1963–71), where the DJ Roger Eagle began to spin his private stash of U.S. rhythm & blues singles and attract an audience of like-minded individuals.[5] Initially, the Northern Soul scene depended on self-directed cultural entrepreneurs such as Eagle to provide the sounds, as American soul imports did not start to enter the UK in any systematic fashion until 1968.[6] Previously, collectors had to rely on individual initiative, private contacts, and trips across the ocean to acquire material. The success of the Twisted Wheel also benefited from the emerging scene in Manchester as the city had come to compete alongside Hamburg as the "Fun City of Europe."[7] The freewheeling atmosphere temporarily abetted that reputation, until an overweening moral panic ensued that focused on drug sales and consumption in public venues as well as an absence of administrative oversight by the owners of those venues. Attention was drawn to these activities by J. A. McKay, Manchester's chief constable, in reports filed in 1964 and 1965.[8] He conjured up an image of unsupervised, adolescent vagrants, wandering from club to club, strung out on hashish or amphetamines.[9] The ensuing melange of "quasi-facts, clichés, innuendoes and indignant moral outrage" that appeared in the local press stirred up politicians to take action and led to the 1965 Manchester Corporation Act.[10] Its statutes responded to the desire on the part of the city council and other forces for regulation and control of errant youths as well as helping promote efforts at modernization of Manchester's city center. Subsequent statutes threatened prosecution of club owners should consumption of illegal drugs take place on their premises, even if the proprietors remained unaware of the purported crime. This and other regulations enabled the powers that be in Manchester to eliminate the kind of behavior that collided with the promotion of civic stability and transformation of the city center into a shopping arena.

Despite these interventions, the Twisted Wheel retained its pre-eminence past the end of the decade as the scene's reputation spread. The visit by music journalist and record promoter Dave Godin to the venue in 1970 led to his promotion of the emerging Northern Soul phenomenon in his column featured in the publication *Blues & Soul*—as well as the initial printed coinage of the appellation Northern Soul. Godin (1936–2004) was the outstanding proponent—one might even say propagandist—for American rhythm & blues in England at the time and a revered figure among aficionados of the genre. Initially a devotee of the Detroit-based

Tamla-Motown affiliated record labels, he founded the Tamla-Motown Appreciation Society, established a professional relationship with the company, acted as its representative, and opened a London-based shop and label, Soul City, as an outlet for the products. In that 1970 column he drew attention to a series of characteristics that typify the Northern Soul scene to this day: how ingratiating and collegial the attendees were—"none of the stand-off-ishness in the North that plagues human relationships in the South"; the expertise of the dancers—"I never thought I'd live to see the day where people could so relate the rhythmic content of Soul music to bodily movement to such a skilled degree in these rigid and armoured isles!"; and the top-notch caliber of the selections chosen by the DJs—"a focal point for that aware and elite minority who are not content with the lifeless pulp that constitutes the bulk of the manipulated 'hit' parade."[11]

Godin's description could apply equally well to the subsequent venues that followed in the wake of the Twisted Wheel and retain to this day their reputation as the *locus mundi* of the Northern Soul universe, principal among them the Golden Torch in Tunstall, Stoke (1971–72), and the Wigan Casino (1973–81).[12] The latter eventually acquired international plaudits when it received the designation of #1 discotheque from the U.S. music industry publication *Billboard* in 1978. It also served as the focus for the 1977 Granada documentary, directed by Tony Palmer, presented on the series *This England*. The opening sequences achieve through parallel editing a painful juxtaposition between the industrial bleakness of the area and the experiential expansiveness of the venue. In particular, the entrancing shots of astonishingly acrobatic male dancers reinforces the virtually utopian dimension of the space as a vehicle that could unclog all manner of bottled-up energy and otherwise assaulted individuality. Some attendees disliked if not loathed the program. They objected to how Palmer had used "unusual camera angles [to] distort and objectify the dancers and (the lights being on) [how] the camera focuses on 'working-class signifiers' such as muscles, sweat and tattoos. Rather than the all-nighter looking fast and exciting, it seems strange, dreamlike and suspended in time."[13] By literally casting light on their countercultural enclave, they felt that Palmer extinguished some of the aura they had attached to its atmosphere. (Tim Wall's 2006 essay "Out On The Floor: The Politics of Dancing on the Northern Soul Scene" provides the most detailed and theoretically sophisticated commentary about the dance floor. Among other things, it does not dwell on the masculine acrobatics and consequently illustrates that there was more than one way to announce one's identity than simply to spin elastically about the floor.)

Palmer's film did illustrate how much Northern Soul remained a nocturnal phenomenon, and that the absence of daylight and banishment of anything affiliated to the diurnal reinforced the specialness of the activity. Oddly enough, the venues were by and large alcohol-free, as local ordinances did not permit the sale of anything other than soft drinks at such a late hour. It should therefore come as little surprise that the scene was routinely drug-enhanced, as the ingestion of amphetamines in particular brought about not only the pleasure of the high but also served as a means of keeping bodies upright long past the crack of midnight. Andrew Wilson, a participant analyst, provides the most detailed and evenhanded study of this dimension of the scene in *Northern Soul: Music, Drugs and Subcultural Activity*. He reinforces how the crowd thought of their drug of choice not as an escape from reality but a means of "being in control, on the ball and smart"; that the absence of moral shibboleths affiliated to their use reinforced the sense of group identity and moral code.[14] As much as anything, amphetamines encouraged if not reinforced "Those experiences— the physiological sensations, confidence, fast thought and talk—together with the upbeat music and sense of camaraderie, all combined in a very real and exciting way."[15]

The incitement of that camaraderie might have been a factor in the absence of sexual predation on the dance floor as well as off. It certainly allowed both men and women the opportunity to express what might otherwise have been submerged portions of their personality. People assuredly sought out partners and physical gratification away from the venue itself, as though to keep the site unsullied and undefined by gender competition. The absence of testosterone-driven feistiness in the Northern Soul scene has been frequently observed. Dave Godin wrote of it in his 1970 article: "There was no undercurrent of tension or aggression that one sometimes finds in London clubs, but rather a benevolent atmosphere of benign friendship and camaraderie." Katie Milestone speaks of the "lack of pressure to conform to heterosexual definitions of masculinity" that made gay men feel welcome and straight men encouraged to drop their guard.[16]

The degree to which dance remained the *raison d'etre* of Northern Soul all-nighters reinforces not only the commanding presence of the DJ but also the crucial dimension of the tracks he chose to play. The phono-centric nature of the Northern Soul community cannot be underestimated.

The participants remain irretrievably entranced by what lies within the grooves of vinyl, the sounds that could be perfected in the recording studio.

That is not to exclude that occasions arose when live performers took to the stage of venues. Kamisi Browne enumerates, in his rewarding and richly detailed 2005 U.C.L.A. Ph.D. thesis *"Soul or Nothing": The Formation of Cultural Identity on the British Northern Soul Scene*, some of the individuals and groups that appeared on the scene. The list incorporates many estimable names, yet remains far from exhaustive.[17] Furthermore, even when filled to capacity, a venue like the Golden Torch, where Chicago-based Major Lance wowed the crowd in 1972 and recorded a widely selling live album, did not exceed much more than fifteen hundred. These occasions, memorable as they certainly were, nonetheless pale in comparison to the impact of one perfect recording after another, the customary fare of all-nighters. One gets the feeling that if the crowd needed to choose between the raw sounds of the stage or the cooked compositions of the studio, they would opt for the latter every time. Their understanding of authenticity encourages the embrace of technology and the perfected manipulation of sound achievable only through the tools available with recording technology.

To some degree, this perspective flies in the face of certain long-standing and emphatically asserted propositions amongst certain popular music audiences. It particularly critiques the antipathy held by many consumers toward corporatism, often expressed in romantically uncritical denunciations of the industry, their stranglehold upon creativity, and promotion of the second-rate at best. It is most persistently addressed in the rhetoric of the "sell-out," an equation of commercial success with creative emptiness, predicated on the assumption that the only bargain that can be struck between an artist and an executive need be Faustian. Northern Soul communities do not typically denounce the marketplace or the players who hope to succeed within it on the basis of its demanding definitions of success. They instead often become obsessed with individual record labels and aim to acquire everything released by them, whereas others who focus on rock music, in particular, as their principal enthusiasm would assume that approach feeds the proposition that too many companies adopt a rubber-stamp mentality and force-feed the public the same kind of product over and over. What one community might denounce as formulae, the other defends as house style.

If advocates of Northern Soul do not renounce the marketplace, they undeniably romanticize and rejoice in the entrepreneurial behavior of small-scale musical enterprises. Therefore, almost as a kind of reflex, they tend to elevate the obscure over the obvious, the unappreciated over the applauded. Should you examine the lists of favorite tracks included throughout the volumes by Winstanley and Nowell, even the more than averagely well-versed fans of rhythm & blues find themselves confronted with a virtually alternate or parallel universe. Many if not most of the names referred to in their books challenge any assumption of the power of commercial charts or the promotional opportunities enhanced by radio airplay. To illustrate, here are some of the artists incorporated by these authors in their respective canons: the Tomangoes, Little Bryant, the World Column, Eddie Foster, Don Thomas, Mel Britt, Sam & Kitty. And a number of the labels remain equally recondite: JJ, Criminal, General American, In, Wise World, Sha-rae, Sassy. Less than a footnote even in the most in-depth histories of the genre, they would remain not simply unknown but obliterated altogether were it not for their resurrection by Northern Soul. Admittedly, this perspective would seem to conflict with the aforementioned attitude toward corporatism. How can you assume that only the best rise to the top if so many who deserve that designation remain prostrate on the floor? Yet the impression given by fans of Northern Soul is that this situation arises out of oversight, not some kind of institutional obliviousness. Were the public only to be made aware of the power of these tracks, their superiority would be undeniable; just look at the dancers that they inspire!

For the fans of Northern Soul, the perfection of these recordings remains a self-fulfilling proposition that requires only an audience's open eardrums. That even extends to recordings that never in fact entered the commercial arena. A number of Northern Soul DJs and collectors valorize test pressings: printed but not merchandised material that, for one reason or another, remained withheld from the public. One of the most treasured and highly appraised items in the Northern Soul canon is Frank Wilson's 1965 "Do I Love You (Indeed I Do)." Written and recorded by the artist for the Soul subsidiary of the Motown label, only two copies are believed to exist and have been appraised for as much as £15,000. Purportedly, having laid down the track, Wilson was challenged by label owner Berry Gordy to choose between performance or production, and he elected (quite successfully, at that) for the latter. Again, even if such items seem to exist outside the commercial process altogether, their eventual success and financial valuation within the Northern Soul community reinforces the assumption that they would have achieved their deserved recognition if only the appropriate circumstances arose.

Acquiring or simply appreciating such discs allows individuals to accrue that non-monetary but undeniably estimable currency that Sarah Thornton famously dubbed *subcultural capital*.[18] The virtually universal anonymity of these recordings outside the Northern Soul community tends to guarantee the membership of that fraternity a kind of desired differentiation from the general audience of mass culture consumers. Not only do their eardrums pick up and respond to rhythms that others fail to apprehend, but they would also appear to operate on another wavelength altogether, a privileged sphere of comprehension that allows them to assimilate compositions that elude their contemporaries. Yet how else did this community benefit, in their eyes, from this perceptual bankroll? One can hypothesize that it permitted them, among other things, to set themselves apart from their neighbors to the south, particularly those from the national center in London, who are assumed (then and now) to act as the nation's cultural barometer. There has been a long-standing cult of Northernness as a region apart and a state of being separate from the rest of the country. George Orwell drew attention to this geographical divide more than seventy years ago in *The Road to Wigan Pier* (1937). He observed that working-class inhabitants of the region have typically characterized themselves as more rooted in the everyday as against the frivolous attraction to fashion and novelty in the South. Orwell writes, "it is only in the North that life is 'real' life, that the industrial work done in the North is the only 'real' work, that the North is inhabited by 'real' people, the South merely by rentiers and their parasites."[19] Commentators on Northern Soul have linked this sense of regional exclusivity with their fascination with such comparatively unknown music. Katie Milestone points to how the region seemed to reject the urban fascination with the counterculture during the 1960s; the North and Midlands of England evidenced "a working-class rejection of the growing middle class culture of hippies, acid and progressive rock."[20] In addition, the fact that many of the recordings they admired came from a city, Detroit, similarly associated with manual labor and industrial technology added to the attraction.

In other words, here was something the elite failed to notice or appreciate, until those off the beaten track laid down the gauntlet. Engagement with Northern Soul also allowed its fans not to be completely defined by their day jobs or the position in the class system to which they were thereby assigned. Neither their salaries nor the substance of their labor could singularly validate their lives or act as means of appraising their worth. Furthermore, as many of the initial denizens of the community either themselves spurned or were turned aside by the community of higher education, their considerable knowledge about the artists they admired and the music they worshipped could be considered a sort of self-conferred higher degree, a means of registering and rewarding their autodidactic proclivities. As the information about this music was, like the discs themselves, not readily available, they had to make the effort as self-motivated researchers to recover the information from oblivion. They could not depend on the music press or other elements of the mass media to sort out that data, but had to dig in the trenches by themselves, and this long before the facilitation of such activities by the internet.

However, as wide-ranging and self-initiating as these enterprises might be, they nonetheless do not comprehensively address the sphere of rhythm & blues. Not only does the Northern Soul community approach the genre in a phono-centric fashion, they also fail to transpose their engagement with the cultural universe conjured up in these grooves to the physical geography from which they originated. While such a gesture could not be considered a requirement, it nonetheless tends to be an activity taken up energetically by many other popular music communities. In the process, various locations acquire virtually totemic resonance as embodying something inalienable from that particular genre. One can observe this phenomenon carried out in various visual representations of music making. To stick to the North American continent, let us consider, for example, the final edition of the *Observer Music Monthly*, which contains a two-page spread of "mythic locations" entitled "Home Is Where the Art Is."[21] It depicts the facades of Sun Studios in Memphis, Chess Records in Chicago, the Capitol Records tower in Los Angeles, and the purported crossroads in Mississippi whereupon Robert Johnson is said to have stood before the devil and delivered over his soul in return for his extraordinary musical proficiency. Or regard the opening sequence of Rachel Liebling's 1994 documentary *High Lonesome: The Story of Bluegrass Music*, which shows the genre's paterfamilias Bill Monroe rummaging through the ruins of his birthplace, as though somehow from among its battered remnants he might extract the very genesis of his genius.

Various communities in the United States have recognized this phenomenon and utilized it successfully to solicit attention to and tourist attendance of their municipalities, among them Chicago, Memphis, New Orleans, and the state of Mississippi, as well as Nashville, Tennessee, which, along with other gestures, advances the Ryman Auditorium as the certified home of country music. Local economics have not suffered in the slightest from the insinuation that to stand upon these sites is to occupy not simply physical space but the end points of communally embraced pilgrimages.

The resonance is hard to resist, as Marybeth Hamilton observes in the introduction to *In Search of the Blues: Black Voices, White Visions*. She, like many others, gravitated to the Southern delta from which the genre is said to have originated. Hamilton endeavored to leave behind all the mythology attached to the region in order "to get a handle on the pilgrim experience, to reconstruct the breathless hunt for the blues' authentic origins."[22] Once there, however, she found herself almost unwittingly succumbing to the enticement of the atmosphere, sucker-punched by what some would dismiss as nothing more than oversold scenery. As she writes, "I found myself wholly caught up in that story. Everywhere seemed to demand to be photographed ... At some level I knew that these photos were hackneyed, that they had been taken by every blues pilgrim before me. But the power of the tale was too strong to resist, that sense of stepping out of history, and entering a mythic, primordial world."[23]

The Northern Soul community seems not to buy into this investment in geographically driven nostalgia. The sounds they revere could well float in an unattached arena, grounded only by the duration of the very grooves from which they emerge. One certainly gets this sense from what collectors anecdotally recount in the volumes by Winstanley and Nowell about their exploits in the United States. They rarely stepped outside the precincts of record stores, where they could rummage through endless boxes of unsold product in search of rare gems. More to the point, even the information compiled about the songs they admired and the artists they incorporated in their canon stayed routinely attached to the fruits of their professional labors, not the communities from which they came or the culture they represented. You do not get the sense of the of the presence of something that resembles what Warren Zanes speaks of as the "imagined South" in his examination of *Dusty in Memphis*, Dusty Springfield's 1969 recording.[24] Zanes draws attention to how a physical location can become enhanced and embroidered for outsiders through its acoustic presence in the cultural landscape. Recordings created in that place—even, as with Springfield, by outsiders, in her case an English woman—are able to assist in the activation of "a particularly *phonographic* kind of seeing, involving a mental framing based on leaving some things in and some things out."[25] Certain sounds, he infers, evoke a sense of place, a kind of geographical aura, which is both rooted in tangible topography and wrenched altogether from it by the imagination. The act of listening to that recording can serve as a virtual passport for the mind to return to the location.

In her 2009 Ph.D. thesis *Performing Fandom on the British Northern Soul Scene: Competition, Identity and the Post-Subcultural Self*, Nicola Smith cogently explains that quite another relationship to cultural geography appears to overtake most participants in the Northern Soul community. She argues that when they listen to these recordings, the individual tracks exist as pretty much little more than sites for the exercise of fandom, not the repository of a whole way of life or the reflection of their geographical origin. These songs might possibly conjure up or allude to a community somewhere on the other side of the Atlantic, but they do not reverberate with the complexities of their point of origin. Consequently, one might argue, to hear the releases of the Motown label does not lead to their decoding into information about Detroit. By listening to them in a new locality and not affixing them to their original home, the Northern Soul community engaged in an act Smith dubs "[re]marking," whereby "a record is able to possess a new identity, and subsequently a new significance, via alterations in the modes of cultural consumption."[26] The artist(s) become thereby more or less absented from their own endeavors, as they achieve consequence only by virtue of what they have left affixed to the vinyl itself. This leads to the paradox that, when artists elevated in this sphere appear live in person, the audience virtually disconnects them from their present circumstances and validates them only as the vehicle for the record they revere. Even if they sing, with all the impact upon their skills of the passage of time, they are then, in effect, virtually lip-synching, for what resonates for the audience remains nothing more or less than the material technologically committed to memory many years before.

If participants in the Northern Soul community were able to accumulate certain kinds of cultural capital through their engagement with the repertoire, to what degree were they simultaneously permitted to test and possibly transform fixed notions of race and ethnicity? As earlier stated, by and large the vast majority of the community was white, and their opportunities for face-to-face interaction with members of other races remained limited, not only by the inherent restrictions of British society but also by the physical separation of those individuals into self-defined enclaves. Therefore, absent an interpersonal avenue for social integration, they opted instead for a phonographically driven metamorphosis. The dance floor itself and the attendant activities of all-nighters became the catalyst through which some kind of osmosis might transatlantically be brought about that would achieve a cultural and potentially an ideological transformation. The anecdotal evidence contained in Winstanley and Nowell, as well as the ethnographic data integrated into Browne's and Smith's theses, validate such a proposition. The respondents' attitudes toward one another, issues of gender, their own bodies, and public manifestations of pleasure underwent a sea change. They consequently found their personalities rendered more elastic and accommodating, as flexible in their identities as the limbs of the most adept dancer. You get some sense of this alteration in the interview with an unidentified young man contained in Tony Palmer's documentary. He speaks eloquently and longingly about his hunger for some alternative to the humdrum routine of his industrial occupation and the undeniable satisfaction of that emptiness at Wigan Casino. The consequences of either an interruption or complete cessation of that way of life baffle him, for he cannot imagine what could replace the means by which his personality is integrated through the community of Northern Soul. He has widened his horizons, and the prospect of collapsing them back into the narrow confines of his residential community horrifies him.

At the same time, how did those horizons incorporate some elaborated understanding of the very individuals who created and performed the repertoire that instigated this fascination with African American music? If the 45s played by DJs triggered some momentous effects, was one of them a realigned sense of race? This question nags at anyone who investigates the sphere of Northern Soul. It seems difficult to believe that the members of this community did not transfer something of their affection for African American music to their comprehension of the complications of race and racism. However, by and large, in most writing about the subject, the issue of the racial position of the community rarely arises. The investigation of the recordings themselves or their creators rarely exceeds the hagiographic. They do not elicit or seem to entertain how these recordings might be part of a larger social context, ideological construction, or racial dynamic. Unlike, for example, the English fans of American blues, they did not translate their appreciation into acts of performance, initially mimicking the material they loved and eventually allow it to become the fuel for their own compositions. The comments made by participants in the community about the repertoire consequently remain, for the most part, effusive rather than interpretive. For them, the incontrovertible superiority of the recordings they treasured required no theoretical or intellectual justification. That should come as no surprise, as even being asked to convey how the scene influenced their personalities appears to have left any number of respondents dumbstruck. They seemed to exclaim without actually stating, "how can one parse out the principles of pleasure?"

By contrast, Kamisi Browne's dissertation provides the most elaborate dissection of the material itself into subcategories and unpacks the manner with which it achieves its effects. He conveys the fact that while the consumers of this repertoire felt overwhelmed by its elements, one can sympathetically dissect the musicological means with which that astonishment was achieved. However skillfully Browne assesses the techniques employed, one simultaneously acquires a sense of the problematic dimension of race that remains encoded within the Northern Soul canon. Some element of the phenomenon one might call a racial imaginary comes across: the conscious and unconscious means by which members of one race imagine the members of another. In the case of the Northern Soul community, some of the means by which this process occurs partake of long-standing conventions that verge on if not exceed the questionable. One of the many means through which audiences construct a sense of another race is through cultural products that are embedded in those communities and carry over into their daily lives the communal patterns and personal characteristics that emerge from the process.

In the case of the rhythm & blues genre, the material most admired by the Northern Soul scene can be broken into two spheres: what Browne calls the "stompers" or "floaters" that enabled many of the dancers, particularly the men, to enact their graceful arabesques; and the slower and often achingly emotional ballads that Browne, Dave Godin, and others have dubbed deep soul. One can extrapolate from these categories a kind of racial imaginary that conceives of African Americans as being alternately rhythmically adept or emotionally assertive. They can command a dance floor and appear to possess abundant reservoirs of soul.

It does not take a great deal of thought to discern how questionable these propositions can be, which implicitly value African Americans not for the wholeness of their identities but, instead, for their capacities for unrestricted physicality and unmediated emotionalism. That is not to imply that the denizens of the Northern Soul sphere overtly caricature the community they so admired, but it does raise the question of just what racial propositions arise from an aesthetic agenda; what polemics reside, implicit or explicit, in pleasure? Can one inadvertently reduce the very identity of a body of individuals while simultaneously becoming personally enlarged by the effusively lauded cultural expressions of that set of people? It could be possible that the white English working class share with their

African American cultural compatriots something of the problematic relationship about which Paul Gilroy inquires between the black people of privilege and the poorer members of that larger community. He wonders: "Maybe privileged people remain dependent on poor people for their soul, or their access to soul comes via the cultures those people erect against their sufferings, which the elite do not share . . . maybe there's a kind of estrangement from the vernacular which the elite experience as form of ambivalence."[27] The ethnographic studies of the Northern Soul community have yet to dig deep and dissect these confounding questions. For the moment, we can only propose that the sphere of Northern Soul undeniably supports and salutes African Americans, but it remains possible that in doing so it also simultaneously incorporates some longstanding and unquestioned assumptions, even generalizations, about those individuals.

While it would be excessive in the extreme to imagine that the Northern Soul community could solve the dilemma of race all on their own, it does bear asking: What might be the ideological dimensions of this phenomenon? Can one unleash some manner of claim about the constitution of society on the dance floor when your principal objective is to engage in acts of pleasure initiated by the commercial products released by the recording industry? The answer to these propositions may not be simple, but it does bear mentioning that ideological claims appear in many guises; even when one does not adopt a form of discourse that overtly engages with polemical gestures, a political proposition may nonetheless emerge. The work of Robin D. G. Kelley, one of the preeminent African American scholars and a cogent chronicler of liberation movements, acknowledges the intractability of political systems, and his work has eloquently given witness to the often, even routinely frustrated efforts of those who batter against oppression. At the same time, however, he advises that we do not allow that struggle to limit the kind of thinking that circumvents the boundaries of immediate circumstances. He inquires, "How do we produce a vision that enables us to see beyond our immediate ordeals?"[28] Kelley elaborates upon this position when he asserts:

> the desires, hopes, and intentions of the people who fought for change cannot be easily categorized, contained, or explained. Unfortunately, too often our standards for evaluating social movements pivot around whether or not they "succeeded" in realizing their visions rather than on the merits or power of the visions themselves. By such a measure, virtually every radical movement failed because the basic power

relations they sought to change remain pretty much intact. And yet it is precisely these alternative visions and dreams that inspire new generations to continue to struggle for change.[29]

Kelley draws inspiration from the proclamation of African American poet Jayne Cortez that we try to envision ourselves "somewhere in advance of nowhere."[30]

Perhaps that is the only place where those "fragile solidarities" that Gilroy speaks of in our epigraph could occur? In *Discographies: Dance Music, Culture and the Politics of Sound*, Jeremy Giulbert and Ewen Pearson take up the issue of how and when these "fragile solidarities" could arise in a dance-centered arena. For them, the answer does not come down to a matter of whether or not some form of dance culture, such as Northern Soul, could topple the destructive consequences of capitalism or race or gender. Instead, they advocate an investigation of at what point that form of culture succeeds in "negotiating new spaces," opening up admittedly limited but nonetheless consequential alternatives to the repressive dynamics of contemporary society.[31] Giulbert and Pearson write, "it is not a simple question of dance culture being 'for' or 'against' the dominant culture, but of how far its articulations with other discourses and cultures (dominant and otherwise) result in *democratizations* of the cultural field, how far they successfully break down existing concentrations of power, and how far they fail to do so."[32] As stated earlier, members of the Northern Soul community did feel that the environment and the recordings it emphasized widened their sense of themselves and the world about them. Whether or not it has also led to the kind of "democratizations" of which Giulbert and Pearson write would require further study and ethnographic engagement with members of the community.

In conclusion, what took place on the turntables of the Wigan Casino and elsewhere on the Northern Soul circuit whenever these recordings were played had an effect on those "concentrations of power," even if it did not issue in explicitly polemical gestures on the part of the participants. While neither the audience nor the DJs involved might have been able to achieve the objective liberation of the creators of the works of music they so admire, what they have incontrovertibly done, time after time after time, is to set free the voices of African American performers and producers who would otherwise remain silenced, erased altogether from history. Some might ask, would not attention have been drawn to the recordings admired by the Northern Soul communities by other individuals if this scene had never come into existence? The chances are narrow, it would seem, for many if not most of the individuals they idolized had fallen off the radar of pretty much the entire North American record-buying public. Conceivably, the activities of later DJs who were engaging in digging in the crates in order to sample unknown sounds could have come across them, but there is no guarantee.

It does not seem altogether an exaggeration to assert that the Northern Soul community transposes the act of emancipation that has yet to occur fully on a social plane for African Americans, and people of color everywhere, into a social context through the vehicle of dance and the communal adoration of commercial recordings. They freed up for consumption and commendation the voices and experiences of the performers who created and marketed the recordings they loved. Pleasure can, it would seem, co-exist with polemics, as I imagine Kelley, and others, advocate. On the dance floors of Britain for some four decades or more, the denizens of the Northern Soul community have launched themselves into this uncontained and endlessly animating sphere wherein we feel in our feet those "moments of affiliation and linkage" Gilroy encourages. At a moment in time when some commentators have announced the dawn of a post-racial age, the continuing friction and outright combat between racial communities reminds us that the fractiousness has not yet been quelled. Therefore, if we can, through affiliation with the Northern Soul community, achieve some acquaintance with the mythic Land of 1,000 Dances, then we might as well more fully imagine, and perhaps then bring into existence, that "somewhere in advance of nowhere" that lures us to believe harmony genuinely can reside in the civic sphere.

Notes

1. Paul Gilroy, Quoted in Richard C. Green and Monique Guillory, "Question of a 'Soulful Style,'" in Richard C. Green and Monique Guillory, eds., *Soul: Black Power, Politics and Pleasure* (New York: New York University Press, 1998), 255.

2. William James, *The Principles of Psychology* (Cambridge: Harvard University Press, 1981), 462.

3. Lawrence Grossberg, "Reflections of a Disappointed Music Scholar," in Roger Beebe, Denise Fulbrook, and Ben Saunders, eds., *Rock Over the Edge: Transformations in Popular Music Culture* (Durham: Duke University Press, 2002), 34.

4. Kate Milestone, "The Love Factory: The Sites, Practices and Media Relationships of Northern Soul," in Steve Redhead with Derek Wynne and Justin O'Connor, eds., *The*

Clubcultures Reader: Readings in Popular Cultural Studies (London: Blackwell, 1997), 157.

5. Dave Haslam, *Adventures on the Wheels of Steel: The Rise of the Superstar DJs* (London: Fourth Estate, 2002), 155–56.

6. Milestone, 154.

7. C. P. Lee, *Shake, Rattle and Rain: Popular Music Making in Manchester 1951–1995* (Devon, UK: Hardinge Simpole, 2002), 68–70.

8. *Ibid.*, 69–70.

9. *Ibid.*, 70–77.

10. *Ibid.*, 79.

11. David Nowell, *Too Darn Soulful: The Story of Northern Soul* (London: Robson, 2001), 44, 46, 48.

12. Milestone, 153.

13. *Ibid.*, 161.

14. Andrew Wilson, *Northern Soul: Music, Drugs and Subcultural Identity* (Cullompton, UK: Willan, 2007), 85.

15. Wilson, 86.

16. Nowell, 47; Milestone, 157.

17. Kimisi Lionel John Browne, "'Soul or Nothing': The Formation of Cultural Identity on the British Northern Soul Scene," diss., University of California, Los Angeles, 2005, 410–11.

18. Sarah Thornton, *Club Cultures: Music, Media and Subcultural Capital* (Hanover, NH: Wesleyan University Press/University Press of New England, 1996), 10–11.

19. George Orwell, *The Road to Wigan Pier* (New York: Berkeley Medallion, 1961), 99.

20. Milestone, 154.

21. "Home Is Where the Art Is," *Observer Music Monthly* 76 (January 2010): 33.

22. Marybeth Hamilton, *In Search of the Blues: Black Voices, White Visions* (London: Jonathan Cape, 2007), 1.

23. *Ibid.*, 2–3.

24. Warren Zanes, *Dusty in Memphis* (New York: Continuum, 2003), 84.

25. *Ibid.*, 86.

26. Nicola Smith, *Performing Fandom on the British Northern Soul Scene: Competition, Identity and the Post-Subcultural Self*, diss., University of Salford, 2009, 136.

27. Green and Guillory, 262.

28. Robin D. G. Kelley, *Freedom Dreams: The Black Radical Imagination* (Boston: Beacon, 2002), x.

29. *Ibid.*, ix.

30. *Ibid.*, x, xii.

31. Jeremy Guilbert and Ewan Pearson, *Discographies: Dance Music, Culture and the Politics of Sound* (London: Routledge, 1999), 160.

32. *Ibid.*, 161.

13

Some Reflections on "Celtic" Music

—Duck Baker

[This article is submitted here as a modest disclaimer by a musician who recognizes the inevitability of the use of the term "Celtic" with regard to music but doesn't like it, for reasons which will be given. Being constrained to use the term in professional situations has created in the author the desire to state some facts about it, whether anyone else is really interested or not.]

Admittedly, the terms used for the marketing of music have never been a matter of scientific exactness. Designations like rock, blues, jazz, and funk have meaning largely because we know what they mean to begin with; in any case they attached themselves to the respective styles soon after they made their appearances, and became familiar almost immediately. In some other cases a term that was originally controversial was embraced (bebop), while in others a name was consciously concocted to replace an undesirable appellation (country and western instead of hillbilly). Other names have been coined by writers or critics, sometimes long after the fact (western swing), while still others have geographic associations of greater or lesser accuracy (Chicago blues or Texas-style fiddling in the first instance, Piedmont blues in the second). A small number of musical genres are related to occupation (cowboy songs, sea shanties).

But while many of these terms actually convey much less than they might seem to at first glance (Mississippi blues is a good example of this, as the term must stretch to include many different musical styles), a term like "Celtic" has problems that go far beyond anything we could attach to any of those above. By the manipulation of a highly inaccurate set of assumptions, it implies musical and cultural links that simply do not exist, and obscures others that do. In America, the term usually amounts to a way to refer to Irish music that leaves room for the occasional tune that comes from Scotland or somewhere else, if the tune fits the performance style. As recently as the late 1980s, Americans operating in this musical realm called what they did "British Isles music." It took that long for them to find out that the Irish don't like being called British. But at the end of the day, this was a far more accurate designation than Celtic.

In fact it was not the Irish or Scots who brought this term into current usage. To a great extent it can be traced to the Breton Alan Stivell. Stivell's vision of a pan-Celtic cultural connection seems to have been with him almost from childhood. His father gave him a recreated Breton harp and encouraged his interest in his own culture, as well as in Irish and Scottish music and legend. During the 1960s Stivell was involved with early Breton folk-rock music, and simultaneously threw himself into the blossoming Breton folk revival. He made his mark with the 1971 record *Renaissance of the Celtic Harp*, an enormous hit in France and internationally.

It is logical that the Bretons nurtured this idea. The history of the Celts in Britain and Ireland is now accepted as having begun with a migration by sea from Spain to Ireland around the sixth century BC. Thence they moved to Scotland and from there to England. At the time of the Roman invasion they were established in England, Ireland, and the Scottish lowlands, while in parts of the Highlands earlier Pictish clans held on. But this state of affairs did not last long, as the Saxon invasions of the fifth and sixth centuries pushed the Celtic Britons into Cornwall and Wales. What is somewhat less well remembered is that this same wave of migrations sent some of the Celtic Britons into northeastern France, where they settled among the largely Celtic population and established the kingdom of Brittany. The medieval Welsh legend of Conan Meriadoc is based on this migration, just as the Arthurian legend has its roots in the displacement of Britons by Saxons in England. In fact, *Great Britain* is a term of differentiation from the lesser *Kingdom of Brittany*, which existed until the late fifteenth century before being absorbed into France. The cultural identity of the Bretons is defined by this history; in remembering the time of their independence from France, they are hearkening directly back to the England of Arthurian legend.

Given this background, it would have been surprising, when Breton folk festivals began to invite international guests to their stages in the 1970s, if Irish and Scottish performers were not among the first to get the call. In short order, these Celtic festivals became popular events, and the timing coincided with the decade that saw a huge explosion of touring by folk performers of all kinds in Europe. Every country had its own folk scene that included people trying to revive their own traditions or write pop-folk songs in their native tongues. And, especially on the Continent, international artists toured extensively, especially those from Ireland and Scotland but also from England, the United States, or almost anywhere else. And, as English revivalists like Martin Carthy, Pentangle, and the High Level Ranters had imported many ideas for the performance of their own music from what had happened in American traditional styles, bands on the Continent looked first to England and then to Ireland for inspiration. Among these groups, very few could generate the excitement created by Irish groups like the Bothy Band or a Scottish outfit like the Battlefield Band.

If this pan-Celtic idea was originally a Breton conceit, it did not take much persuasion to get Irish musicians on board, at least for as long as the party lasted. The seventies folk festival circuit provided a wonderful opportunity for the Irish and Breton musicians to discover each other, along with a feeling of commonality that is a positive development and not something anyone wants to disparage. At the same time, we should ask how much of the relationship is based on any historical or cultural fact—and the moment that that is done, the Kingdom of the Celt is in serious trouble.

If we were to borrow the term *Gaelic* from linguists, and use it to refer to the Scots and Irish, there would be no problem. Irish and Scottish history and culture are interwoven from antiquity, and the two nations have always felt themselves to be cousins. This is reflected in the music. Apart from general tendencies, there are a great many tunes and songs that are shared, some of which are not easily ascribed to either nation. But the modern term *Celtic* was pretty much intended from the start to include the Bretons, which would mean that the Welsh and Cornish were aboard without even having to fill in an application form. And, of course, it did not stop there. Any group who identified themselves as Celts, like the Galicians in Spain, could now claim a share in this great mystical heritage. Presumably the lad I encountered in Friulia, in northeastern Italy, who claimed to be a Celt should be included, even though his actual knowledge of the ancient Celts was such that he was quite insistently mistaken about the direction of their migration. He thought that they originated in Ireland and crossed Europe on their way to India. This is only slightly more wrongheaded than the entire issue here, and typical of the depth of knowledge involved.

After all, the Celts were spread over Northern Europe just before the time of the Roman Empire. There was certainly no hegemony felt between the different Celtic peoples of two thousand years ago. Someplace like Friulia has since that time been overrun by so many different races that to single any one out—Romans, Goths, Vandals, Austrians—is amazingly silly. The fellow I met could just as well have thought of himself as a Hun as a Celt. Perhaps his neighbors do. In any case it makes much less sense to call a contemporary Irishman a Celt than it does to refer to Mexicans as Aztecs.

The problem is that vendors of the "Celtic" mythology have convinced their audience that there was once a wonderful race that was somehow nobler, purer, and more soulful than the baser peoples who pushed them out of their rightfully held domains, back in a golden age we have forgotten because the Truth has been suppressed. The music is only one aspect; the mythology is also fundamental for much contemporary fantasy fiction, not to mention the modern revivals of pagan religion. A large percentage of the audience for Celtic music buys into the whole package, and certainly some of the bands providing the soundtrack do as well, dressing and even acting the part. (This is not true of the Irish and Scottish bands so much as lesser-known groups playing the smaller venues and festivals around the United States and Europe.) The question no one asks is whether the music played 1,500 years ago by people in Ireland, Scotland, Wales, Brittany, or Galicia sounded anything like the music we now call Celtic. The answer, of course, is that there is no reason to suppose that any of it sounded like any of the music we know today. Nor is there any reason to believe that such music as did exist sounded radically different from the music played by people like Angles or Saxons.

One could argue that all of this is harmless fun, and as long as it is understood to be that, there really should be no problem. But of course, nothing of the sort is understood; this idea has become so pervasive that any attempt to inject any real history into the discussion is usually viewed as an unwelcome intrusion. Celtophiles will typically respond to someone who makes the attempt with a mixture of pity and condescension, and wave objections aside with statements about how the history in history books does not tell the true story. Presumably the history in New Age bookstores, music fanzines, or adult fantasy novels does.

What we have in traditional music is the ongoing creation of a community of musicians, who can be seen as bearers of the culture of a larger community. That racial musical tendencies run deep can be seen by any consideration of African American music. But anyone who knows anything about that music will admit that the sense of melody displayed in the spiritual folk songs of the slaves owes a great deal to an assimilation of

Anglo-Scottish folk melody. Does this make their music Celtic? There is no doubt that Irish tradition has brought a spectacular body of music to the world, unsurpassed in melodic grace and depth. But is it a slander to the musicians responsible to imply that this is the result of neither diligence nor inspiration, or indeed of their cultural inheritance, but of their DNA (in fact only to certain specific strands of it)? I am reminded of the view of old-line southern racists who credited with innate musical abilities the Negro they regarded as only half human.

A consideration of American music might shed light on something important, which is that when blacks and whites heard each other making music, they often picked up things from one another and, as a result, their own musical traditions underwent radical transformations. The truth of the matter is that someone working within the framework of an inherited musical system that expresses something of a people's collective spiritual depth has a chance to contribute to that system (even if they were born to an altogether different culture), and that a folk musical tradition is the result of untold thousands of such contributions. We do not know who wrote most of the classic tunes of the Irish repertory, nor is it seen as important. What is valued is devotion to the tradition—the dedication to mastering instrument and repertoire, the drive to maintain the language nurtured by previous generations. (Obviously this has little to do with the showbiz aspirations of some current stars of the Celtic scene.)

How old is the Irish tradition? There are some general references that date from medieval times, but scholars consider it rash to think that any of the tunes we know are older than three or four hundred years. We might assume that some general characteristics go back further, but even the earliest references are over a thousand years removed from any connection to the Celts of Galicia or Spain.

It is intriguing to imagine that the Breton bombard and binou tunes, which seem older and more mysterious than folk music in some other regions of France, might be related to a root that also nurtured Galician music, but it is hard work to find any particular similarity to Welsh music, let alone Scottish or Irish. One might just as easily imagine that there was once a common prototypical European music that eventually was driven to the outlying areas, but whether such an idea would stand up to hard scrutiny is open to question. The problem with trying to see any real similarity between Breton and Irish music becomes apparent when we look at the songs of the Bretons, which seem largely to be light tunes, similar in fact to the sorts of ditties common in all kinds of French folk song. Not that there is anything wrong with Breton or French songs, but they certainly do not sound anything like Irish songs.

This of course brings us to something the Celtic label more or less deliberately tries to obscure: the very palpable relationship between Irish music and English music. Dance music in most of England is not generally as interesting as it is in Ireland (though the relationship is obvious), but English folk song is a spectacular tradition that anyone should be proud of, and anyone with less reason than the Irish for antipathy would be proud of this connection. This assessment of English dance music may seem sweeping and unfair, and no doubt there is plenty of room for disagreement (in any case, this generalization would not apply to the music of Northumberland and the northeast).

Whether a lengthy treatise could resolve such an issue or not, I will outline why I think it to be true and leave the reader to draw his/her own conclusions. The fact is that the development of Irish musical styles really escalated during the eighteenth, nineteenth, and early twentieth centuries (the noted authority Reg Hall sees it as something that did not begin to take off until well into the 1800s). When the musical tradition was in the hands of the rural population, there were few opportunities for an exceptionally talented youngster to earn a living at any kind of music, and almost none by playing music that was not traditional unless they lived in one of the large cities. Thus the talent pool was not drained by the kinds of opportunities that would have been available to rural people in England, where there were many more urban centers that provided opportunities for an easier kind of employment than could be found on the farm: dance bands, theater orchestras, etc. Moreover, the effect of the Industrial Revolution on the development of traditional culture of every kind was devastating, as was the Great War; English revivalists asking older people about folk music in their youth heard repeatedly that it was never the same after World War I.[1] As hinted above, much the same is true all over western Europe, and we generally find folk music developing to its greatest heights in areas that are remote, like southwestern Norway, Dalarna in Sweden, Andalusia, Sardinia, etc. The levels of virtuosity we associate with many of the instrumental traditions of these regions are the result of a longer period of development, which led to a great evolution of the dance music.

But singing traditions do not depend on the development of virtuosic styles. There is no way to deny the depth and richness of the English folk song, and as indicated above, the relationship between this tradition and that of the Irish is unmistakable. Some song tunes we think of as Irish have an English origin, including those of famous rebel songs. There is an implied swipe at the English with all this "Celtic" blarney. While the Irish and Scots have earned the right to bitter feelings toward the English, there is quite a bit wrong with Americans boarding this particular bandwagon, but I'll return to that. The body of Anglo-Scottish folk song studied by Francis Child in the nineteenth century, now known as the Child ballads, demonstrates a wealth of beautiful melody in both countries as well as textual relationships to songs and legends over much of Europe, particularly the Scandinavian nations.

It should also be said that not every Irishman was an oppressed mystic, nor every Englishman a highborn Philistine. The one people who arguably suffered more at the hands of the English than the Irish are the English themselves. Engels's study of the English working class or George Orwell's writings could be entered as evidence, but it is a complex argument and the point that needs making is simple: oppression is an economic issue that does not depend on national boundaries. Scottish history is so full of feudal wars (even after the English conquest), betrayals, and class divisions of their own that seeing the English as the only bogies takes real desire. Not that that is entirely lacking; the simplistic Hollywood-style view of it all has been embraced to the extent that a recently erected statue of William Wallace in Scotland bears a strong resemblance to—who else?—Mel Gibson.[2]

The Scandinavian relationship to Irish and especially Scottish music is quite a bit more obvious than any presumed ties to Brittany, but because this does not jibe with the Celtic idea it is conveniently ignored. This is unfortunate, not least because the Norwegian Hardanger fiddle tradition, for instance, is spectacular but still relatively unknown. Topic Records in the early eighties did devote an excellent album, *Ringing Strings*, to the connection between Shetland and Norwegian fiddle music, but the fundamental defining rhythmic characteristic of Scottish music, the "snap" exemplified in the Strathspey dance tunes, is remarkably like Scandinavian rhythms. I don't hear much direct connection between Scandinavian and Irish dance music, but the similarity between traditional Norwegian and Irish Sean Nós singers is uncanny. Did repeated Viking invasions during the period before the congealing of the modern Irish style have any influence? This in my view is an interesting possibility, but one not often discussed, presumably because to the modern mind Vikings are not cuddly like Celts.

The great English collector Cecil Sharp discovered during his 1916–18 travels in the Southern Appalachian Mountains that English and Scottish folk songs were quite alive. There were also Irish and Scottish tunes among the dance repertoire of mountain fiddlers brought over by early Scots-Irish settlers. An important later American connection is the fact that many of the performers on the early minstrel show circuit were Irish musicians; mid- nineteenth-century five-string banjo tutorials contain a high number of jigs. Later the tenor banjo was taken back and introduced in Ireland, where it has found a happy home.

All of this points us toward one of the oddest, and in a way most troubling, aspects of the current Celtic palaver: the manner in which the relationship of Scottish and Irish music to old-time mountain music and its progeny, bluegrass, is completely ignored. It is easy to name a dozen Irish or Scottish tunes commonly played by old-time musicians, and almost any bluegrass fiddle tune you can name is obviously related to those traditions, while the traditional repertoire shared by Irish and Breton players is nil. Many hill people are racially as purely Scots-Irish as the inhabitants of Derry. Are they excluded from the kingdom of Celts for the sin of singing English folk songs, for playing instruments of African descent, or simply because they are just thought of as half-witted inbred hicks whose musical abilities are, again, "innate" (like the youth in the 1972 film *Deliverance*)? One hates to burst bubbles, but the Hatfield-McCoy feud, symbolic of hillbilly backwardness, was a picnic compared to the murderous sprees the noble Kennedys of Ayrshire indulged in.[3] It is hard not to be suspicious of Americans who embrace all things Celtic while turning up their noses at the purveyors of their own direct link to that culture.

I also suspect that Americans who participate in Anglo-bashing as if it were a prerequisite to appreciating Irish and Scottish music are largely living up to the reputation of buffoonery that the rest of the world has come to expect of us. To a great extent Americans are just English people who stayed away from home too long.[4] Our cultural base is predominantly British, and this is true of any ethnic group to the extent that they participate in mainstream American society. It is foolish for Americans to pretend to be some kind of Celtic soulmates by proxy, and if we have not been guilty of oppressing the Irish or Scots, we have more than made up for it elsewhere.

It is also worth noting that, a couple of generations ago, Americans wanting to find musical relations to some sort of fount of white soulfulness looked not to the Celts but to the English. Folk song collectors in the wake of Cecil Sharp began hunting high and low for Child ballads, and while this was certainly important and valuable work, much of it smacks of unbridled Anglophilia. One group turned their attention to shape note and related hymnody, some with the misguided attention of proving the spirituals of black America were nothing more than direct borrowings from white songs. These scholars, headed by the industrious if slightly daft George Pullen Jackson,[5] seemed to quiver at the very idea of English folk song. But at least Jackson did not try to relate the music of the Anglo-Saxon to that of ancient cousins in Thuringia or some such.

It is interesting to note that Canadians from Quebec and Cape Breton do get covered by the Celtic umbrella. In the latter case it would be impossible to exclude them: not only are the inhabitants overwhelming of Scottish descent, they have maintained and nurtured their fiddling traditions with at least as much care as the folk back home. In the case of the Québécois, they have added a great many Irish and Scottish tunes to their own traditional repertoire, and play them in a style much closer to contemporary Irish practice than do American old-time players. So they qualify in terms of what their music actually sounds like, which seems perfectly sensible; this is certainly a far saner criterion when discussing musical styles than making specious claims on the basis of the bloodlines.

Notes

1. According to the Northumbrian musician Alistair Anderson, this story was told, with variations, over and over. A village band of eight might typically have been reduced by more than half its members, and the survivors often did not feel like carrying on. When the age of radio was ushered in during the ensuing decade, people were just as glad to adapt to new popular musical styles that did not hold such painful associations for them.

2. When this article was written, the statue of Wallace by Tom Church was on display at the Wallace Monument near Stirling, but it proved controversial and eventually was removed to the property of the sculptor in 2008.

3. Scottish history is full of accounts of blood feuds, dating back at least to the times when early Celtic arrivistes were vying with the Picts. The feud between Cassalis and Barganey factions of the Kennedy clan ran from about 1570 to 1610. The popular writer S. R. Crockett drew on this history in the very entertaining novel *The Grey Man* (1896), which one still finds in Scottish bookstores. Walter Scott also wrote a fictionalized account, *The Ayrshire Tragedy* (1830). Probably the most useful account, though the most difficult to find, is William Robertson's *The Kings of Carrick* (1890).

4. This is a slightly streamlined expression of the basic premise of the excellent book *Albion's Seed* by David Hackett Fischer (1989). He holds that mainstream

American culture is formed by the confluence of four distinct British folkways; the Puritans of New England, Pennsylvania Quakers, the combination of Cavaliers and indentured workers who settled Virginia, and the Scots-Irish who settled in Appalachia. Simplistic as it might seem in outline, Fischer develops this idea in impressive depth in this invaluable volume—but apologies to my fellow American contributors Kaufman, Cohen, Schwartz, and Cataliotti!!

5. The American educator and musicologist (1874–1953) and author of, among others, *White Spirituals in the Southern Uplands* (1933). Jackson's *Spiritual Folk-Songs of Early America: Two Hundred and Fifty Tunes and Texts with an Introduction and Notes* (1937) is a valuable book despite this bias. It should be noted that his basic premise has merit; there are indeed several African American spirituals that are obviously derived from shape note hymns (the best example I know of involves a well-known shape note hymn "Parting Friends" and a fairly obscure spiritual, "Somewhere Around the Throne"). But I think the real point is that African Americans absorbed the basic sense of Anglo-Scottish melody and incorporated it in their own music, in much the same way, and at the same time, that white musicians began to syncopate their fiddle tunes and play the banjo.

Contributors

"Duck" Baker (Richard R. Baker IV) is an accomplished and influential American finger-style guitarist who plays everything from rags, blues, country, gospel, and bluegrass to Celtic music, ballads and jazz. He has made many recordings, written reviews, and regularly performs in America and Europe—recently playing at the American Roots Guitar festival in Salisbury, England. Among his latest recordings is the collection *The Roots and Branches of American Music* (Les Cousins, 2009).

Robert H. Cataliotti, Ph.D., is a professor in the Department of Humanities at Coppin State University in Baltimore, Maryland, where he teaches courses in American and African American literature. He is a music critic/historian, the winner of a 1983 ASCAP Deems Taylor Award. He has written two books, *The Music in African American Fiction* (1995) and *The Songs Became the Stories: The Music in African American Fiction, 1970–2007* (2007). He is the producer and annotator of the compact disc that accompanies *Call & Response: The Riverside Anthology of the African American Literary Tradition* (1998) and the Smithsonian Folkways compact discs *Classic Sounds of New Orleans* (2010), *On My Journey: Paul Robeson's Independent Recordings* (2007), and *Every Tone A Testimony: An African American Aural History* (2001), and annotator of *A Voice Ringing O'er the Gale! The Oratory of Frederick Douglass Read by Ossie Davis* (2009).

Ronald D. Cohen is emeritus professor of history, Indiana University Northwest, Gary, Indiana. He is the author and/or editor of numerous books, including: (editor) Agnes "Sis" Cunningham and Gordon Friesen, *Red Dust and Broadsides: A Joint Autobiography* (1999); *Rainbow Quest: The Folk Music Revival and American Society, 1940–1970* (2002); (editor) *Alan Lomax: Selected Writings, 1934–1997* (2003); (with Robert Lichtman) *Deadly Farce: Harvey Matusow and the Informer System in the McCarthy Era* (2004); *Folk Music: The Basics* (2006); *A History of Folk Music Festivals in the United States: Feasts of Musical Celebration* (2008); (with Bob Riesman) *Chicago Folk: Images of the Sixties Music Scene: The Photographs of*

Raeburn Flerlage (2009); *Work and Sing: A History of Occupational and Labor Union Songs in the United States* (2010); (editor) *Alan Lomax, Assistant in Charge: The Library of Congress Letters, 1935–1945* (2011). He has also co-produced recordings, including: (with Dave Samuelson) *Songs for Political Action: Folk Music, Topical Songs and the American Left, 1926–1954* (Bear Family, 1996); (with Jeff Place) *The Best of Broadside: 1962–1988: Anthems of the American Underground From the Pages of Broadside Magazine* (Smithsonian Folkways, 2000). He is the editor of the American Folk Music and Musicians book series for the Scarecrow Press.

John Hughes teaches English at the University of Gloucestershire. He has published widely on nineteenth-century literature and on twentieth-century literary theory and philosophy. His publications include *Lines of Flight: Reading Deleuze with Hardy, Conrad, Gissing, Woolf* (1996), *Ecstatic Sound: Music and Individuality in the Work of Thomas Hardy* (2001), and "*Affective Worlds*": *Writing, Feeling, and Nineteenth-Century Literature* (2011).

Will Kaufman is professor of American literature and culture at the University of Central Lancashire. Originally from New Jersey, he is a graduate of Montclair State College and was a Marshall Scholar at the University of Wales, Aberystwyth. He is the author of *The Comedian as Confidence Man: Studies in Irony Fatigue* (1997), *The Civil War in American Culture* (2006), *American Culture in the 1970s* (2009), and *Woody Guthrie, American Radical* (2011). He is the series editor for the ABC-Clio *Transatlantic Relations* Encyclopaedia Series and, with Heidi Slettedahl Macpherson, edited the three-volume title in that series, *Britain and the Americas: Culture, Politics, History*. As a professional folk musician and singer, he has given hundreds of presentations on Woody Guthrie throughout Europe and the USA. In 2008 he was the recipient of a BMI Woody Guthrie Research Fellowship.

Andrew Kellett earned his doctorate in modern European history in 2008 from the University of Maryland–College Park, and is now a visiting assistant professor of history at Harford Community College in Bel Air, Maryland. His research and teaching specializations include transatlantic cultural exchange, the use of myth and ritual in political culture, and expressions of masculinity in popular culture. He has written articles for *African American National Biography* (Oxford University Press, 2008), and his first published monograph, *Fathers and Sons: American Blues and British Rock Music, 1960–1970*, is forthcoming.

Erich Nunn is assistant professor of English at Auburn University, where he teaches American Studies with an emphasis on race, popular music, and the U.S. South. His essays on such figures as William Faulkner and Jimmie Rodgers have appeared in the *Faulkner Journal* and *Criticism: A Quarterly for Literature and the Arts*. He is currently working on a book project entitled *Sounding the Color Line: Race, Music, and American Vernacular Modernism*.

Christian O'Connell is a research student at the University of Gloucestershire working on a Ph.D. thesis entitled "The British 'Bluesman': Paul Oliver and Blues Historiography." After taking his first degree from the University of Leeds in geography. he completed an M.A. in American Studies at King's College, London, including a thesis on "The Impact of the Recording Industry on the Blues during the Race Records era, 1920–1942".

Paul Oliver is an international scholar, reviewer, broadcaster, and musicologist whose influence has been enormous in two areas—vernacular architecture and Afro-American music. He has written numerous publications in both areas, including the award-winning book *Blues Fell This Morning*, and is the winner of a Sony Radio Award and the Grand Prix du Disque for his programs on blues music. His most recent publication is *Barrelhouse Blues* (2009), and his many other publications include: *Savannah Syncopators, Yonder Come the Blues, Screening the Blues*, and editing the *Blackwell Guide to Blues Records*. He is the editor of the four-volume *Encyclopedia of Vernacular Architecture of the World* (Cambridge University Press, 1997). Oliver has been connected with Oxford Brookes University for many years, and was associate head of the School of Architecture between 1978 and 1988. Among his many honors is the MBE awarded by the Queen in 2003 in recognition of his contribution to architectural education.

David Sanjek has been professor of music and director of the Popular Music Research Centre at the University of Salford since 2007. Before that, he was the Director of the BMI Archives in New York City from 1991 to 2007. He recently published "Bank Accounts and Black Narcissus: Jimmie Rodgers and the Professionalization of American Popular Music," in *Waiting for a Train: Jimmie Rodgers' America* (2009), and completed "'What's Syd Got to Do with It?': Syd Nathan, Henry Glover and the Complex Achievement of Crossover" (*Hidden in the Mix: African American Country Traditions*, Duke University Press); "You Can't Always Get What You Want: Riding the Medicine Ball Caravan" (*Sights & Sounds: Interrogating the Music Documentary*, University of Edinburgh Press); "Putting It Together: The Institutionalization of the American Music Theatre" (*Keywords in American Musical Theatre*), and "Hard of Hearing: Acoustic Legacies and Public Policies" (*Popular Music and Society*). He is preparing two volumes for publication: *Always on My Mind: Music, Memory and Money* and *Stories We Could Tell: Putting Words to American Popular Music*. [Sadly, David died suddenly in November 2011 on his way to a meeting of the National Recording Preservation Board at the Library of Congress in Washington, D.C. –Ed.]

Roberta Freund Schwartz is an associate professor of historical musicology at the University of Kansas, and advising director of the University of Kansas Archive of Recorded Sound. Her areas of specialization include the music of the Spanish Renaissance, patronage studies, and African American popular music—jazz, blues, gospel, and rock and roll. She has produced articles on the Spanish melomane and composer Saint Francis of Borja, the patronage of music by the Spanish nobility in the Renaissance, blues rock songwriting, Meredith Willson's *The Music Man*, and the role that British jazz critics played in popularizing African American music in that country. Her recent monograph, *How Britain Got the Blues: the Transmission and Reception of American Blues Style to the United Kingdom* (2007), was named the best book on historical research on blues, R&B, or soul recordings by the Association of Recorded Sound Collections in 2008.

Jill Terry is head of English and Cultural Studies at the University of Worcester, England. Her publications focus on orality in American literature from the South and she has a long-held interest in folk music, originally as folk singer and dancer, latterly as academic. Her chapter "Transatlantic Folk Exchanges in 1959—the Revival Year" is collected in Richard Gray and Waldemar Zacharasiewicz, eds., *Transatlantic Exchanges: The American South in Europe—Europe in the American South* (2007). Other publications include "'Reads kinda like jazz in they rhythm': Gayl Jones' recent Jazz Conversations," in Fiona Mills and Keith Mitchell, eds., *After the Pain:*

Critical Essays on Gayl Jones (2006); and "Oral Culture and Contemporary Fiction by Women," in Richard Gray and Owen Robinson, eds., *The Blackwell Companion to the Literature and Culture of the American South* (2004).

Brian Ward is professor of American Studies at the University of Manchester. His major publications include *Just My Soul Responding: Rhythm and Blues, Black Consciousness and Race Relations* (1998), which won several prizes, including the Organization of American Historians' James A. Rawley Prize for the best book on the history of U.S. relations and an American Book Award for "outstanding literary achievement." His 2005 book *Radio and the Struggle for Civil Rights in the South* earned a CHOICE Outstanding Academic Title Award from the American Library Association and was named the best history book of the year by the Association for Education in Journalism and Mass Communication. In 2009 he published *The 1960s: A Documentary Reader*. He is currently working on a book about the relationship between the American South and the world of British popular music.

Neil A. Wynn is professor of twentieth-century American history at the University of Gloucestershire, England. He has published several works on African American and American history, most notably *The African American Experience during World War II* (2010), *The Afro-American and the Second World War* (1976; paperback 1993), and *From Progressivism to Prosperity: American Society and the First World War* (1986). His work as editor includes *"Cross the Water Blues": African American Music in Europe* (2007) and *America's Century: Perspectives on U.S. History Since 1900*, co-edited with Iwan Morgan (1993). He has also produced two historical dictionaries and written numerous articles and reviews, including pieces on American society and World War II, transatlantic race relations, Mike Tyson, and on *The Sopranos*.

Index

ABC Television, 209
Acuff, Roy, 156
Adams, Derroll, 131
Adams, James Taylor, 65
Adins, George, 31
African American literature, use of, in blues scholarship, 42–43, 46–48, 51
Air India, 34
Aldan, Jeff, 12
Alexander, Alger "Texas," 156
Ali, Muhammad, 64
Almanac Singers, 81, 90
Alvin Ailey Dance Company, 31
American Columbia, 26
American Embassy (London), 31, 134
American Folk Blues, 31
American Folk Blues (and Gospel) Festivals, 10, 32–34, 161, 183
American Folk Song and Folk-lore: A Regional Bibliography, 7
American Folklore Society, 5
American Roots Music (PBS), xi, 3
American School of the Air (CBS), 120
American Troubadours, The, 23
American Victor, 26
Ammons, Albert, 26
Anderson, Ian, 143
Andrews, Inez, and the Andrewettes, 33
Animals, The, xiii, 11, 96, 141, 153–59, 166–73, 187, 217, 221–22; "The House of the Rising Sun," xiii, 155, 158, 166, 194. *See also* Burdon, Eric
"Another Man Done Gone," 126
Anthology of American Folk Music, 95

Anthony, Ted, 155–56
Appalachian ballads, 57, 108; identity, 62; isolation, 62; Cecil Sharp trips to, 6, 57, 252
Arhoolie (records), 31
Arlen, Harold, 85
Armed Forces Radio Service, 16, 121
Armstrong, Louis, 11–13, 123
Arnold, Billy Boy, 141
Arnold, Jerome, 190–91
"Arthur MacBride," 109
Arthurian legend, 247
Asch, Moses, 87
Ashley, Clarence "Tom," 156
Atlantic Monthly, The, 62
Atlantic Records, 185
Attenborough, David, 128
Auden, W. H., 94
Aynsley Dunbar Retaliation, The, 149

"Baby Let Me Take You Home," 153
"Baby Scratch My Back," 145
"Back Where I Come From," 120
Baez, Joan, 11, 102
Baker, Ginger, 196
Baker, Josephine, 13–14, 25
Baldry, "Long John," 30
Baldwin, James, 208
"Ballad of Hollis Brown, The," 97, 105
Ballads and Blues, 8, 11, 97, 125–26
Bane, Michael, 170, 219-20; *White Boy Singin' the Blues*, 219
Baraka, Amiri. *See* Jones, LeRoi
"Barbara Allan," 66, 109

263

"Barbara Allen," 80
Barbee, John Henry, 32
Barber, Chris, 29, 123, 130
Barry, Margaret, 126–27
Basie, Count, 12, 84
Battlefield Band, The, 248
BBC, 7, 12–14, 28–29, 78, 94, 120–22, 124–28, 133–34, 145–46; home service, 121, 123, 128; Third Programme, 124–25, 128
Beatles, The, 11, 95, 153, 170, 184, 192, 196, 198, 205, 208–11, 213, 217, 223
Bechet, Sydney, 12, 24
Beck, Jeff, 145, 182–83, 192, 197–98, 214
"Bedtime Blues," 145–46
Behan, Dominic, 125
"Bells of Rhymney, The," 109
Below, Fred, 183
Berea Alumnus, 66
Berry, Chuck, 140, 166–67, 194, 207, 209–10
"Big Boss Man," 140
Big Fella, 14
Big John's (club), 190
Big Rock Candy Mountain, The, 131–32
Bikel, Theodore, 102, 127
Billboard, 232
Bishop, Dick, and His Sidekicks, 77
Bishop, Elvin, 186, 191
Black and White Minstrel Show, The, 23
Black Arts Movement, 211–13, 217
Black Divas (Channel 4 documentary), 14
"Black Power," 211
Blackbirds, 12–14, 25
Blackwell, Scrapper, 123
Blake, Eubie, 25
Blanchett, Cate, 110
Bland, Bobby "Blue," 213
Bland, James, 22
Blind Faith, 223
Blitzstein, Marc, 85

Bloomfield, Michael, 180–81, 183, 185–99; *The Electric Flag*, 198
"Blowin' in the Wind," 94
Blues and Gospel Records Discography, 28
"Blues in the Mississippi Night," 124
Blues Incorporated, 139
Blues Project, The, 181, 193, 195
Blues Records 1843 to 1970, 28
Blues Unlimited, 27, 142, 162, 164–65, 214, 216
Blues World, 27, 162, 214
Blues-Rock Explosion, 218
"Bo Diddley," 140
"Bob Dylan's Dream," 96
Bohee Brothers Colored Minstrel Company, 23
Bond, Graham, 140
Booker T and the MGs, 167, 190
"Boom Boom," 141, 217
Booth, Stanley, 209–10
"Boots of Spanish Leather," 96
"Born Under a Bad Sign," 147
Borneman, Ernest, 27
Bothy Band, The, 248
"Bound for Glory," 121
Bowie, David, 96, 149
Bowman, Pete, 24
Boyd, Eddie, 30, 48
Boyd, Joe, 195
Boyes, Georgina, 14, 38, 41, 132
"Brave Wolf," 122
Bray, Jim, 126
Brewer, James, 102
Bridges, Harry, 88
Bridson, Geoffrey, 122
"Bright Lights, Big City," 140
British Invasion (bands), 38, 52, 179, 184, 192, 208, 210–11, 213
Britt, Mel, 235
Brocken, Michael, 9
Broonzy, Big Bill, ix, xiii, 3, 9–10, 17,

28–29, 42, 48, 49, 123–26, 130, 132, 139, 141, 159–61, 186, 207
Broven, John, 27, 162
Brown, James, 212
"Brown Adam," 98
Browne, Kamisi, 234, 240–41
Browning, Robert, 57
Brubeck, Dave (Quartet), 34
Bruce, Jack, 195–96
Brunning, Bob, 170
Brunswick, 26, 158
Bryden, Beryl, 30
"Buffalo Skinners, The," 122
Burdon, Eric, 153–59, 161, 166–74, 188–89, 194, 221; *Winds of Change*, 171. *See also* Animals, The
Burke, Kenneth, 83
Burnett, Lillie, 214
Butterfield, Paul (Blues Band), viii–xiv, 102, 179–81, 183, 185–99; *East-West*, 198; *Fathers and Sons*, 197

Callahan, Homer, 156
Callender's Minstrels, 22
Calloway, Cab, 13–14
Cameron, Isla, 125–26
Campbell, Olive Dame, 6
"Canadee-I-O," 109
Cannon, Geoffrey, 154, 169
Cantwell, Robert, 8
"Cape Cod Girls," 122
Caravan, 125
Carawan, Guy, 126
Carry Me Back to Old Virginny, 22
Carter, Clarence, 140
Carter Family, 63
Carthy, Martin, xi, 78, 96–99, 101, 248
Case, George, 148
Cash, W. J., 71
"Cat's Squirrel," 146
Cavell, Stanley, 112
CBS, 103, 120

Centralia mining disaster, 80–81
Chandler, Chas, 166
Charles, Ray, 166, 183
Charters, Samuel, 7, 41, 161
Chauvard, Marcel, 31
Checkerboard Lounge, 217
Checklist of Recorded Songs in the English Language in the Archive of American Folk Song to July, 1940, 7
Chess Records, 140, 184–85, 187, 191, 197, 216–17, 237
Chicago Blues Festival, xi
Child, Francis James, x–xii, 5–6, 17, 57, 60, 63, 66, 95, 98–100, 108, 125, 132, 252; English and Scottish Popular Ballads, 5, 57
Children's Hour, The (BBC), 78
Chilton, Charles, 27
"Chimes of Freedom," 101
Chisholm Trail, The, 121
Chocolate Dandies, The, 13, 25
Christian, Charlie, 84
Civil Rights movement, viii, 11, 95, 121, 164–66, 210
Civil War (U.S.), 61
Clancy Brothers, The, 100
Clapton, Eric, xiv, 142–44, 146–47, 161, 172–73, 180, 182–84, 187–89, 191–92, 195–99; and the Bluesbreakers, 192; *Riding with the King*, 223. *See also* Cream
Clarke, Mick, 145, 147
Clinch Mountain Boys, The, 34
"Clothes Line Saga," 111
Club A-Go-Go, 168
Cochran, Charles B., 25
Cocker, Joe, 96
Cohen, Phil, 144
Cohen, Ronald, x, xiii, 16
Cold War, 7–8, 16, 181
Cole, Bob, 23
Coleman, Fitzroy, 127

Collins, Shirley, 7, 128–29
Coltrane, John, 212
Columbia Records, 121, 143
Colyer, Ken, 45
"Come All You Fair and Tender Ladies," 109
communism: in Britain, 10, 78, 119, 125, 128; in U.S., 82–84, 87, 121, 134; Young Communist League, 125
Congress of Industrial Organizations (CIO) 15, 82–84, 88
Conservative Party, 124
Cook, Bruce, 215
Cook, William Marion, 24
Cooke, Alistair, 7, 120, 123
Coon Creek Girls, The, 121
Copeland, Johnny, 223
Copeland, Shemekia, 223
Copland, Aaron, 85
"Copper Kettle," 108
Cortez, Jayne, 243
Coser, Lewis, 85
Cott, Jonathan, 194
Cox, Ida, 12
Crawdaddy (magazine), 183, 192
Crawdaddy Club, The, 141
"Crawling King Snake," 140
Cray, Ed, 81
Cream, 146–48, 169, 196, 206, 210, 219, 222–23; *Disraeli Gears*, 147, 196
"Creole Love Call," 13
Criminal (label), 282
Crissman, Maxine, 87
"Crosscut Saw," 147
"Crossroad(s) (blues)," 147, 195
Cuban missile crisis, 97
"Cuckoo Is a Pretty Bird, The," 109
Cumberland Empire, The, 65
Cyp Landreneau's Cajun Band, 34

Daily News, 84
Daily Worker, 126

Dallas, Fred, 132
Dark Doings, 14
Davies, Cyril, 30, 139
Davies, Ray, 198
Davis, Belle, 24
Davis, Francis, 179
Davis, Miles, 212
Davison, Howard, 28
DC Comics, 103
Decca, 140, 143, 216
Delauney, Charles, 27–28
Deliverance, 253
Delta Interpretive Center, 205
Dem Golden Slippers, 22
Demetre, Jacques, 27, 31
Denning, Michael, 82–85, 88; *The Cultural Front: The Laboring of American Culture in the Twentieth Century*, 82
Denisoff, R. Serge, 84–85
Depression, the (1930s), 15, 81
Derek and the Dominos, 223
Desanto, "Sugar Pie," 32
Dickens, Charles, 21
Diddley, Bo, 140, 145, 166, 170, 208
"Dimples," 140, 142
Disc Records, 16
Discophile, 28
Dixieland Jug Blowers, The, 26
Dixon, R. M. W., 28
Dixon, Willie, 32, 188, 207
"Do I Love You (Indeed I Do)," 235
Donegan, Lonnie, 16, 45, 77, 123, 133, 157
Donovan, 96
Dorothy Norwood Singers, The, 33
"Double Crossing Blues (Time)," 143
Dover Street to Dixie, 12
Down Beat, 191, 211
Downliners Sect, The, 140
"Drifting Too Far from the Shore," 108
Du Bois, W. E. B., 45
Dunbar, Scott, 162–64

Duncan, Johnny, 132
Dupree, "Champion" Jack, 30, 34, 207
"Dust My Broom," 141, 144
Dusty in Memphis, 238
Dylan, Bob, xi–xiii, 78, 94–113, 157–58, 192, 196; *Another Side of Bob Dylan* 118; and The Band 111; *Basement Tapes*, 107, 111; *Blonde on Blonde*, 104, 106; *Bringing It All Back Home*, 102; *Chronicles*, 99, 102–4; *Don't Look Back*, 109–10; *Highway 61 Revisited*, 101–4; *John Wesley Harding*, 111; *Nashville Skyline*, 111; *Self-Portrait*, 111; *Time Out of Mind*, 108

Eagle, Roger, 231
Eat the Document, 109–10
Ebony, 166
Ed Sullivan Show, 221
Edison Bell, 24
Edwards, Dave "Honeyboy," 35, 169
Egan, Sean, 170
"Eileen Aroon," 109
Elektra Records, 191, 193, 195
Ellington, Duke, 11, 13, 26, 34, 84
Elliott, Bill, 12
Elliott, June, 131
Elliott, Ramblin' Jack, 77–78, 104, 111, 131, 157; *Woody Guthrie's Blues*, 78
Ellison, Ralph, 43
Emancipation, 23
Emerson, Ralph Waldo, 106, 111–13; "History," 112
Emmett, Dan, 21
Engels, Friedrich, 252
English Folk Dance and Song Society (EFDSS), 5, 119, 122
Ennis, Seamus, 119, 125–27
ENSA (Entertainers' National Service Association), 13
Esquire, 26
Estes, Sleepy John, 32

"Eternal Circle," 100
Ethiopian Serenaders, The, 11, 21
European Blues Association, 35
Evans, David, 37, 40
"Everlasting Circle, The," 100
"Everything's Gonna Be Alright," 146, 147

Fairport Convention, 96
Fame, Georgie, 192
"Far Away in Shanty Town," 14
"Farewell," 100
Farlowe, Chris, 192
Fickle Pickle, 190
Filene, Benjamin, x, 4–5, 7
First World War, 6, 11, 24, 251
Fisk Jubilee Singers, 11, 22
Fisk University, 10, 22
Fitzgerald, Ella, 34
Five Musical Spillers, The, 24
Fleetwood Mac, xiv, 146, 149, 169–70, 210, 218, 222
Folk Song of the American Negro, The, 10
Folkways, 16, 87
Ford, Mark, 111–12
44 Skiffle and Folk Song Group, 77
Foster, Eddie, 235
Foster, Harriet, 133
"Four until Late," 147
"4th Time Around," 95
"Froggie Went a Courtin'," 109
Frost, William Goodell, 62, 65
Fuller, Blind Boy, 123

Gable, Dorothy, 70–71
Gaslight, The, 99
General American, 235
Gerde's, 97
Gershwin, George, 85
Gershwin, Ira, 85
Gibson, Mel, 252
Gibson guitars, 143

Gillespie, Dizzie, 84
Gilmore, David, 149
Gilroy, Paul, 227–28, 230, 242–44
"Gimme a Pigfoot," 139
"Ginger Blues," 22
"Girl from the North Country," 96, 99
"Git along Little Dogies," 122
Giulbert, Jeremy, 243
Glamorous Night, 14
Glover, Tony, 99
"God Save the Queen," 110
Godin, Dave, 140, 231–33, 241; *Blues & Soul*, 231
Godrich, John, 28
Golden Chords, The, 103
Golden Gate Quartet, The, 120
Golden Torch, 232, 234
Gomelski, Giorgio, 188
"Gonna Send You Back to Georgia," 153
"Gonna Send You Back to Walker," 153, 155
"Good Morning Little Schoolgirl," 195
"Goodnight Irene," 16, 122
Gordon, Robert, 197
Gordy, Berry, 235
Gospelaires, The, 33
"Got Love if You Want It," 141
Granada TV, 129, 232
Grand Ole Opry, 63
Grapes of Wrath, The, 79
Grappelli, Stephane, 30
Gray, Michael, 103, 108
Green, Archie, 4
"Green Onions," 190
Gregory, David, 8, 122, 124, 129
Griffith, Andy, 157
Grist, Leighton, 171–72
Groom, Bob, 27, 216, 219; *The Blues Revival*, 216, 219
Grossberg, Lawrence, 228
Grossman, Albert, 119–20
Gruning, Thomas, 17

Guardian, The, 154
Guralnick, Peter, 187, 191, 197, 221; *Feel Like Going Home*, 220
Guthrie, Marjorie, 80
Guthrie, Mary Jo, 80
Guthrie, Woody, ix–xiii, 8–9, 15, 77–90, 94–95, 104–6, 108, 112, 120–21, 124, 129, 131–33, 157; *Dustbowl Ballads*, 8
Guy, Buddy, 32, 142, 146–47, 161, 183, 189, 217, 221, 223; *Folk Festival of the Blues*, 142
"Gypsy Davey," 104

Hall, Adelaide, 13–14
Hall, Reg, 251
Hall, Vera, 124
Hamilton, Marybeth, 38, 40–41, 155, 238; *In Search of the Blues*, 238
Handle, Johnny, 158
Handy, W. C., 22
Hangen, Tona, 49
Hankins, Esco, 157
Harburg, Yip, 85
"Hard Rain's a Gonna Fall, A," 99, 104
Hardanger fiddle tradition (Norway), 252
Harker, Ben, 9
Harlem Renaissance, 48
Harmonizing Four, The, 39
Harmony (guitars), 68
Harriet and Her Harmonium, 133
Harris, Rex, 160
Harrison, George, 198
Hasted, John, 78, 130
Haverly Colored Minstrels, 22
Hawks, The, 109, 187
Haynes, Todd, 110
"He's Gone Away," 7
Henderson, Hamish, 119
Henderson, Rosa, 22
"Here 'Tis," 140
"Hey Crawdaddy," 140

Heylin, Clinton, 97, 100–101
Hicks, Bert, 13
Hicks, Michael, 149
"Hideaway," 143
High Level Ranters, The, 248
High Lonesome: The Story of Bluegrass Music, 237
"Highlands," 108
Higley, Dr. Brewster, 59
"Historical America in Song," 125
HMV, 26
Hobsbawm, Eric, 41
Holcomb, Roscoe, 34
Holiday, Billie, 84
Hollywood, 86–89, 252
Home Office (UK), 134
"Home on the Range," 58–61, 68–69, 73
"Honey What's Wrong," 140
"Hoochie Coochie Man," 141–42
Hooker, John Lee, 32–33, 140, 143, 160–61, 166, 168, 187–89, 193, 207, 217
Hopkins, Lightnin', 31–32
Horne, Lena, 13
Horton, Walter "Shakey," 33
Hot Discography, 28
House, Eddie "Son," 33, 103, 209
"House Carpenter," 109
"House of the Rising Sun, The," xiii, 155–58, 166, 174, 194
House Un-American Affairs Committee, 16
Houston, Cisco, 121
"How Long, How Long Blues," 139
"How Many More Times (Years)," 148, 209
Howard, Rosetta, 12
Howe, Irving, 85
Hughes, Langston, 31, 48, 120
Hunter, Alberta, 25
"Hunter, The," 148
Hurston, Zora Neale, 48

"I Ain't Got You," 140, 142
"I Can't Give You Anything but Love," 13
"I Don't Believe You," 96
"I Got Rhythm," 13
I Hear America Singing, 7
"I Left My Heart in San Francisco," 29
"I Wanna Be Your Lover," 95
"I Wanna Be Your Man," 96
"I Want to Know," 195
"I Wish You Would," 141
"I'm a King Bee," 141
"I'm a Little Blackbird Looking for a Bluebird," 12
"I'm a Man," 140
"I'm in the Mood for Love," 13
I'm Not There, 129
"I'm So Glad," 147
In (label), 235
"In an English Country Garden," 128
In Dahomey, 24
Industrial Revolution, 251
Industrial Workers of the World (IWW), 85, 88
International Folk Music Council, 16
Invisible Man, 43
Isle of Wight festival, 111
"It Ain't Right," 148
"It Hurts Me Too," 146
"It's All Meat," 171
"I've Got My Brand on You," 141
"I've Got My Mojo Working," 141
Ives, Burl, 86–87, 120–21, 125, 129

J. Geils Band, 193
Jackson, Edgar, 12
Jackson, George Pullen, 254
Jacobs, "Little Walter," 30–31, 33, 148, 169
Jagger, Mick, 148, 161, 180, 190, 194, 196, 206, 216–18. *See also* Rolling Stones, The
James, Elmore, 141, 143–44, 146, 218
James, Jesse, 26

James, (Nehemiah) Skip, 33, 147, 222
James, William, 228
Jazz Collector, 26
Jazz Hot, 27, 31
Jazz Journal, 27, 38, 139
Jazz Monthly, 27, 38–39, 139
Jazz Music, 133
Jazz News, 27
Jazz Records 1897–1942, 28
Jazz Singer, The, 70
Jean Ritchie in Kentucky, 125
Jefferson, Blind Lemon, 42, 44–45, 49
"Jesse James," 133
"Jesus Gonna Make Up My Dying Bed," 146
Jim Crow, 44, 64. *See also* segregation
"Jim Jones," 109
JJ (label), 235
John, Elton, 149
"John Brown," 99
Johnson, Blind Willie, 174
Johnson, J. R., 23
Johnson, Lonnie, 29, 32, 45, 139
Johnson, Pete, 12, 26
Johnson, Robert, 4, 50, 52, 103, 143, 146, 161, 183, 209, 218, 221–22, 237
Jokers, The, 103
Jones, Brian, 140, 161, 184, 196, 209
Jones, Curtis, 27, 30, 33
Jones, Edgar, 23
Jones, Evan, 94
Jones, Gayl, 260
Jones, LeRoi (Amiri Baraka), 211–12, 217; *Blues People*, 211; "Changing Same, The," 211
Jones, Loyal, 71–72
Jones, Max, 27, 29, 160
Jones, Paul, 195
Jones, Quincy, 185
Jones, Wizz, 77
Joplin, Janis, 218
Joplin, Scott, 20

Joseph, Anthea, 97
Journal of American Folk-Lore, 59
"Jump Jim Crow," 69

Karpeles, Maud, 6, 16
Kazin, Alfred, 110
Keats, John, 109
Kelley, Robin D. G., 44, 242–44
Kelsey, Bishop Samuel, 33
Kennedy, Douglas, 122
Kennedy, John F., 97
Kennedy, Peter, 119
Kennedys of Ayrshire, 253
Kersands, Billy, 22–23
KFVD, 87
"Killing Floor," 145–46
Kincaid, Bradley, xii, 62–73; *My Favourite Mountain Ballads and Old Time Songs*, 64
King, Albert, 147, 213, 222
King, B.B., xiv, 34, 147, 161, 166, 193, 205–7, 210, 212–13, 216, 220–24; *Blues All Around Me*, 206; *Riding with the King*, 223
King, Freddie, 143, 147, 215, 222
King, Martin Luther, Jr., 210
King Edward VIII, 25
King George V, 26
Kingston Trio, The, 16
Kinks, The, 198
"Kitty Wells," 70
Klein, Joe, 81
Ku Klux Klan, 167
Kooper, Al, 101
Korda, Alexander, 13
Korner, Alexis, 30, 123, 139, 148–49, 171, 192

La Chapelle, Peter, 82, 87
Laine, Frankie, 157
"Lakes of Pontchartrain, The," 99, 109
Lampell, Millard, 88

Landy, Elliott, 111
Lane, William Henry "Master Juba," 21
Late Junction (BBC), xi
"Lawdy Mama," 146–47
Lay, Sam, 190
"Lay Down Your Weary Tune," 110
Leadbelly, ix, 5, 8–10, 16, 28, 30, 83, 122–23, 129, 133, 139, 157, 174
Leadbitter, Mike, 27–28, 164–65
"Leaving of Liverpool, The," 100
Leberman, Henry, 59, 61
Led Zeppelin, 148–49, 169, 223
Lee, C. P., 110
Lennon, John, 96, 110, 181, 206
Lenoir, J. B., 162
"Let's Go to Town," 121
Lewis, Jerry Lee, 167, 207
Lewis, Meade Lux, 26
Library of Congress, 6–7, 90, 120, 122, 129, 133; Archive of American Folk Song, 6–7, 120
Liebling, Rachel, 237
"Like a Rolling Stone," 112
Lippman, Horst, 32–33
Little, Reverend John, 33
Little Bryant, 235
Little Esther, 143
Little Milton, 213
"Little Red Rooster," 141, 198
Littlewood, Joan, 131
"Liverpool Gal," 98–99
Living Blues, 27, 214
Lloyd, A. L. (Bert), 10–11, 97, 119, 123, 125–28, 131, 133–34, 184; *Folk Song in England*, 123; "Lo and Behold," 111
Locke, Alain, 48
Logsdon, Guy, 82
Lomax, Alan, x–xi, xiii, 4, 6–8, 10, 12, 16–17, 29, 78, 84–85, 90, 97, 102, 119–35, 156–57, 219; *American Folk Songs*, 120; *The Art of the Negro*, 124; *A Ballad Hunter Looks at Britain*, 124; *Columbia World Folk Music*, 129; *Folk Music of Italy*, 124; *Folk Songs of North America*, 129; *The Land Where the Blues Began*, 219; *The Midnight Special: The Songs of Texas Prisons*, 8; *Negro Folk Songs as Sung by Lead Belly*, 10, 120; *Negro Sinful Songs Performed by Lead Belly*, 8; *Reminiscences of a Folk Song Collector*, 124; *Spanish Folk Music*, 124; "World Folk Songs," 124
Lomax, John, x–xii, 5–6, 10, 57–64, 68–70, 72–73; *Adventures of a Ballad Hunter*, 5, 61, 72; *American Ballads and Folk Songs*, 6, 120; *Cowboy Songs and Other Frontier Ballads*, 6, 58–62; *Cowboy Songs of the Mexican Border*, 60
Lomax, Johnny, 133
Lomax, Shirley, 128
Lomax Hawes, Bess, 81
London Jazz Club, 29
London Times, 123
"Lonesome Death of Hattie Carroll, The," 100, 105
"Long Time a' Growing, A," 109
"Lord Franklin," 96
"Lord Randall," 99
"Lost Woman," 145
Lott, Eric, 69, 218; *Love and Theft*, 218
"Louise," 141
Louisiana Troupers, The, 23
"Lover Man," 13
Lovin' Spoonful, The, 195
Lucas, Sam, 22–23
Lynn, Vera, 13
Lyttelton, Humphrey, 130

MacColl, Ewan, xi, 8–9, 11, 97, 119, 125–29, 131, 133–34
MacLeod, Sheila, 195
MacMillan, Harold, 97

Madhouse on Castle Street, The, 94, 96
Magoo's Club, 190
Mainer, Wade, 121
Major Lance, 234
Man Who Went to War, The, 120
Manchester Corporation Act (1965), 231
Manfred Mann, 96, 195
Marcus, Greil, 102, 109
Marquee Club, 139
Marqusee, Mike, 112
Marsh, Dave, 84
Marshall (amplifiers), 143
Martin, Lou, 146
Martin, Sara, 22
Martin (guitars), 68
Martins and the Coys, The, 121
"Mary Hamilton," 110
"Mary of the Wild Moor," 109
"Masters of War," 97, 104–5
Matrix, 28
"Matty Groves," 122, 155
May, Phil, 166
Mayall, John, xiv, 96, 143, 149, 184, 192, 196, 219, 222; and the Bluesbreakers, 192, 196; and Eric Clapton, 192
McCarthy, Albert, 27
McCartney, Paul, 184, 208, 215
McCarty, Jim, 145
McDevitt, Charles, 130
McDowell, Mississippi Fred, 32, 174, 214, 222
McGhee, Brownie, 10, 29, 33–34, 48, 83, 121, 129–30, 207. *See also* Terry, Sonny
McKay, Claude, 43, 47
McKay, J. A., 231
McKechnie, Andy, 188
McStravick, Summer, 218
McTell, Blind Willie, 48
McTell, Ralph, 77, 80
Melly, George, 30, 141
Melody Maker, 12, 139, 153, 159–60, 166, 169
Meriadoc, Conan, 247
Miles, Lizzie, 26
Milestone, Katie, 229, 233, 236
Miller, Aleck "Sonny Boy Williamson No. 2," 27, 31–32, 144, 166, 187–89, 192
Miller, J. D., 164–65
Miller, Jimmy. *See* MacColl, Ewan
Miller, Karl Hagstrom, x, 4, 8
Miller, Yola, 131
"Million Dollar Bash," 107
Mills, Florence, xi, 12–14
"Minnie the Moocher," 13
minstrelsy, xi, 23, 25, 63, 69–70, 174, 217–18
Minstrelsy of the Scottish Border, 5
Mississippi Sheiks, The, ix, 146
Mitchell, Gillian, 41
Mitchell, Mitch, 197
"Molly Bawn," 122
"Mona," 140
Monroe, Bill, 237
Montgomery, Eurreal "Little Brother," 29, 32
"Moon Is Rising, The," 140
"Moonshiners," 122
Morrison, Toni, 68, 70–71, 222–23; "Rootedness: The Ancestor as Foundation," 222
Morrison, Van, xiv, 154
Morton, Jelly Roll, 124
"Motorpsycho Nitemare," 105, 107
Motown (label), 235, 239
"Mr. Tambourine Man," 101
"Mrs. McGrath," 100
Murphy, Matt, 32
Murray, Charles Shaar, 147, 218
Music Mirror, 27, 38–39, 47, 51
Musicians Union Ban, 29
Musselwhite, Charlie, 186
Mutual Broadcasting System, 121

"My Girl," 167
"My Mammy," 221
"My Mind Can Rest Easy," 146
"My Western Home," 59

Naftalin, Mark, 191
Napier, Simon A., 27, 142
Nazi Germany, 15
"Nazz are Blue, The," 144
Neal, Larry, 211–12; "The Ethos of the Blues," 212
New Lost City Ramblers, The, 34
New Musical Express, 166
New York Syncopated Orchestra, 24
Newell, William Wells, 5
Newport Folk Festival, 101–3, 196
Newport Jazz Festival, 13
News (Jackson, Miss.), 66
"Nine Hundred Miles," 78
Nixon, Hammie, 32
No Direction Home, 108
Norfolk Jubilee Company, The, 23
Northern Soul: Music, Drugs and Subcultural Activity, 233
"Norwegian Wood," 96
"Nottamun Town," 97
Novello, Ivor, 14
"NSU," 148
Nymph Errant, 14

"O Rosie," 148
Observer Music Monthly, The, 237
Odeon, 24
Odum, Howard, 10
Oedipus, 107
Office of War Information (OWI), 120
Oliver, King, 123
Oliver, Paul, x–xii, xiv, 7, 12, 14, 37–52, 78, 160–61, 169, 213; *Bessie Smith*, 38; "Blue-Eyed Blues," 213; *Blues Fell This Morning*, 37–38, 46; *Conversation with the Blues*, 37; *Savannah Sycopators*, 37; *The Story of the Blues*, 31, 37
"On Top of Old Smokey," 16, 122
"One of Us Must Know," 107
oral history, 48–51
Original Dixieland Jazz Band, 11–12
Original Five Blind Boys of Mississippi, 33
Orwell, George 236, 252; *The Road to Wigan Pier*, 236
Oscher, Paul, 186
Otis, Johnny, 143
Our Singing Country, 120
"Out on the Floor: The Politics of Dancing on the Northern Soul Scene," 232
"Outside Woman Blues," 147

Page, Jimmy, 142–43, 161, 173, 188
Panassie, Hughes, 27–28
Palmer, Robert, 217; *Rock & Roll: An Unruly History*, 217
Palmer, Tony, 232–33, 240
Parker, Charley, 84, 183
Parlophone, 26
Parry, Harry, 158
"Parting Glass, The," 100
Pastor, Tony, 94
Paton, Caroline, 125
Paton, Sandy, 125
"Patriot Game, The," 100
Patton, Charley, 33, 52, 103
"Pawn in Their Game, A," 105
Pearson, Ewen, 243
Peer, Ralph, 8
Pennebaker, D. A., 109–10
Pentangle, 248
People's Song Book, The, 127
People's Songs, 121, 127
Performing Fandom on the British Northern Soul Scene, 239
"Personal Manager," 147

Peterson, Oscar (Trio), 34
Philips, 143
Philips, Sister Lena, 33
Place, Jeff, 82
Plant, Robert, 148, 223
"Please Mrs. Henry," 111
"Po Lazarus," 122
Polizotti, Mark, 101, 104
"Polly Vaughan," 109
Popular Front, 82–85, 88
Porter, Cole, 14
Powell, Enoch, 172
Powerhouse, The, 195
"plantation revues," 12
Presley, Elvis, 70, 103
"Pretty Peggy-O," 109
"Pretty Polly," 122
"Pretty Thing," 140
Pretty Things, The, 140
Price, Alan 155, 166; Rhythm and Blues Combo, 168
Principles of Psychology, The, 228
Prior, Snooky, 145
Professor Longhair, 167–68
Progressive Party, 121
Pye, 140, 142, 145

Queen Victoria, 23

R & B All-Stars, 139
R & B Live at the Marquee, 139
R & B Monthly, 27
Rachell, Yank, 32
"Rack My Mind," 145
Radio Rhythm Club, 158
Rainey, Gertrude "Ma," 49, 125
Ram Jam Band, The, 190
Ramblers, The, 129; *The Skiffle Album*, 129
Ramsey, Frederic, 161
Rau, Fritz, 31–34
Razaf, Andy, 25

RCA Victor, 16
REA (Rural Electrification Act), 163
Record Mail, 154
Recorded Jazz: A Critical Guide, 160
Red Channels, 121, 124
Redding, Otis, 167
Reed, Jimmy, 33, 140, 142, 213
Reinhardt, Django, 30
Renaissance of the Celtic Harp, 247
"Restless Farewell," 100
Reuss, Richard, 81, 83–84, 88
Reynolds, Blind Joe, 147
Rice, T. D., 69–70
Richards, Keith, 148, 173, 183–84, 196, 206–9. *See also* Rolling Stones, The
Ringing Strings, 252
Rising Sun, The, 156–57
"Rising Sun, The," 156
Rinzler, Ralph, 126, 129
Ritchie, Jean, 125–26
Roach, Joseph, 155
"Road and Miles to Dundee, The," 100
"Road Runner," 140
Roberts, Chris, 153
Roberts, Robin, 121–25
Robertson, Jeannie, 126
Robeson, Paul, 14–16, 25, 121
Robinson, Bill "Bojangles," 14
"Rock Island Line," 16
Rodgers, Jimmie, 63
Rolfzen, Boniface J., 103
"Rollin' and Tumblin'," 147
Rolling Stone, 206
Rolling Stones, The, xiii–xiv, 11, 139, 158, 169–70, 183–84, 188, 192, 196, 205–11, 214, 216, 220, 222–23; *Beggar's Banquet*, 148; *Exile on Main St.*, 183; *True Adventures of the Rolling Stones*, 209
Romans, the, 247–49
romanticism, 15; in interpretations of the blues, 38–39, 41, 52, 161–66, 172, 183, 220; of Northern Soul, 234–35

Roos, John, 218
Roosevelt, Franklin D., 15
Roosevelt, Theodore, 62
Ross, Dr. Isaiah, 146
"Rounder's Luck," 156
Roundhouse, The, 96
Roy, William, x
Rush, Otis, 32, 142, 161, 195, 215
Rushing, Jimmy, 48
Russell, Tony, 27
Rust, Brian, 28, 160
Rye, Howard, 28

Said, Edward, 181–82
"Salt of the Earth," 148
Sam & Kitty, 235
"Sam Bass," 122
Sandburg, Carl, 6
Sassy, 235
Saville, Philip, 94
Savoy Brown Blues Band, 170, 210
"Say It Loud, I'm Black and I'm Proud," 212
Scarborough, Dorothy, 10
"Scarborough Fair," 96, 98
Scorsese, Martin, 108
Scott, Frank, 165
Scott, Walter, 5
Schwartz, Roberta Freund, 11
Sears-Roebuck, 68
Seeger, Charles, 84, 129
Seeger, Peggy, 97, 127, 129, 132–33
Seeger, Pete, ix–xi, 85, 101–3, 120–21, 132–33
segregation, 8, 164–65, 167, 206. *See also* Jim Crow
Sellers, Brother John, 42, 48, 130
Shadow Blasters, The, 103
"Shame, Shame, Shame," 140
Sha-rae, 235
Sharp, Cecil, 5–7, 17, 41, 57, 63–64, 119, 122, 129, 132, 167, 252–53; *English Folk*

Songs of the Southern Appalachians, 6, 57. *See also* Appalachian mountains
Shaw, Timmy, 153
Shepp, Archie, 212
Shines, Johnny, 4
Shuffle Along, 13, 25
Silber, Irwin, 84
Simone, Nina, 157, 166, 212
Sinatra, Frank, 16
Sing, 119, 132–34
Singers' Club, The, 11, 97, 114, 126
Singing Country, 121
"Sittin' on Top of the World," 146–47
Sissle, Noble (Colored Entertainers), 25
Six-Five Special, 130
skiffle, 45–46, 77–78, 119, 125–27, 129–33
"Sky Is Crying, The," 146
Slaven, Neil, 27–28
Slim, Memphis (Peter Chatman), 30, 32, 129, 195, 207
Slim Harpo, 141, 145, 213
Smith, Bessie, 12, 26, 38, 104
Smith, Chris, 22
Smith, Geoffrey, 183
Smith, Nicola, 239
Smith, "Pinetop," 26
Smith, Trixie, 12
Smithsonian Global Sound Collection, 17
Smithy's Corner, 216
"Smokestack Lightning," 141, 209, 217
"So Long It's Been Good to Know Yuh," 77
Sollors, Werner, 60, 64
"Solomon," 14
"Someone to Love Me," 145
Song Hunter (BBC), 8, 127
Soul City, 232
Soul or Nothing: The Formation of Cultural Identity on the British Northern Soul Scene, 234
Sources of Afro-American Music, 27

Southern, Eileen, 218
Southern Syncopated Orchestra, The, 24
Spann, Otis, 27, 30, 32, 188, 207
Spector, Phil, 198
Spencer, Jeremy, 146
Spencer, Jon Michael, 39
Spencer Davis Group, 141–42, 195, 218
Spivey, Victoria, 32
"Spoonful," 148, 193
Springfield, Dusty, 238
"Springfield Mountain," 133
"St. Louis Blues," 25
Stax Records, 190
"Steal Away," 148
Steel, John, 158, 168–69, 172
Steele, Tommy, 130
Steinbeck, John, 79
Stepney, Bill, 32
Steve Miller Band, The, 181, 193
Stewart, Rod, 96
Stewart-Baxter, Derrick, 27, 38
Still Dancing, 25
Stivell, Alan, 247
"Stormy Monday," 145
"Stormy Weather," 14
Strachwitz, Chris, 31
"Strange Brew," 147
"Stray Cat Blues," 148
"Street Fighting Man," 220
"Streets of London," 77
Stuart, Marty, 3
Sumlin, Hubert, 143
Sun Studios, 217, 237
"Sunday Morning," 145
Sundowners, The, 157
Sunnyland Slim (Albert Luandrew), 32, 186, 188
"Sunshine of Your Love," 148
Sweers, Britta, 127
Sykes, Roosevelt, 29, 32

"Take This Hammer," 122
"Talking Columbia Blues," 124
"Talking Hard Work," 81
Tamla-Motown, 232
Taste, The, 149
Tatum, Art, 13
Taylor, Eddie (Blues Band), 33
Taylor, Eva, 12
Taylor, Hound Dog, 33
Taylor, James, 65
Taylor, Ko Ko, 32
T-Bones, The, 187–88
"Tell Me Momma," 110
Tempo, 26
Ten Years After, 149, 169, 210
Tennyson, Alfred, 57
Terry, Sonny, 10, 29, 33–34, 48, 83, 121, 129–30, 141, 207. *See also* McGhee, Brownie
Tharpe, Sister Rosetta, 34, 130
"That Old Triangle," 109
This England, 232
"This Is My Country," 212
Thomas, Don, 235
Thomas, Rufus, 213
Thomson, Virgil, 85
Thornton, "Big Mama," 32
Thornton, Sara, 236
Tin Pan Alley, 63, 86–87, 89, 123
"Tinmaker-Man," 133
Titon, Jeff Todd, 39–40
"To Be Young, Gifted and Black," 212
"Tom Dooley," 16
Tomangoes, The, 235
"Tombstone Blues," 111
"Tomorrow Is a Long Time," 99
Topic Records, 119, 131, 134, 252
Traill, Sinclair, 27
Transatlantic Call: People to People, 120
"Travelling Riverside Blues," 195
Trip to Coontown, A, 23
Troubadour, The, 96–97, 114

"Trumpets of the Lord," 124
"Try to Understand," 146
Turner, Bruce, 126, 129
Turner, Ike, 210, 216
Turner, (Big) Joe, 12, 26, 32
Turner, Tina, 210, 216
Twisted Wheel, 231–32
2.19 Skiffle Group, The, 77
Tye, Otis, 59

UNESCO, 16
"Unfortunate Rake, The," 155
"Unquiet Grave, The," 98

Valentine, Hilton, 157–58
Van Ronk, Dave, 157
Vernon, Mick, 27
Vietnam War, 111
Vikings, The, 252
Vipers, The, 77, 130
Vocalion, 26
Vogue, 213
Von Schmidt, Eric, 97

"Wabash Cannonball," 78
Wald, Elijah, 4, 38–39, 41, 114, 220; *Escaping the Delta*, 220
Walker, George, 24
Walker, T-Bone, 33
Wall, Tim, 232
Wallace, Henry, 121
Wallace, Sippie, 32
Wallace, William, 252
Waller, Thomas "Fats," 13, 20
"Walls of Red Wing," 100
Ward, Brian, xiii–xiv, 12
Washington, Geno, 190
Washington Post, 66
"Water Is Wide, The," 109
Waterman, Dick, 209
Waters, Ethel, 13, 25, 121
Waters, Muddy, 10, 29–30, 32, 44, 103, 129, 139–41, 143, 147, 160–61, 180, 183–86, 188, 189–93, 197, 207–9, 213, 215, 217, 220, 222; *Electric Mud*, 197; *Fathers and Sons*, 197; *London Sessions*, 197
"We Shall Overcome," 102
Weavers, The, 16, 77
Webber, Harry, 99
Weeks, Seth, 23
Weissman, Dick, 9, 88
Welch, Elizabeth Margaret, 13–14
Wells, Junior, 32, 146–47, 217
"Wellsprings of Music," 120
"West Virginia Boys," 122
"Westron Wind," 99
"What Do You Want," 145
What's Shakin'!, 195–96
Wheatstraw, Peetie, 42–43, 45
"When a Man's in Love," 109
Whisnant, David, 9
White, Josh, ix, 12, 28, 45, 83–84, 88, 121, 129, 139, 157–61, 207; *Singer Supreme*, 158
White, Newman, 10
White Top Festival, 9
Who, The, 206
"Who Do You Love," 145
"Who Killed Cock Robin," 100, 122–23
"Who Killed Davey Moore," 100
"Wild Mountain Thyme," 109
Williams, Bert, 24
Williams, Big Joe, 32–33, 186, 188
Williams, Gospel Joe, 33
Williams, Paul, 192
Williams, Ralph Vaughan, 16
Williamson, Sonny Boy. *See* Miller, Aleck
Wilmer, Val, 160
Wilson, Andrew, 233
Wilson, Edmund, 13
Wilson, Frank, 235
Wilson, Jackie, 212

Winstanley, Russ, 235, 238, 240
Winwood, Steve, 180–81, 184, 195, 197, 199, 218
Wise World, 235
"With God on Our Side," 100
WLS (Chicago, Ill.), 63, 68, 70
Wolf, Howlin' (Chester Burnett), 31–32, 103, 141, 143, 147–48, 174, 180, 183–84, 186–91, 197–99, 209–10, 214–17; *London Sessions*, 197
Wolf, Peter, 193
Wolfe, Karl Michael, 162–63
Womad, xi
Wood, Hally, 121, 157
Woods, Fred, 126
Woodstock festival, 111
Work, John Wesley, Jr., 10
Workers Music Association (WMA), 78, 119, 127
Works Progress Administration (WPA), 15
World Column, The, 235
World War II, 8, 10, 15, 26, 37, 78, 80; influence on popularity of American music in Europe, 15
Wright, Richard, 40, 43, 46–48; *Black Boy*, 43; *12 Million Black Voices*, 46
WSM (Nashville, Tenn.), 63
Wyman, Bill, 158, 214

Yancey, Jimmy, 24
Yardbirds, The, xiii, 140–42, 144–45, 184, 187–88, 195–98, 217; *Roger the Engineer*, 145
Yarrow, Pete, 102
"Yea, Heavy and a Bottle of Bread," 111
"You Can't Judge a Book by Looking at the Cover," 140
"You Got to Move," 146
"Young but Daily Growing," 109
Your Ballad Man, 121

"Your Own Fault Baby, To Treat Me the Way You Do," 148
YouTube, 17
"You've Got to Hide Your Love Away," 96

Zanes, Warren, 238

mN